The Buddhist Religion

The Religious Life of Man Series
FREDERICK J. STRENG, *Series Editor*

Understanding Religious Life, Third Edition
Frederick J. Streng

African Cosmos: An Introduction to Religion in Africa
Noel Q. King

The Buddhist Experience: Sources and Interpretations
Stephan Beyer

The Buddhist Religion, Third Edition
Richard H. Robinson and Willard L. Johnson

Chinese Religion: An Introduction, Fourth Edition
Laurence G. Thompson

The Chinese Way in Religion
Laurence G. Thompson

The Christian Religious Tradition
Stephen Reynolds

The Hindu Religious Tradition
Thomas J. Hopkins

The House of Islam, Third Edition
Kenneth Cragg and R. Marston Speight

Islam from Within: Anthology of a Religion
Kenneth Cragg and R. Marston Speight

Japanese Religion: Unity and Diversity, Third Edition
H. Byron Earhart

Religion in the Japanese Experience: Sources and Interpretations
H. Byron Earhart

The Life of Torah: Readings in the Jewish Religious Experience
Jacob Neusner

The Way of Torah: An Introduction to Judaism, Fifth Edition
Jacob Neusner

Native American Religions: An Introduction
Sam Gill

Native American Traditions: Sources and Interpretations
Sam Gill

The Buddhist Religion
A Historical Introduction

THIRD EDITION

Richard H. Robinson
formerly of
University of Wisconsin

Willard L. Johnson
Oberlin College

Assisted by
Kathryn Tsai, Shinzen Young

Wadsworth Publishing Company
Belmont, California
A Division of Wadsworth, Inc.

Religion Editor: Sheryl Fullerton
Production Editor: Judith McKibben
Managing Designer: Lois Stanfield
Copy Editor: William Waller
Cover Design Adaptation: Chris Werner

Printed in the United States of America

11 12 13 14 15—99 98 97 96 95 94 93

Library of Congress Cataloging in Publication Data

Robinson, Richard H., 1926–1970
The Buddhist religion.

(The religious life of man series)
Bibliography: p.
Includes index.
1. Buddhism I. Johnson, Willard L. II. Title.
III. Series: Religious life of man series (Belmont, Calif.)
BQ4012.R6 1982 294.3 81–16059

ISBN 0–534–01027–X AACR2

To Sītā and Neil,
my daughter and my son,
kuladuhitre ca kulaputrāya
(RHR)

In this life, hate is never
calmed by hatred,
But by love.
This is the primordial Dharma (sanātana-dhamma).
Dhammapada
(WLJ)

To Ven. Dr. Thích Thiên-ân, 1926–1980
Supreme Patriarch of the Vietnamese
Buddhists in America, Educator, Friend
(KAT, SZY)

Contents

Foreword

THE RELIGIOUS LIFE OF MAN series is intended as an introduction to a large, complex field of inquiry—human religious experience. It seeks to present the depth and richness of religious concepts, forms of worship, spiritual practices, and social institutions found in the major religious traditions throughout the world.

As a specialist in the language and culture in which a religion is found, each author is able to illuminate the meanings of a religious perspective and practice as other human beings have experienced it. To communicate this meaning to readers who have had no special training in these cultures and religions, the authors have attempted to provide clear, nontechnical descriptions and interpretations of religious life.

Different interpretive approaches have been used, depending on the nature of the religious data; some religious expressions, for instance, lend themselves more to developmental studies and others more to topical studies. But this lack of a single interpretation may itself be instructive, for the experiences and practices regarded as religious in one culture may not be the most important in another.

THE RELIGIOUS LIFE OF MAN is concerned with, on the one hand, the variety of religious expressions found in different traditions and, on the other, the similarities in the structures of religious life. The various forms are interpreted in terms of their cultural context and historical continuity, demonstrating both the diverse expressions and the commonalities of religious traditions. Besides the single volumes on different religions, the series offers a core book on the study of religious meaning, which describes different study approaches and examines several modes and structures of religious awareness. In addition, each book presents a list of materials for further reading, including translations of religious texts and detailed examinations of specific topics.

During a decade of use the series has experienced a wide readership. A continuing effort has been made to update the scholarship, simplify the organization of material, and clarify concepts through the publication of revised editions. The authors have been gratified with the response to their efforts to introduce people to various forms of religious life. We hope readers will also find these volumes "introductory" in the most significant sense: an introduction to a new perspective for understanding themselves and others.

Frederick J. Streng
Series Editor

Preface to the Third Edition

After scholarly review and extensive revision and augmentation, we produced this third edition with an eye to making the textbook easier to use and more interesting to the beginning student of the Buddhist religion. Limitations of space led us to cut many sections from the previous editions, while requirements for completeness led us to include many new sections and features. Further, we critically reviewed the entire work both before and after the revision.

Specific chapters and sections, especially in Part Two on Buddhism beyond India, have been revised extensively or expanded, including those on Theravāda and Tibetan Buddhism. Dr. Kathryn Tsai completely revised the chapter on East Asian Buddhism and added a new section on Central Asia in Buddhist history. Shinzen Young wrote an appendix on Buddhist meditation. We added much to the glossary, increased and diversified the bibliographic materials, and provided an analyzed index. The line drawings of the previous edition have been replaced in large part by photographs. There are also additional charts and diagrams and improved maps.

Many friends helped us in this task. We especially thank series editor Fred Streng for his surveillance of the entire project and for putting his editorial stamp on the work during final revision, and William Waller for his copy editing of the manuscript. Many others aided us, and they deserve our gratitude: Professors Ingrid Aall, Harvey Aronson, Jeffrey Hopkins, Charles Prebish, and Denis Sinor, along with Professors Jeffrey Broughton of California State University, Long Beach, James H. Foard of Arizona State University, G. W. Houston of Indiana University at Kokomo, F. Stanley Lusby of University of Tennessee, and

Donald K. Swearer of Swarthmore College, who reviewed the manuscript at various stages. Boris Erwitt, Richard Martin, Ruth Meserve and Hannah Robinson also contributed, while Sheryl Fullerton, religious studies editor for Wadsworth, oversaw the entire project. We thank all these who helped produce this book, as our debt to them is great.

Nonetheless, we remain solely responsible for this text. We ask all readers to excuse the remaining misleading statements, ill-founded ideas and interpretations, or other errors, and would like that comments or corrections be sent to us in care of the publisher. These will help us in preparing for the fourth edition. Personally, I (WLJ) thank Oberlin College for employing me during this revision, and my wife, Livia Diane Berg, for her assistance.

We thank the following individuals and organizations for contributing important visual materials to this work: Merilyn Britt, Harvey Aronson, the International Buddhist Meditation Center, the San Jose Buddhist Church, the Sino-American Buddhist Association, the Information Office of Vajradhatu (Boulder, Colorado), and the Zen Center of Los Angeles. We thank Boris Erwitt for permission to use photographs from the collection he made during 1966 and 1967 for his Survey of Buddhism in the U.S.A., sponsored by Dr. Kenneth Morgan of Colgate University. Finally, we thank the Research Institute for Inner Asian Studies of Indiana University (Bloomington, Indiana 47405); Distinguished Professor Denis Sinor, Director; Professor Stephen Halkovic, Assistant Director; and Ruth I. Meserve, photographer, for permission to use illustrations made from the Antoinette K. Gordon Collection of Tibetan Art, Professor Thubten J. Norbu, Curator, and from the Institute's manuscript collection.

Willard L. Johnson, Oberlin College

Kathryn Tsai, Vista, California

Shinzen Young, International Buddhist Meditation Center, Los Angeles

Note on Linguistics

Terms transliterated from foreign languages in this book often appear with diacritical marks. Occasionally, when a transliterated word may not be recognized and has an accepted English spelling, proper transliteration form is dropped (as Krishna for the more proper Kṛṣṇa).

The reason for diacritical marks is that only by using them can our orthography (writing system) closely approximate the original spelling of these foreign terms. For instance, the term *nirvana*, when spelled without diacritics indicating that the first *ā* is long and that the *ṇ* is retroflex (represented by the dot under the n), is not a close approximation of the original spelling of the term, since Sanskrit distinguishes long *ā* from short *a* and a retroflex *ṇ* from a dental *n*.

Buddhists have used many and quite diverse languages for canonical purposes, ranging from the north Indian languages of Sanskrit and one of its literary vernaculars, Pali (in which the oldest Buddhist Canon is preserved), to Chinese, Korean, and Japanese. To simplify matters this text uses Sanskrit so as to present the basic vocabulary of Buddhism in one of its original languages, although terms transliterated from other non-Indic languages also occur.

Though Pali was the first canonical language of Buddhism, all Indic words and names are given in their Sanskrit rather than their Pali form so that the beginning student will not have to learn two forms for each term. The few exceptions to this rule occur when a word has been left in Pali because it is misleading to use its less usual Sanskrit form. In such cases the word is either marked clearly as being Pali or is required by the context to be in its Pali form. Many words are identical in the two languages, for example: *Bodhi, Buddha, Māra, Piṭaka, Rāhula, samādhi, Saṅgha, Tathāgata, Vinaya.* Common Sanskrit-Pali correspondences: *Abhidharma—Abhidhamma, arhant—arahant, bhikṣu—bhikkhu, bodhisattva—bodhisatta, dharma—dhamma, dhyāna—jhāna, Gautama—Gotama, Kauṇḍinya—Koṇḍañña, Kuśinagara—Kusināra, maitrī—mettā, Maitreya—Metteya, nirvāṇa—nibbāna, prajñā—pañña, Śakra—Sakka, Siddhārtha—Siddhattha, skandha—khandha, śramaṇa—samaṇa, sthavira—thera, Sūtra—Sutta, Udraka Rāmaputra—Uddaka Rāmaputta, vijñāna—viññāna, yakṣa—yakkha.* Sanskrit /ś/ and /ṣ/ become Pali /s/—for example: *Aśoka—Asoka, Tuṣita—Tusita.*

PART ONE

The Buddhism of South Asia

INTRODUCTION

Buddhism arose out of early classical Indian civilization in the sixth century B.C.E. The first Indic culture existed during the Harappā period in the Indus Valley. It began around 2300 B.C.E. when a sophisticated urban life started to spread along the Indus River. About a thousand years later, bands of semi-barbarian nomadic cattle herders, the Indo-Aryans, began filtering into the Indus Valley, bringing an Indo-European culture and religious cult, an early form of Sanskrit, and a tripartite social system. These peoples absorbed what survived of the indigenous civilization. The resulting hybrid civilization gained in strength and creativity, moving into the subcontinent to overspread the Ganges River Valley.

These two religious traditions fed the classical cultural synthesis. Our knowledge of the religion of the Indus Valley is incomplete because its sparsely recorded language has remained undeciphered. More information exists about the Indo-Aryan religion, since it was recorded in the *Vedas* (manuals of ritual and religious knowledge, composed circa 1500 B.C.E. to 1000 B.C.E.). By 800 B.C.E., northern India was swept up in a period of spiritual efflorescence.

Out of this double heritage, India's major religious traditions came into being. First, rallied by the powerful charisma, image, and biography of the Buddha, a party of people of unorthodox religious persuasion organized itself. They became a *Saṅgha*, or order of wandering monks and nuns—the first Buddhists. Second, reacting to this new spiritual precipitate, the orthodox Brahmanical traditions (of the *Upaniṣads* and the *Bhagavad Gītā*) gave rise to Hinduism.

Part I traces this development of Buddhism. Buddhism began with the enlightenment of the Buddha, which the tradition later retold in his biography as an epic transformation. Early Buddhist history saw the death of its founder (around 480 B.C.E.) and the establishment of its community, its standard Canon, and its common goal—to bring enlightenment to the world.

The tradition later divided into two major divisions, which separated the earlier Elders' traditions (the Hīnayāna) from the later Mahāyāna developments. The Elders' sects survived on the subcontinent until the end, and succeeded in transplanting themselves (in the Theravāda form) to Greater India (Southeast Asia, discussed in Part II). The Mahāyānists also created a vibrant religious life throughout India and found a home in Central and east Asia, and, in Tantric form, in Tibet as well.

Buddhism of both forms contributed to classical Indian religion, art, literature, and culture. Finally, about sixteen hundred years after its founder's death, Buddhism disappeared as a separate religious form within the Indic tradition, though it survived in the subsequent culture that it had influenced or originated.

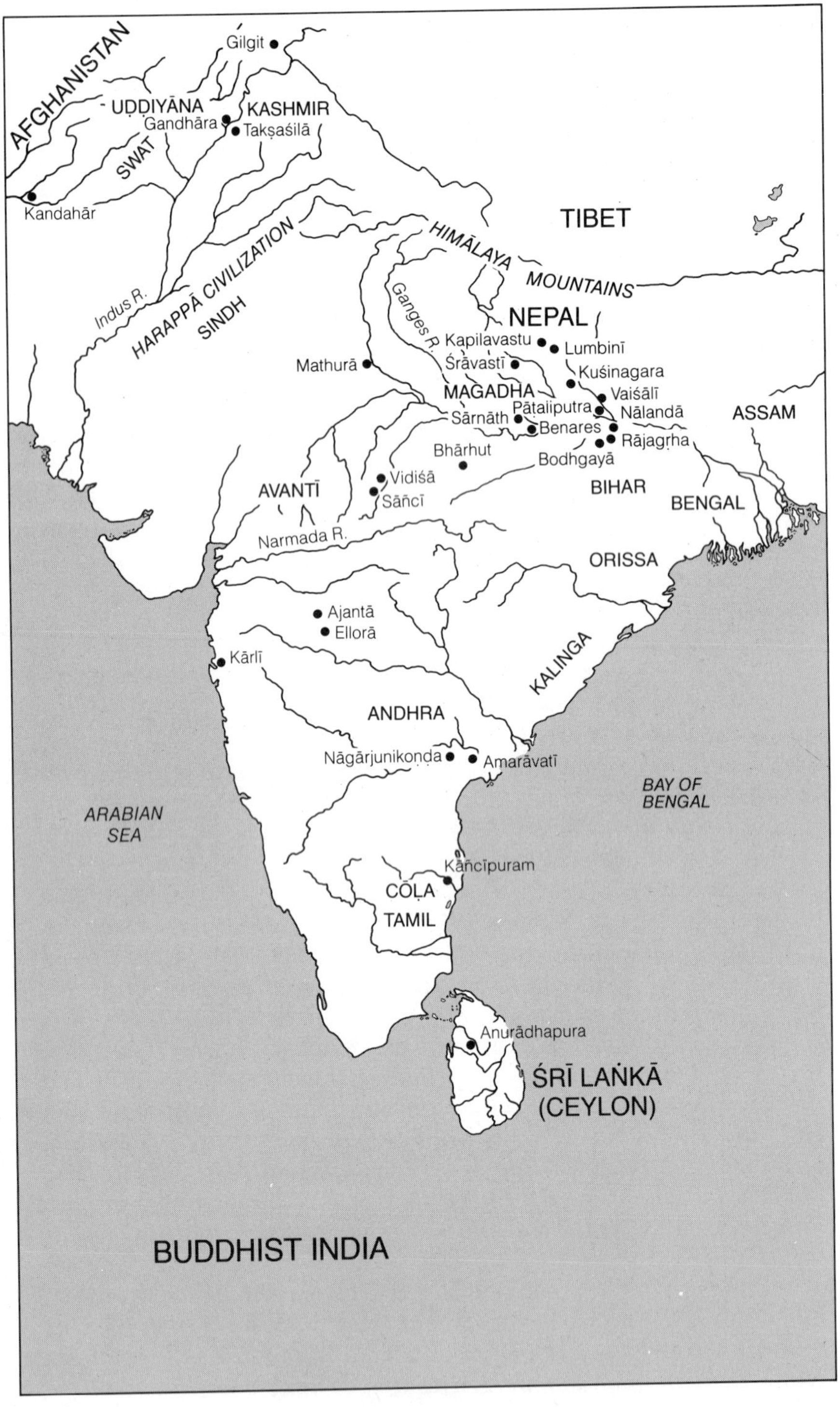

BUDDHIST INDIA

CHAPTER 1

Gautama's Enlightenment

The extant versions of the complete life of the Buddha were all composed 500 or more years after his death. They draw on much earlier material from the canonical *Sūtras* ("Discourses") and *Vinaya* ("Discipline") for events after he left home and began his religious quest.

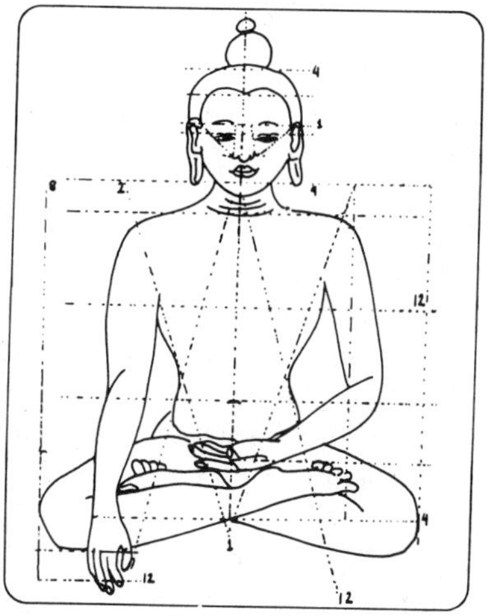

The enlightened Buddha, here sketched according to the Tibetan tradition to show the traditional proportions of the Buddha-image. His right hand touches the earth to recall the drama of Enlightenment. By this gesture he called Mother Earth to bear witness to his merit and thus to his power to defeat Māra and gain salvation from Māra's realm of recurrent birth and death. *(See p. 11.)*

Except for sporadic incidents, they give a legendary account of his earlier life, a fabric of myth and literary invention. The authors viewed the Buddha as an epic hero, and their purpose was to celebrate his deeds; they were not chroniclers but poets. Nonetheless, Aśvaghoṣa (first century C.E.), in his *Acts of the Buddha*, saw Gautama as a genuine human being; and even where the narrative is not historical, it is dramatically authentic. The hero is a man experiencing conflicts; undergoing genuine temptations; trying, and ultimately rejecting, false courses; at every point exercising choice; and prevailing, not through fate or the intervention of other men or gods, but through his own action. He is motivated by compassion for suffering humanity; and he exhibits the martial virtues of courage, steadfastness, initiative, and self-discipline. Throughout his ordeals he sustains a delicate sensitivity and an unshakable dignity.

How close is this attractive character to the historical person? Probably as close as Aśvaghoṣa could make it with the data and concepts at his disposal. The quest for the objective Gautama, like that for the historical Jesus, is foredoomed to a measure of failure. We cannot get behind the portraits that the early communities synthesized for their founders; their reports are all we have. But though the *Saṅgha* ("Community") created the image of the Buddha, the Buddha created the Saṅgha and in so doing impressed upon it his personality. The master exhorted his disciples to imitate him, and they formulated and transmitted an image of him, along with his teachings, as a model for later generations to imitate. Though the process of formulation entailed distortion, the purpose of transmission ensured a measure of fidelity.

THE RELIGIOUS CONTEXT DURING BUDDHA'S LIFETIME

By the sixth century B.C.E. India had gone far in developing its distinctive hybrid civilization, which united two streams of civilizing influence. The first came from the northwestern area of the Indus Valley, known as the Harappā civilization (circa 2300 B.C.E. to 1600 B.C.E.). It was a great riverine civilization like those to the west (Egypt and Mesopotamia) and later to the east (China). Harappā's writing remains undeciphered, so we know little of its religious ideas, but they certainly influenced following ages. A second stream entered northwest India over the Khyber Pass beginning around 1600 B.C.E. It was brought by Indo-Aryan invading peoples speaking an early Vedic form of Sanskrit and carrying Indo-European forms of culture. Their priests, the brahmins, recited verses (*mantras*) during their sacrificial rituals and spread a religious form ancestral to later Hinduism called Brahmanism (circa 1500 B.C.E. to 500 B.C.E.).

Thus, by the time of the Buddha's birth, north Indian religion was a complex made up of local indigenous cults in most part probably derived from Harappā times; the Brahmanical overlay, considered an "orthodox," or rather "orthoprax," (enjoining proper action) tradition; and organized nonorthodox groups of ascetic religious seekers called *śramaṇa* (literally, "striver"). These groups generally denied the authority of orthodox Brahmanism, in both ritual forms (seen in their *Vedas*) and speculation (contained in the *Upaniṣads*, early pre-Hindu texts). They abandoned the family and its orthoprax ritual life, generally giving up normal work and social status to live by begging. These strivers wandered around, dwelling outside the villages in forest *āśramas* ("places of spiritual striving") and forming unstable congregations around masters who propounded a wild diversity of teachings.

BIRTH AND YOUTH OF THE BODHISATTVA

The Śākyas were a warrior (*kṣatriya*) tribe inhabiting a border district on the northeastern Gangetic plain just below the Himālayan foothills. For some unknown reason, they used the brahmin clan name Gautama ("descendent of the sage Gotama"). The future Buddha's father, Śuddhodana, was a king of Kapilavastu, a town whose remains archaeologists lately have tentatively identified.

Śākyamuni ("Sage of the Śākyas"), was born about 560 B.C.E. Buddhists celebrate his nativity on the full moon of Vaiśākha ("April–May"), the fourth month in the Indian calendar. The legend says that he was conceived when his mother, Māyā, dreamed that a white elephant entered her body. When her time was approaching, she retired to the wooded garden of Lumbinī, near Kapilavastu, where, standing with her upstretched right hand on the branch of a tree, she gave birth to the *Bodhisattva* ("future Buddha"). The newborn child stood up, strode seven paces, and declared that this was his last birth—that he was destined for enlightenment. Asita, an aged sage, came, examined the marks on the infant, and prophesied that he would become a *Buddha* ("an enlightened one"). Other accounts specified that he would become such only if he chose to leave the palace to become a wandering ascetic; otherwise, he would become a world-ruling monarch. They called the boy Siddhārtha, "he who has achieved his goal."

The purpose of all the mythic elements in the nativity cycle is to show that the Bodhisattva was innately different from ordinary men. The view that normal procreation and birth are impure betrays a body image in sharp contrast to the Upanisads, which liken copulation to sacrifice.

Seven days after giving birth, Māyā died. Śuddhodana married her sister, Prajāpatī, who brought up the young Bodhisattva. When he came of age, he was married to a bride, usually called Yaśodharā, whom his father had selected. The legend embellishes this phase with epic folklore motifs, saying that Śuddhodana tried to prevent his son from leaving the palace and becoming an ascetic by tying him down with sensual pleasures, not only arranging his marriage but surrounding him with song-and-dance girls and every delight a man could desire.

In due course Yaśodharā bore Siddhārtha a son, whom they named Rāhula, "The Fetter," an indication that the young father's heart was already turning away from the household life.

THE GREAT RENUNCIATION

The legend tells that Prince Siddhārtha, sheltered by his overprotective father from every hint of sorrow and suffering, went out for a chariot ride and for the first time saw a decrepit old man. Shocked, he asked his charioteer about the man's condition; the charioteer declared that such is the destiny of all humans. The prince turned back to the palace and brooded in melancholy, taking no relish in the gaiety and pleasure around him. On a second ride, he saw his first diseased man and reflected that people are foolish to revel under the constant threat of disease. On the third trip, he saw his first corpse; dismayed, he marveled that people could forget the fear of death and live heedlessly.

The life of princely pleasure provides effective counterpoint to the traumatic encounters with impermanence and suffering. Aśvaghoṣa exploits the theme skillfully; then, in the conventions of Sanskrit drama, he composes a dialog between his hero and a confidant, the king's counselor, who advises him to follow the example of bygone heroes and sages and pursue the pleasures of erotic love. The Bodhisattva's reply is an eloquent statement of the ascetic case against the sensual life. Sensual joys are fleeting; death casts its long shadow back over life and blights all transient happiness.

The brooding prince rode out again, observed the peasants plowing, and, unlike the ordinary patrician, was moved to grief at the suffering of toilers and oxen and even at the slaughter of worms and insects by the plow. He sat under a tree, entered the first meditative trance (*dhyāna*), and found some peace of mind. He meditated on the truth of suffering. After a while he saw a religious mendicant and made up his mind to leave the household life.

The legend poignantly describes how in the depth of night the prince took a last look at his wife and infant son, mounted his horse, and rode out of the sleeping city, accompanied by his charioteer. Siddhārtha dismounted, sent his charioteer back to Śuddhodana with his ornaments and a message, then cut off his hair and exchanged clothes with a passing hunter.

The kernel of this episode, the Great Renunciation, is the conflict between the household and the mendicant practitioner's (śramaṇa) ways of life. Far from encouraging his son to become a monk, Śuddhodana had done everything in his power to prevent him. And at each point, Siddhārtha recognized his duty and expressed strong affection toward his father. Aśvaghoṣa puts into the Bodhisattva's mouth a speech justifying departure for the homeless life as fidelity to an even higher *dharma* ("duty, norm").

THE BODHISATTVA'S STUDIES

The new mendicant, then twenty-nine years old, went first to a teacher called Ārāḍa Kālāma, who apparently taught a kind of meditation leading to "attainment of the state of nothing at all." His means were confidence, enthusiatic exertion, mindfulness, concentration, and understanding wisdom. Gautama practiced the method and quickly attained the goal. Kālāma then set him up as his equal and coteacher. But Gautama concluded that this dharma did not lead to the spiritual experience that was ultimately satisfying to him and went away. He then studied under Udraka Rāmaputra, who taught the way to the "attainment of neither perception nor nonperception." Gautama mastered this dharma, was acclaimed a teacher, found it, too, unsatisfactory, and abandoned it.

The canonical account of Gautama's study under these two teachers is an old one, formulated in the concepts and literary modes of the early Buddhist church, but otherwise plausible. What the teachers and their illustrious disciple were pursuing was not contemplative identification of the soul and the world spirit (like the Upaniṣads), not starving out impurities through abstinence and asceticism (like the Jains), but attainment of *bodhi* ("enlightenment") and *nirvāṇa* ("emancipation") through cultivation of meditative trances. This path is known in later Hinduism as *rāja-yoga*, "the royal discipline." But the earliest clear references in the Upaniṣads to this method are later than the Buddha, the fullest archaic Hindu description of it being found in the *Bhagavad Gītā* (circa 200 B.C.E.); and it became part of the systematization of yoga in the *Yoga Sūtras* of Patañjali (circa third or fourth century C.E.). Rāja-yoga came into Buddhism not from Brahmanism but from the ascetic wanderer sects of ancient India.

These episodes in the biography indicate that Siddhārtha sought out teachers and learned the spiritual disciplines then current. The two taught him how to attain two very deep states of *samādhi* ("meditative concentration"), which they considered to be ultimate, but Siddhārtha felt dissatisfied, as deep samādhi alone was not the ultimate experience he sought. Gautama forsook the dharma of the two teachers because it did not conduce to "aversion, dispassion, cessation, tranquility, superknowledge, enlightenment, and nirvāṇa," says the Sūtra. These seven quasi synonyms taken together show the main features of the goal that Gautama sought: pacification of mental turbulence, perfect direct knowledge, and attainment of the unconditioned realm.

HIS AUSTERITIES

The Bodhisattva then went eastward to Uruvelā near Gayā, where he found a pleasant spot and settled down to austerities. He practiced stopping his breath to induce trances and was not deterred by the violent headaches that resulted. He fasted and came as close as he could to eating nothing at all, becoming utterly emaciated. He was joined in his strivings by five ascetics, and he continued in this painful course until six years after the Great Renunciation. Realizing that by this severe mortification he had not achieved sublime knowledge and insight, he tried to think of another way. He remembered an incident in his childhood when he sat under a shady tree while his father was plowing. His mind had happened on a dispassionate equilibrium, and he had entered the first dhyāna, a pleasant and zestful state. Perhaps this pointed to a fruitful method. But his body was too weak and lean, he realized, to gain this blissful exaltation.

The later legend says that Gautama then sat under another sacred tree. A woman named Sujātā had vowed a yearly offering to this tree if she bore a son. The wish was fulfilled, and she prepared as offering a fine bowl of rice and milk. Her maid came upon the Bodhisattva sitting there, mistook him for the spirit of the tree, and reported the apparition to her mistress, who came and presented the food to Gautama. The earlier Pali text says simply that Gautama took solid food, rice, and yogurt. The five mendicants then left him in disgust, saying that he had given up striving and was living in abundance.

Gautama's rejection of extreme austerities hinged on a critical moment when he realized that in his childhood he had known a state of happiness free from sensual desires and immoral thoughts. It dawned on him that there was nothing wrong with being spiritually happy. He went on to recognize that a healthy body is necessary for the pursuit of wisdom. In so doing, he turned toward enlightenment and took the first step on the Middle Way, which became the central point of his Dharma. While rejecting both mortification of the flesh and sensual indulgence, he accepted happiness as good. Moreover, the act of breaking his fast affirmed that the person is not a soul-substance alien to the body, but an organic entity in which both physical and psychic factors participate.

TEMPTATION BY MĀRA

According to the legend, on the fourteenth of Vaiśākha, Gautama dreamed five dreams indicating that he was about to become a Buddha. The next day he accepted the meal from Sujātā. He went and sat under the Bodhi Tree, facing east, and resolved not to arise until he attained enlightenment. Māra ("Death") was alarmed at the prospect of the Bodhisattva's victory, which would allow him to escape from Death's realm, and came to assail him with an army of fearful demons. The Bodhisattva was protected, though, by his accumulated merit and his friendly love (*maitrī*). After failing to shake him, the hosts of demons fled in defeat. Māra then invoked his own magic power to overthrow the Bodhisattva. But Gautama invoked his own superior merit, amassed through many previous lives. Māra called on his retinue to witness his merit; and Śākyamuni, having no other witness on his side, touched the earth with his right hand (a pose often shown in Buddhist art), and called Mother Earth to testify to his merit. The earth quaked in response. Then Māra, having failed with intimidation and compulsion, turned to temptation. He sent his three daughters, Discontent, Delight, and Desire, to seduce the future Buddha, who remained as impervious to lust as he had to fear. As the sun set, Māra and his hosts gave up and withdrew.

This temptation episode is quite a late addition and entirely mythical. The myth, though, is a suitable expression of an experience common to most contemplatives. The seeker eventually is committed to an integral attempt, overcomes doubt and inertia, and sets to work. This conjures up the demons of fear from the unconscious. All the habit-hardened dispositions protest against their coming destruction. But good habits sustain the seeker's resolve. The waves of fear pass, and doubts arise about whether the candidate is really equal to the challenge. If the seeker possesses genuine self-confidence, the doubts are vanquished. The last peril is of course the rosiest and the deadliest. Perfect love (maitrī) may cast out fear, but it all too easily changes into personal pleasure.

THE ENLIGHTENMENT

On the night of the full moon, the Bodhisattva ascended the four stages of dhyāna. The first trance is produced by detaching from sense objects and calming the passions. It is marked by zest and ease, and thinking in it is discursive, focusing and gazing at the mental images as they pass. Similar trances sometimes occur spontaneously when the mind is concentrated, stimulated, and focused steadily on one object by love or hate, intellectual discovery, or artistic inspiration. The second trance is nondiscursive. There is one-pointedness of mind, serene faith, zest, and ease. The third trance is dispassionate rather than zestful; it is mindful and conscious, with a feeling of bliss in the body. The fourth trance is free from opposites such as pleasure and pain, elation and depression. It is pure awareness and equanimity.

All of the trances are characterized by concentration and insight. The insight they facilitate is not theoretical knowledge but direct perception. Attainment of the fourth dhyāna leads to the six superknowledges (*abhijñā*): (1) magic powers (such as levitation and walking on water); (2) the divine ear; (3) knowledge of others' minds; (4) memory of one's former lives; (5) the divine eye; and (6) extinction of the *āsrava* ("outflows," or "binding influences")—namely, sensual desire, desire to exist, wrong views, and ignorance. The first five are mundane, while the sixth is realized only by the *arhant* ("perfected saint") who has completed the Holy Eightfold Path. The attainment of the sixth superknowledge distinguishes the liberated adept from the mere wizard.

The progress toward release from the conditions of bondage is also described in terms of unusual kinds of cognition. During the first watch of the night (evening), Gautama acquired the first cognition, that of each of his own previous existences, seeing them one by one, just as they had been.

During the second watch (midnight) he acquired the divine eye (the fifth superknowledge and second cognition), with which he surveyed the decease and rebirth of living beings everywhere. The whole universe, it is said, appeared to him as in a mirror. He saw that good *karma* ("acts") leads to a happy rebirth and evil karma to a miserable next life.

During the third watch (late night), he acquired the third cognition (and sixth superknowledge), that of the extinction of the outflows. He perceived the Four Holy Truths, noting, "This is suffering, this is the source of suffering, this is the cessation of suffering, and this is the path that leads to the cessation of suffering." According to Aśvaghoṣa, he realized the principle of *pratītya-samutpāda* (dependent co-arising), and meditated on the twelve preconditions (*nidāna*) for the arising of existence. His mind became free from the outflows, and, as the Sūtra says, "In me emancipated arose knowledge of my emancipation. I realized that rebirth has been destroyed, the holy life has been lived, the job has been done, there is nothing after this."

The new day dawned on Gautama, now the Buddha. According to

legend the animate and natural worlds celebrated the event with prodigies. The earth swayed, thunder rolled, rain fell from a cloudless sky, and blossoms fell from the heavens. Gautama's ancestors, then sages in paradise, observed his victory and offered him reverence. The Buddha thus acquitted on a higher level the family obligation that, as a Bodhisattva, he had forsaken in the worldly sense.

INTERPRETATION OF THE ENLIGHTENMENT

What actually happened on the night of the Enlightenment? The oldest account is stylized and exhibits typical mythic features. It purports, though, to be autobiographical. First-person reporting of "peak experiences" was not a genre in pre-Buddhist Indian literature and flourished only sporadically in later centuries. Implicit in it is the affirmation that the particular experiences of a historical person are of outstanding value. The dignity, economy, and sobriety of the account not only highlight the magnitude of Gautama's claims but also strongly suggest a remarkable man behind the style, self-assured and self-aware, assertive but not bombastic. If disciples put such words into the mouth of their master, then who put into their minds such an image of him?

Later doctrine elaborates the idea of "the silence of the saints" and holds that nirvāṇa is indescribable; but nowhere does the early Canon say that the content of the Enlightenment is nonintellectual or that it is inexpressible. However splendid the visions and however exalted the mystic state of mind, the Enlightenment consisted of the discovery of communicable ideas. It is described as the realization in trance of the specific destinies of all living beings and of the general principles governing these destinies. The first cognition, memory of one's own former lives, is a shamanic power, documented even among the Amerindians. The second cognition, perception of living beings everywhere dying and being reborn, is likewise a variety of shamanic power—unobstructed cosmic vision— widely attested in archaic cultures. It evidently involved seeing the past and future condition of others, as well as the present, a power universally attributed to prophets. The specifically Buddhist feature is correlating good deeds with happy births and bad deeds with miserable ones. The third cognition is a philosophical theory (Greek *theōria*, "a seeing, a vision, a contemplation"). It is presented not as the fruits of speculation but as a direct perception, like the first two cognitions. The phrasing looks rather abstract to the modern reader, but clearly it was intended, for all its generality, to be experiential and concrete. The universals that Gautama saw were simply the aggregates of observable particulars.

The content of enlightenment is thus two-thirds shamanism ethically transformed and one-third philosophy, a feature found in civilizations but not in archaic and primal cultures.

The sequence of nocturnal watches matched with the three cognitions and the coincidence of daybreak and enlightenment are mythic but not necessarily fictitious. Many a person has sat rapt in thought all night and, quickening to the new day, has seen a solution in a flood of light. The initiate into Mediterranean mystery cults sat in darkness until engulfed by a great light. Darkness is an objective aid to sensory withdrawal without which the inner light cannot burst into radiance. The Eskimo aspirant to shamanhood passes long hours in solitary meditation and, in the climactic moment, feels aglow with a mysterious, brain-centered light that enables the meditator to see in the dark as well as to see the future and other occult things. The light in question, with shaman and *bhikṣu* ("Buddhist monk"), is not just a figure of speech but a physical experience of overwhelming radiance. The experience is described often and vividly in meditation manuals. It has obvious analogies with certain experiences facilitated by psychedelic drugs and may perhaps have a similar physiological basis. In any event greatly heightened sensitivity is a factor.

The full moon may be a ritual and symbolic element in the story. The nights when the moon changes phase, especially the new and full moons, were considered ominous in ancient India and marked with fasts and rites. Other wanderer sects were celebrating these dates by assembling and preaching their doctrines, so at the instance of his followers the Buddha prescribed that his Community should do likewise. The ritual high point of the month, the night of the full moon, would have seemed most appropriate for the Enlightenment, and the event may in fact have taken place then. One can imagine the effect on Gautama's psyche of the cool, moonlit, tropical night scene, but that it also is a time of ritual celebration may have induced biographers to select the special time as the date of the founder's achievement. Symbolically, too, the night of the full moon has meaning extending back into Sanskrit literature. At that time, the ever-being-reborn moon achieves a paradoxial fullness, for one night imitating the sun and immutable existence, indicative metaphysically of achieving enlightenment and release from mutability.

As already remarked, the Enlightenment fused archaic shamanic attainments with an ethical and philosophical vision. The primitive elements are in service to the higher ones. The first and second cognitions, rememberance of former lives and cosmic vision, constitute an empirical verification of the doctrines of transmigration and retribution for deeds. In Gautama's view the materialists, who say that there is no afterlife and that there is no fruition of past deeds, are as wrong as the dualists, who hold that there is a soul separate from the body. What determines one's rebirth, though, is not sacrifice or mere knowledge, as in the Upaniṣads, but the quality of one's entire life. Those who do good in deed, word, and thought, who speak well of the saints and hold right views, are reborn in a happy state, in paradise. Those who do evil are reborn in a wretched state, in hell.

The idea of moral causality seems only in the sixth century B.C.E. to have become dissociated from notions of the efficacy of ritual and ascetic acts. There is no assurance that Upaniṣadic passages expressing the idea are pre-Buddhist. If, as is probable, Gautama discovered this comprehensive moral world view, it is no wonder that the vision burst upon him with relevatory force, that he saw the principle enacted in a cosmic panorama of doing, dying, and rebirth.

One novel feaure of early Buddhist ethics is that it gives primacy to intention. Good and bad are not quasi-physical as in Jainism but are assigned to a distinct moral dimension. Unintentional deeds have merely common-sense consequences, not karmic ones. The *Vinaya* ("Discipline") regularly distinguishes deliberate from inadvertent violations of the rule. In contrast to later Hinduism, the physical act is of itself neither pure nor impure. Gautama's achievement in freeing ethics from ritual and tabu was as momentous as Paul's emancipation of Christianity from the Jewish Torah.

THE WORLD VIEW OF EARLY NORTH INDIAN THOUGHT

By the time of Siddhārtha's enlightenment, north Indian thought had accepted at a presuppositional level certain basic ideas about the world. This world view, which framed early Buddhism's soteriology, made basic assumptions about five aspects of life.

1. It assumed that time and space are endless. Time is measured in aeons (*kalpas*), incomprehensibly long cycles that repeat themselves endlessly. The drama of human life and salvation takes place within this temporal frame.

2. Further, this view assumed that death is recurrent—and that personhood and identity extend beyond this lifetime, being continuous both from the past and into the future. Mortality does not mean that one dies once but that one transmigrates and dies endlessly, or until one escapes into the deathless realm.

3. A third set of hypotheses concerned individual identity. One's identity is morally determined by the influences of karma taken in this and previous lives. These influences extend into this life and potentially into subsequent lives unless stopped by counteractive measures.

Everything that one is depends on the moral choices one made in previous lifetimes. Everything that one will become depends on the continuation of this process in the current lifetime. The individual is totally responsible.

4. It was believed that the world system into which the individual is repeatedly reborn is transient and ever-changing, perilous like an ocean or a swiftly moving stream. Called *saṃsāra*, "that which turns around forever," it is the mortal realm into which karma-laden beings are reborn to experience endlessly transforming destinies determined totally by their prior choices and actions in this and previous lives.

5. Yet another underlying belief was the existence of an alternative to saṃsāra, an escape from endlessly recurrent death and karma. This nirvāṇa or *mokṣa* (release), the transcendent, deathless state, salvation, the ultimate goal, respite from suffering and the trials of mortality. The ultimate goal (*artha*) of moral betterment in Indian thought, whatever the intervening stages, is this escape. Western readers should note that heaven (*svarga*) is not nirvāṇa, in the Indian world view, but a part of the saṃsāric world system.

THE TWELVE PRECONDITIONS OF DEPENDENT CO-ARISING

The variant accounts of what Gautama realized during the third watch agree that he found the causes and the cure for miserable bondage to rebirth in saṃsāra ("the round of existence"). The twin causes are invariably *tṛṣṇā* ("desire") and *avidyā* ("ignorance"), and the cure is knowledge.

The formula used to explain the origin and interdependent causes of this bondage to "old age, death, grief, lamentation, physical and mental pain, and despair" is pratītya-samutpāda (dependent co-arising). Insight into this, according to Aśvaghoṣa, immediately preceded Gautama's release from saṃsāra. Pratītya-samutpāda is equated with Dharma (see glossary); whoever sees one, sees the other. It is thus a subject of paramount importance to Buddhists and a subject of constant meditation.

Dependent co-arising, or the Buddhist law of moral cause and effect, is expressed in its twelve preconditions (*nidāna*) leading to continued *duḥkha* ("suffering") and bondage to rebirth. These are: (1) ignorance, (2) dispositions, (3) consciousness, (4) name-and-form, (5) the six sense fields, (6) contact, (7) feeling, (8) desire, (9) appropriation, (10) becoming, (11) rebirth, and (12) aging and dying.

Causation, a central problem throughout the history of Indian philosophy, first drew consideration in early archaic speculation about creation. The question was, simply and vaguely, how the world came into existence. Gautama's question, though, was not how the manifested world came to be projected or created from the unmanifest, but what suffering depends on and how it can be stopped. He began at the end of the chain and worked backward, observing that:

12. Aging and dying depend on rebirth (if there were no rebirth, then there would be no death).
11. Rebirth depends on becoming (if life *X* did not die and come to be life *Y*, there would be no birth of *Y*).
10. Becoming depends on appropriation (if the life process did not appropriate phenomenal [observable] materials just as a fire appropriates fuel, then there would be no transmigration).
9. Appropriation depends on desire (if one did not thirst for sense objects, for coming to be after this life, and for ceasing to be after this life, then the transmigrant process would not appropriate fuel).
8. Desire depends on feeling (if pleasant and painful feelings were not experienced, then one would not be conditioned to seek continuing experience of the pleasant or cessation of the unpleasant).
7. Feeling depends on contact (the meeting of sense and object is necessary before pleasure or pain can be felt).
6. Contact depends on the six sense fields (the six pairs of sense and datum—namely, eye-visible form, ear-sound, smelling-smell, tongue-taste, body-touchable, mind-dharma).
5. The six sense fields depend on name-and-form (mind and body; as the sense fields are equivalent to name-and-form, some lists of the preconditions omit the sense fields).
4. Name-and-form, the whole living organism, depends on consciousness, which here means the spark of sentient life that enters the womb and animates the embryo.
3. Consciousness depends on the dispositions accrued throughout life as karmic residues of deeds, words, and thoughts.
2. The dispositions, or karmic legacy that produces rebirth, depends on ignorance of the Four Holy Truths.
1. Ignorance.

Gautama's prescription is: When ignorance ceases, dispositions cease, and so on until aging and dying cease.

Each precondition depends on the one before it, and evidently ignorance is held to depend on aging and dying, so that the twelve preconditions form a circle, represented in Buddhist art as the Wheel of Life. The logical character of the chain is shown by the affirmative and negative forms: If *B* exists, then *A* has existed. If *A* does not exist, then *B* will not exist. The relation between the links is implication. As a theory of causation, this "dependent co-arising" concerns the formal concomitances among things rather than their material derivation from one another. It resembles a medical diagnosis in several ways. By showing that the ailment depends on a series of conditions, it indicates the point at which the series can be broken and so facilitates a cure. This counteracts the theory that the disease is a fortuitous happening, against which no remedy would be effective. It also opposes the view that the ultimate cause of the malady is some entity outside the process such as God or an immutable soul. Salvation from transmigration is to be found in the process of transmigration itself.

THE WHEEL OF LIFE AND THE HIERARCHY OF BEINGS

Just as Gautama realized the causal links in this third night watch, in the previous watch he observed with his "pure divine eye" the details of saṃsāra, or the world system. He saw, according to Aśvaghoṣa's account, "beings appear and pass away according to their kąrma." His

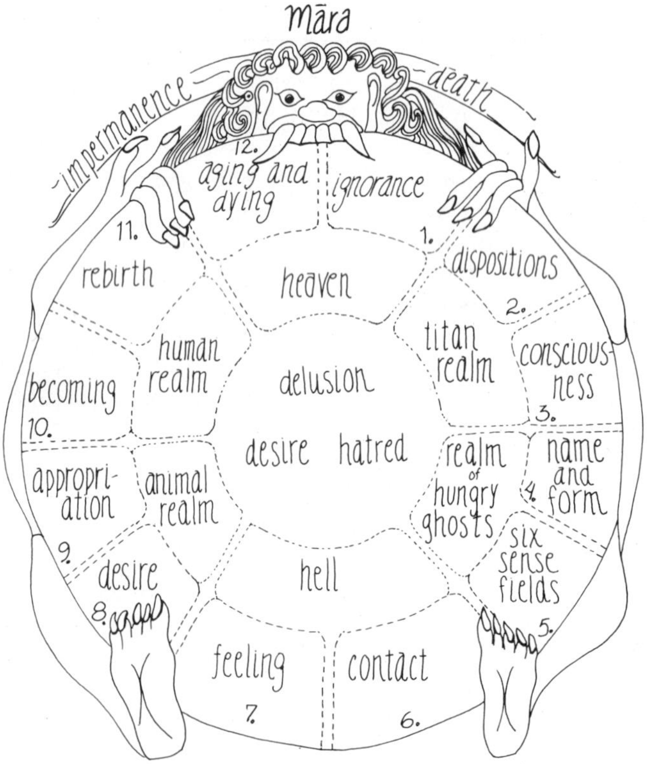

Figure 1. The Buddhist Wheel of Life.

vision, combined with the twelve preconditions, was systematized in later Buddhist art in the figure of the Wheel of Life. This image (see Figure 1) is the map Buddhists use to make their existence intelligible.

Buddhist texts present no prominent account of creation. Rather, it is assumed that it is more important for the individual seeking release to understand the proximate cause of bondage and to take actions in this life that will alleviate duḥkha (suffering). The Wheel of Life is the Buddhist creation myth. Psychological in its basis, it is an attempt to account for a person's world experience; it presents the drama of personal choice and consequence. One Buddhist text describes the Buddha instructing his disciples to paint such a wheel over the gateway of a monastery. In Tibetan monasteries it was often conspicuously painted in the vestibule or on hanging scrolls for meditation, showing graphically how the individual is bound to saṃsāra, the endlessly turning Wheel of Life.

The whole wheel is held in the mouth and claws of the demon Death, or Impermanence, and its perimeter is ringed with the twelve preconditions. In its nave are three animals: the cock, symbolizing desire; the snake, hatred; and the pig, delusion. They are the propelling forces of the cycle of existence, in which karmic retribution determines where on the wheel each individual will be reborn.

There are six rebirth realms, or destinies, within the wheel. The three lower destinies result from evil acts; the three upper reward good. The most degraded beings are the inhabitants of the hells, hot and cold subterranean places of age-long but not everlasting retribution. Buddhist hells are purgatorial: once the ripening of the karma (deeds) is complete, a process accomplished only through passage of time, the condemned individuals can ascend and reach the human realm, where again they must face moral responsibility for their future. Next lowest is the realm of hungry ghosts. These beings haunt the earth's surface, continually tormented by insatiable hunger. They stand outside walls and gates, mutely pleading to be fed. The realm of animals is considered to rank just above the hungry ghosts. Individuals reborn as animals have to suffer the cruelties to which dumb creatures are subjected.

The three upper, fortunate destinies reward good karma. Of these the human destiny is considered the lowest but also the most important, since only here can virtue and wisdom be increased. All other realms are retributions or rewards for choices and actions taken in the human realm. Even when someone attains nirvāṇa while sojourning in a heaven, it is due to the ripening of merit won as a human being. Human beings stand in the middle of the animate hierarchy, not, as in the post-Darwinian world view, at the top.

The two highest rebirth realms are those of the gods and the demigods, or titans (beings of a slightly lower order than gods). Both of these realms are inhabited by a diversity of beings, but all are there by virtue of their karma and, when traces of their actions run out, are subject to reincarnation. Thus, even the gods, those born in one of the heavens, suffer death and expulsion from their transient dominion. Their loss of pleasure is painful. Lacking sufficient merit, they may be reborn even in realms lower than the human. Because of his superior merit, the Bodhisattva was reborn from a heavenly domain for his last rebirth as Gautama among humans, and attained there the completion of his saṃsāric destinies. All the realms of saṃsāra are transient and subject to recurrent death. Buddhism's final goal is release from the Wheel of Life entirely. Nirvāṇa is nowhere on the wheel but utterly transcends it. The continual appearance of gods and spirits in early Buddhist texts is a fact to be seriously considered, even though the texts insist that the Buddha and the arhants (perfected saints) are superior to all the gods since technically they have transcended saṃsāra. The existence of spirits is taken for granted; their members frequently have transactions with human beings; and human beings, too, go to rebirth in these incorporeal destinies. All, even the highest gods, are included within the wheel's system of karmic retribution, and no being holds a rank forever. Even the great gods of the popular religion of the time, Indra and Brahmā, are not eternal persons but merely karmic individuals born into those positions. The spirit world is given an ethical basis and thus rendered rational and more benign. The frequent theme in Buddhist literature of the ogre's conversion expresses the conviction that human virtue can overcome even the most malignant nonhuman beings. Accordingly, the proper mode of transaction is to make food offerings to a spirit just as if it were a human guest, a brahmin, or a monk. If the being is malign, it should not be appeased with sacrifice but rather tamed through the power of a holy individual. Buddhists do not consider the spirit world especially sacred and in fact treat it as a gaseous extension of the animate realm.

What is striking about the Wheel of Life's version of the moral drama of creation is the central place human volition holds in it. No one but the individual is the author of rebirth in a lower or higher realm, and no one else can bring about the individual's ultimate salvation. The human person stands at the center of creation with the assurance that whatever destiny is suffered or enjoyed is fully merited. The image accounts for every turn of one's life experience.

CHAPTER 2

The Buddha as Teacher

THE DECISION TO PROPAGATE THE DHARMA

Tradition says that the Buddha spent forty-nine days in the neighborhood of the Bodhi Tree. Then two merchants en route from Orissa passed close by and were advised by the spirit of a dead relative to make offerings to the new Buddha, who was sitting at the foot of a certain tree. They offered honey cakes and sugar cane and "took refuge" in (formally committed themselves to the authority of) the Buddha and his Dharma, thus becoming the first Buddhists and the first lay devotees in the world. In this case Gautama did not preach Dharma to the two men but merely received their reverence and offerings. Worship of holy persons was in many instances nonsectarian and did not necessarily involve subscribing to their ideas. Buddhist lay cult is here shown developing naturally out of pre-Buddhist practices.

The canonical account says that the Buddha at first thought that humanity, addicted to its attachments, would find it hard to understand his Dharma. If he tried to propound his doctrines and they did not understand, this would weary and vex him. Brahmā, the highest god in the popular religion of the time, read the Buddha's mind, left the Brahmā-world, appeared before the Buddha, and pleaded: "May the Blessed One teach the Dharma. May the Well-gone One teach the Dharma. There are living beings with little dust in their eyes who fall away through not hearing the Dharma. They will be recognizers of the Dharma." Then, out of compassion for living beings, Śākyamuni surveyed the world with his Buddha-eye and saw that some beings had little impurity and some had much, that some had keen faculties and some had dull ones. Realizing that there was a suitable audience, he decided to proclaim the Dharma.

In the Buddhist myths Brahmā claims to see everything, so it is appropriate that he should tell the hesitant Gautama that there were living beings ready to recognize the Dharma. Then and only then did Gautama use his Buddha-eye to confirm this fact. The Canon commonly presents inspiration as a message from a god.

Either Gautama actually experienced an apparition, or this tale is a fiction. In either case, it expresses a critical choice that he must have made. If he had not decided to return and act in the world, his renunciation would have been insignificant for human history. The stated motive for his reconsideration was compassion. This virtue, the peer of wisdom and superior to all others, figures prominently in Mahāyāna Buddhist doctrine but also is regularly ascribed to the Buddha earlier, in the Pali Canon. The Buddha, furthermore, observes the Aryan gentleman's etiquette. He does not thrust his doctrine on those who are unready to accept it; he waits for an invitation. Since he was to be the teacher of gods and men, who else but Great Brahmā was worthy to invite him?

THE FIRST SERMON

Having decided to proclaim his doctrine, Gautama thought first of telling his two former teachers; but a deity informed him that Arāḍa had died a week before and that Udraka had died the previous night. The Buddha confirmed this with his superknowledge, then thought of the five mendicants who had shared his austerities. With his divine eye he saw that they were staying near Benares, so he set out to enlighten them.

On the road Gautama met an ascetic who remarked on his clear eyes and radiant complexion and asked about his religion. The Buddha declared that he was a Victor, that he had no equal in the world of gods and men, that he had become omniscient and had reached nirvāṇa. The ascetic answered in one word, which means either "it may be so" or "let it be so," shook his head, and walked away on another road. This curious encounter seems like historical fact rather than pious invention. Gautama's first proclamation of his Buddhahood was ignored.

The Blessed One walked by stages to Benares, about 130 miles from Gayā. Four miles north of the city, in the Deer Park at Sārnāth, the five ascetics saw him coming and resolved not to show more than the

The Buddha preaching the first sermon at the Deer Park of Sārnāth, hands in the "turning the Wheel of Law" posture. (A fifth-century C.E. *Sārnāth sculpture.)*

minimum courtesy to the backslider who had taken to the easy life. But his charisma was too strong for them. Against their own resolve they saluted him, took his bowl and robe, prepared his seat, and gave him implements with which to wash his feet. The impact of his spiritual presence preceded any word.

The five mendicants called him "Friend Gautama," but he told them not to do so, since he was now a *Tathāgata,* an arhant, a perfectly enlightened one. He declared that he had attained the immortal; that he was going to teach Dharma; and that if they practiced as he taught, they would quickly realize it for themselves. The five were dubious, protesting that one who quit striving could not have attained the superhuman Dharma. The Buddha denied that he had given up striving, and reasserted his claim. Eventually they admitted that he had never spoken to them in this way before and agreed to listen willingly and receptively.

Whether the Buddha actually preached on this occasion that discourse the Canon attributes to him is as moot as whether Jesus pronounced the Sermon on the Mount as a single discourse. The doctrine of the Middle Way, though, is entirely appropriate to the task of persuading the five ascetics that one who had abandoned extreme austerities had not necessarily forsaken the ascetic quest.

The Blessed One condemned two extremes, saying that sensual indulgence is low, vulgar, worldly, unspiritual, and useless, while self-torture is painful and also unspiritual and useless. The Tathāgata had avoided these extremes and so had discovered the Middle Way, which leads to enlightenment and nirvāṇa. This Middle Way is the Holy Eightfold Path: (1) right views, (2) right intention, (3) right speech, (4) right action, (5) right livelihood, (6) right effort, (7) right mindfulness, and (8) right concentration.

The Buddha then declared the Four Holy Truths. The first is the truth of duḥkha, or suffering, found in every aspect of existence. Birth, illness, decay, death, conjunction with the hated, and separation from the dear—in short, the experienced world, made up of the five skandhas (groups of material and mental forces), entails suffering. The second Holy Truth is the truth of the source of suffering. This is thirst or craving for sensual pleasure, for coming to be, and for ceasing to be. The third is the truth of the cessation of suffering. When craving ceases entirely through dispassion, renunciation, and nondependence, then suffering ceases. The fourth is the truth of the path leading to cessation of suffering, the Holy Eightfold Path. Suffering must be thoroughly understood. The source of suffering must be forsaken. Cessation must be realized, made actual. The Eightfold Path must be cultivated.

Gautama testified that he attained supreme, perfect Enlightenment when, and only when, he had acquired purified true knowledge and vision of these Four Truths. He had understood suffering, forsaken its cause, realized its cessation, and cultivated the path.

The five monks welcomed the discourse; and during it, one of them, Kauṇḍinya, acquired the pure Dharma-eye and saw that whatever is subject to arising is subject to cessation. Then the Buddha declared, "Kauṇḍinya has caught on! Kauṇḍinya has caught on!" Kauṇḍinya asked the Buddha for full ordination, which he received with the simple formula, "Come, bhikṣu, the Dharma is well proclaimed. Walk the holy course to the perfect termination of suffering." Thus he became the first member of the Order of Monks. The Buddha, having already experienced such an awakening, could recognize it in another and publicly indicated Kauṇḍinya's new state of mind before the others.

The other four mendicants took turns begging alms for the group and listening to the Buddha's instruction. Very soon all four attained the Dharma-eye and received admission to the Order.

The Buddha then preached a discourse on the five skandhas, briefly mentioned earlier under the First Truth. Form, feeling, conception, dispositions, and consciousness are each *anātman* ("devoid of self"). They are impermanent and so are subject to suffering. Hearing this exposition, the five monks overcame their infatuation for the five skandhas and were freed from the outflows; thus they, too, became arhants, or saints.

COMMENTARY ON THE FIRST SERMON

It is noteworthy that Gautama proclaimed and insisted on his own status. He used two terms current among the ascetic (śramaṇa) sects—*Jina* ("Victor") and *Tathāgata* ("he who has gone thus, or he who has reached what is really so"). The claim of a hairless ape in bare feet and saffron rags to be omniscient and immortal is virtually incredible to the post-Darwinian world. It was scarcely less preposterous to professional ascetics in the sixth century B.C.E. Unable to convince the stranger whom he met on the road, Gautama eventually prevailed with his old friends only by appealing to their knowledge of his responsible character.

Gautama's apparent motive in self-proclamation was not vanity but a desire to prepare the listener to receive the doctrine. He did not proceed to instruct the five mendicants until they acknowledged his authority and were disposed to assent. His style in the first sermon, as in many later discourses, was didactic rather than demonstrative—elaborating the points but not attempting to prove them. The chief guarantee of their truth is that they are the testimony of an Enlightened One. It is assumed that men with keen faculties will find them self-evident. The tone is earnest and exalted, free from sentimentality and hyperbole. Gautama's manifest desire to convince his hearers never shakes his gravity.

Faith in the Buddha as revealer of the Dharma is a first step on the Path. Faith is not a substitute for knowledge but is the seed that grows into confirmatory realization. It is willingness to take statements provisionally on trust, confidence in the integrity of a witness, and determination to practice according to instructions. It is not a mental state of boiling zeal but rather of serenity and lucidity. Śāriputra, one of the great disciples, explained that the confidence, like that of a lion, with which he proclaimed the Doctrine came not from his own superknowledge but from the faith inspired in him by hearing Gautama teach. "I, understanding that Dharma, perfected the quality of faith in the Teacher. And I confessed in my heart: The Blessed One is supremely awakened; the Dharma is well proclaimed by him; the Saṅgha (Buddhist Community) has followed it well."

The fruit of faith is not just progress in wisdom. The saintly disciples who possess faith in the Three Jewels (Buddha, Dharma, and Saṅgha) may predict for themselves that they will never go to rebirth in hell, as animals, among the ghosts, or in any state of woe. They are "stream-winners," lowest of the four grades of saint, and they are confirmed in the course of enlightenment. The objects of faith are not credal statements (faith is not belief) but holy persons (the Buddha and the Saṅgha) and the Truth (Dharma), of which their statements are just expressions. The decisive efficacy of faith is not that it stimulates its objects to act supernaturally but that it transforms the subject.

The ideas of prediction and confirmation played a conspicuous part even in early Buddhism, as it was propounded in the Pali texts, and then underwent progressive embellishment after the rise of Mahāyāna, or later Buddhism. The Pali texts often show the Buddha declaring that such-and-such a disciple has become an arhant; has become a "nonreturner," who will sojourn in the highest heavens until attaining nirvāṇa; has become a "once-returner," who will attain arhant-ship on rebirth as a human being; or has become a stream-winner, who is assured of not relapsing until attaining enlightenment. Confirmation is not an externally imposed predestination but an irrevocable change in the karmic endowment of the subject. The Buddha, or any arhant, can predict a person's destiny by reading the dispositions in the person's mind, a feat that is possible through the superknowledges.

Closely related to prediction is certification of attainment. The Buddha's declaration "Kauṇḍinya has caught on!" is the first instance of this formal act. Identifying the saints has always been important for the Buddhist devotee, whose chief religious authority is the word of an Enlightened One. Enlightenment is recognized by a teacher, who has achieved it, in another, who is striving for it. Once the sainthood of the Buddha is granted, as it is when one professes the Buddhist faith, it is a convenience to have the Buddha's or an arhant's certification that so-and-so is a saint of such-and-such a degree. Like many other early Buddhist institutions, this is a legal solution to a spiritual problem.

THE FOUR HOLY TRUTHS	THE HOLY EIGHTFOLD PATH	THE THREEFOLD TRAINING
1. Of suffering		
2. Of the source of suffering		
3. Of the cessation of suffering		
4. Of the path leading to the cessation of suffering	1. Right views 2. Right intention	Wisdom-Prajñā
	3. Right speech 4. Right action 5. Right livelihood	Morality-Śīla
	6. Right effort 7. Right mindfulness 8. Right concentration	Concentration-Samādhi

Table 1. The Middle Way.

What is the Middle Path proclaimed in the First Sermon? (See Table 1.) It is, like the Greek and Chinese Middle Way, or Golden Mean, a course of moderation in which the bodily appetites are fed sufficiently for health rather than indulged or starved. But it comprises much more than this. The Eightfold Path is equivalent to a shorter formula, the Threefold Training: namely, morality (right speech, action, and livelihood), wisdom (right views and intention), and concentration (right effort, mindfulness, and concentration). We have already seen all three as strands in the Enlightenment. Morality goes beyond mere self-denial because it involves intention and the effects of one's acts on others. Wisdom here means clear understanding of the Doctrine of the kind obtained through thinking, study, and meditation. To discipline the intellect is a higher asceticism than merely to hold the breath and keep fasts. Concentration is achieved through specific techniques apparently known to Gautama's two teachers but not favored by the five mendicants. It requires not the mortification of the body but the cultivation of psychic skills. The Three Trainings are dependent on one another. A Pali text (*Dīgha Nikāya* 16) says: "Concentration suffused with morality becomes very fruitful; wisdom suffused with concentration becomes very fruitful; the mind suffused with wisdom is quite freed from the outflows." The Middle Way is not only moderate but comprehensive, engaging the whole person. It is nonetheless a stringent discipline, a yoga, going against the current of habit.

In the Eightfold Path, right action means abstaining from the three bodily wrong deeds: taking life, taking what is not given, and sexual misconduct. Right speech means abstaining from lying, slander, abuse, and idle talk, the four vocal wrong deeds. Right livelihood is abstention from occupations that harm living beings—for example, selling weapons, liquor, poison, slaves, or livestock; butchering, hunting, fishing; soldiering; fraud; soothsaying; and usury. Right intention is marked by dispassion, benevolence, and aversion to injuring others. Right views means knowledge of the Four Truths. This explains the otherwise abrupt transition in the First Sermon from the Path to the Truths. Another implicit connection is that the Path is the Fourth Truth.

We have already seen that ignorance of the Four Truths is the first of the twelve preconditions and that knowledge of them is the antidote to transmigratory misery (duḥkha). By realizing them during the third watch, Gautama extinguished his karmic "outflows," or "binding influences" (āsrava): sensual desire, desire to exist, wrong (or speculative) views, and ignorance; he understood that he had overcome rebirth. Just hearing them, Kauṇḍinya "caught on," had an opening of his religious vision. The Word of the Buddha was no ordinary word, and his Four Truths were no mere worldly theses. These statements were proclaimed to people many of whom believed that the Primal Being produced Speech out of himself, then copulated with her to produce all other creatures. Human speech was considered objectively effective, too; mantras (incantations) were the chief stock in trade of the brahmin ritualist. The propositions of archaic Indian philosophy were just one step removed from mantras. The Holy Truths, like the Great Statements of the Upaniṣads, were not premises for a deductive system but enunciations of *gnōsis* ("saving knowledge"), to be meditated upon until the hearer "catches on" and breaks through to another plane of being.

For such meditation the Buddha declared that the five skandhas—that is, the phenomenal world-and-person—are duḥkha. His first Holy Truth states essentially that all conditioned states involve this duḥkha, experienced either as actual physical or psychological pain or as the various concomitants of attachment to conditioned states that result from the five skandhas making up the fiction of a "real self." These concomitants include all human insecurities and anxieties, which are present even during states of so-called happiness. It is difficult to select any single word to translate the term *duḥkha*, because it means all the unsatisfactoriness of existence in the material realm. Discomfort, "dis-ease," suffering, or even German *Angst* are acceptable near-equivalents.

In this first Holy Truth, the Buddha specified the crucial attribute of the five skandhas, duḥkha, as the object of meditation, designed to achieve eventual mastery over the skandhas. Why, though, did Gautama single out suffering? One of the mendicant teachers held that there are several eternal substances, including happiness, suffering, and the self. But Gautama did not say that suffering is a substance, much less that it is everlasting. This would have expressed true pessimism. The point is that attachment to worldly pleasures is the cause for rebirth; it blocks attainment of the immortal. So meditation on suffering is a therapeutic exercise to counteract tṛṣṇā (desire), which, with avidyā (ignorance), is the source of attachment and rebirth.

The frequent charge that Buddhism is pessimistic because it declares life to be suffering is inaccurate. An early text glowingly praises the blessings of the good householder's life—the company of the wise, honoring the honorable, living in a congenial country, erudition and skill, good manners and speech, looking after one's family, having a peaceful profession, giving alms, doing good deeds, practicing the religion, and becoming immune to worldly sorrow and defilement. The delights of life among the gods are also praised highly, and it is never denied that there is much happiness in the world. It is only asserted that sooner or later one must suffer because of separation from dear things, that worldly happiness is yoked to suffering. This observation is a preacher's commonplace, but its acceptance in one form or another is inescapable when bereavement occurs.

The Third Truth affirms that there is a happy state free from suffering. When craving ceases, suffering ceases. But is this not tantamount to saying that happiness is a purely negative state consequent upon the extinction of life, an absolute death? And is it not better to live and suffer than to escape at the price of total annihilation? How can there possibly be positive happiness if all desire is destroyed?

In Buddhism, as in Hindu Vedānta, the pairs of opposites are not exhaustive. They are contraries rather than true contradictories. To be or become means to be or become in the realm of saṃsāra. To "disbecome" or "not be" means to pass out of one form (and on to another) within the phenomenal world. In the earliest Indian thought, *being* was the solid, reified state of things, and *nonbeing* was their subtle, unmanifested state. The meaning of the terms changed shortly before the Buddha's time, and *being* came to mean that which endures as against that which changes, the ground or essence in contrast to its modifications. The Buddha is reported to have denied the two widespread extremes of eternalism and annihilation, saying that the Enlightened One, seeing how the world arises, rejects the idea of its nonbeing, and seeing how it perishes, rejects the idea of its being. The Middle Path that avoids these extremes is "dependent co-arising": "When *A* exists, *B* comes to be." The formula of the twelve preconditions is the usual elaboration of this principle. It is the Middle Way in metaphysics, just as the Eightfold Path is the Middle Way in ethics.

The term *exist* has been used here in two senses: (1) to occur at one time after arising and before ceasing and (2) to exist at all times without beginning or end. The second sense is impossible given the Buddhist position that no substance exists apart from its modifications. The Upaniṣad says that the clay is real and the pots are mere modifications created by "naming." The Buddhist says that no clay ever exists apart from particular forms, so the unchanging substratum is unattested and does not exist. Existence in the first sense means manifested existence, and no form of Buddhism has ever denied that commonsense things exist in this relative way, though there has been continual apprehension lest this admission lead people to believe in the second, absolute kind of being.

Cessation, it is plain, is transcendence rather than annihilation. Early Buddhism accepted the axiom that being cannot come from nonbeing and cannot go to nonbeing. Thus, it ruled out genuine annihilation. Transcendence, though, would not seem to accommodate happiness in any mundane sense. This is congruent with the basic pattern of early Indian negation. Suffering and happiness are paired opposites of finite extension, so to achieve perfect felicity one must rise not only beyond misery but beyond ordinary bliss as well. The notion of "positive happiness" is a finite, contingent one. But so long as the five skandhas have not dissolved, the arhant lives and between his or her enlightenment and death certainly is happy. The Canon pictures the Buddha and his liberated disciples vividly as calm, cheerful, spontaneous, even humorous, free from strife, and humane: "Let us live happily, hating none in the midst of men who hate. Let us live happily, then, free from disease. Let us live happily, then, free from care. Let us live happily, then, we who possess nothing. Let us dwell feeding on joy like the Radiant Gods" (*Dhammapada*, verses 197–200).

FOUNDING THE SAṄGHA (THE BUDDHIST COMMUNITY)

After the Second Sermon, there were six arhants in the world, counting Gautama himself. Soon Yasa, son of a rich merchant of Benares, waking up during the night in a state of anxiety, went out to Sārnāth, where the Buddha comforted him and taught him the Dharma suitable for laymen, namely, the merit of donation, the moral precepts, heaven, the wretchedness of sensual desires, and the blessings of forsaking them. Then he preached the higher Dharma, the Four Truths, to the young man, who attained arhant-ship and then took full ordination as a monk. Later, Yasa's father took the Three Refuges (rites of entry) and thus became the first lay devotee (*upāsaka*) in the strict sense; the two merchants who had brought offerings to Gautama at Bodhgayā had not been able to take refuge in the Saṅgha, since it did not yet exist. Yasa's mother and sisters took the Three Refuges and became the first female devotees (*upāsikā*). The young man's friends came, listened to the Buddha, took ordination, and became free from the outflows until there were sixty-one arhants in the world.

The Buddhist Saṅgha consists of four assemblies: monks, nuns, laymen, and laywomen. The rites of entry into these assemblies are both legal and sacramental in character, hence the great importance that the Vinaya (books on moral discipline) attaches to their institution. Going for refuge is a formal act of submitting to the authority and claiming the protection of a powerful patron, whether a man or a god. The formula is uttered three times to make it solemn and magico-legally binding. Traditionally those who take refuge in Buddha, Dharma, and Saṅgha are Buddhists. Though it has been said that the monastics are the only true Buddhists, this is not the case. All who have taken the Refuges belong. The commitment is formal and definite. Though it does not require credal assent to tenets such as the Four Truths, it does constitute a profession of faith in the Buddha's wisdom, the truth of his teaching, and the worthiness of the Saṅgha.

When the cadre of sixty enlightened monks was consolidated, the Buddha sent them out as missionaries, charging them to travel and proclaim the Dharma for the benefit of the many, out of compassion for the world, for the welfare of gods and humans. Beings with keen faculties would attain liberation if, and only if, they heard the doctrine.

The historic success of Buddhism stems from its concern for the many, regardless of race, caste, class, or sex. Compassion is not just feeling the suffering of others but acting to alleviate it, and the foremost act is "Dharma-donation." The Brahmanical schools kept their teachings as secret as possible, and their teachers retained personal control over the students. In contrast the Buddhists broadcast their message to the multitudes, aiming it specifically, though, to those most ready to receive it. Good Dharma-preachers use their divine eye (or lacking that, the science of character analysis) to discern whether people are dull, ordinary, or keen minded and to adapt the teaching to the hearer's capacity. In the Quaker phrase, they "speak to the condition" of their audience. The Buddhist missionaries aim not only to proclaim their doctrine but to communicate it.

Only Buddhas attain enlightenment without receiving the gift of Dharma from another, and even they, according to later theory, heard it many lives ago from a former Buddha. (There have been many Buddhas in the past and another is expected in the future.) Thus, no one works out personal salvation unaided: "You yourself must make an effort. The Buddhas, for their part, are the revealers" (*Dhammapada* 276). The later disputes over self-power versus other-power concern the price of salvation and do not deny that it takes two parties for anyone to achieve it. Every form of Buddhism has held that guides are necessary; and though the Buddhas are the highest guides, the other saints and even some worldlings perform the office.

The sixty missionaries were soon so successful that many converts came long distances to receive ordination. The Buddha noted the hardship this caused them and so granted his monks permission to confer ordination themselves wherever they went. This made the Saṅgha self-propagating and enabled it to spread far beyond the area within which the Buddha or any pontiff could have exercised personal control. Even during his lifetime, Gautama entrusted his Community with management of its own affairs, serving as lawmaker when his disciples consulted him on problems but otherwise not imposing his authority. By the time of his decease, the Saṅgha was consolidated as a republican society, a loose federation of little democracies bound together by a common code, a common oral tradition, and the constant coming and going of itinerant monks.

Śākyamuni spent the first three-month rainy season after his enlightenment at Sārnāth, near Benares. This summer monsoon retreat became an institution and is observed to the present day throughout the Buddhist world; it is particularly important in Theravāda countries. After the rains he returned to Uruvelā, where he had practiced austerities. The Vinaya relates that there he encountered and converted three brothers of the Kāśyapa clan who, with their hundreds of disciples, belonged to the Jaṭila sect of Brahmanic ascetics.

This tale shows how Buddhism grew not merely through individual conversions but by incorporating whole sects. It is remarkable that all the early converts speedily became arhants. In later centuries Buddhists attributed this to the superior capacities of people born in the auspicious age when a Buddha was alive. The arhant-ship of individual famous disciples is uncontested in the tradition even though the attainment is sensed only by the person and others who had achieved it. Doubtless Gautama's personal charisma enormously facilitated realization. Furthermore, his good news burst like a sudden light in a milieu thronging with expectant seekers.

The Buddha went on to Rājagṛha, capital of Magadha, where he was greeted by King Bimbisāra and a large crowd. The king entertained him and donated the Bamboo Grove park just outside the northern gates of the city. Soon Śāriputra of Nālandā, about ten miles north of Rājagṛha, and his friend Maudgalyāyana were converted. They became the two chief disciples, Śāriputra being foremost in wisdom, and Maudgalyāyana foremost in psychic powers. They died before the Buddha did, and relics said to be theirs are now enshrined in a new temple on the ancient site at Sāñcī. Among other famous disciples there was Mahākāśyapa, foremost of those who keep the ascetic rules, who shortly after the Buddha's decease convened the Council of Rājagṛha and superintended standardization of the recitation of the Sūtras. Subhūti, foremost among those who dwell in peace, supreme in practicing the samādhi (concentration) of emptiness and paramount among those worthy of offerings, attained arhant-ship by meditating on friendly love (maitrī). Kātyāyana, a brahmin and court priest from Avantī in western India, was sent by his king on a mission to the Buddha, who sent him back as a bhikṣu (monk) and arhant to spread the Dharma in Avantī. He was the father of Buddhist exegesis, known as "foremost of those who analyze at length what the Buddha has stated concisely." Upāli, the barber of Kapilavastu, became "foremost among those who keep the Vinaya," which he recited at the First Council. Tradition says that Gautama's own son, Rāhula, received ordination and became an arhant. He was considered unrivaled among those who love to train the new monks and novices.

Gautama's cousin Ānanda became a monk and was the Buddha's favorite disciple and constant attendant for the last twenty years of his life. Ānanda figures often in the account of the Buddha's last weeks and was present at his death. He alone among the great disciples had not become an arhant, so Mahākāśyapa excluded him from the First Council, admitting him after he had retired and overnight achieved extinction of the outflows. His exceptional memory enabled him, it is said, to recite accurately the dialogs of the Buddha that then composed the *Sūtra Piṭaka*.

The Order of Nuns is said to have been instituted by the Buddha at Ānanda's repeated plea. Gautama's foster mother, Prajāpatī, and her attendants became its first members. Queen Kṣemā, wife of King Bimbisāra, was converted and became a prominent nun. Despite the example of such wise and saintly women, the female order never became nearly so important as the male one.

The early lay converts included a good array of kings, princes, and rich merchants. Of the latter, Anāthapiṇḍika donated the land for the famous Jetavana monastery at Śrāvastī. Two wealthy laywomen also donated to the Saṅgha, the courtesan Amrapālī giving her garden at Vaiśālī and the matron Viśākhā giving land for a monastery in Śrāvastī. Thus, even during the Buddha's lifetime, his Saṅgha became a wealthy landowner.

THE DEATH OF THE BUDDHA (ATTAINMENT OF FINAL NIRVĀṆA)

For forty-five years the Buddha journeyed around the central Gangetic plain, staying in the Saṅgha's parks, receiving all callers—ascetics, brahmins, princes, and commoners—and answering their questions, spreading the Dharma, and aiding followers in spiritual growth.

In his seventy-ninth year, Gautama set out on his last journey. He left Rājagṛha and moved by stages north and west until he reached Vaiśālī, where he fell seriously ill. The *Sūtra of the Great Decease* says that he told Ānanda that through magic powers he could stay alive for an aeon (kalpa), but Ānanda failed to request him to do so. Then Māra approached and told Gautama that it was time for him to attain final nirvāṇa. The Buddha agreed, saying, "Trouble not, Evil One. Very soon the Tathāgata's parinirvāṇa will take place. After three months he will enter parinirvāṇa."

These episodes betray the notions of a later age puzzled by the seeming failure of the dying master to avert his own death. Control of one's life span is a yogic power, and even today India and the Buddhist world are full of reports about holy men who have lived well beyond a hundred years. Great holy men similarly can predict or determine the date of their death. Gautama might well have answered, "My immortality is not of this world." But his editors stated that it was

Ānanda's fault for not taking the hint and asking the Buddha to stay alive.

The Tathāgata's last meal was at the home of Cunda the smith. After eating a quantity of pork (later commentators say mushrooms), he became very sick, blood flowed, and he suffered sharp dysentery pains. He bore it calmly, arose and went to Kuśinagara, where he lay down between two śāla trees. There he received the wanderer Subhadra, to whom he recommended the Holy Eightfold Path. Ānanda then received this last of Gautama's converts into the Saṅgha.

The dying Buddha asked the assembled monks three times whether they had any last doubts or questions, but all kept silent. So the Blessed One delivered his last exhortation: "Conditioned things are perishable by nature. Diligently seek realization." Then he entered the first dhyāna and ascended the trance states up to the fourth, from which he passed into parinirvāṇa. The Buddha thus died in meditative calm, as he had learned to live.

The legend says that earthquakes and thunder marked the moment of death. Brahmā and Śakra recited stanzas, and the monks (except the arhants) burst into lamentation until Anuruddha reminded them that doing so was not in keeping with the Buddha's teaching.

The people of Kuśinagara came the next day and held a six-day wake for the Blessed One. They danced, sang, made music, and offered garlands and scents. The body was wrapped in alternate layers of cloth and cotton wool. On the seventh day, eight chiefs of the Malla clan

Reactions of distress at the death of the Buddha, as portrayed in a Tun-huang cave wall painting on the Chinese border with Central Asia.

carried the bier in through the north gate and out the east gate of the town to a tribal shrine. There they cremated the body.

When they asked Ānanda how the remains of the Tathāgata should be treated, he replied: "Like those of a king of kings. Cremate the body and build a *stūpa* (memorial mound) at the crossroads to enshrine the relics." The country at that time was dotted with shrines (*caitya*) and stūpas of deceased holy men, at which worship was offered by the people. The stūpa is a form of the round barrow, the tomb of bronze-age chiefs and kings from Ireland to Japan. The funeral rites are similar to those of Homeric Greece, for example the cremation of Hector in the *Iliad*. Continuity with the Indo-European heritage is apparent in many aspects of Buddhism, but in none more so than in the mortuary rites of its founder.

The cultic appropriation of royal cremation and burial forms is an instance of that interpenetration of sacred and secular that typifies Buddhism as a religion. Modern European languages require use of different words where Sanskrit and Pali use the same one in both social and religious contexts. Ārya means "noble, aryan" socially, but "holy, a saint, a nonworldling" in the context of Dharma. Pūjā means "honor, reverence" in one sphere, and "worship" in the other. Dharma means "social custom-law," and also "the truth-content of religion." Going for refuge is a political act, as well as the religious rite of commitment. In effect, the sacred and the profane were considered different dimensions of one and the same reality. But the modern translator who chooses the secular equivalents will muffle the numinous light that glows from the original.

Simple worshippers believe that the physical relics radiate a spiritual force. In fact the sense of physical continuity evokes such a power in the devotee's mind. But Gautama is reported to have said, "What is there in seeing this wretched body? Whoever sees Dharma sees me; whoever sees me sees Dharma." The immortality of the Buddha is that he is immanent in his Word.

INTERPRETING THE LIFE OF THE BUDDHA

The story of the Buddha's life is the cornerstone of the Buddhist religion. All else is organized around this ideal biography. As with the life of Christ, an example for Christians everywhere to imitate, it is the model life. The Buddha found in an ignorant world a comprehensive vision allowing a way out of saṃsāra's sufferings.

A religion is a means of ultimate transformation. It asserts values, placing higher worth on one or another outcome of the actions that fill one's daily living. Values orient action, allow personal control over one's life, and determine the outcome of one's most important and consequential choices.

The symbolism of the story of Gautama's Enlightenment presents these values and actions to Buddhists. He is portrayed as an epic hero, a warrior in the struggle for self-control and redeeming knowledge. His battle is not to conquer enemies but to achieve spiritual growth and maturity.

As a prince, Gautama stood to inherit the physical world. During his youth he had everything anyone could desire. The palace symbolizes the material world, which is also the fleeting world ending in painful death. The first period of Gautama's life is one of indulgence, the privilege of innocent immaturity.

Gautama's first encounters with old age, sickness, and death made him realize the impermanent character of the world he had chosen to value above all else by remaining in the palace as the heir apparent. His response was to change his life. At the age of twenty-nine be became an itinerant seeker, practiced self-discipline, and learned the techniques of spiritual self-transformation current in his time, particularly meditation and asceticism.

In the context of his entire life, this period of six years was a therapeutic process, a time for learning and self-reflection during which Gautama transformed himself. It allowed him to take responsibility for his values and actions. It was a time of spiritual maturation, leading to his Enlightenment when, again making choices (against extreme asceticism, for the Middle Way), he decided on the values that would orient his life's actions. Based on his Enlightenment visions, his life was ultimately transformed by the culminating experience of his therapy.

He returned to the world—to his companions, family, and countrymen—to share these new values and to exemplify the spiritually mature and humanly responsible actions they recommended. After a fulfilling forty-five years, he faced death with impressive composure. Unlike the painful death of one still immaturely bound to what must inevitably be lost, it was calm and dispassionately meditative.

The life of the Buddha exemplifies the threefold structure of the Buddhist Path. Everyone is born into a family and culture (the palace) and makes accommodations and adjustments, often defensive and stereotyped, to it. Life experiences result in a karma, a propensity to act in a certain habitual way. The Buddha's life shows how one must come to terms with this heritage, becoming aware of it and counteracting it. Otherwise, there can be no spiritual maturity and no free individual. The ideal Buddhist way of dealing with one's karma is patterned directly on the Buddha's experience. It begins with śīla, a set of moral rules to purify, and begin the transformation of, one's nature. Śīla increases the individual's self-insight and mindfulness (smṛti), essential since karma cannot be counteracted without its being brought to full consciousness. Then, samādhi, the cultivation of meditative calm (śamatha), and finally one-pointedness of concentration, comes. Only from this state of mental control can the third step, prajñā (wisdom), be attained. Then, correct insight (vipaśyanā) can properly fathom the correctness of Buddhist truths (Dharma) and affirm trust in Buddhist life values. The ideal Buddhist course, for laity and monk alike, follows this progression modeled on the life of Gautama, the only difference being that the layperson's progress to the ultimate goal will take longer.

The inscription reads, "Anāthapiṇḍika dedicates Jeta Grove, purchased with a layer of gold." Anāthapiṇḍika, a rich merchant, bought Prince Jeta's grove with as much gold as would cover the ground. (The gold is being unloaded from the cart.) At the center the merchant presents the grove by pouring water over a tree symbolizing the Buddha. Thus the Saṅgha quickly became a corporate landowner. (From a second century B.C.E. *Bhārhut stūpa medallion.)*

CHAPTER 3

Development of Indian Buddhism

FORMATION OF THE CANON

Just before the Buddha died, he reportedly told his followers that thereafter the Dharma would be their leader. The early arhants considered Gautama's words the primary source of Dharma (doctine, teaching) and Vinaya (rules of discipline and community living), and took great pains to formulate and transmit his teachings accurately. Nonetheless, no ungarnished collection of his sayings has survived. The versions of the Canon (accepted scripture) preserved in Pali, Sanskrit, Chinese, and Tibetan are sectarian variants of a corpus that grew and crystallized during three centuries of oral transmission. From our perspective, ancient Indians were capable of prodigious memorization. The resulting Pali texts, as anyone who has tried to read any of them knows, based themselves on such mnemonic devices as formulaic repetitions, numeral lists, and other techniques to guarantee ease and accuracy of transmittal. The style of the Pali Canon differs considerably from the Mahāyāna, which was from the first a literary, textual composition. The Buddhist chronicles present an anachronistic and idealized story of the First Council, held at Rājagṛha during the three-month monsoon retreat after the Final Nirvāṇa. Mahākāśyapa, it is said, first questioned Upāli, who stated when and under what circumstances the Buddha had promulgated each rule of the Vinaya, the first of the three collections or Piṭakas ("Baskets") that comprise the Buddhist Canon. Textual analysis, though, shows that, while some of the material in the Vinayas of the various *Hīnayāna* ("small vehicle or course") sects may go back to the first generation of disciples, the literary form and much of the content had their origins centuries later.

Ānanda is said to have recited in order each of the five *Nikāyas* ("collection of Sūtras", also called *Āgamas*) in the second collection, the Sūtra Piṭaka ("Basket of Discourses"). Four *Nikāyas* are recognized by all the early sects: the Long (*Dīgha*), the Medium (*Majjhima*), the Connected (*Saṃyutta*), and the Item-More (*Aṅguttara*) *Nikāya*. But the Little (*Khuddaka*) *Nikāya* as a collection is found only in Pali and not in the Chinese translations, even though many of its texts (such as the *Dhammapada*) exist in Chinese as separate works or parts of other *Āgamas*.

The canonical texts are chiefly in prose, except for stanzas interspersed through the first four *Nikāyas* and the anthologies of verse (*Dhammapada*, *Sutta-nipāta*, and so on) in the fifth *Nikāya*. In the prose texts, the early disciples seem to have been concerned with the substantive content rather than with the exact words. Individuals were allowed to recite the scriptures in their own dialect. We do not know precisely what language the Buddha spoke, but it was probably the precursor of the Māgadhī dialect in which most of Aśoka's inscriptions are couched. The complete Canon of the Theravāda sect has been preserved in Pali, a vernacular descended from Sanskrit and most likely spoken in west India, whence it was taken to Ceylon. Tradition says that the Pali Canon was written down in Ceylon during the first century B.C.E. Probably the Canon was reduced to writing in north India during the second century B.C.E.

Sectarian bias undoubtedly has occasioned distortions, additions, and omissions. Nevertheless, a large fund is common to all versions, and the Saṅgha seems from the first to have striven to exclude spurious texts and to maintain purity of transmission.

Both strictness in preserving the essential kernel and liberty to expand, vary, and embellish the expression characterize Buddhist attitudes through the ages toward not only texts but also art, ritual, discipline, and doctrine. The perennial difficulty lies in distinguishing the kernel from its embodiment. The Buddha is said to have told Ānanda that, if the Saṅgha wished, it might revoke the minor rules; but Ānanda forgot to ask which rules were minor, so the First Council, it is said, decided to retain everything in the Vinaya.

Prodigious amounts of energy have gone into preserving and reproducing the Canon. In the early centuries, certain monks specialized in reciting a particular collection. But to memorize only one, such as the *Majjhima Nikāya*, which yields 1100 pages of modern printed text, is not merely an exercise but a vocation. And to copy such a collection by hand demanded ample donations to support the scribes. Short summaries of the Dharma have been available from the earliest times, nor does its essence require voluminous expression. But the very bulk of the Canon conveys the prestige of the Dharma. Hearing, learning, reciting, and copying the scriptures are a religious exercise for which, the longer the Canon, the greater the benefit. And the diversity of teachings, while frustrating the desire for unanimity, affords interest and options to the seeker. The Buddhist Canon, like the American system of government and the Japanese script, generates a surplus of energy through its fascinating unwieldiness. Buddhists have always been solicitous of their Canon, providing amply for the copying (or printing) and storage in monastic libraries of their precious texts.

The third collection in the Pali Canon is the *Abhidhamma* (Sanskrit, *Abhidharma*) *Piṭaka*, consisting of seven scholastic works. Among these are the *Enumeration of Dharmas*, which analyzes mental and bodily dharmas (constituents); the *Divisions*, which discuss the skandhas, dependent co-arising, the fetters, and meditation; and the *Subjects of Discussion*, which is a polemical treatise discussing the theses in dispute among Hīnayāna schools. Other segments of the *Abhidhamma Piṭaka* list the dharmas; investigate causal relations; classify personality in terms of the preponderance of desire, hatred, and delusion; and give fuller explanations of matters left imprecise in the other collections.

Early Buddhist meditation focused on the dharmas as a means of reducing bondage to conditioned reality and thus produced a large literature. This Abhidharma literature, though composed by scholars of later centuries (beginning circa 350 B.C.E.) and not the word of the Buddha, is an important part of the Buddhist Canon. The term *Abhidharma* implies "that which is above or about the Dharma," the teaching of the Buddha. Thus, it explains and orders the key ideas of the Buddhist religion in a systematic, more authoritative fashion. Couched in technical language, Abhidharma literature defines and explains both materials presented in ordinary language in the other texts and the experiences generated in meditations on the dharmas. In this sense, it provides an essential means for understanding Buddhist thought.

The Abhidharma literature of the Theravāda school was composed and preserved in Pali. Later, especially in the fifth century C.E. in Ceylon, commentaries were written on the Pali Abhidharma that came to define the orthodox Theravāda position on Buddhist doctrine. The famous south Indian, Buddhaghosa, went to Ceylon and wrote commentaries on all seven works. Today the Pali Abhidharma remains a living literature, especially among Buddhist scholars in Burma and Ceylon. Many early Buddhist sects composed their own Abhidharma literatures in Sanskrit. Most of these were lost over the centuries; only two survive in entirety because they were translated into Chinese.

EARLY SCHISMS AND SECTS

Tradition says that a hundred years after the Final Nirvāṇa, (that is, about 380 B.C.E.), the monks of Vaiśālī proclaimed ten theses concerning discipline—some trivial (for example, storing salt in a horn vessel is permissible) and some significant (a monk may make use of gold and silver). When these monks went so far as to take up a collection of money from the laity on Observance Day, one monk protested and advised the laypeople not to donate. The Council assembly censured him and required him to apologize. He did so but continued to assert his opinion until the laity of Vaiśālī were convinced, whereupon the monks suspended him for preaching without permission. He fled to the west and lobbied his case until an impressive group of eminent monks convened in Vaiśālī, vindicated him, and censured the monks who had accepted money and had punished him. The importance of this Council lies in the indication it gives that there were differences among the early followers of the Buddha. It made apparent some of the conflicts and tensions that were beginning to split the Community. Many consider that the first great schism in Buddhism began there, dividing the Buddhist tradition into two groups that differed on points relating to discipline and the separation of monastic and lay matters.

The early teaching admitted that laypersons could attain the first three degrees of sainthood (stream-winner, once-returner, and non-returner); but whether they could become arhants was a disputed point. The Buddha reportedly declared that he took no categorical stand, that with the laity as with the monks it is conduct that counts. The Sūtras list twenty lay followers who attained the highest goal without ever becoming monks. Their case, though, is rarer than that of monks becoming arhants, and the household life is not considered propitious for the highest attainment.

The arhant monks formed an elite guild in the early Saṅgha and alienated many other monks and laymen by insisting that they alone knew the True Dharma and were qualified to pronounce on the correctness of views and the holiness of others. Some opposed this monopoly by declaring that a householder could become an arhant and keep his lay status. And some opponents belittled the arhants, maintained that they were liable to relapse, and contradicted claims that they were in every way perfect. In the second century after the Final Nirvāṇa (circa 340 B.C.E.), a set of propositions circulated that challenged the arhants' saintliness, claiming that they could be seduced in dream, could have doubts, could wonder about their arhant-ship, could be guided by another along the path to salvation, and could utter spontaneously the word *suffering* (duḥkha) while meditating. None of these propositions really dethrones the arhants, but they contradict claims that saints are in every way omnipotent and omniscient. Even the Buddha was not accorded such powers in the early teaching. At the same period, there was a universal tendency to attribute more and more extraordinary powers to the Buddha, such as the ability to live for a whole aeon and knowledge of all facts.

During the second century after the Buddha's Nirvāṇa, the Community split into sects (see Figure 1), dividing first into the *Sthaviras* (Pali *Thera*, "Elders") and the *Mahāsāṅghikas* ("Great Assembly-ites"). The Mahāsāṅghikas admitted lay followers and non-arhant monks to their meetings and were sensitive to popular religious values and aspirations. Two out of three basic strands in the Mahāyāna are of Mahāsāṅghika origin (see p. 65). They claimed to be truer to the primitive teaching than did the Elders. They kept the earlier open, permissive structure as against the bureaucratic exclusivism of the Sthaviras. And they refused to gild the lotus of arhant-ship. But they carried the transfiguration of the Buddha much further than the Sthaviras did, holding that he is supermundane and perfectly pure. His body is infinite, his power boundless, and his life endless. He educated living beings tirelessly, awakening pure faith in them. Furthermore, apparition-bodies (conventional human forms) of the Buddha appear and act in different world-realms at the same time.

Half a dozen subsects came out of the Mahāsāṅghikas, partly as a result of doctrinal disputes and partly through geographic separation.

The Elders, or Sthaviras, claimed to conserve the true teaching and discipline of the Buddha by emphasizing the value of monastic life for personal enlightenment and the authority of monks in the Buddhist community. They, however, underwent another major schism about two hundred years after the Buddha's death. The schismatics were *Pudgalavādins* (Personalists), who asserted on the one hand that there exists a person or self (*pudgala*) who is neither identical with the five skandhas nor different from them but who nonetheless knows, transmigrates, and enters nirvāṇa. They said, on the other hand, that the skandhas that constitute the phenomenal person are mere designations, not real substances. The Sūtras contain many statements that can be cited in support of these views. The person of the Personalists is rather like the consciousness (*vijñāna*) that, according to an early teaching, transmigrates and enters nirvāṇa. Furthermore, the canonical expositions of the anātman (no-self) doctrine are ambiguous. They deny that any one of the skandhas is the ātman (self or person), and so conclude that the five taken together are not the ātman.

The Personalists said that the person is to the skandhas as fire is to the fuel, neither identical nor different. If it were other than the skandhas, it would be eternal and unconditional, which is a heretical view. If it were the same as the skandhas, it would undergo annihilation, also a heretical view.

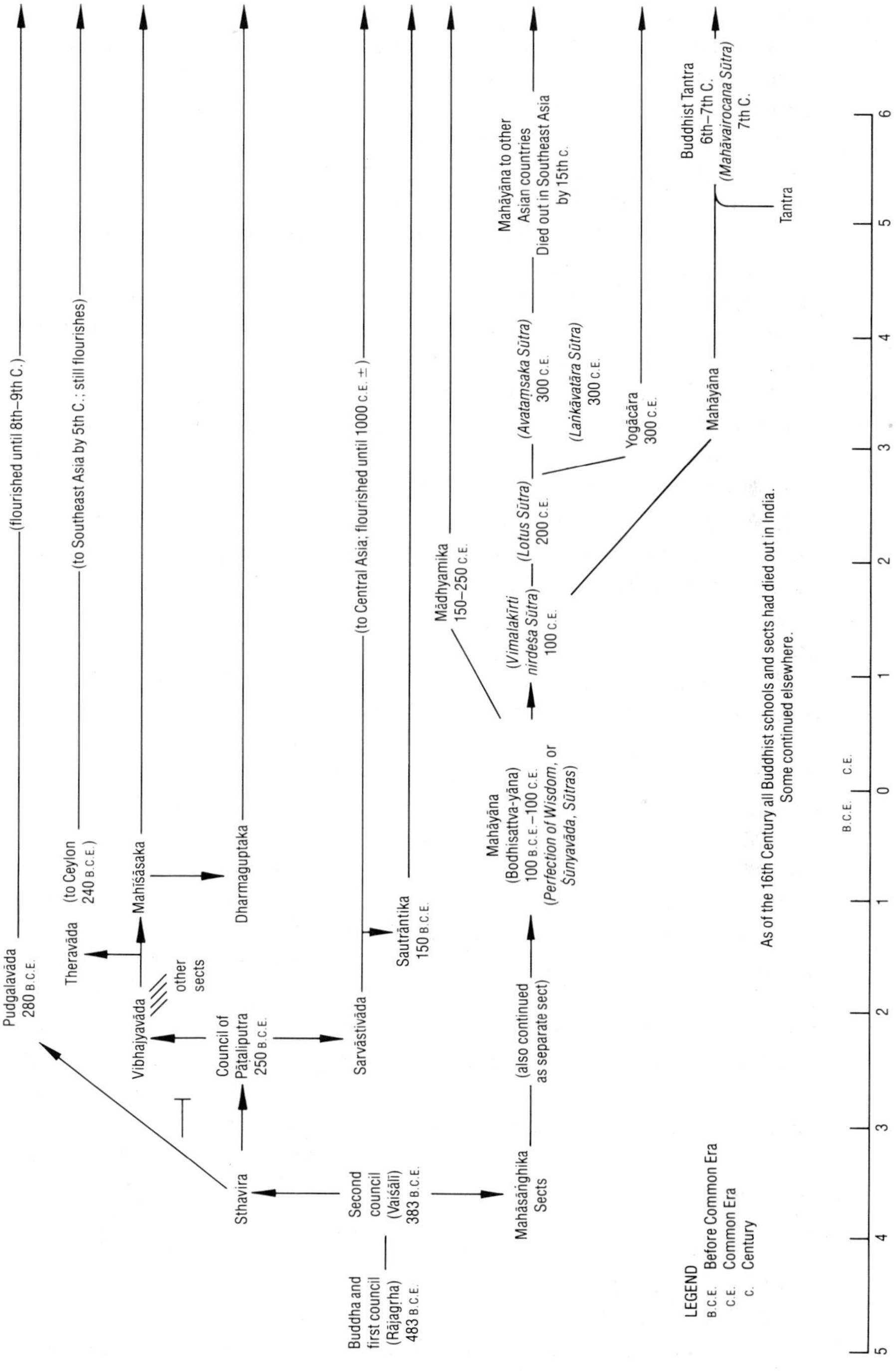

Figure 1. Major Buddhist Sects in India, 500 B.C.E.–600 C.E.

The Abhidharma masters of the Sthavira schools declared that the dharmas (elements) are real things (*vastu*) or substances (*dravya*), while the person is just a designation. The Personalists denied that either dharmas or persons are real things, while affirming that both exist as designations—that is, as objects of commonsense knowledge and statements. It is also the position that Mahāyāna later took.

The Personalists maintained that nirvāṇa is neither really the same as nor really distinct from dharmas (phenomena). If the person is neither the same as nor other than its elements, then its cessation must be neither the same nor different. Saṃsāra, also, is to nirvāṇa as the fuel is to the fire. It would be going rather far to make an active principle out of nirvāṇa, even for the Personalists, but this is just what the Mahāyāna sect called *Yogācāra* (see p. 71) later did. The Sthavira tradition emphasized the utter transcendence of nirvāṇa and refused to concede that it is immanent in sāṃsara even when the Sūtras used worldly symbols for immanence such as the fire and the ocean. The Tathāgata who dies is like the fire that goes out. Gautama's hearers believed that fire is an indestructible element latent in every bright or warm thing, but especially in fuel. It alternates between manifestation and "going home" to its occult source. In the Brahmanical literature, the ocean is the reservoir from which the streams of differentiated existence proceed and to which they revert when the liberated one merges back. So the Tathāgata, residing in this nirvāṇa-realm, is subtler than the subtlest (like fire) and greater than the greatest (like the ocean). These are precisely the predicates of the ātman (self) and *brahman* (cosmic essence) in the Upaniṣads. The Personalists were more cautious than the Upaniṣads in asserting immanence, but they kept alive this aspect of the early ontology and prepared the way for Mahāyāna doctrines such as that all living beings are endowed with suchness and with Buddha-nature. As a sect the Personalists thrived for over a thousand years.

This seemingly obscure philosophical dispute really has vital relevance to a cardinal religious issue: the value to be placed on this world. Buddhism, like Christianity, has passed its centuries in a continual quandary on this point. If a spiritual reality dwells in and suffuses this world, then worldly and secular activities such as raising a family and scientific research have inherent worth. But if the worldly and the spiritual realms are mutually alien and exclusive, then profane things and activities have no intrinsic value and are significant only insofar as they contribute to escape from the profane realm into the spiritual. Christianity sided wholeheartedly neither with the orthodox Jewish affirmation nor with the Gnostic rejection of this world. Buddhism similarly preferred an enigmatic Middle Way against the easy-to-understand, dead-end extremes of mere worldliness and mere other-worldliness.

A third schism further rent the Elders' school at the Council of Pāṭaliputra about 250 B.C.E. The two factions were called Distinctionists (*Vibhajyavādins*) and All-is-ists (*Sarvāstivādins*); the latter's chief thesis was that past and future things really exist, as do present things.

The Council of Pāṭaliputra, and possibly Emperor Aśoka himself, decided against the Sarvāstivādins, some of whom migrated west and north. They established a strong center in Kashmir, which flourished for a thousand years. They were numerous between Mathurā and Gandhāra. Buddhism flourished in this region under the Indo-Greek kings during the second century B.C.E. The greatest of these kings, Menander (Milinda), is said to have become a Buddhist. The Indo-Greeks and their successors, the Śakas (first century B.C.E. through first century C.E.) and the Kuṣāṇas (first century C.E. through mid-third century), were all invaders from Bactria and Parthia. They retained their connections with Central Asia and so enabled Buddhism to spread to the developing city-states along the silk route between China and the West. The Sarvāstivādins were in a favorable position and so came to dominate the cities on the northern branch of the trade route: Kashgar, Aksu, Kuchā, and Karashahr. From there, they entered China and exerted a powerful influence.

It is doubtful whether the Sarvāstivādin theories about time and being are religiously important. This school did, however, nourish a doctrine that became one cornerstone of the Mahāyāna: the perfections. The bodhisattva, they said, fulfills six perfections—donation or generosity, morality, patience, vigor, meditation, and wisdom. Each of these virtues is frequently commended in the Sūtras, but they become perfections only when carried out fully. The *Tales of the Previous Lives of the Buddha* (Jātaka), attested to in the art of the second century B.C.E. relate how Gautama in his former lives accomplished each *pāramitā* ("perfection"). Reborn as a hare, he resolved to practice giving (*dāna*), especially on Observance Day. Disguising himself as a brahmin, the god Indra decided to test the Bodhisattva hare and requested food. The hare realized that he could not offer grass as food to people, so he instructed the brahmin to make a fire, roast him, and eat him. Indra lit the fire, but when the hare jumped into it, the flame did not singe a single hair. Indra revealed himself and praised the hare. Reborn as a mariner, the Bodhisattva became blind but achieved great feats of navigation through the practice of prajñā (wisdom). Reincarnated as a caravan leader, he exemplified vigor (*vīrya*) by persisting in the search for underground water when his caravan ran dry in the desert.

Living one of his former lives as an ascetic, the Bodhisattva was staying in the pleasure grove of a dissolute king of Benares. The king entered with a flock of dancing girls, and when he fell into a drunken sleep, the girls wandered off and discovered the ascetic. On awakening, the ruler was enraged to find his girls gathered round the mendicant and listening to his sermon. He asked the Bodhisattva what doctrine he professed and was told patience (*kṣānti*). So the king summoned his executioner, had the Bodhisattva severely flogged, then asked, "What do you profess?" The answer was still "patience." So the king had his victim's hands and feet cut off, then his nose and ears. To the end, the Bodhisattva professed patience and felt no anger whatsoever. The Earth, however, ran out of patience. As the tyrant was leaving his pleasure grove, the Earth opened up beneath his feet and toppled him to the lowest hell. These popular tales urged the listeners to imitate the Bodhisattva but did not tell them to become a bodhisattva, a step that was taken by early Mahāyāna doctrine.

AŚOKA

In 321 B.C.E., roughly when the Mahāsāṅghikas and the Sthaviras were dividing, Candragupta Maurya succeeded to the throne of Magadha after a campaign of harassment and gradual erosion of his predecessors' power base. By 303, he controlled everything from Bengal to eastern Afghanistan and as far south as the Narmadā River. He exchanged ambassadors with the Seleucid rulers of Persia, whom he had defeated in battle, and adopted technology and political institutions from these successors of Alexander. Candragupta's son, Bindusāra, acceded to the throne in 297 B.C.E., conquered the Deccan and Mysore in central India, and in the far south brought the Tamil country under his suzerainty. He died in 272, succeeded by his son Aśoka, who consolidated his power for some years. In 260, Aśoka conquered Kaliṅga in northeast India, the only area still refusing to submit. Extensive bloodshed and destruction filled the emperor with remorse. He began to study the Dharma of various sects, became a lay follower of Buddhism, and gave up the royal pastime of hunting because it infringed on the first precept not to take life. He visited monks frequently, learned from them, and spent some time in retreat as a lay brother.

The emperor's life as a Buddhist began, appropriately, with a pilgrimage to Bodhgayā, the site of the Buddha's Enlightenment. Legend says that he erected stūpas there, at Sārnāth, site of the First Sermon, and Kuśinagara, on the spot where Śākyamuni was cremated. In the same region, in 253, he ordered the enlargement of the stūpa dedicated to the former Buddha Kanakamuni. The inscription recording this act is the earliest datable evidence for the doctrine and cult of Buddhas who had lived previous to Gautama. Aśoka's first wife came from Vidiṣā, which is apparently why he sponsored the construction of the oldest stūpa on the nearby hill of Sāñcī, the most extensive and perhaps the loveliest of all early Buddhist holy places in India. Legend continues that Aśoka built 84,000 stūpas, but even the more modest tally of history and archaeology abundantly testifies that honoring the Buddha ranked as highly as ethical conduct in Aśoka's religion.

Five years after attacking Kaliṅga, Aśoka proclaimed a new policy, that of peaceful Dharma-conquest, which he had come to prefer over military conquest. He had a series of fourteen edicts engraved on rocks throughout his empire, and he instructed his officials to read them to the public on festival days. Thirteen years later he began issuing another series of seven edicts, which were inscribed on polished stone pillars. These inscriptions are the earliest surviving compositions of a Buddhist lay follower. Aśoka's favor enriched the Saṅgha, caused recruits to flock to the Order, and demonstrated the oft-repeated rule that the survival and prosperity of Buddhism have usually depended on its ability to enlist the support of rulers.

His motive in adopting Buddhism was a blend of personal conviction and political astuteness. In the plain and personal style of the edicts sincere concern with the welfare of his subjects and his neighbors' subjects shows through more clearly than in any other royal pronouncements of the ancient world. He inherited a strong bureaucratic state, which not only regulated commerce, industry, and agriculture but acted as entrepreneur itself. Centralized government served to strengthen the craft guilds, and the handicraft industry and interregional trade increased. Thus, craftsmen and merchants, whose interests were tied to the Maurya state, especially supported Buddhism. So Aśoka in supporting that religion was strengthening a bond with an already loyal class but was also trying to bridge the gulf between the state and all its people. To achieve this, he sought an ideological common denominator, utilizing available means of communication to propagate it.

The Dharma commended in the Rock Edicts is the common core of the orthodox and ascetic religious traditions, not just the particular teachings of the Buddha. Aśoka proclaimed that he honored and made gifts to ascetics and householders of all sects. His aim, he said, was the growth of religious essence in all sects, which means not praising one's own and not disparaging others. He recommended that the different schools listen to and learn from one another. Dharma meant to him chiefly the first four perfections—donation, morality, patience (tolerance), and vigor. He said nothing about meditation or wisdom, topics not usually the concern of the laity. His edicts encouraged willing obedience to and honoring of one's parents, teachers, and other elders; generosity to relatives, acquaintances, and religious persons; abstention from killing of animals; moderation in accumulating and spending wealth; and kindness to serfs and servants. To his subjects he commended the mental qualities of self-control, gratitude, devotion, compassion, and truthfulness and took specific steps in his personal life to carry out his program. For his subjects, he established dispensaries and medicinal herb gardens and improved highways for travelers. Rather than going on pleasure tours, he instead went on Dharma-tours, visiting holy places, giving to people of religion and the aged, and discoursing with the people of the country on moral custom. Yet there is one glaring omission, compared with other civilizations of the time, in the list of Aśoka's good works: he founded no schools, no colleges, no academies.

Aśoka left the propagation of the specifically Buddhist Dharma to the Saṅgha, though he did preach in some of the edicts. According to Buddhist tradition, he dispatched his son Mahinda and his daughter Saṅghamittā as missionaries to Ceylon, but they went as monk and nun rather than as prince and princess. The Dharma of his edicts is not just humanistic morality. Aśoka asserted that he had caused gods to mingle with men as they had never done before. This may mean that by fostering offerings to holy individuals and deities and by promoting Dharma he had propitiated the spirits and drawn them down to the altars and homes of his people. He sponsored religious shows in which the people saw models of the paradises with images of the gods, showing how with zeal in Dharma they could attain life in those heavens.

One of his edicts says that in 256 and 255 he sent Dharma-envoys to the Greek rulers of Syria, Egypt, Macedonia, Cyrene, and Epyrus, as well as to the Tamils in south India. His missionaries left no traceable impression on the Mediterranean world, but they succeeded to some degree closer to home. A bilingual Greek-Aramaic inscription of Aśoka at Kandahār in Afghanistan records the measures he had taken to "make men more pious" and concludes, "Acting in this way, during their present life and in their future existence they will live better and more happily together in all things." Aśoka did much more for the Buddhist tradition, however. He can be considered its second founder, since his example established the influential model of the Buddhist state and the dedicated layperson. Later Buddhists never forgot the pious monarch who ruled as a Buddhist king and lived the model life of the lay follower of the Buddha's Dharma. Thus, alongside the Saṅgha and its monastic ideals there developed a parallel tradition whose goals involved achieving the Dharma's ends within the worldly structures of political and social reality.

RELIGIOUS LIFE IN THE EARLY CENTURIES

The Canon furnishes evidence for the practices of the Community, lay as well as monastic, during the second century B.C.E. The Pali Vinaya (which is still in theory the rule in Theravāda monasteries, though large parts of it have fallen into disuse) prescribes the correct life for the monk and describes, in telling the origin of each rule, the colorful abuses against which the Order had to protect itself. Areas in which the Saṅgha was well established were divided into districts, each approximately twenty miles square. Each district had one observance (*uposatha*) hall, at which all monks resident within the district were required to assemble on the last day of each half-month for recitation of the Rules of Discipline (Pali, *Pāṭimokkha*).

Rules of Discipline for Monks

This code defines five classes of offense, prescribes rules of deportment, and establishes some procedural principles. Four offenses warrant permanent expulsion: fornication, theft, killing a human being, and falsely claiming spiritual attainments. Similar rules, appropriately modified for the subordinate role of women in Indian society of that period, govern the lives of nuns.

Thirteen offenses require a formal meeting of the Saṅgha chapter, with a quorum of at least twenty monks, and are punished with probation. The first five of these concern sex: intentional ejaculation, touching a woman, speaking suggestively to her, urging a woman to earn merit by yielding to a man of religion, and serving as a go-between. Two rules deal with the prescribed size and the approved site of monks' dwellings. Six rules pertain to concord in the Order. For example, it is an offense to harass a fellow monk by false accusations of an offense that merits expulsion or to support such an accusation with misleading testimony. And it is an offense to persist in fomenting discord within the Saṅgha after the assembly has three times formally warned the culprit to desist. Likewise it is a misdeed for other monks to persist in supporting a schismatic and for a monk to persist after the third warning in being obtuse and ignoring what the assembly tells him. An evil-living monk whose influence is pernicious to the laity is to be asked to leave the district. If, after the third request, he has not reformed his ways or taken leave, he is guilty of an offense that requires probation.

The probationer forfeits many privileges: he must not allow monks in good standing to offer salutation, provide seats for him, carry his robe or bowl, or shampoo him. He must not walk or sit in front of a rule-abiding bhikṣu. He must announce that he is on probation to newcomers, when he enters a new residence, on Observance Day, and at the ceremony terminating the rainy season retreat. His residence is restricted, and he has few options for changing it. He is required always to take the lowest seat, the worst bed, the worst room.

A monk must not take a seat with a woman, either in private or in public. If he does so, the assembly may decide whether the offense requires probation or merely confession.

Thirty of the enumerated offenses require expiation and forfeiture of the article involved. They deal mainly with robes, alms bowls, and seat-rugs. The obedient monk must not have more than one of each of these at a time. He must not allow a nun to do his laundry, give him a robe, or prepare wool for a rug. When his begging bowl is broken in five places, he can exchange it for a new one. He may store medicinal foods only for seven days. He may not receive gold or silver, buy, sell, or barter.

Ninety-two of the designated (monk's) offenses require expiation. The list is quiet miscellaneous: lying, abuse, slander, stealing another bhikṣu's sleeping space, taking more than one meal at a public rest house, sporting in the water, or eavesdropping while other monks quarrel. It is prohibited to dig the ground, destroy any vegetable, or sprinkle water with living creatures in it. Thus the monk could not practice agriculture. These rules, ostensibly to protect worms and bugs, also safeguarded the religious against lapsing into peasanthood and neglecting the Dharma. Another group of rules prohibits the monk (except for good cause) from going near an army drawn up for battle, staying with an army more than two or three nights, and watching the troops on parade. The idea seems to be that the monk should not be an accessory to bloodshed. The prohibitions were doubtless also intended to prevent him from engaging in espionage or diplomatic intrigue.

Unlike killing a human being, taking animal life deliberately does not warrant expulsion, but merely expiation. The monk must not even drink water that contains living things. But eating meat is not forbidden in the Rules of Discipline, though drinking liquor is an offense to be expiated.

A monk who tells a layperson or another monk that he has extraordinary spiritual powers, even when it is true, commits an expiable offense, and so does one who tells a nonmonk that a bhikṣu has committed a grave offense. Nevertheless, every monk is duty-bound to inform the assembly of any serious transgression committed by a fellow monk. Since the Vinaya provides formal procedures for judging the accused and prescribing penance and since an unconfessed and unexpiated sin is considered an affliction that is aggravated the longer it goes unabsolved, the informer is doing the accused a kindness. On the other hand, the code treats false accusation as a serious offense and forbids harrying another with insinuations that he is transgressing. These rules taken together demand that the Saṅgha keep its own counsel; shun both the adulation and reproach of outsiders; and compel honesty, conformity, and goodwill from its members.

Some of the seventy-five rules of deportment regulate the conduct of the monk while going on his begging rounds among the homes of the laity, receiving alms, eating, and excreting. He must at all times be properly clothed, keep his eyes downcast, not sway his limbs or body, not loll or slouch, refrain from loud laughter and noise, and observe good table manners—neither stuffing his mouth, smacking his lips, talking with his mouth full, nor tossing the food into his mouth. He must not excrete while standing up, onto growing grass, or into water. Sixteen rules forbid the monk to preach Dharma to a monk or layperson whose deportment is disrespectful: carrying a parasol, staff, sword, or weapon in the hand; wearing slippers, sandals, a turban, or other head-covering; occupying a higher seat than a monk; sitting while the monk is standing; or walking on a path either in front of or beside the monk.

The overall purpose of the rules of deportment is to render the monk worthy of reverence and of offerings and to ensure that he receives the formal respect to which he is entitled. The bhikṣu must himself maintain impeccable conduct and allow the laity to choose their response. If they revile him, he suffers it with gentle dignity. If they behave like pigs, he withholds the pearls of the Dharma. The good monk is indifferent to success and failure, gain and loss. But he does the things that are most conducive to success in fulfilling the Dharma and sticks to his principles even when so doing places his life in danger. Monks, and presumably nuns too, have starved; died of disease; been killed by robbers, tyrants, and ferocious beasts; and been mocked and humiliated by hostile unbelievers. But wherever the Vinaya has been observed in spirit and in letter, the Saṅgha as a whole has earned respect and has prevailed.

In themselves the rules of deportment seem trivial and quaint. The Saṅgha, it must be remembered, accepts recruits from all social classes and peoples. It has to refine vulgar boys and civilize uncouth barbarians. Etiquette alone does not suffice, of course, but it is a necessary part of the complete discipline through which character is shaped, good habits built, and external observances converted into inner discipline.

A noteworthy feature of the Vinaya rules is that they are utterly free from prerational tabus of the sort so common in the Brahmanical and Near Eastern lawbooks. There is no idea that certain foods are impure, that bodily wastes pollute spiritually, or that certain acts or objects are lucky or unlucky. The authors of the Vinaya certainly thought that spirits and gods exist, yet no place is given to tabu plants and animals associated with particular divinities, a department in which Classical Hinduism rivals the cults of the ancient Near East. Nevertheless, the two dominant ethical concerns of the code—not taking life and continence—are carried to extremes not justifiable on humanistic and pragmatic grounds. The implicit premises are that life breath (or life-blood) and semen are tabu. Animal sacrifice offers up the sacred life substance, while nonviolence (*ahiṃsā*) earns merit by saving life and then devotes the merit to holy objectives, while ascetic continence saves the force of Eros and applies it to spiritual goals.

The Vinaya does not see the monk as working out his own salvation unaided, like the self-made man of nineteenth-century capitalist folklore. Each monk is his brother's keeper; and, when the ordinand joins the Saṅgha, he surrenders some liberties and submits to the collective authority of the Community. Several disciplinary procedures are laid down for reducing the obstinate and the wayward to conformity. A strife-maker may be placed under an act of rebuke, which excludes him from participating in ordinations, guiding novices, exhorting nuns, censuring monks, commanding a junior, or associating with the other bhikṣus. An ignorant or foolish monk may be put under an act of subordination that suspends the same privileges and, in addition, places him in the care of a tutor until he has learned the Dharma. Acts of banishment are directed against those who cause scandal to the Saṅgha. A monk who offends the laity may be made to submit to an act of reconciliation, under which he forfeits privileges until he has asked and obtained the pardon of the layperson whom he has wronged. An act of suspension is directed against the monk who refuses to renounce a pernicious doctrine. He is not allowed to eat or dwell with the Saṅgha, and notice of his banishment is sent to neighboring districts, in which he is likewise to be denied food and shelter. All these acts remain in force only until their object has mended his ways.

A few features of the Vinaya, or Discipline, merit comment. It insists throughout on due process of law. The offender is warned, reminded of the rules, and, if the unacceptable behavior persists, is formally charged and duly tried by a jury consisting of the whole chapter. A transgressor cannot be tried while absent, may speak in his own defense, but must accept the sentence once it has been passed. The code, like the Talmud and the New Testament exhortations, is designed to compel expiation of sins and reconciliation of conflicts. Nevertheless, the Vinaya's insistence on confessing one's misdeeds is inimical to most present-day Hindu and Buddhist cultures, in which preserving appearances rates higher than solving the problem. One last point: the punishments prescribed in the Vinaya, while stringent, constitute a middle way between laxity and cruelty.

The Discipline presupposes a high degree of earnestness and integrity. It will work only if most candidates enter voluntarily and in good faith. For this reason, full ordination (*upasampadā*) is not granted to anyone under twenty years of age. Eight years, though, is the minimum age for the novitiate ordination, which even adult candidates must undergo before proceeding to full ordination. In the "going forth" ceremony, the ordinand is invested with the saffron robes, has his head shaven, and takes the Three Refuges and the Ten Precepts. The Ten Precepts for a moral life are to abstain from (1) taking life; (2) taking what is not given; (3) sexual misconduct; (4) lying; (5) drinking liquor; (6) eating after noon; (7) watching dancing, singing, and shows; (8) adorning oneself with garlands, perfumes, and ointments; (9) using a high bed; and (10) receiving gold and silver. The ordinand is then a novice and has left the household life. If under twenty, the novice must live with a preceptor until of age. The preceptor must have passed ten years since full ordination and must be of good character and competent. The novice also receives instruction from a tutor.

Ordination is conferred by an assembly of at least ten bhikṣus. The candidate, accompanied by one of his tutors, comes before the president of the assembly, whom he petitions for admission to the Saṅgha. Then he retires to the foot of the assembly, his alms bowl strapped onto his back, and his two tutors examine him to ascertain that he has his bowl, under robe, upper robe, and mantle. Then one of the tutors asks him in the hearing of the whole assembly whether he is free from certain diseases and whether he is a free human male, debtless, exempt from military service, furnished with his parents' permission, and at least twenty years of age. The candidate is then made to go forward, kneel, and ask the assembly for ordination. The assembly signifies assent by silence, so the candidate stands up, and the tutors put him through the interrogation again. One of the tutors reports that the candidate desires ordination, is free from disqualifications, has a bowl and a set of robes, asks for ordination, and that the assembly grants ordination. The public proclamation is made: "If any approves, let him be silent. If any objects, let him speak." When the assembly keeps silent through the third repetition of this proclamation, the two tutors announce to the president that the candidate has received ordination. The date and the hour are then noted, since seniority in the Order commences from the time of ordination. The new monk is given an exhortation, in which he is told that henceforth his four reliances are to be on alms for food, on old rags for clothing, on the shade of a tree for shelter, and on cow's urine for medicine. Actual monastic life is usually much less austere; the laity prepare good food for the monks and donate new robes annually, just after the rainy season retreat. A Buddhist nun's ordination is similar in most respects to a Buddhist monk's.

Life of the Monks

The Buddhist monk owned nothing but clothes, which consisted of an undergarment, outer garment, cloak, waist-cloth, and belt and buckle. The robes, donated by the laity, were red or ochre. He also wore sandals and carried a begging bowl, a razor, tweezers, nail clippers, ear- and toothpicks, some gauze for filtering water, a needle, a walking stick, and a bag of medicines. He was also allowed an umbrella against the sun and a fan against the heat. Every other month the monk shaved his hair without using a mirror, forbidden to him, as were adornments, cosmetics, and perfumes, along with profane music and song. The Buddhist nun's personal possessions were equally meager.

Originally, the Buddhist monk was a wanderer, having no fixed domicile. He lived under a tree or in a natural mountain grotto, on a hillside or in a glen or forest glade, even on a haystack. Naturally, he stayed near some village or town to beg, sometimes living in a thatched hut or some other humble temporary dwelling. For three months out of the year the rainy season made travel impossible, and very soon recluses and monks tended to group their dwellings together. The Canon reports that on occasion the Buddha accepted groups of dwellings and parks from local merchants to house monks during the rain retreat. There they could pursue their spiritual development and conduct communal ceremonies relatively undisturbed. The site selected for such resting places had to be secluded to ensure a proper atmosphere for meditation but also close enough to a village or town so that the monks could go on their begging rounds.

About 200 B.C.E., they began to receive from wealthy donors rock-cut residences (*vihāra*), in which the features of the wooden prototypes—pillars, joists, and rafters—were imitated in stone. About the same time, residences of fired brick came into general use. Doubtless humble dwellings of wood and thatch, like the typical village residence in modern Śrī Laṅkā, continued to outnumber the imposing brick and stone ones that survive for archaeological study. The remains of the brick residences at Sāñcī, Sārnāth, and Nālandā and their rock-cut counterparts at Kārlī and Ajantā exhibit a common plan. Four rows of cells, each eight to ten feet square, a half dozen or more cells to a row, surround a central courtyard, which was part of the cave in the rock-cut residences and was probably enclosed with thatch or a canopy in the brick ones. The cells each contained one or two brick or stone benches, which were covered with rugs and used both as seats and as beds like modern Indian benches. Apparently only elders and perhaps their personal attendants lived in the cells; the junior monks and novices slept in the central courtyard, which also served as a classroom and a refectory.

At Ajantā (fifth to sixth century C.E.) walls surrounding the rock-cut monastery courtyards were covered with brightly colored paintings of Jātaka stories (*Tales of the Previous Lives of the Buddha*), donors, foreign visitors, celestial beings, beautiful princes and princesses, and formal designs. The monks who lived amid this aesthetic splendor were forbidden by their rule to discuss women, chariots, elephants, kings, and battles, but were permitted to see all these subjects exquisitely painted on their dwelling walls. They were exhorted to avoid even the thought of sexual love, yet the doorways to their residences were carved with consummately voluptuous loving couples. The paradox of the beauty of the walls and the austerity of the monks who found refuge within them remains today to puzzle the observer. Whatever its valuation of sensual things, Buddhism has never allowed its distrust of attachment to beautiful things to intrude and prevent the beautification of sacred premises. Buddhists used other sorts of pictures didactically. Paintings of hell, where the wicked suffer punishment for their evil deeds, were painted on the walls of monastery bathrooms and sweat baths. A picture of the Wheel of Life was sometimes painted over the monastery door or in a hall where passersby could see it, and a monk was appointed to explain it.

Some bhikṣus evidently lived alone in huts, either near a village or deep in the jungle. The Vinaya specifies the maximum size for such huts. Solitary residence was more favorable for meditation and the practice of austerities than was the communal life of the larger residences, where the daily routine comprised many activities other than meditation and where most bhikṣus did not practice more than the mild austerity required by the Vinaya.

Another important structure associated with early Buddhist monastic residences was the hall housing a stūpa (*caitya-gṛha*). The stūpa is the principal object of worship for Buddhists, especially when it enshrines relics of the Buddha or of an important or locally revered monk. Stūpa worship includes circumambulation in the auspicious clockwise direction around the monument, prostrations, and offerings of flowers. When housed in a special structure, the stūpa was placed at the end of a long hall, with a nave in front in which worshippers could gather and an apse containing the stūpa itself. Outside aisles demarcated by a colonnade made circumambulation possible. In addition to stūpas, monastic residences, and such stūpa halls, Buddhists also built temples, few of which have survived in India.

The main outlines of the daily monastic routine seem to have varied little through the centuries in India and to have undergone no major changes in China. The Siṅhalese commentator Buddhaghosa in the fourth century C.E. based his account of the Buddha's daily habits on the standard monastic routine. The Buddha, he says, got up at daybreak, rinsed his mouth and went to the toilet; then he sat quietly until it was time to go on the begging rounds (nowadays, in Theravāda countries, at daybreak), when he put on his robes, took his bowl, and entered the village or town for alms. The bhikṣu's residence was supposed to be near enough to a village that he could easily go there to beg and far enough away that he would not be distracted by noise and company. The Buddha, says Buddhaghosa, was usually received with honor by householders, who vied to invite him and his companions to lunch. They would seat him and place food reverently in his bowl. Then when he had eaten, he would discourse on Dharma to his hosts. Returning to the monastery, he sat in the refectory pavilion while the monks who had not been invited to dine in their donors' homes finished eating. Then he withdrew to his cell, called "the perfumed chamber," washed his feet, and rested. Following the siesta period he came out and preached to the monks who had gathered outside his cell. Then he responded to individual requests for guidance in meditation, after which the monks dispersed to their dwellings. The Buddha took another rest in the late afternoon, then preached to the lay donors and worshippers who came to call on him. Afterward he went to the bathhouse for a cool bath, then paced back and forth in the courtyard or garden and meditated. He concluded the evening (first watch of night) by granting interviews to individual monks. During the second watch of night, he received deities who came for instruction; during the third, he rested.

This schedule alternates rest and activity, retirement and sociability, covering a long and busy day at a leisurely pace. It is with good reason that the Vinaya and the elders in charge of the monasteries have consistently emphasized the daily routine and guarded its observance. Buddhism as a way of life is concretely realized in the monastic routine, with its provisions for cultivating morality, wisdom, meditation, and worship; with its scrupulous attention to the correct performance of everyday acts; and with its faith that in the still of the night the gods come down and converse with holy monks in the Saṅgha's moonlit groves.

The yearly monastic routine followed the rhythm of the seasons. During the monsoons (June/July to October/November [*varṣa*, Pali *vassa*]), the monks retreated to their monasteries for study and meditation. Some were assigned specific functions to ensure efficient operation of the monastery. A senior member supervised the details of the structure's physical survival, and a layman acted as a liaison agent between the Community and the outside world. The dry season's return was marked by ceremonies that preceded the departure of the monks for their wandering and preaching. The laity presented gifts of cloth to the assembled monks, invited them to midday meals, and participated in processions. Only a few monks remained behind to maintain the monastery.

Buddhist Nuns

The Order of Nuns (*bhikṣuṇī-saṅgha*) was said to have been instituted reluctantly by the Buddha at the request of his aunt and foster mother, Prajāpatī, and upon the intercession of Ānanda. The Blessed One conceded that women are able to attain arhant-ship but laid eight special regulations on the nuns, subordinating them strictly to the Order of Monks. A nun shall honor all monks as her seniors. She shall not reside in a district where there are no monks. The nuns shall celebrate Observance Day on its appointment by the assembly of monks and under the supervision of a monk. A nun shall invite criticism at the end of residence from both the nuns' and the monks' assemblies. She shall undergo penance for a serious offence toward both assemblies. A female postulant must undergo a two-year novitiate and then seek ordination from both assemblies. A nun shall not revile or abuse a monk. And whereas monks are allowed to reprove nuns formally, nuns may not reprove monks. The Buddha is said to have stipulated this strict subordination of the bhikṣuṇī to the bhikṣus because "When women retire from household life to the houseless one, . . . that religion does not long endure." The True Dharma, for this reason, will only last five hundred years. It is perhaps not surprising that an order founded so reluctantly should not have flourished. After the first generation few distinguished nuns are mentioned.

The Laity

We have already noted that the first two worshippers of the new Buddha were laymen (p. 21). We have also observed (p. 41) that all sects agreed that the laity could attain the first three degrees of sainthood and remain in the household life; the Sūtras and some Hīnayāna sects, however, affirmed that arhant-ship was open to the laity, though some insisted that immediately after attainment they must either die or become a monk or nun.

In ancient India, the layman dressed in white, as opposed to the colored robes of the monk, and lived as a married householder. Though he followed the Buddhist way of life, taking refuge in it and supporting the monastic community, he was not compelled to forgo other religious practices common among members of his social class. He was required to follow the ethical code of the Buddhist layman, but his chief virtue was generosity in giving to the monks. Since he remained involved in the world, he was not expected to excel in meditation or wisdom. He could enhance the practice of his lay virtues by fasting four days every month—that is, eating nothing after his one prenoontime meal. These special days would be devoted to recitations, reading of the scriptures, and preaching sermons. The layman was also expected to be without personal luxury, which meant giving up fine furniture, flowers, perfumes, singing, dancing, and dramatic performances. For further spiritual advance, he could abstain from sex and generally follow the practice of novices and monks. Finally, he could take the ultimate step and join the Order, trading his white robes for those of the novice monk.

The laity in early Buddhism were thus assigned arduous functions and promised ample rewards in this life and subsequent ones. The monastic orders depended on their donations, and in return they instructed them in Dharma, especially in giving, morality, heaven, the wretchedness of sense-desire, and the benefits of overcoming sense-desire. By taking the Five Precepts and having profound faith in Buddha, Dharma, and Saṅgha, the layman and laywoman were surely to become *srotāpanna* (stream-winners), have only happy rebirths, and speedily attain full enlightenment. The virtuous householder was assured increase of wealth because of his zeal, a fine reputation, confidence in handling public affairs, a calm and unbewildered death, and rebirth in a heaven. Girls were told to become good wives, to be willing and sweet tempered, to honor their husbands' relatives and guests, to be skillful at homecrafts, to manage the servants well, and to protect their husbands' valuables. As a reward, after death they would be born among the Gods of Lovely Form.

In the Saṅgha, today as in antiquity, males are segregated from females and monastics from laity, resulting in a fourfold organization. Relations among members of the four orders are restricted, so that they will not corrupt one another. The relations are expressed in formal

Female donors. (From a Central Asian wall painting, circa eighth century C.E.*)*

gestures like bowing and proper address, so that due honor and seniority will be observed. Though the individual layman may well be more moral and more spiritual than any given monk, the former must give precedence to the latter, because the yellow-robed orders are superior to the white-clad laity. The nun must look up to the monk and the laywoman to the layman, because the male sex per se is considered superior to the female regardless of whether particular women are better than any individual man.

This uncomplimentary view of womankind is doubtless the product of both prevailing cultural prejudices and monkish anxiety, but it is not an essential Buddhist doctrine. Reading the *Songs of the Elder Women* (the Pali Canon's *Therīgāthā*), we find that in Buddha's time women were recognized as having attained full arhant-ship, a state of liberation equal to that of the Master. The scriptures do not present much of a case for male superiority, and their case for the ceremonial precedence of the monastics is fragmentary and weak. The homeless life is more favorable for attaining sainthood, because it is free from the distractions, temptations, and worries of family life. Hence, it is presumed that, in general, monks are more moderate in eating and drinking and more zealous in following the moral precepts than the laity.

The householder is encouraged to take the first five of the ten śīla (precepts) undertaken by the novice (see p. 53). *Śīla* is defined as suppressing unwholesome conduct of body and speech in pursuance of a resolution made either in private or before witnesses. The first precept is to refrain from killing living beings (*prāṇin*, "having life, breath"). Animals of all sorts are intended, but plants are not. The sin is to know that something is a living being, intend to kill it, attempt to do so, and succeed. Unintentional killing is not a sin as killing, though it may constitute sinful negligence. The layman cannot avoid inadvertently killing small creatures while practicing agriculture, but if he undertakes this precept, he is supposed to minimize the destruction of small lives.

The second precept is to refrain from taking what has not been given. The sin consists in taking the property of another by force or by stealth. The offense is committed when one knows that the thing belongs to another and intentionally attempts and successfully executes the act of taking it. If the ownership of an object is unknown, there is an obligation to try to find out whether it is the property of another before taking it.

The third precept is to refrain from misconduct in sexual matters. It concerns intercourse with a forbidden woman (the wife of another, a woman under the care of a guardian, a betrothed woman, a nun, a woman under a vow of chastity), as well as intercourse with one's own wife "by a forbidden passage," in an unsuitable place (that is, a public place or a shrine), or at an unsuitable time (that is, when the woman is pregnant, is nursing, or has taken a vow of abstinence). Factors considered here are the rights and obligations of others, the wishes of the woman herself, her health, and that of her child. The elaborate commentaries of this precept do not consider intercourse with a courtesan forbidden unless she has become betrothed to another. Notice that the entire discussion on sexual matters pertains to a man's actions. Ancient India commonly assumed that women were by nature wanton and that, consequently, the responsibility for keeping them out of trouble sexually lay with their guardians.

The fourth precept is to refrain from lying speech. The sin consists of intentionally concealing the truth or stating what is known not to be so in order to deceive another person.

The fifth precept is to refrain from drinking liquor. The reasons given are that liquor does the body little good and much harm and that by weakening self-control it occasions other sins.

Some Sūtras indicate that the laity were not usually given instruction on the more technical aspects of wisdom and meditation. Abhidharma scholasticism and the more abstruse contents of the Sūtras were reserved for monks. This is in part not the case in contemporary Buddhist countries, where lay Dharma-study and meditation groups function as an important institution. Laypersons were not allowed to study the Vinaya, by definition the rules of the ritually elite Saṅgha members. One ostensible reason is that the ordinary layperson does not have time to understand, let alone practice, such deep and difficult doctrines. But what of the extraordinary householder? Most of the Greek philosophers, the Talmudic sages, the philosophers of classical and imperial China, and the masters of the Hindu Nyāya-Vaiśeṣika and Mīmāṃsā schools were householders. Perhaps some monks feared that householders would rival them if they became too proficient in the deeper Dharma.

We know next to nothing about the life-cycle ceremonials of the Indian Buddhist laity. There were apparently Buddhist funeral and memorial rites, but there is no evidence of a Buddhist wedding ceremony. The Buddhist monk, even today, is not a caterer to mundane liturgical needs, like the brahmin. Weddings and other rites of passage may have been purely social ceremonies without participation of religious specialists, or brahmins may have been employed, or there may have been non-brahmin specialists. In the official Buddhist view, such matters were not religious.

We can infer from modern Theravāda customs that at some period Indian Hīnayāna (early Buddhist sects) must have celebrated calendrical festivals like New Year's (mid-March or mid-April) and Offering to the Ancestors (fifteenth of the seventh month—that is, the beginning of October). The dates and many features of the festivals are close to the corresponding Hindu celebrations. But we do not have direct evidence that such festivals were in vogue in the second century B.C.E. They are just not the sort of thing that Hīnayāna monks wrote about, as can be seen from the works of modern Theravāda bhikṣus. A Tibetan student of Christianity would have equal trouble learning how Americans celebrate Christmas, New Year's, and Easter from the writings of contemporary theologians.

As the early extracanonical accounts of the lives of the Buddha regularly place both his Birth and Enlightenment on the full moon night of Vaiśākha (April–May), describing how the population of the whole cosmos worshipped and rejoiced with hymns and flower offerings at both events, it is likely that the festival to celebrate these events was already celebrated in the last centuries before Christ. This festival is the greatest in the modern Theravāda calendar.

Sacred Places

We do know something of ancient Buddhism's sacred places, forms of worship, and symbols, especially from its early art. Evidence indicates that at the popular level Buddhism integrated local religious forms and the cults present in its environment. These had a long ancestry, extending in part back to the Indus civilization and other levels of Indian prehistory, in part deriving from Vedic and Brahmanical customs and lore. Buddhists and the followers of the Brahmanical religion shared the same world view, and both conceived the world system on the model of the Wheel of Life. Cults of trees and tree spirits, serpents, fertility goddesses, and reliquary mounds all entered early Buddhism from the preexisting religious tradition. These became part of Buddhist cult practice and lore. For example, in the myth of the Buddha, Queen Māyā gave birth to her son under a sacred tree. In art, she is shown standing under it in a posture traditionally associated with female fertility.

In cult practice and holy places, Buddhism adopted much of the popular village religion. The considerable veneration paid to the sacred Bodhi Tree derived from Indus Valley fertility cults and before that perhaps from shamanism. Characteristically, a sacred tree stood in every village; it became for followers of the Buddhist religion the Bodhi Tree under which the great hero was enlightened. (Notice that he was born under a tree and died resting between two trees.) At the base of the tree was an altar, usually surrounded by a fence or railing of wood and stone. This Bodhi Tree (a type of fig, *Ficus religiosa*, *pipal* or *aśvattha* in Sanskrit) has since the earliest times been a major object of veneration for Buddhists throughout Asia. Aśoka, tradition says, paid such inordinate attention to the tree at Bodhgayā that his queen out of jealousy tried to have it destroyed. By virtue of Aśoka's devotion, Bodhgayā was improved physically and became a major Buddhist shrine and place of pilgrimage. Also at this sacred site, in front of the tree, is a carved stone seat, the "diamond seat" (*vajrāsana*, so-called because here Gautama achieved stability) which, though empty, symbolizes his presence.

We have already mentioned two most important sacred Buddhist monuments, the cave temple and the stūpa. People met and honored the Buddha in the cave temples, faithfully performing the ceremonial clockwise circumambulation (*pradakṣiṇā*) around the reliquary stūpa in the central nave at the back of the cave. Stūpas were also erected in the open air. In countries practicing the Buddhist religion, the stūpa remains today the most venerated of all its monuments. Deriving from funerary origins, stūpas were traditionally set up over the ashes of holy men, as in the case of the Buddha; over relics belonging to them (the cult of relics being important in itself); or to commemorate a miracle, mark a sacred spot, or gain merit from sponsoring the construction. Its dome rests on a square or circular base. From its top rises a stone umbrella, symbol of the Buddha's spiritual royalty. Unfortunately, the iron pillar supporting the umbrella serves as a lightning rod and has

General view of the great stūpa at Sāñcī.

resulted in the destruction of many monuments. During the ceremonies consecrating the shrine, the relics or holy articles were placed in the stūpa's interior in a specially constructed box, the tunnel leading to the box then being sealed permanently. The symbolism of the stūpa is complex, but ultimately it represents the Buddha. Even though, technically, he has left saṃsāra, it is a concrete reminder of him. The dome is called the "egg" (*aṇḍa*), thus suggesting that the stūpa commemorates not only his death but his second spiritual entrance into final nirvāṇa, too.

Forms of Worship

From early Buddhist sculpture we gain some idea of the religion's worship forms. We see people (and even serpents and celestial spirits) gathered around a sacred tree or a stūpa, their hands reverentially folded before them in Indian fashion, either standing or kneeling. Often they have placed garlands of flowers (especially lotus petals) on the stūpa, hung them on the tree, or laid flowers or other offerings on the shrine before it. A fervent religious mentality ran deep in traditional India's consciousness. Perhaps the presupposition that every act, however minor, necessarily led to good or bad consequences encouraged this ardent religiosity. It expressed itself in bending, adoring, venerating, serving, and sacrificing (flowers and offerings) before the holy shrine. These acts acknowledge or "remember" the sacred presence manifested by the shrine. The Bodhi Tree, revered because the Buddha was enlightened under it, also functioned as the pan-Indian "wish-fulfilling tree," bringer of all desires.

In these early representations of Buddhist worship, we see many

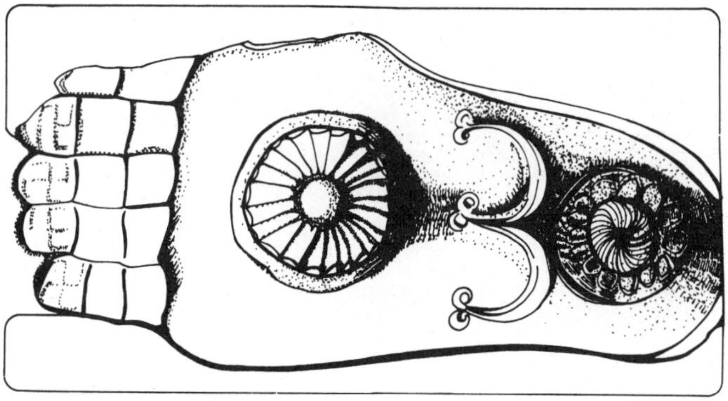

Symbols on an early representation of the Buddha's footprint, including svastikas (meaning "well-being" in Sanskrit) on his toes, a wheel, a symbol of the three jewels (Buddha, Dharma, and Saṅgha), and a lotus.

symbols used instead of actual figures of the Buddha, which came into general use only after 100 C.E., probably in response to devotionalism fostered by Mahāyāna, a later form of Buddhism. The objects for worship included the empty throne, a pair of footprints, a wheel or lotus, a shrine with a turban on it, or even a circle under a tree. The empty throne recalled the spot on which the Buddha had attained Enlightenment; the pair of footprints reminded worshippers that he walked among people and, even though he entered nirvāṇa, left his Path and his continuing influence in the world. The turban symbolized what he had renounced, his royal worldly inheritance; the wheel stood for his First Sermon as well as the Wheel of Life. The lotus, which appears often, has a complex symbolism all its own. It grows from the mud of mundane existence yet transcends it in its purity—its leaves and beautiful petals appear not even to touch the waters (of becoming). Thus, the lotus, like Buddhahood, is self-created out of the defilements of existence. Frequently, we see lotus flowers on the altar before an enshrined Bodhi Tree or in garlands draped over the dome of a stūpa or the branches of the tree. We can only speculate why the Buddha was not depicted in human form for almost 500 years after his nirvāṇa. Perhaps prior to that time, symbols were sufficient to recall his memory and establish his presence for the worshipper; or, perhaps respect for his attainment of nirvāṇa, a state entirely beyond representation, motivated the use of alternate symbols. Much of this cult practice and symbolism survives in Buddhist religious life today throughout Asia.

Worshippers with garlands and offerings of leaves and lotus flowers at altar in front of a sacred Bodhi Tree. Some stand with folded hands, others kneel. (From the Bhārhut stūpa, second century B.C.E.*)*

CHAPTER 4

Beginnings of Mahāyāna Buddhism in India

THE RISE OF MAHĀYĀNA

During the two centuries from 100 B.C.E. to 100 C.E., there arose within Buddhism a movement that called itself the Mahāyāna, the "Great Vehicle or Course" (*yāna:* a going, a course, a journey; a vehicle), in contrast to the Hīnayāna,* the "Inferior Vehicle." The Great Course, said its adherents, was that of the bodhisattva, which leads to Buddhahood (supreme, perfect enlightenment), while the Inferior Course leads only to arhant-ship. It appears that the Mahāyāna arose within the Mahāsāṅghika sects, which from the first had disparaged the arhant and had championed doctrines later typical of the Great Course, such as that phenomena are *māyā* (illusory) and *śūnya* (empty), that the true Buddha is transmundane, and that the historical Buddha is a mere apparition of him (see p. 83). The idea of the bodhisattva, the future Buddha, was accepted by all the early sects. The Mahāyāna innovation was to proclaim that the bodhisattva course is open to all, to

* "Hīnayāna" originated as a Mahāyāna pejorative for those who did not accept the new Sūtras and their doctrines. As the conservatives answered the Mahāyāna propaganda and polemics with silence, they did not adopt any name for themselves *vis-à-vis* Mahāyāna. Consequently modern European, Japanese, and Indian scholars have given them the name their enemies gave them, "Hīnayāna," though without implying any deprecation. Modern Theravādins do not like being called Hīnayānists, but there is no other current term that designates the whole set of sects that arose between the first and the fourth centuries after the Parinirvāṇa. Continued usage may expunge all derogatory connotations of the term. "Quaker," "Mormon," and even "Christian" started out similarly as labels sarcastically attached by outsiders.

lay out a path for aspiring bodhisattvas to follow, and to create a new pantheon and cult of superhuman bodhisattvas and cosmic Buddhas who respond to the pleas of devotees.

The hallmark of Mahāyāna is its Sūtra (Pali, *Sutta*) literature rather than any one doctrine or practice. All Buddhists accept the authenticity of the Pali Suttas. When the early Canon was committed to writing in the second century B.C.E., it more or less fixed the corpus of the Sūtras but did not extinguish the preachers' old habits of embellishing the kernel of a Dharma-theme with their own innovations. These embellishments began the development of a new Buddhist literature that was accepted by some and rejected by others as normative for life and thought in the Buddha's Way. They are continuous with the last phases in the formation of the Hīnayāna Canon. The new Sūtras, written in Sanskrit rather than Pali, like the old claimed to report dialogs of the Buddha; and in the earliest extant "expanded Sūtras," the discussants are well-known figures of early Buddhism. Those who deny that the Mahāyāna Sūtras are the word of the Buddha are Hīnayānists; those who accept them are Mahāyānists. As there is no special Mahāyāna Vinaya, a monk could follow the advice for spiritual training and morality in the new Sūtras without drastic change in his mode of life. If he happened to be a Mahāsāṅghika, he could accept the new literature without much alteration of his doctrinal convictions. The very earliest Mahāyāna Sūtras—for example, *The Small Perfection of Wisdom*—do not disparage Hīnayāna and in fact place the teachings of the bodhisattva course in the mouths of the great arhants. Eventually a wider rift developed between Mahāyānist attitudes and those of Buddhists who did not accept the new Sūtras as normative. For example, the *Vimalakīrti-nirdeśa*, a somewhat later Sūtra, ridicules the arhants and says that even the worst sinner still has a chance to become a Buddha, while the arhant is at a dead end in an inferior nirvāṇa. The still later *Lotus Sūtra* is even more vehemently hostile to Hīnayāna but adopts a seemingly conciliatory posture, affirming that the arhant is not really condemned to an inferior goal since there is in reality just one nirvāṇa, that of a Buddha, which even arhants will reach in due course. There could not have been much conflict between the two Courses in 100 B.C.E. However, the rift between them widened more and more, until in 200 C.E. the *Lotus Sūtra* betrays a clear schism.

The switch from oral to written sacred literature contributed to the genesis of the Mahāyāna Sūtras, some of which were perhaps composed orally and some in writing. In either case, manuscripts freed the author from the constraints of oral transmission and facilitated the dissemination of longer and more complex texts. But writing had also enabled the community to stabilize the older literature, and even with the inconveniences of manuscript libraries it was now fairly easy to check whether a text was really included in the official Sūtra Piṭaka ("basket"). The *Lotus Sūtra* castigates wicked people who say that the expanded Sūtras are not the word of the Buddha. Well it might, as much of the Buddhist community believed on good grounds that such texts were recent forgeries. Mahāyānists then claimed that their Sūtras had been preserved for five hundred years by the Nāgas (mythological serpentine spirits) in their underwater palaces, to be divulged when the world was ripe for them. Such tales probably did not convince many opponents.

The composition of Mahāyāna Sūtras continued from 100 B.C.E., until 400 C.E., reflecting changes in doctrine and religious life, regional and sectarian differences, and sociocultural factors, some of which can be identified from the evidence of the Sūtras themselves. There are no firsthand historical sources on this literature and the movement that produced it.

In the second century C.E. Mahāyāna authors started publishing treaties (*śāstras*) in their own names. Although they cited the Sūtras as proofs, and so encouraged the composition of new Sūtras to validate new doctrines, they also relied substantially on experience and rational inference. These treatises served to present the Buddhist case to non-Buddhists who rejected the testimony of the Sūtras, and the newer Buddhist doctrine to Hīnayānists who denied the authenticity of the Mahāyāna Sūtras. The new respect for human authors stemmed from a crucial change in Indian elite culture—the emergence of a secular literature (fiction, poetry, and nonfiction), individual authorship, advances in science and knowledge, improvements in techniques of debate and logic, and greater confidence in people's ability to achieve knowledge without the aid of gods or superhuman saints. But the middlebrows and lowbrows continued to crave revelations and stimulate the composition of new Sūtras. The Hindus, likewise, went on writing Upaniṣads, Purāṇas, and Āgamas and attributing them to gods and ancient sages. Shortly after the Buddhists stopped writing Sūtras, they started composing *Tantras* (esoteric scriptures, manuals of ritual observances and meditations), likewise anonymous and somewhat casually attributed to the Buddha.

There is a Mahāyāna theory of revelation that covertly justifies attribution of these discourses to Śākyamuni. Whatever the enlightened disciples teach is to be considered Buddha's own teaching, because they have themselves realized his Dharma, and nothing that they teach deviates from it. Early Buddhism, too, had maintained that the words of the arhants agree with those of the Buddha, a confidence somewhat shaken by the frequent falling-out of arhants. The Mahāyānists introduced the notion of the Buddha's inspiration, or charisma (*adhiṣṭhāna, anubhāva*), through which he infuses thoughts into the minds of individuals and sustains the advocates of his Dharma. Since the Mahāyāna Buddha is eternal, omnipresent, and omniscient, it seemed reasonable that his influence would pervade the thoughts of individuals in the centuries after the Parinirvāṇa and that their inspirations would have the value of scripture. Early Buddhism had a definite notion of Gautama's charisma (see p. 23), and inasmuch as the Buddha and other arhants can read one another's minds (the third superknowledge, see p. 12), it was not a big step to the idea that the Buddha can implant thoughts in the mind of another. This theory, though, was never openly used to defend the Mahāyāna Sūtras, because to do so would have meant giving up the false historical claim the Mahāyānists had foolishly made—that their Sūtras were from the mouth of the Buddha.

Much obscurity surrounds the origins of Mahāyāna. We do not know where it first arose, but the most likely areas are those where the Mahāsāṅghikas were strong, Āndhra and Gandhāra. Scholars who think Iranian and Hellenistic influences played a major part in engendering the Great Vehicle favor northwest India as its birthplace. Considering, though, that bhikṣus wandered the length and breadth of India and stayed freely as guests in the monasteries of all sects, early Mahāyāna ideas doubtless spread rapidly throughout the whole country. The laity, furthermore, were mostly nonsectarian, and as the Great Vehicle developed among them, as well as among the monks, the evolution likely took place in many areas far removed from the spot where it first arose.

The first historical glimpses of Mahāyāna are afforded by Chinese sources pertaining to the Serindian missionaries of the second century C.E. At that time, northwest India and adjoining regions of Central Asia were under the powerful Kuṣāṇa dynasty, whose great monarch Kaniṣka (late first or early second century C.E.) is renowned in Buddhist sources as a patron of the Dharma. The Kuṣāṇa domain had been a Buddhist stronghold since the second century B.C.E., when the Indo-Greek kings favored it. It included Kashmir and Gandhāra, both Sarvāstivādin, and the oasis kingdom of Khotan, a powerful Mahāyāna center where certain aspects of the movement and certain Sūtras may have originated. The earliest Mahāyāna texts came to China from the Kuṣāṇa realm, and especially from Khotan. Wherever it originated, the Great Vehicle first flourished notably in northwest India, where it exhibited its greatest strength at 400 C.E., when the Chinese pilgrim Fa-hsien passed through.

The northwest was inhabited by many peoples, Iranian and Greek as well as Indo-Aryan, Zoroastrian and Brahmanical as well as Buddhist. Buddhism appealed more strongly to non-Indians than did Brahmanism, though one inscription records the devotion of a Greek to Krishna. Several Hīnayāna sects had achieved missionary successes long before Mahāyāna appeared on the scene. Nevertheless, the contact of peoples and cultures seems to have affected the complexion of Buddhism, to have favored ideas and cults closer to the previous religions of Greece and Persia, and to have loosened the bonds of conservative tradition.

THE TEACHING OF EMPTINESS

The *Prajñā-pāramitā* ("Perfection of Wisdom") *Sūtras* are dialogs between saints who are said to be "coursing in the Perfection of Wisdom." The perfection of wisdom consists in the direct realization that all the dharmas, whether conditioned or unconditioned, are śūnya (empty). Saṃsāra is empty, and nirvāṇa is empty; the Buddhas are empty, as are the beings whom they guide. Thus, there is no essential difference between the relative and the absolute. But what is *śūnyatā* (emptiness), the common predicate of all things? It is absence of *svabhāva* (own-being), a term that means something (1) existing through its own power rather than that of another, (2) possessing an invariant and inalienable mark, and (3) having an immutable essence.

Early Buddhism had ascribed to all conditioned dharmas three universal marks: suffering, impermanence, and no-self (duḥkha, anitya, and anātman). Early Mahāyāna added a fourth, emptiness. The addition is not really an innovation, since the effort to describe the personality-in-existence as a composite of dharmas was to indicate the emptiness of an essential self (*ātman*). Its importance lies more in the value-tone of the word *empty* than in its formal doctrinal content. The early Buddhist emphasis on suffering and impermanence is intended to arouse aversion to worldly life.

The Mahāyāna advocates of emptiness (Śūnyavādins) insisted on emptiness in order to summon the hearer to reevaluate transmigration and achieve release within it rather than fleeing it while still considering it real and important. Intellectually, "own-beings" are false reifications, conceptual figments. Emotionally, they are the foci of obsessions, the illusory idols that enslave the passions. The contemplation of emptiness is an intellectual and emotional therapy. The aim is not to deny commonsense reality to things as experienced in the commonsense world, but to cleanse one's vision of false views and so to see the world "as it really is"—that is, to see its "suchness" (*tathatā*). Emptiness is not an absolute substance, not a stuff out of which all things are made. Rather, it claims that no immutable substance exists and none underlies phenomena. Emptiness is equivalent to dependent co-arising, the principle that Gautama enunciated as the Middle Way between being and nonbeing (see p. 16).

Emptiness has far-reaching consequences for the religious life. Monks in training who are ridden with feelings of guilt and shame because they have infringed the Vinaya are told to appease their guilt by meditation on its emptiness. This does not give them license to sin, but it liberates them from the burden of evil. The bodhisattva can work and play in the secular world without fear of contamination from sense objects, because he knows that intrinsically they are neither pure nor impure. He associates with merchants, kings, harlots, and drunkards without falling into avarice, arrogance, lust, or dissipation. He accepts and excels in the arts and sciences, welcoming them as good means to benefit and edify living beings. He recognizes the religious capacities of women, listening respectfully when they preach the Dharma, because he knows that maleness and femaleness are both empty.

Some proponents of the emptiness-teaching used logical arguments to convince those who did not accept the emptiness Sūtras. A notable example is Nāgārjuna (circa 150–250 C.E.), who was the founder of the Mādhyamika, or Madhyamaka, school, so-called because it claims to maintain the Middle Path (*Madhyamā Pratipad*) between being and nonbeing that the Buddha declared in his sermon to Kaccāna (see p. 29). Nāgārjuna's best-known work is the *Middle Stanzas (Madhyamaka-kārikās)*, a polemical treatise of about 450 verses in which he refutes a wide range of "wrong views." He uses a kind of reduction-to-absurdity argument (*prasaṅga*), in which he shows that all the implications of the opponent's thesis are unacceptable in light of the opponent's own assumptions.

The opponent objects: If emptiness (śūnyatā) is not real, then your whole system is baseless. Nāgārjuna replies: If emptiness were real-in-itself, then things would not be empty, and my system would be baseless. But emptiness, too, is empty. My system is without foundation, because nothing has any ultimate resting place. But the claim "all things are empty" is with me not an absolute claim on which to build a systematic philosophy; it expresses the highest truth only if one does not assume that it expresses some "thing" called "emptiness" having own-being (svabhāva).

Nāgārjuna did not deny that reason is valid for mundane purposes, but words and sentences are just designations or indicators, complex actions like fingers pointing at the moon. One must look beyond the finger to the moon and not confuse the naïve concreteness of the perceived indicator with the dependent co-arising nature of existence. The meaning is not found in the utterance itself—as in an oath or magical formula—nor in some supposed referent corresponding to words. The goal is realized when thinking no longer binds a person to thought-construction, when nameables are not assumed to be more real than nonnameables and the "cinema of thought-constructs" ceases. Nāgārjuna's philosophy, like several others, achieves its goal when the thinker is no longer grasped by thought.

Nāgārjuna's immediate disciple, Āryadeva, carried on the polemic tradition, and Mādhyamika became quite popular. But it did not make qualitative advances until about 500 C.E., when Bhāvaviveka adopted the epistemology and logic of the logician Dignāga and confronted a host of problems that his school had previously ignored. Candrakīrti (sixth century C.E.) then attacked Bhāvaviveka, severely criticizing his use of logic and going back to the position of the earlier Mādhyamika commentators. Bhāvaviveka wrote one of the first handbooks of the Indian philosophical systems, and Candrakīrti composed an excellent compendium of the bodhisattva path, the *Introduction to Madhyamaka*. Both authors display a superb style and rigorous thought.

THE DOCTRINE OF MIND ONLY

The Śūnyavādins were not concerned with the phenomenology of mind, but in their assertion that all phenomena are illusion (māyā), cinematic fictions, and dreamlike, they accorded the mind a major role in creating the seeming world. Conventional things, they said, are not purely objective entities but concepts or discriminations constructed by the mind under the limitations of ignorance. This raises several questions that the Śūnyavādins did not answer. What, in worldly scientific terms, is the process by which the mind creates and objectifies fictions? What is the real nature of error? If the sense-consciousnesses arise and perish moment by moment following their evanescent objects, which of them imagines the objects, and how is the process of world construction passed on from moment to moment? How do memories take place? And what is it that experiences the absolute truth free from discrimination?

The attempt to answer such questions gave rise to a new school called Yogācāra ("Yoga Practice") or Vijñānavāda ("Teaching of [Fundamental] Consciousness"). Its doctrines appeared first in several Sūtras about 300 C.E.: the *Avataṃsaka*, the *Sandhinirmocana*, and the *Laṅkāvatāra*. The earliest Vijñānavādin treatises are attributed to Maitreyanātha, who may have been either a human philosopher or the Bodhisattva. He inspired the two brothers Asaṅga and Vasubandhu (circa fourth century), who commented on his treatises and brought the school to its definitive form.

The Sautrāntikas, an early Buddhist sect, maintained that the effects of deeds are transmitted as a series of "seeds" until they ripen. The

Yogācāra school named this stream of "seeds" the store or foundation consciousness (*ālaya-vijñāna*). The Yogācārin Sūtras equate the store-consciousness with the womb of Tathāgatahood (*tathāgatagarbha*), a concept of great soteriological importance. *Garbha* has a twofold general meaning: first, the womb, and by extension, an inner room, the calyx of a lotus; and second, the womb's contents—that is, an embryo, fetus, child. In the first sense, the purified store-consciousness is the womb where the tathāgata (the Enlightened Being) is conceived and nourished and matured. In the second sense, the womb of Tathāgatahood is the embryonic Buddha consisting of the pure dharmas in a person's store-consciousness.

The later Sūtras originating in India specify that the womb of Tathāgatahood is innate to all living beings, since they are irradiated by the pervading power of the Buddha and since through time without beginning they have grown a stock of good dharmas under the influence of this radiating grace. If this womb did not exist, a person could not take religious initiative, could not turn from saṃsāra and aspire to nirvāṇa. This womb is always intrinsically pure and is synonymous with suchness, which is identical in everyone. In ordinary beings, it is covered with adventitious defilements; in the bodhisattvas, it is partly pure and partly impure; and in the Buddhas, it is perfectly pure.

The womb of Tathāgatahood is described in a series of similes as being like honey covered by bees, a kernel of grain in the husk, gold in the ore, a treasure hidden in the earth, and the fruit in a small seed. It contains the causes from which pure as well as impure dharmas arise; it is the source of the phenomenal world, of good things and bad alike. This follows from its office as a storeroom for the seeds of past karma. Likewise, the store-consciousness is both individual and collective. It receives the impressions of individual deeds, harbors them, and projects the phenomenal world, which consists of (1) the "receptacle world" of space-time and (2) the psychophysical individual. The purified mind of the saint no longer projects a phenomenal world of its own, but it sees the world projected by the minds of ignorant people.

Whereas Mādhyamika posits two "truths," the relative and the absolute, Yogācāra sets up three "natures" (svabhāva), the absolute, the relative, and the imaginary. Practice of the Path purges the imaginary out of the relative and so refines it into the absolute. Mādhyamika ridicules the idea of a coupling of the real and the unreal, but this is just what the Yogācārin relative nature is. Furthermore, the imaginary has its basis in the absolute. After all, where else could illusion have its source except in reality?

The Yogācāra introduced the doctrine of the three bodies of the Buddha. The first is the apparition-body (*nirmāṇa-kāya*), which corresponds to the apparition or form-body (*rūpa-kāya*) of Siddhārtha of the earlier teachings. The third is the Dharma-body, the unconstructed, unlimited, and perfectly pure reality, a Mahāyāna formulation of nirvāṇa. The second is a Yogācārin innovation, the recompense or enjoyment-body (*sambhoga-kāya*). It is the glorified body that the Buddha attains as a reward for his bodhisattva practices, and it is the transfigured body that the great bodhisattvas apprehend when they see the Buddha. For example, the Buddha Amitābha in his Pure Land is apprehended in his enjoyment-body by the bodhisattvas there, while he appears in his apparition-body to favored persons in this world.

Vasubandhu, coarchitect of the Yogācāra system, was also the greatest of the Abhidharmists. He wrote the *Abhidharmakośa* (*Compendium of Abhidharma*), a brilliant polemical work that became the standard Mahāyāna Abhidharma text. For better or worse, the new school took over the Abhidharma enterprise, pulled together all the classifications, subclassifications, lists, and numbers that appeared in the Sūtras and treatises, and proceeded to invent more and more.

CHAPTER 5

Soteriology and Pantheon of the Mahāyāna

THE BODHISATTVA PATH

Mahāyāna is synonymous with the course (*yāna*), or career (*caryā*), of the bodhisattva. In the early Mahāyāna Sūtras (composed before the second century C.E.), this is a simple path beginning with arousing the thought (that is, aspiration) for supreme, perfect enlightenment, and practicing the six pāramitās (perfections) until the goal is reached. Between 100 and 300 C.E., the doctrine of the ten bodhisattva stages (*bhūmi*) was introduced, and an elaborate schema of paths and stages was devised.

The Mahāyāna Sūtras address their teaching equally to the monastics and laity, exhorting both to recite, copy, and explain the Sūtras, an enterprise that monasticizing Hīnayāna sects reserved for the monks and nuns. But though the laity and monastics were regarded as equal in some respects, both sects still maintained that the monastic orders were superior, and the layman still had to pay formal honor to the monk. Only some Sūtras, the libertarian ones, authorize the laity to preach Dharma to monks. The most famous of such Sūtras, the *Vimalakīrti*, shows that householder-bodhisattva encouraging a crowd of young patricians to leave the household life. When they protest that they cannot do so without their parents' permission, Vimalakīrti tells them to arouse the thought of enlightenment and practice diligently, since that is equivalent to "going forth." Far from diminishing the monastic vocation, this concession is a second-best for those unable to take the yellow robe.

The householder-bodhisattva Vimalakīrti. (From a wall painting of the Tun-huang caves in China, eighth century C.E.*)*

Nothing like European anticlericalism is found in the Sūtras of the Great Vehicle. Nevertheless there is one lurid description of corruption in the monasteries, of wicked monks who, "destitute of shame and morality, impudent as crows, arrogant, ill-tempered, consumed by jealousy, conceit, and presumption," engaged in commerce and litigation and cohabited with women. And documents found in Central Asia show one monk giving his daughter in marriage to another, monks disputing with one another in the secular courts, and monks buying and selling. Evidently some monasteries fell into the hands of opportunists who disregarded the Vinaya while enjoying use of the Saṅgha's property and privileges.

Though the literature reveals a number of lay preachers, it mentions no legitimate noncelibate communal life and no householder clergy. The householder-bodhisattva was welcome to study meditation and philosophy and probably was allowed to spend protracted periods of retreat in the monasteries. He could teach the doctrine and was encouraged to propagate it. But so far as we know, the Mahāyāna Sūtras were composed by monks, and there is not a single important treatise attributed to any Indian Buddhist layperson.

The bodhisattva saṅgha was evidently a fraternity within the general Buddhist Community. It had no special monastic rule, and its householder sections were probably loose-knit associations like those that gather around modern Hindu holy men and temples. There was also an ordination rite for the lay bodhisattva, modeled on the bhikṣu's ceremony rather than on the less solemn Hīnayāna lay initiation.

The bodhisattva path begins with instruction from a Buddha, a bodhisattva, or some other spiritual friend. Seeds of virture are planted in the mind of the hearers, and from much hearing they come to perform good deeds, through which they acquire more and more roots of goodness. After many lives, thanks to the infused grace of the various teacher-saviors and the merit earned by responding to them, a person becomes able to put forth the *bodhicitta* ("thought of enlightenment"). The two motives for this aspiration are one's own desire for bodhi and compassion for all living beings who suffer in saṃsāra. Initially the motivation is both egotistic and altruistic, but along the path one realizes the sameness of self and others and transcends the duality of purpose. Arousing the bodhicitta is an extremely meritorious deed. It cancels past bad karma, increases merit, wards off bad rebirths, and ensures good ones. In these respects, it corresponds to "winning the stream" in early Buddhism, since the srotāpanna, too, will never be reborn in the woeful destinies and is confirmed in the course of enlightenment (see p. 25). "Arousing the thought of enlightenment" is a decisive conversion experience with profound psychological effects. It is compared to a pearl, the ocean, sweet music, a shade-giving tree, a convenient bridge, soothing moonbeams, the sun's rays, a universal panacea, and an infallible elixir.

New bodhisattvas proceed to consolidate their bodhicitta and advance on the Path by cultivating good qualities and working for the welfare of living beings. They make a set of vows or earnest resolutions (*praṇidhāna*). Some vows are quite general—for instance: "When we have crossed the stream, may we ferry others across. When we are liberated, may we liberate others." Some bodhisattvas' vows are very specific and pragmatic—for example, those of Dharmākara, who later became the Buddha Amitābha. He made three or four dozen vows in the form "May I not attain supreme, perfect enlightenment until [such-and-such a benefit] is assured beings who are born in my Buddha-land" (where he [Amitābha] lives and teaches the Dharma). Taking the precepts is an early Buddhist forerunner of Mahāyāna vow-making, in that it is a formal act of commitment and involves a greater forfeiture of merit if one transgresses than if one had not made a vow. Bodhisattva vows are usually binding until the end of he bodhisattva career, a matter of aeons. Even when the great bodhisattva has passed beyond dualistic cognitions and intentions, he is motivated, as if on automatic pilot, by the force of his original vows.

The bodhisattva is supposed to declare his vows in the presence of a Buddha, which means that he must wait until a Buddha appears in the world. The Tathāgata then gives the bodhisattva a prediction (see p. 26) that after *x* number of ages he will become a Buddha of such-and-such a name, reigning in such-and-such a Buddha-land, (a world created by a particular Buddha for the salvation of his devotees), which will have such-and-such excellences. Ordinary bodhisattvas who have not yet had the good fortune to be born in the same generation as a Buddha make their vows in the presence of other human bodhisattvas or even with the Buddhas and bodhisattvas of the ten directions as their witnesses.

The six pāramitās are the main course of the bodhisattva career. As we have noted (p. 45), these virtues are all advocated in the early Buddhist Canon, and graphic instances of them are extolled in the *Lives Tales (Jātakas)*. Mahāyāna differs from Hīnayāna in making the extremes the model for ordinary devotees.

A virtue is practiced to perfection when the most difficult acts are executed with a mind free from discriminatory ideas, without self-consciousness, ulterior motives, or self-congratulation. The perfect giver, for example, does not think "I give" and has no fictive concepts about the gift, the recipient, or the reward that ensues from the act. Thus, prajñā-pāramitā (perfection of wisdom) is necessary in order to attain the other five perfections.

The perfection of giving (dāna) consists of giving material things, Dharma-instructions, and one's own body and life to all beings, then in turn transferring or reassigning the ensuing merit to supreme enlightenment and the welfare of other beings, rather than allowing it to earn one future bliss in the world. The bodhisattva practices giving and stimulates others to do likewise.

The perfection of morality (śīla) consists of following the ten good paths of action, transferring the merit, and prompting others to do likewise. The ten are not killing, stealing, fornicating, lying, slandering, speaking harshly, chattering frivolously, having covetous thoughts, having hostile thoughts, or having false views.

The perfection of patience (*kṣānti*) is founded in nonanger and nonagitation. It means patient endurance of hardship and pain, forbearance and forgiveness toward those who injure and abuse the bodhisattva, and patient assent to difficult and uncongenial doctrines, a virtue encouraged in the Mahāyāna scriptures for the purpose of promoting their acceptance as authentic Buddha-word.

The perfection of vigor (*vīrya*) means unremitting energy and zeal in overcoming one's faults and cultivating virtues, in studying Dharma and the arts and sciences, and in doing good works for the welfare of others. *Vīrya* is derived from *vīra* ("a martial man," "a hero"). It corresponds to right effort, the sixth member of the Holy Eightfold Path of early Buddhism, but more explicitly signifies heroic endeavor to benefit other living beings.

The perfection of meditation (dhyāna) consists of entering all the meditative trances, concentrations, and attainments, yet not accepting rebirth in the paradises to which such states normally destine one in the next life.

The perfection of wisdom (prajñā-pāramitā) is personified as a goddess, because *prajñā* is grammatically feminine. She is the mother of all Buddhas, since through her they become Enlightened Ones. A famous hymn endows her with feminine traits and maternal loving kindness.

The *Perfection of Wisdom Sūtras* say over and over again that the doctrine that things neither arise nor cease is surpremely difficult, that it causes fear and aversion in the tender-minded, and that the bodhisattva who can accept it is a great hero (*mahāsattva*). Three degrees of assent are distinguished. The first is acceptance of the words of the teaching. The second is conforming assent, attained in the sixth bodhisattva-stage and consisting of an intense but not definitive conviction. The third is ultimate acceptance of the fact that the dharmas are nonarising. It is said by later texts to be attained in the eighth stage, and it is concomitant with reaching the nonrelapsing state.

The early theory of stages seems to have recognized just seven bodhisattva-stages, with acceptance that the dharmas are nonarising and that the nonrelapsing states occur coming in the seventh stage. The number of stages was increased from seven to ten about 200 C.E. Variant lists of stations and stages circulated for a while, but ten became the standard.

There are some differences of opinion about the duration of the bodhisattva career, but the prevalent view was that it takes three immeasurable aeons: one to or through the first bodhisattva-stage, one from there through the seventh stage, and one for stages eight to ten. The doctrine of three immeasurable aeons was taken literally by Indian schoolmen, but it was rejected by some Chinese schools and bypassed in later Indian sects. It may be hyperbolic, serving to make graphic how long and arduous the course is and how great a distance stands between the beginning bodhisattva and the great savior bodhisattvas on the highest stage.

THE CELESTIAL BODHISATTVAS

The Mahāyāna pantheon contains the personages to whom the Mahāyānist should offer worship, veneration, and propitiation. The chief innovation in this Mahāyāna pantheon is the class of great bodhisattvas, also called great beings (*mahāsattvas*). The *Lotus Sūtra* mentions by name twenty-three; the *Vimalakīrti* names some fifty. Of these, four become most important: Mañjuśrī, Avalokiteśvara, Mahāsthāmaprāpta, and Maitreya. All four figure as interlocutors in Mahāyāna Sūtras, where they appear as men and converse with the great disciples and Śākyamuni. These great beings are nonhistorical; there is no evidence that any one of them is an apotheosis of a human hero, as Rāma certainly was and Krishna probably was. Strangely, no Sūtra preaches devotion to a celestial bodhisattva until the third century C.E., a full three centuries after these beings entered the literature. The strategic function of these bodhisattvas is to serve as Mahāyāna counterparts to the great arhants in the Pali Sūtras.

Maitreya

Maitreya is the earliest cult bodhisattva. A Pali Sutta predicts that in the distant future there will arise in the world a Blessed One named Metteya (Pali for Maitreya), who will have thousands of disciples just as Śākyamuni has hundreds. All Hīnayāna sects acknowledged Maitreya, and the Theravāda tradition recognizes no other bodhisattva in the present age. He was conceived of as a historical bodhisattva.

Maitreya, unlike the Buddhas before him, is alive, so he can respond to the prayers of worshippers. Being compassionate, as his name indicates (its Sanskrit root means "benevolent"), he willingly grants

Maitreya, in a late seventeenth-century or early eighteenth-century Tibetan representation. (Photo: Antoinette Gordon Collection.)

help; and being a high god in his present birth, he has the power to do so. His cult thus offers its devotees the advantages of theism and Buddhism combined.

Mañjuśrī

Mañjuśrī shares with Maitreya preeminence among the bodhisattvas in Mahāyāna Sūtras up to 300 C.E. In the *Lotus Sūtra* he remembers deeds of former Buddhas that were unknown even to Maitreya. In the *Vimalakīrti* he alone of all Śākyamuni's disciples has wisdom and eloquence enough to stand up to that formidable householder, Vimalakīrti. The name Mañjuśrī means "gentle or sweet glory." He is also called *Mañjughoṣa* ("Sweet Voice") and *Vāgīśvara* ("Lord of Speech"). Mañjuśrī's standard epithet is *kumāra-bhūta,* "in the form of a youth," or "having become the crown prince." The former meaning is the earlier, and it applies equally to a celestial being (Gandharva), who like all angels never grows old, and to Brahmā, whose epithet is "Forever-a-youth." Mañjuśrī is the crown prince of Dharma, because, like other tenth-stage bodhisattvas, he will next become a King of Dharma, a Buddha. The Sūtras mention Mañjuśrī as residing in diverse Buddha-fields in the present and in the past and as being in other world-realms now, as well as ages ago.

Mañjuśrī usually appears to human beings in dreams. The chronicles record that a dozen or more great masters "saw the face of Mañjuśrī." Merely hearing Mañjuśrī's name subtracts many aeons from one's time in saṃsāra. Whoever worships him is born time and again in the Buddha-family and is protected by Mañjuśrī's power. Those who meditate on Mañjuśrī's statue and his teaching will be similarly fortunate and will reach enlightenment. If a devotee recites the *Śūraṃgamasamādhi Sūtra* and chants Mañjuśrī's name, then within seven days Mañjuśrī will come to the worshipper, appearing in a dream if bad karma hinders the supplicant from receiving direct vision. Mañjuśrī also takes on the form of a poor man or an orphan and appears to those who are devoted to him. The wise man should contemplate Mañjuśrī's superhuman physical marks. If he does so, he will soon see the Bodhisattva.

Avalokiteśvara

Avalokiteśvara (Chinese, Kuan-yin) first appears as a mere name in the lists at the beginning of the *Vimalakīrti* and, later, the *Lotus Sūtra*. His first significant role is in the *Sukhāvatī-vyūha Sūtra,* where he and Mahāsthāmaprāpta are Amitābha Buddha's chief attendants. They are the only Bodhisattvas in Sukhāvatī (see pp. 86–89) whose light is boundless; owing to them, that world-realm is luminous always and everywhere. The two of them used to be men in this world, and on dying they went to Sukhāvatī.

The *Avalokiteśvara Sūtra* was incorporated into the *Lotus Sūtra* as late as the third century C.E. To this day, though, it circulates as an independent work in China and Japan, where it is the main item in the liturgy of the Kuan-yin cult. A few verses at the end describe Sukhāvatī and say that Avalokiteśvara stands now to the left of the Amitābha and fans him. The rest of the text says nothing about Amitābha but shows Avalokiteśvara as an omnipresent, omnipotent savior-deity subordinate to no one. He has purified his vows for countless aeons under millions of Buddhas. He possesses all virtues and is especially rich in love and compassion. His skill in means is infinite, and through it he takes whatever form will help living beings. He adopts the guise of a Buddha, a bodhisattva, a disciple, Brahmā, Indra, and other gods. Like Mañjuśrī, he has played the role of a Buddha and will play it again, without getting trapped in extinction. In this respect the celestial bodhisattvas are superior to the Buddhas.

Avalokiteśvara grants multifarious boons to those who remember him and recite his name. The merit from adoring him is equal to that from worshipping and serving an incredible number of Buddhas. Those who adore him are saved from lust, hostility, and folly. A woman who worships him will give birth to a son or daughter,

The Bodhisattva Avalokiteśvara, who holds a lotus in his hand (Padmapāṇi), his eyes looking down out of compassion for beings. (From a wall painting in Cave 1 at Ajantā. Sixth century C.E.)

whichever she wishes. Anyone in distress will be freed from danger and anxiety. For example, if you fall into a fire, think of Avalokiteśvara and it will be quenched. Similarly, he rescues those who invoke him from shipwreck, falling off a precipice, missiles, armed robbers and enemies, execution, chains and shackles, witchcraft, demons, wild beasts, snakes, and thunderbolts.

The origin of this bodhisattva-figure is obscure. The name is composed of *avalokita* ("observed, looked down upon" or "observing, looking down") and *īśvara* ("lord"). The general idea is that the Bodhisattva observes the world and responds to the cries of living beings. He is also called Lokeśvara, "Lord of the World," and a variant name, *Avalokitasvara* (where *svara* means "sound, voice"), underlies the Chinese short name Kuan-yin, "sound-regarder." The longer Chinese name, Kuan-shih-yin "regarder of the world's sounds," is beautifully clear but does not translate any known Sanskrit form. Avalokiteśvara is praised for his voice; which is like a cloud's voice, like thunder, like the tides. This Bodhisattva is usually represented in art as a bejewelled layman wearing a high crown with a cross-legged image of Amitābha in the front of it. He often holds a lotus in his hand. In the Tantric period (600–1200 C.E.), he came to be represented with eleven heads, or with four, ten, twelve, twenty-four, or a thousand arms.

In Tibet, Avalokiteśvara was revered as the country's patron, or protector. Tibetans everywhere worshipped him for his compassionate response to the sufferings and trials of life, particularly through his mantra, *"Oṃ maṇi-padme-hūṃ"* (see p. 94). In China, Avalokiteśvara was eventually represented as a woman. At present she is worshipped as a madonna of gentle compassion throughout east Asia. The Chinese call her Kuan-yin, the Japanese, Kannon; in Korea she is Kwanŭm, and in Vietnam, Quan-ân. Porcelain figures of her have found their ways onto the bric-a-brac shelves of many American homes.

Mahāsthāmaprāpta

Mahāsthāmaprāpta is mentioned in the lists at the beginning of the *Lotus Sūtra* and the *Vimalakīrti*. Śākyamuni addresses a discourse to him in Chapter 19 of the *Lotus*, and as already noted, the *Sukhāvatīvyūha Sūtra* places him on a par with Avalokiteśvara as an attendant of Amitābha's. In Far Eastern art he is frequently represented standing on the right of Amitābha while Avalokiteśvara stands on the left.

Samantabhadra

Samantabhadra ("Universal Sage") became popular rather late. He is not mentioned at the beginning of the *Lotus Sūtra*, but in Chapter 26, a late addition, he comes to the world with a fabulous retinue to ask Śākyamuni to expound the *Lotus Sūtra*. He promises to protect the monks who keep this Sūtra, to avert the menaces of human enemies and demons. Mounted on a white elephant with six tusks, he will accompany the preacher and will appear and remind him when he forgets part of the text. If the devotee circumambulates for twenty-one days, then Samantabhadra will show his body on the twenty-first, will inspire the devotee, and will give him talismanic spells.

In Buddhist symbolism, Samantabhadra represents daily practice and application, which must proceed by gradual but firm steps like the elephant upon which he is depicted. Samantabhadra is often paired with Mañjuśrī, the personification of prajñā-wisdom, whose lion leaps and roars with the confidence that comes from experiential understanding. Together the two bodhisattvas thus symbolize the twin requisites of spiritual growth, understanding and application.

THE CELESTIAL BUDDHAS

Śākyamuni was reportedly the object of adoration even during his lifetime. He reproved Vakkali, "the highest of those who have faith," for being so attached to the Tathāgata's person and told him to concentrate instead on the Dharma. The idea was, "Whoever sees the Dharma sees me (the Buddha)." He also said, "Those people, enthralled by ardent desire, who saw me by [my] form and followed me by [my] voice, do not know me." He regularly referred to himself not by his name but as the Tathāgata, "he who has come or gone to the True," or "he who has come or gone thus—that is, on the path of all the Buddhas."

Multiple Bodies of the Buddha

From the first the Buddha was held to have two bodies (kāya), the physical or form-body (rūpa-kāya) and the Dharma-body (Dharma-kāya). In addition, he could conjure up apparition-bodies (nirmāṇa-kāya) through his magic powers, and in mind-made bodies (manomaya-kāya) he could travel to the heavens. Devotion to Dharma was encouraged, but adoration of form (rūpa) was disparaged as a sensual fetter. Nonetheless, over the centuries piety glorified Śākyamuni's body, ascribed to it the thirty-two major and eighty minor marks of a superman, extolled its radiant complexion, and stated that rays of six colors constantly shone from it and that it exuded sweet perfume.

Dharma was from the first a transcendental principle immanent and operative in the world. It is the constant, the real, the true, the good, the valuable, the harmonious, and the normative. Perception of Dharma in the moral sphere is the Buddhist version of conscience.

Intellectual penetration of the Dharma-realm is bodhi, the goal, enlightenment. The nature of things, Dharma-ness (*Dharmatā*) is like the medieval idea of natural law. It is the fixity, regularity, and necessity in phenomenal occurrences. The Buddha taught Dharma—it is in some sense expressible—but Dharma is not just doctrine. It is a real and holy force that governs the destiny of individuals and peoples. It should be not merely respected but worshipped and sought as a refuge. The Buddha and the Saṅgha are to be revered because they "have become Dharma." When the early sects agreed that the real Buddha is the Dharma-body, it was not that they were personifying the Teaching, but that in their view the Buddha actualized the Dharma, which his Teaching then revealed.

Among the early schools, it was the Mahāsāṅghikas (see p. 42) who maintained that the Buddha is supermundane and yet forever active in the world, infinite and eternal, transcendental and immanent. Since Dharma is all these things, it stands to reason that his Dharma-body should be likewise. Though Buddhism denied that there is a personal Creator, it assigned the same functions to Dharma (=pratītya-samutpāda), and by emphasizing the fictive, insubstantial, and transient character of phenomena, came to view the conditioned world as a figment of cosmic imagination. So when the historical Buddha was considered an apparition, he was not held to be less real than anything else in the world. (See Yogācāra classification of the three bodies, p. 72).

Once granted that the historic Gautama was an apparition of the everlasting Dharma-body, it seemed reasonable that there should be apparition-bodies in all times and places, that benevolent omnipotence should respond to the needs of all suffering beings. There must be Buddhas elsewhere in the universe, as well as in the past and future of this world-realm.

Early Buddhist cosmology had posited just one world system (*loka-dhātu*), consisting of four continents on earth and assorted hells below and heavens above. Later it came to be held that a universe in which a Buddha acts consists of one billion such worlds (a so-called great chilicosm). In the ten directions (East, Southeast, South, Southwest, West, Northwest, North, Northeast, Nadir, and Zenith), there are universes "as numerous as the sands of the Ganges." Some but not all of these universes are Buddha-lands, in each of which a Tathāgata lives and teaches the Dharma.

The Buddha-lands differ from the heavens of the gods in that they are presided over by a Buddha so that the inhabitants can practice the Way, earn merit, and gain wisdom. In the heavens of the gods, a nonreturner can attain arhant-ship only through the maturing of merit previously earned as a human being. But the characteristics of the celestial Buddha-lands are very much like those of the heavens of the gods. The inhabitants of both are freed from labor, and the necessities of life come to them for the mere wishing. Sex is attenuated or entirely eliminated, and birth takes place without coitus or gestation.

Certain features of the Mahāyāna paradises deserve comment. Their penchant for jewels, jewel-trees, and diamond bodies indicate a low opinion of organic matter, because it is so perishable and "impure." Minerals, in contrast, are durable and pure. Jewels, moreover, possess occult properties and radiate spiritual forces. They are visionary substances. Concentrating on them induces trances, and paradise visions tend to be bright, with gem-like colors and shapes.

The pure Buddha-lands differ from the Iranian, Christian, and Muslim paradises in that their delights are a means to a goal of bodhi rather than an end in themselves. All who go to there are assured that they will attain enlightenment, but residence is neither an equivalent nor a substitute for nirvāṇa. Some inhabitants are disciples (*śrāvakas*), and they become arhants and enter final nirvāṇa, which of course is not localized in any world-realm. Others are bodhisattvas; being bound by their vows, they do not enter cessation when they attain the highest stage but appear at will throughout all the worlds in order to benefit living beings.

The Mahāsāṅghikas very early asserted that there are Buddhas in all directions and in all the universes. In Mahāyāna, the drama of salvation was no longer confined to this world-realm, and help from outside might be expected. Śākyamuni's followers were not spiritual orphans, because extraterrestrial friends stood always ready to protect them—not only gods like Śakra, Brahmā, and the Four Great Kings but also great bodhisattvas and Buddhas. This feeling of endless space populated by spiritual beings is perhaps part of the nuclear world view of classical Indian civilization.

Akṣobhya

Akṣobhya is the earliest attested of the nonhistorical celestial Buddhas. In *Vimalakīrti-nirdeśa* Gautama says: "There is a country named Abhirati and a Buddha named Akṣobhya. This Vimalakīrti died in that country and came to birth here." To satisfy the Assembly's longing, Vimalakīrti entered samādhi, grasped Abhirati, and set it down in this world to be seen. Afterward it returned to its proper place, in the East. In the *Small Perfection of Wisdom,* Śākyamuni exerts his wonder-working power and enables his Assembly to see Akṣobhya and his retinue. Neither Sūtra advocates devotion to Akṣobhya. Apparently, though, rebirth in Abhirati was sought by some people. It could be attained through moral acts or even through hearing the name of Akṣobhya. This Buddha became moderately popular in Tantrism. In art he is represented as blue, holding a "diamond" (*vajra*) in his right hand, his left hand in the earth-witness gesture (*bhūmi-sparśa-mudrā*), with a blue elephant for his mount. The name Akṣobhya means "immovable" or "imperturbable." Legend says that, while he was just a bodhisattva, he made a vow to practice deeds without anger. The bodhisattva who does likewise will go to birth in Abhirati.

Amitābha (Amita)

Amitābha ("Unlimited Light") and Amitāyus ("Unlimited Lifespan") are alternate names for the same Buddha. Chinese A-mi-t'o and Japanese Amida are rendered from the short form, Amita. The cult of this Buddha goes back at least to 100 C.E.

The spiritual development of Amita begins with a bhikṣu named Dharmākara ("Mine or Treasury of Dharma"), who countless aeons ago heard the Buddha Lokeśvararāja preach and expressed a fervent desire to become a Buddha like him. He implored the Buddha to teach him the way to supreme perfect enlightenment and the qualities of a pure Buddha-field. The Tathāgata then taught him for ten million years the excellences and amenities of innumerable Buddha-lands. Dharmākara took all these good qualities, concentrated them all on one Buddha-land, and meditated on them for five aeons. Then he went to his future Buddha-land.

In his Buddha-land, said Dharmākara, there will be no evil destinies (hell, animals, ghosts). In other words, everyone born there will be at least a stream-winner (see p. 25). There will only be a nominal difference between men and gods in that Buddha-land. All beings born there will be almost, but not quite, arhants. They will all be destined for consummation in nirvāṇa, and unless their bodhisattva vows bind

The Buddha Amita. (From a twelfth-century Japanese silk painting.)

them to more rebirths, they will only be reborn once. But their life span in Sukhāvatī ("happiness-having") will be unlimited. Evil will not be known there even by name. All beings will be able to hear automatically whatever Dharma-theme they wish; but there will be neither teaching nor learning, because all will possess direct cognition and will be able to recite the Dharma informed by all-knowledge.

The Buddha Amita will have unlimited light and unlimited life. His congregation of disciples will be countless, and innumerable tathāgatas in other Buddha-lands will proclaim his fame and praise him. In return, bodhisattvas from Sukhāvatī will travel everywhere to visit and worship the other Buddhas, while beings who stay in Sukhāvatī have merely to think of making offerings to Buddhas elsewhere and the gifts will automatically spring into being and be accepted. Bodhisattvas in that country will be able to convert their merit into precious substances, incense, robes, umbrellas, flags, lamps, dancing, and music. Just by wishing, the bodhisattvas will produce masses of superb ornaments from the jewel-trees of the land. There will be myriad incense burners always emitting fragrance.

Dharmākara, when he becomes a Buddha, will exercise tremendous outreach. Other Buddhas everywhere will declare his name and fame, and from hearing his name living beings will derive manifold benefit. Women who hear the name of Amita will never again be reborn as women. (This is not just masculine arrogance but a judgment on women's life in ancient Asia with which women generally concurred.) Living beings in other Buddha-lands who hear Amita's name will be released from birth and gain knowledge of the spells (*dhāraṇīs*). Through hearing his name they will attain birth in a noble family. Bodhisattvas who hear Amita's name will be honored by gods and men if they worship him. They will attain a samādhi in which they will dwell continually, seeing countless Buddhas, until they reach bodhi. They will earn merit by rejoicing in the bodhisattva course. No bodhisattva who hears Amita's name will ever relapse or forsake the Three Jewels, Buddha, Dharma, and Saṅgha.

The most crucial question concerning a Buddha-land is how to attain rebirth there. Dharmākara's vows give a specific answer to this, though different versions of the Sūtra vary significantly. The second-century Chinese translation says that if those who have aroused the thought of bodhi always meditate on Amita with a faith-filled mind, then at their death Amita and his retinue will come to escort them to Sukhāvatī. Likewise, if those who have done evil in former lives hear Amita's name and sincerely aspire to birth in his land, they will not endure bad destinies when they die but be reborn in Sukhāvatī.

The third-century translation distinguishes three classes of candidates for rebirth: evildoers, good Buddhists, and practicing bodhisattvas. The general prerequisites for rebirth are a desire to be reborn in Sukhāvatī and good conduct (with dedication of the resultant merit to rebirth and bodhi). The sinner must hear Amita's name and repent and reform. The ordinary devotee has to perform worship and donation. The bodhisattva must meditate, presumably on Amitābha and his paradise. Note that faith is not mentioned at all.

The Chinese version attributed to K'ang Seng-k'ai (third century C.E.) appears to be a fifth-century paraphrase by a Chinese monk rather than a direct translation from Sanskrit. It was adopted as orthodox by the Chinese and Japanese Pure Land sects, perhaps because they preferred its simple doctrine and emphasis on faith. In this text the eighteenth vow says that all living beings in the ten directions who with sincere faith desire rebirth in Amita's country, calling this desire to mind only ten times, will attain it. Only those who have committed atrocities or slandered the True Dharma are excluded. The nineteenth vow says that all living beings in the ten directions who arouse the thought of bodhi, cultivate all the virtues, and wholeheartedly vow to be reborn in Amita's country will, when they die, see Amita and a large retinue before them. The twentieth vow says that, if living beings in the ten directions hear Amita's name, fix their thoughts on his country (that is, meditate on it), plant all the roots of virtue, and wholeheartedly dedicate (the resulting merit) desiring rebirth in his country, then it will happen that way. Here the general prerequisites are a desire for rebirth and good conduct. (Presumably dedication of merit is required by all three vows.) No distinction is made between classes of devotees. One may meditate with sincere faith as little as ten times. Or one may arouse the thought of bodhi. Or one may hear Amita's name and meditate on his country. But faith alone is not stated to suffice for rebirth.

The foregoing excursion into textual criticism has been necessary because the whole dogmatic edifice of the East Asian Pure Land school (see p. 172) rests on the interpretation of these three vows. The issue is whether salvation requires both faith and works or faith alone. On the evidence of the Sūtra in all surviving versions, faith is just an adjunct to meditation. The concentrated, aspiring mind is faith-filled. Salvation, furthermore, is not effected by Amita's power alone. The candidate, too, must make an effort.

Having proclaimed his vows, Dharmākara practiced the bodhisattva course for a trillion years. He established innumerable living beings in supreme perfect enlightenment. He worshipped countless Buddhas. Gradually his body became transformed, a sweet scent issued from his mouth and pores, and he acquired the signs and marks of a Great Person. Finally, ten aeons ago, he became the Tathāgata Amitābha presiding over the world-realm Sukhāvatī, a trillion Buddha-fields away to the West, a realm endowed with all the virtues he had vowed that it would have.

In India Amitābha never became as popular as Śākyamuni. He is not very frequently represented in art. The Chinese belief that Nāgārjuna and Vasubandhu were devotees of Amita rests on the attribution to these authors of treatises that are unknown in Sanskrit and Tibetan and are probably later Central Asian or Chinese writings ascribed to earlier authors. Chinese pilgrims in the seventh century, though, reported that the worship of Amitābha was widespread in India. In the *Lotus Sūtra* and in Tantrism he figures as one of the Five Tathāgatas who rule the cardinal points and the center. There is no separate Amitābha sect in Tibet, where the popular saviors are Avalokiteśvara and his consort Tārā. It was in the Far East that the Buddha of the Western Paradise became the dominant object of cultic reverence.

Vairocana

Vairocana ("Shining Out") is an epithet of the sun. Originally it was just an epithet of Śākyamuni, but in due course the name acquired separate identity as a celestial Buddha. In the Tantric set of the Five Tathāgatas, he occupies the center, which is Śākyamuni's position in the exoteric Mahāyāna *maṇḍala* ("sacred circle"). The Chinese scholastic view that Vairocana is the Dharma-body of Śākyamuni thus reaffirms the identity from which Vairocana had historically been derived.

We have seen that solar traits characterize the early accounts of Śākyamuni's Enlightenment (pp. 12–14). Ignorance was paired with darkness, and knowledge with light. Daybreak and the Enlightenment were synchronized. The *Lotus Sūtra* represents the Buddha's revealing act as a beam of light shooting from the wisdom-eye between his brows. Amitābha's very name signifies that he is a luminary deity, and his Buddha-land is suffused with radiance in all the hues of the rainbow. It is a land of eternal daylight, devoid of shadows.

The *Mahāvairocana Sūtra*, a Tantric work composed in about the seventh century, consists of Vairocana's revelations to the Tantric equivalents of bodhisattvas. Vairocana did not become popular either in art or in cult until the seventh century, when his role as Śākyamuni's transcendental counterpart gave him preeminence in the Tantric cosmoplans (*maṇḍalas*) and the associated rites.

Mahāvairocana ("Great Illuminator") is a distinctly Tantric form. Though well known in Tibet, he is less popular there than the "high patrons" such as Hevajra, Heruka, and Saṃvara, who are creations of a somewhat later period. However, he is of central importance in the early form of Tantra, which was introduced into Japan in the ninth century by Kūkai and Saichō. Called Dainichi ("Great Sun") in Japanese, he is conceived of as the "Cosmic Buddha," or "Cosmos as Buddha," whose body, speech, and mind pervade the universe. In some ways this is the closest traditional Japanese equivalent to a monotheistic concept. "Dainichi" was even used for a short time by sixteenth-century Jesuit missionaries as a translation for the word God.

Maitreya, in a twelfth-century representation from Bengal.

CHAPTER 6

Buddhist Tantra

MIXED ORIGINS

Buddhist Tantra is a mysticism mixed with magic, amalgamating some elements distinctly Buddhist, others traditionally quite non-Buddhist. Tantra, like yoga and *bhakti* ("devotionalism"), is a pan-Indian religious form, not limited to any one Indian religion. There were Hindu and Jain Tantrisms, just as yoga and devotionalism were a part of all three.

Buddhist Tantra originated primarily in the frontierlands of classical India, somewhere around the sixth century C.E. It flourished both in the far northwest, where it was influenced by Brahmanical and perhaps Chinese and Central Asian elements, and in the northeast—in Bengal, Orissa, and Assam. There Tantra drew inspiration from local magic and occult arts. Buddhist Tantra especially prospered from the eighth century on, under the Pāla dynasty of Bengal (circa 750–1150 C.E.). At Nālandā, the great center of Buddhism at that time, Perfection of Wisdom ideas combined with Tantra, uniting metaphysics with ritual, magical practices. Tantra was exported throughout Southeast Asia, from Ceylon and Burma to the Indonesian isles, where it found its greatest success; but eventually it failed, either defeated by Theravāda, syncretized with Śaivism and then disappearing, or repressed by Islam. Since the Buddhism of the Tibetan culture area was imported from India during this period, it is predominantly Tantric. In the eighth century, three Indian monks took a school of ritualized Tantra (*Chen-yen*) to China, where it won favor at the court of the T'ang emperors but did not last more than a century. At the beginning of the ninth century, Kūkai introduced it into Japan as the Shingon school. It first became popular among the nobility and continues to be generally popular to the present day.

Part of the amalgam of Buddhist Tantra is the culmination of trends long present in Buddhism. Magic was explicitly allowed by the Buddha and the early Canon in the spells (Pali, *paritta*), which, when repeated, offered protection from such dangers as snakebite. Magic spells (dhāraṇī) also occur in the Mahāyāna Sūtras as early as 200 C.E. These were supposed to epitomize the doctrine of the Sūtras and thus make available a shortcut to enlightenment to those who repeated them. By the seventh century, Buddhism had also incorporated the Hindu notion of inherently efficacious sounds such as *Oṃ* (Aum) and had elaborated a set of magical syllables, associating one with each major figure in the Tantric pantheon and with each "center" (*cakra*) in the mystic physiology of the meditator's body.

Another specifically Buddhist feature was the maṇḍala, or magic circle. It derived many of its features from the early religious architecture of the stūpa. The first of these shrines, with their railings separating sacred from profane ground, were intended as replicas of the cosmos. When the Buddha-image came into use, about 100 C.E., images were placed on the stūpa or at its cardinal points or those of the courtyard surrounding it. The shrine thus became a three-dimensional maṇḍala.

The Tantric innovation was to turn the creation of maṇḍalas into an "actualization," a rite in which the agent becomes the deity conjured up. Probably Yogācāra meditation, which specialized in elaborate investigation of meditative states, greatly facilitated this development. Even in the beginning, the Canon indicates that monks meditated on external figures (*kasiṇa*) such as colored circles as supports for their practice of meditative visualization. All this fed the growth of Buddhist Tantra. Maṇḍalas can be depicted in painting; in three-dimensional models; by a troupe dramatically acting one out; or by a yogin visualizing the setting and the figures, basing the imaginative recreation of the mystic diagram on an external text or painting (such as a hanging scroll) for meditative support.

The maṇḍala is a divine cosmoplan and a theophany, able to manifest divinity itself when used by the meditator as a meditative object. Like the Vedic altar, it received the gods into its sacred space, making the divine immediately accessible to human beings. It was the site of communication with other worlds and the invisible gods. In its center, and in its complex design—consisting of variously colored circles, squares, and triangles—were placed the gods, as if residing in their labyrinthine, divine palace complete with rooms, towers, and gardens.

On its periphery were four entrances or doors through which the meditator could enter, symbolically receiving thereby initiation into the exclusive world of divine reality. The complex symbolism of the maṇḍala was fully used in Tantric meditations.

Tantric practices had a venerable Brahmanical ancestry as well. Buddhist Tantra was a radical departure from the classical Buddhist tradition, allowed primarily by Mādhyamika metaphysics, which had declared the world empty, hence in principle essentially pure. This permitted, for one, incorporating unorthodox components into Buddhist ritual, including sexual elements. A considerable amount of esoteric yoga practice was taken over from independent circles of yoga practitioners, including Haṭha yoga, along with elements of popular and magical ritualism. Perhaps mostly from the northwest, traditionally a stronghold of Brahmanism, came such forms of Hindu ritualism as magical rites, instructions for ceremonies, and their formulas (mantras). Another influence was the Hindu emphasis on the necessity for having a *guru*, or preceptor, to direct one's difficult learnings and transformations. These were prefigured in the Bhagavad Gītā's emphasis on Krishna as the divine teacher from whom mystic vision comes and on the earlier Vedic preceptor. Even the rationale of the Vedic sacrifice was adopted, since we read of a fire sacrifice that would impart immortality in an early text from the northwest, the *Śatapathabrāhmaṇa*. The highest purpose of Tantric ritual actualizations, though, is attainment of enlightenment, the conventional Buddhist goal. If magic power also resulted, this was nothing new, since Buddhist meditators from the beginning had experienced extraordinary powers (*siddhi*) born of their contemplative disciplines.

MEDITATION AND RITUALS

Mantras were so much a part of Tantric meditation that Tantra (Buddhist as well as Śaivite) received the alternate name *Mantrayāṇa*, the "Mantra Vehicle, or Course." To call the use of mantra a *yāna*, or vehicle, accorded it the dignity of being a legitimate, distinct path to salvation. The term *mantra* was first used in Vedic Sanskrit to designate a verse, particularly one used to invoke or call up a deity or to bring the gods from afar to the sacrifice for whose success their presence was required. From the beginning, mantra was not prayer but an "instrument of mind" (its etymological meaning), which, via speech, influenced cosmic forces. In the *Ṛg Veda*, mantra is also associated with the safety or protection that comes from the god's response to the recited "mantra of the praising poet." These meanings are remarkably continuous with Tantra. The scholar Jan Gonda's definition of mantra according to its etymology and earliest textual meanings applies almost as well to the much later Buddhist use: "word(s) believed to be of 'superhuman origin,' received, fashioned, and spoken by the 'inspired' seers, poets, and reciters in order to evoke divine power(s) and especially conceived as means of creating, conveying, concentrating, and realizing intentional and efficient thought, and of coming into touch or identifying oneself with the essence of the divinity which is present in the mantra." The continuity of the Vedic use with that of Buddhist Tantra recalls the remarkable resistance Indian traditions have had to extinction.

In Buddhist Tantra, mantras were used as a means of evoking the deity so that the meditator might become one with him or her. In this sense their full soteriological import becomes apparent. They were also a means of protection against evil forces and adverse events. A mantra could be used as a meditative object from which to gain insight or to induce mental calm through repeated repetition, silent or vocal. One of the most famous Buddhist mantras, recited literally uncountable times, is "*Oṃ maṇi-padme hūṃ*." Often a mantra's form is so compressed that it even fails to conform to ordinary Sanskrit grammar, but this one means, roughly: "Oṃ in the lotus a jewel, hail!" Its symbols are thoroughly Buddhist: The lotus (padma) is the material world, the Wheel of Life, saṃsāra. But in it is the jewel (maṇi), which may be colored by an adjacent object (as a diamond would reflect a nearby rose) but which is not in its essence of that color. Uncut by any other substance but itself, the jewel is a symbol of the unconditioned, nirvāṇa, or of the natural, essential purity of mind (citta).

Another famous Buddhist mantra, "*Gate, gate, pāragate, pārasaṃgate, bodhi svāhā*," evokes the Goddess of Perfect Wisdom at the end of the *Heart Sūtra*, by far Buddhism's best-known and most concise statement of its wisdom, to summarize and evoke Prajñā-pāramitā, the perfection of wisdom. It means: "Gone (gaté), gone, gone beyond, completely gone beyond, enlightenment hail!" This mantra can open the mind to enlightenment. The "beyond" it refers to is nirvāṇa, the other side of saṃsāra, the ocean of existence. Hsüan-tsang recited this mantra while traversing the Gobi desert to fend off demons and goblins. Tārā's mantra, "*Oṃ, tāre tuttāre ture svāha*" (untranslatable but verbally playing on her name), evokes protection of the goddess Tārā from dangers, both physical and spiritual. A mantra that avows the truth of the teaching of emptiness goes: "*Oṃ śūnyatā-jñāna-vajra-svabhāvātmako 'haṃ*"—"Oṃ, I am a self whose essence is the diamond knowledge of emptiness." A similar mantra states: "*Oṃ svabhāvaśuddhaḥ sarva-dharmāḥ svabhāvaśuddho 'haṃ*." This mantra, encapsulating the teaching of the emptiness of self and dharmas, means: "Oṃ by essential nature all the dharmas are pure, by essential nature I am pure!"

Many have observed that some Tantric ritual procedures, including the sexual and magical practices that its emptiness metaphysics allows, are incongruous in the Buddhist context. But this view runs counter to the way religions actually develop and evolve. Tantra was the result of both Buddhist and non-Buddhist influences. Some of its rites, while violating traditional Buddhist precepts, still sought the traditional Buddhist goal, although they imbued it with new doctrinal significance and converted it into a sacramental means of realization. Tantric masters systematized these rites and eventually wrote them down in the form of Tantras (ritual manuals). The Tantras were intended as aids for initiates training under a master. They were not for public perusal, and their secrets were safeguarded by an argot called "twilight speech," in which, for example, semen was called "camphor," "*bodhicitta*" (thought of enlightenment), and "elixir"; the male and female genitals were called "thunderbolt" and "lotus"; and the corpse of an executed criminal was called a "banner."

It is not surprising that Tantra has been excoriated by many modern writers. It has been said that Tantrism was a degeneration, that it grafted the Hindu cult of female energies onto Buddhism, and that the graft became a parasite that in due course crushed the life out of its host.

What happened was in fact the reverse. The main Buddhist tradition assimilated diverse non-Buddhist elements, restructuring and reinterpreting them, until it would be more correct to say that pure Buddhism crushed the life out of the Tantras. By 800 C.E. Tantric studies had achieved the dignity of an academic discipline. Learned scholars in Bengal and Bihar were writing commentaries; giving glosses for the twilight speech; explaining the symbolic meanings of the ritual objects, persons, and acts; and suffusing the subject with a refined and ethical tone. The practitioners who wrote the Tantras considered that the accompanying mental exercises were more important than the physical acts of the rites. It was a commonplace that everything is mind, so it was not always necessary to perform the rites in imagination. After a time, most Tantric schools ceased to perform those rites that infringed the precepts. Tantra became respectable exercises in pure contemplation.

A typical contemplative visualization uses the characteristic devices of Tantric meditation. An alternate reality, a "maṇḍala-world" peopled by divinities, is generated by chanting and thinking of mantras and by meditative visualization. The process is not so different from the early Buddhist contemplative practice of visualizing various kinds of circles, only the meditative object is more complex. The meditator envisions himself as the central Buddha of the maṇḍala, as if to abide in an "interior castle" or divine mansion strikingly similar to the one experienced in meditation by the medieval Spanish mystic, St.

The bell and vajra *(''diamond''), items held in various Tantric ritual meditations. They symbolize, respectively, effective compassion and liberating insight.*

Teresa of Avila. The meditator's purpose is to gain access to the knowledge and divine power of Buddhahood by a direct, ritual assault on Buddhahood itself.

Tantric practice is based in part on the Mādhyamika principle that saṃsāra and nirvāṇa are not different. As Nāgārjuna said, ''The limit of saṃsāra is the limit of nirvāṇa. Between these two there is not even the subtlest something.'' Also, ''Unrelated to the pure there is nothing impure with reference to which we can designate the pure. Therefore even the pure is not a matter of fact.'' An early Buddhist maxim says: ''Living beings are defiled through defilement of the mind, and purified through purification of the mind.''

Reference back to a popular Mahāyāna Sūtra, clearly not Tantric, shows how Mahāyāna metaphysics could provide a basis for Tantric practice. The *Vimalakīrti-nirdeśa Sūtra* shows the great bodhisattva accepting gifts of maidens and garlands that the monks had refused, fearing they would be contaminated by them. The blossoms stuck to the arhants, because they discriminated lawful and unlawful, but did not stick to the bodhisattvas, who discriminated nothing. Many sayings in this Sūtra have a very Tantric ring: "Only for conceited men does the Buddha preach that separation from lewdness, anger, and folly is liberation. For men without conceit, the Buddha preaches that lewdness, anger, and folly are indeed liberation," "The bodhisattva seems to proceed in precept-breaking, yet persists in pure morality and feels great fear even at the smallest sin. He seems to proceed in the passions, yet is always pure in mind. He seems to have wives and concubines, yet always keeps far away from the mud of the five lusts." "Just as lotus flowers do not grow on a high plain of dry land but only where there is low, moist mire, even so, only in the mire of passions are there living beings to produce the Buddha-qualities." "He appears to indulge the five lusts, but also seems to practice meditation. A lotus blossom that grows in a fire has to be described as a rarity. One who lives in lust yet meditates constitutes as great a miracle."

The Tantric poet Saraha says: "Here there's no beginning, no middle, no end, no saṃsāra, no nirvāṇa. In this state of supreme bliss, there's no self and no other." "Just as water entering water becomes of the same taste, so when the sage thinks vices and virtues the same, there's no polarity." In other words, the enlightened man is beyond good and evil.

The crux of the matter is skill in means. The *Hevajra Tantra* says, "The unknowing worldling who drinks strong poison is overpowered; he who has expelled delusion, with his mind on the truth, destroys it utterly." What is licit under the direction of a preceptor (guru) and within the consecrated maṇḍala is still illicit for ordinary people. When the tabus are broken, they must be broken with a pure mind and not for worldly pleasure.

The aim of the Tantric devotee is to destroy the passions by means of the passions. As the *Hevajra* says, "The expert in poison repels poison by that very poison, a little bit of which kills most people. . . . Those who have 'means' are liberated from the bondage of 'becoming' through the very thing by which wicked people are bound. The world is bound by lust, and released by the same lust."

Who should ritually break the tabus, and who should not? Tantric doctrine classifies people into five "tribes," or "families," according to personality type and prescribes a different method of meditation for each tribe. Earlier meditation manuals recommended different meditations depending on the student's dominant passion. The lustful type should meditate on impurity, the hostile type on compassion, and the foolish type on causal relations. The classical prescription for the hostile type is cultivation of compassion and friendly love. Tantrism prescribes for such a one the performance of erotic rites. "Compassion" is twilight speech for "sexual love." Tantra fuses spiritual and physical love, in idea and in practice.

Already, in the *Perfection of Wisdom Sūtras*, Mahāyāna thinkers had held that enlightenment requires perfection of wisdom (prajñā) and development of skill in means (upāya). Wisdom soon became a goddess (see p. 78). The Tantras made Means a male divinity. The union of Wisdom and Means produces the thought of enlightenment (bodhicitta). In the maṇḍala of Hevajra, the goddess Nairātmyā ("No-self") stands for Wisdom, and Hevajra stands for Means. When the maṇḍala is acted out, the yogin impersonates Hevajra, and his consort takes the part of Nairātmyā.

The rites are practiced long and thoroughly in contemplation before they are actually performed. The yogin imagines the maṇḍala and the goddess around the circle and mentally envisages the rites with himself as the deity. Having conjured up this vivid drama, he contemplates that these phenomena, like all others, are empty—that there is neither subject nor object, thought nor thinker.

Such visualizations are a considerable psychological feat. Images and paintings are used to support the imagination, and in turn the artist pictures the themes mentally before executing the painting or the statue.

The body, which earlier Buddhism tended to devalue in one way or another, received its due in Tantra. Saraha says: "Here's the Jumna, river of the gods, and here's the Ganges' flood; here are Prayāga and Benares, here are the Moon and Sun. In wandering, I've visited all kinds of Tantric meeting-places, but never have I seen another holy place as blissful as my body." Tantric physiology is mystical rather than anatomical. It confounds the circulation and nervous systems, for example. It posits four psychic centers (navel, heart, throat, and brain) and three main channels, one corresponding to the spinal column and the other two to the jugular veins. It says that the bodhicitta ascends at the moment of Great Bliss (orgasm) until it reaches the highest center.

The Tantras do not advocate murder, even ritually, and they observe the general Buddhist prohibition against animal sacrifice, which Hinduism allowed as an exception to its precept against injuring sentient things. But the Tantras do make use of illicit and even incestuous sexual relations, and they do prescribe drinking wine and eating the flesh of men, cows, elephants, horses, and dogs. Early Buddhism was not vegetarian, but during the fourth century C.E. Mahāyāna adopted vegetarianism from the Hindus. Cow slaughter had become a heinous crime by Tantric times, so for an upper-caste Indian, whether brahmin or Buddhist, eating beef was virtually as repugnant as cannibalism.

Much Western horror at Tantric practices stems from cultural astigmatism. The imagery of human sacrifices and the eating of human flesh underlie the greatest of all Christian sacraments. If a Tantric deity holding a skull filled with blood seems morbid, consider the phrase "washed in the blood of the Lamb" and its origins in the animal sacrifices and ancient Hebrew belief in the purifying power of blood.

The Tantric spirit brought a needed revival to Buddhism in its later Indian stages, in the same way that Zen masters cut through the oversystematized Mahāyāna Buddhism of China to its essentials. The effectiveness of the Tantric path is witnessed by the great saints it produced. Each major Buddhist movement has created its own type of holy individual and incited the zeal of its followers by pointing to living exemplars. In the Buddha's day, many attained arhant-ship. As the generations went by, the ideal faded and fewer attained it. Then in early Mahāyāna the bodhisattva path offered human saints of modest attainment fellowship with celestial bodhisattvas. But the latter were so extolled that they eventually robbed earthly bodhisattva-hood of all glamor. Seventh-century China circumvented the scholastic claptrap concerning the bodhisattva course and created a new type of holy man in the Zen master. The Tantric accomplished one (*siddha*) combined features from most of the preceding Indian types of wizard and saint and added some new traits, both bizarre and admirable. They usually lived and operated outside the regular monastic communities, which continued their old style of life throughout the Tantric period. Some achieved success with very little instruction, and some went through many years of ordeals under stern and capricious masters. The one great rule for the Tantric student was absolute obedience and devotion to his guru, whom he must revere as a very Buddha. Success depended on the preceptor's ability to identify the student's problems and understand his karmic states of mind, manipulate him through personal interaction, and use charisma to overcome blocks that the student could not surmount by himself. The Tantric preceptor is thus a variant of the pan-Buddhist teacher-savior type.

CHAPTER 7

Facets of Later Indian Buddhism

THE DEMISE OF INDIAN BUDDHISM

In the seventh century, Buddhism was fairly strong in most parts of India. Hsüan-tsang, the seventh-century Chinese pilgrim who studied there, reported quite a few deserted monasteries, but prospering centers were numerous and widely distributed. However, archaeology tells the tale of a steady decline over the next several centuries in most regions. The latest of the Buddhist cave-temples at Ellorā are eighth century, contemporary with the magnificent neighboring Hindu temples. In south India, Hindu temples in stone began to be built in the sixth century, but no great Buddhist edifices were erected since then. After 600, Buddhism in the south gradually gave way to the devotional Hinduism of the Tamil minstrel saints. It left its influence on Tamil theism, however, fostering the idea of a compassionate God.

The White Hun invasions of the sixth century devastated the monasteries of Gandhāra. Buddhism continued to prosper in nearby Kashmir, but by the ninth century, Buddhism and Śaivism became intermingled there. Muslim rulers finally stamped out Kashmiri Buddhism during the course of the fifteenth century. In Sindh, the Ganges valley, and Orissa, Buddhism flourished until the Muslim invaders sacked the monasteries and butchered the monks. Nālandā was pillaged and burned in 1198, and, though it continued to function on a reduced scale for several decades, repeated attacks by Muslim marauders eventually exterminated the institution. Buddhism lingered for a few centuries as a folk cult in Bihar, Bengal, and Orissa, then disappeared. In south India, a renowned Buddhist center was located at Kāñcīpuram (Conjeeveram), and as late as the fifteenth century a Theravāda community existed there.

It has been said that Buddhism vanished from India because it was imprudently tolerant and gradually became so Hinduized that it lost all reason for a separate existence. This is at best a partial truth. Mahāyāna was quite hostile to theistic Hinduism. A householder-bodhisattva pledged himself never on pain of death to worship Vishnu and Śiva. Āryadeva reportedly entered a south Indian temple and tore the eye out of a baleful idol of Śiva. The mutual antipathy was still evident about 1000 C.E., when a Bengali brahmin family strongly opposed the marriage of their daughter to Nāropa, who came from a Buddhist family. A Kashmiri play of the same general period takes the rivalry among Buddhism, Jainism, and various Hindu sects as its theme. It evinces both a strong sense of the distinctions among sects and a genial spirit of conciliation. The element of truth in this theory is that institutional Buddhism had grown self-centered, conservative, and unresponsive to the needs of the people. The great monasteries depended not on widows' mites but on landed estates and royal grants, so they neglected to maintain popular support and became divorced from the rural populace; and when the monasteries lost royal support or were destroyed by invasions, the general population had little interest in either preserving the Dharma or restoring the Saṅgha.

Theistic Hinduism had its large temples and monasteries, which were just as vulnerable to Muslim onslaughts. But every village had its brahmins, whose services were necessary for the life-cycle rites. And the devotional cults were spread by mendicant hymn singers, who achieved maximum outreach while offering a negligible target for persecution. The Buddhist Tantrics were similarly mendicant, and they popularized their teachings in vernacular hymns no less lively and appealing than those of the Hindus. In fact, Buddhist, Hindu, and Sufi popular didactic verse share a common vocabulary and a common spirit. It has been observed that legalistic Islam and mystical Sufism are at once antithetical and interdependent. The same is probably true within Buddhism. The charismatic Tantric tradition did not survive long after the bureaucratic monastic system was obliterated.

It is not unnatural that Buddhism should have died out in India. Mithraism and Manichaeism, widespread and powerful in their day, perished, yet scholars are not overly amazed. The Vedic religion died about the time that Buddhism arose, Christianity vanished gradually from its Oriental homelands under Muslim occupation, and in this century Confucianism has ceased to be a religion. From very early, Indian Buddhists had expected the Dharma eventually to decline and disappear. Though Buddhism in its homeland finally went the way of all conditioned things, it had by then lighted the lamp of the Dharma in many other parts of Asia and had endured several times as long as any empire that has ever held sway in India. Curiously enough, the story of contemporary Asian Buddhism includes a rebirth in India. Bhimrao Ramji Ambedkar, late leader of Maharashtra's Untouchables, led 600,000 of his followers into the Buddhist fold in a mass conversion in 1956. Though identified with political strategy and the attainment of equal rights by Untouchables, this conversion means that some Indians have become Buddhist again.

CENTRAL ASIAN BUDDHISM

An interesting episode of Buddhist history directly linked to later Indian Buddhism is that of Central Asian Buddhism, unearthed in archaeological and textual studies during this last century. Central Asia, from Samarkand to Tun-huang, has a glorious past as the highway between East and West. The great Silk Road was an artery of trade and communication between three ancient centers of civilization: India, China, and the Mediterranean. Central Asia is now an oblong desert, running from east to west. (See map on p. 156). But two thousand years ago the climate was much wetter and therefore favorable for settlement and agriculture. Major oasis city-states started as early as the third century B.C.E. Chinese pacification of the area under the Han dynasty (206 B.C.E.–220 C.E.) gave a further impetus to growth. Some cities in the eastern reaches, however, had been abandoned and lost to the desert as early as the end of the second century C.E., and by the seventh century there were clear signs of desiccation. When the Muslim armies overran the area in the tenth and eleventh centuries, they gave the death blow to an already dying area and age.

In its heyday, however, Central Asia was an extraordinary international blend. The population of the city-states was Indo-European, speaking languages related to Greek, Latin, Celtic, Farsī ("Persian"), and Sanskrit. If the surviving frescoes are accurate, and there is no reason to think they are not, many of these people were fair-haired and blue- or green-eyed. Their languages were written in modified Indian script, indicating Indian influence throughout Central Asia, and their literature and religion (Buddhism) were also Indian. Other material aspects of the culture were closely related to pre-Muslim Persia. More surprising are the clear remains in paintings executed in the second half of the third century C.E. of Gandhāran, and therefore, of Greco-Roman influence as far east as the borders of China (Niya and Mirān, see map, p. 156). The Gandhāran art style from northwestern India is a blend of Buddhist subjects and Greco-Roman stylistic features, which developed as a result of the vigorous trade that then linked the cultures of Rome and the East.

Our knowledge of the long-vanished Central Asian civilization comes from two major sources: Chinese documents and recently uncovered archaeological artifacts, including manuscripts and paintings.

The Chinese dynastic histories deal with affairs of state and therefore include sections on foreign relations. These chapters tell much about the political ups and down within Central Asia as these affairs impinged on the Chinese. The records begin in the former Han dynasty with the account of the expedition of Chang Ch'ien, an officer in the Chinese army sent by Emperor Wu of Han in 139 B.C.E. to make an alliance with a people to the west. The interplay among China, the nomadic hordes, and the western kingdoms of Central Asia created an equilibrium—not a stable and constantly peaceful one, but a fluctuating balance. This balance was not finally upset until the decline of Chinese power in the area coincided with the rise of Islam.

Several Chinese Buddhist pilgrims and travelers to India left detailed records, most of which have been translated into either French or English (see bibliography). No summary can do justice to the works themselves. Among the earliest of eyewitness accounts is that of Fa-hsien, who left China in 399 C.E. to return in 414. The most famous traveler is Hsüan-tsang, who, in addition to displaying indomitable zeal and determination was also a keen observer. His geographic and ethnographic notes give us a lively, detailed glimpse of those golden, but dangerous, times. Lest we think the trip easy, we need only recall Hsüan-tsang's report that in some places his only guide was the bones of previous travelers.

Religious Life

The religious makeup of Central Asia was mixed, with Buddhism predominating in most areas but not driving out other beliefs. Iranian fire worship (Zoroastrianism), Manichaeism, and Nestorian Christianity also had many adherents. Both Hīnayāna and Mahāyāna Buddhism flourished. Hīnayāna, of the Sarvāstivāda school, was found along the northern and part of the southern Silk Road; Mahāyāna was found along the southern.

From the third century C.E. on, we have positive evidence of the presence of Buddhism in Central Asian kingdoms. About 260 C.E. a Chinese named Chu Shih-hsing went west to search for "more complete" texts of *Perfection of Wisdom* scriptures and got as far as Khotan, where he found a copy of the Sanskrit text he was seeking. Although Khotan was later a Mahāyāna center, at the time of Chu Shih-hsing's visit both Hīnayāna and Mahāyāna were represented. Tradition says

Hīnayānists tried to keep him from taking a pernicious Mahāyāna text back to deceive the people of China.

Reports of all the Chinese travelers agree: Khotan was a large and prosperous center with a well-developed silk industry along with production of felt, wool fabrics, and taffeta. The area also produced fine jade. The urbane and sophisticated population used Sanskrit as the religious and literary language. Khotanese artists impressed the Chinese and were welcomed to the Sui and T'ang capital of Ch'ang-an. Khotanese artistic tradition also influenced later Tibetan painting. The Khotanese were skilled in music and were dedicated (for the most part) to Mahāyāna Buddhism, which eventually showed Tantric influence. Some five thousand clerics lived in about one hundred monasteries, each with its own legend of origin and founding. Khotanese monasteries followed Indian models of organization and discipline, as did Central Asia as a whole.

Fa-hsien and Hsüan-tsang left accounts of Buddhist festivals such as processions of images and relics through the city. More interesting are the tales of the arhants meditating in the mountains to the south of the city. Centuries-old arhants sat in samādhi in the many caves and grottoes, according to the accounts, and monks from Khotan shaved them regularly as a religious duty.

Kuchā, on the northern branch of the Silk Road, had a brilliant material culture of Iranian inspiration and was as sophisticated as Khotan. Its predominant religion was Hīnayāna Buddhism, received from Sanskrit sources. Monks followed Indian discipline in their monasteries. Chinese travelers noted more than once that monastic discipline in Central Asia was very rigorous, much more so than in China.

Close ties between Kao-ch'ang (Turfan) and China did not submerge the separate identity of Kao-ch'ang. The religious composition of the area was diverse, with Manichaeism, Iranian fire worship, and Nestorian Christianity all present. A wall painting from Kao-ch'ang shows a Palm Sunday procession of worshippers. Biographies of monks and nuns from Kao-ch'ang are included in Chinese Buddhist biographies. These records indicate, if they are to be believed at all, that many monks and nuns from Kao-ch'ang possessed extraordinary powers such as clairvoyance and clairaudience. They also practiced bodily mutilation such as burning off fingers in honor of the Three Treasures. A strong streak of asceticism seems to have been part of Central Asian Buddhism, as well as magical practices, medicine, and general wonder-working in shamanic modes.

Tun-huang, being a Chinese outpost, was different in culture and practice from other Central Asian centers. Nonetheless, it had a large non-Chinese population and was an important Buddhist city. Lying as it did at the eastern end of the Silk Road, it was the gate through which Buddhism passed into China. The remarkable cave paintings there reveal the merging of different artistic traditions; the caves are not purely Chinese in inspiration.

As early as the third century C.E. Tun-huang could boast a translation center under the leadership of Dharmarakṣa, the "bodhisattva from Tun-huang." His family was of Central Asian origin and had lived in Tun-huang for generations by the time of Dharmarakṣa's birth around 230 C.E. He studied in a monastery under an Indian teacher, traveled in Central Asia, and learned many languages. His center translated Sanskritic texts into Chinese. In other Central Asian cities similar work went on, with Buddhist texts being translated from Sanskrit into the several Central Asian languages. The flow of texts seems to have been constant and strong, and there is evidence of Chinese translations having been made from Central Asian languages and vice versa. There is little evidence, however, of texts having been translated into Sanskrit. Clearly a religious work of major importance in Central Asia was spreading the written as well as spoken message of the Buddha.

Islam exterminated the Buddhist culture of Central Asia around the tenth century C.E. Marauding, fanatic devotees of Allah destroyed the followers of the Buddha along with their temples, monasteries, shrines, and scriptures. They hacked apart priceless statues and whitewashed wall paintings. Some consolation is found in the few remnants that survive.

A cave in Tun-huang, sealed about 1000 C.E., perhaps in fear of invading nomads, yielded the finest of the Central Asian manuscripts, including the oldest extant printed book in the world—a Chinese translation of the *Diamond Sūtra*, printed in 868 C.E. These manuscripts include texts and fragments in long-dead languages, translations of religious and philosophical works of different traditions, historical documents, such as the Chinese account of the famous debate at Samye in Tibet (see p. 140), contracts, financial statements, songs and poetry, expanded vernacular Chinese versions of Buddhist writings, (which filled a huge gap in the history of Chinese popular literature), and documents that clarify the history of the development of Ch'an Buddhism in China (see p. 181). These all give us more detailed information about the presence and influence of Buddhism in Central Asia, and clarify the crucial role that Central Asia held in the transmission of Buddhism from India to China.

PART TWO

The Development of Buddhism Outside India

INTRODUCTION

From its beginnings on the eastern frontier of India, Buddhism was carried through missionizing activity to people of varying languages and cultures. Indian spirituality, both Hindu and Buddhist, spread to most of Asia east of Iran, dominating in the areas where it did not meet China, the other east Asian civilizing force. In several areas such as Vietnam, China prevailed. In others such as Tibet, a mixing of influences added Chinese elements to the Indianizing of culture. Elsewhere, as in most of Southeast Asia all the way to Java and Bali, Indian influences prevailed in religion. Islam transformed some of the Indianized areas after the eighth century, effectively making them Muslim with an Indic underlay (as in Central Asia, and eventually Indonesia).

Buddhism in the various areas of the world to which it has spread, including the Western world, is diverse because the source, Indic Buddhism, changed in its homeland through the centuries. Thus, as exportations came about, differing forms of Buddhism became predominant in different areas. Very early in its history, old Buddhism spread across the Indian subcontinent, first in Hīnayāna sectarian traditions and soon in early Mahāyāna variants. These various sectarian movements covered the subcontinent from Ceylon to Nepal and Kashmir, and they reached Central Asia through the Indo-Greek kingdoms of the western borderlands. China received various transmissions from the latter, mostly classical Mahāyāna. By the time of the aggressive spread of Indic civilization through Southeast Asia, differing schools and areas sent missionaries, so that Hīnayāna and Mahāyāna, including Tantrism, came to be represented. Clearly, by the end of the first millennium, Buddhism for export was Tantrism, as witnessed in Tibet and Indonesia.

By the end of the fourteenth century, a declining Indian Buddhism could no longer provide the impetus for missionary endeavors. Transmissions of the Dharma continued, nonetheless, among the countries already converted. A remarkable interchange of pilgrims and scholars knit together the widely spread branches of the Buddhist world, a process that continues today with our greatly enhanced communications. Finally, after Europeans and Americans had discovered the East, Buddhism was brought from various sources into the stream of Euro-American culture—from India (brought first by scholars and Theosophists), from Japan, and now from Southeast Asia and Tibet. The mix of schools and forms of Buddhism in the United States somewhat resembles the various strands that have always spread to foreign lands.

This successive spread of Buddhism can be represented in chart form in Figure 1; it will be described in detail in the following chapters.

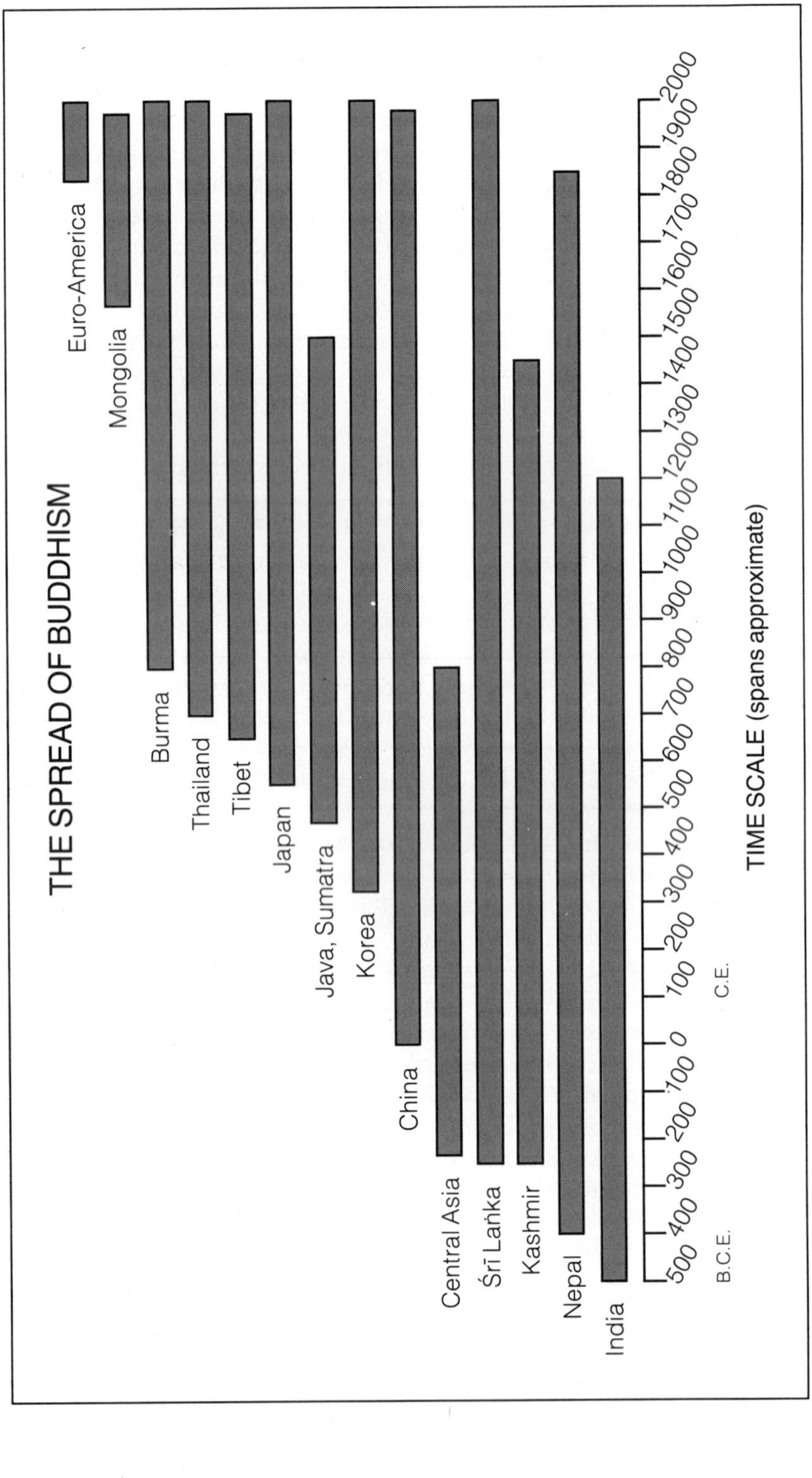

Figure 1. The Spread of Buddhism.

CHAPTER 8

The Buddhism of Southeast Asia

BUDDHIST MISSIONARIES

According to the Pali Canon, the Buddha instructed all his monks to become missionaries and to spread his Word in the languages of the people they visited, far or near. In ancient India this meant using vernacular variants of the Buddha's own dialect, but it could apply to any situation, however far-flung. It was not until Aśoka's enthusiastic royal patronage, however, that Buddhist missionaries began taking the religion beyond the Indian subcontinent. One record indicates that in 256 and 255 B.C.E., Aśoka sent Dharma-envoys to various Greek rulers in the West, and later—about 247—to Ceylon (today called Śrī Laṅkā), reportedly at the request of the island's ruler, Devānaṃpiyatissa. Tradition also tells us that he sent a mission to Burma, where the proselytizers founded a Buddhist community. Though nothing came of the missions to the West, Aśoka's missionaries had begun the gradual spread of Buddhist and Indian culture to Southeast Asia.

After the first century C.E., Indian expansion into the area increased, until by the eighth century the entire stretch of Southeast Asia from India's eastern coast all the way to Campā (Annam in Vietnam) and Bali in the Indonesian archipelago was Indianized. There is reason to believe that the entire region was somewhat related to India before this time by a partially shared substratum of culture (perhaps Austro-Asiatic). Vigorous Indian expansion resulted in a Southeast Asian religious culture that had both a Hindu and Buddhist overlay (including Theravāda, Mahāyāna, and Tantric elements). Eventually the

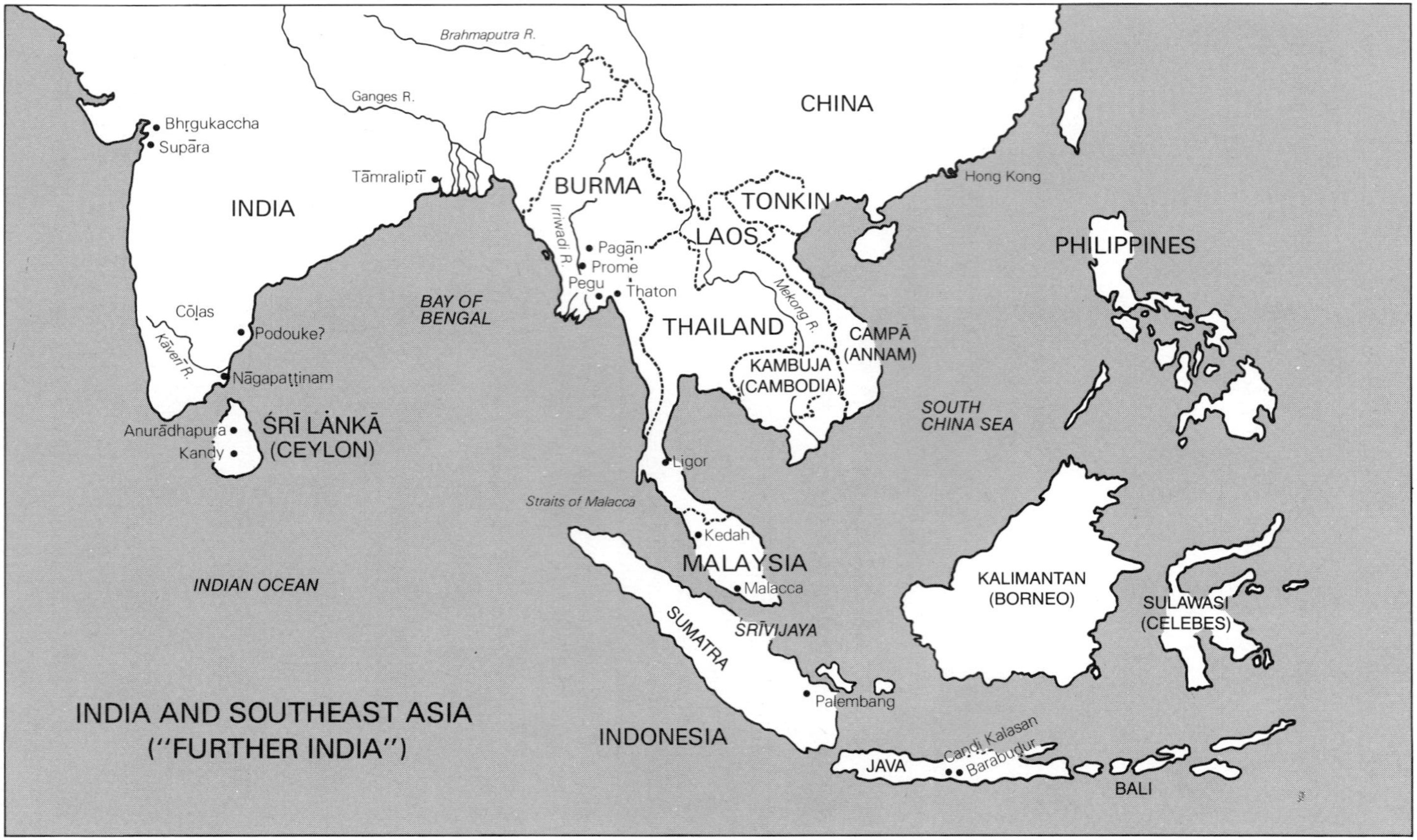

INDIA AND SOUTHEAST ASIA
("FURTHER INDIA")

Theravāda Buddhists prevailed, amidst varied survivals of older religious cultures, the ancient spirit cults, and Brahmanical customs. Only Vietnam did not retain Theravāda but adopted Mahāyāna, because of its proximity to China, while Indonesia became largely Islamic after the fifteenth century. The history of Buddhism in this area of "further India" is an important chapter in its development.

ŚRĪ LAṄKĀ (CEYLON)

Before Aśoka's missions to Ceylon in the third century B.C.E., Indo-Aryan clansmen had come to the island from the northwestern or northeastern Gangetic plain, bringing with them Brahmanical customs and political institutions. The Sinhala clan dominated and founded a royal dynasty. It was their king, Tissa, who was converted by Aśoka's son and other missionaries about 247 B.C.E. The work of popular conversion took more time, but by the second century B.C.E. the Sinhalese had thoroughly accepted the Dharma. King Tissa had well prepared the way for this victory by patronizing Buddhist missionaries and giving Buddhists a royal pavilion in a city park of his capital, Anurādhapura, from which they organized their conversions of the royal entourage and the people. A great monastery was established, a shoot of the Bodhi Tree was brought from Bodhgayā by Aśoka's daughter (who also founded an order of nuns), and a huge stūpa was constructed for popular worship.

Thus, from the beginning the Buddhist Saṅgha in Ceylon maintained close relations with the government, becoming the state religion. Buddhists had no trouble accepting the Brahmanical political institutions of the ruling dynasty. Kings became practicing Buddhists and patrons of Buddhist works of art, learning, culture, and worship. They had shrines and monasteries built and helped regulate the affairs of the Saṅgha. Nobles and commoners supported Buddhism too; beautiful monuments were built, adorned with Buddhist art, and monasteries became centers of culture and learning. For over two millennia Theravāda has been closely linked with the fortunes of the Sinhala monarchy. Its conservative, archaistic character has been preserved through the common efforts of kings and elders to guard a perennially threatened national heritage. Buddhism in Śrī Laṅkā has had a longer continuous existence than anywhere else in the world. Throughout its history the island has relied heavily on India for its literate culture. From the early centuries of the Christian era on, Hindu Tamils migrated there from nearby southern India, so that it came to have both Buddhist and Hindu populations under a Brahmanical-style monarchy.

The history of Ceylon has been a continual struggle against foreign invaders. South Indian Coḷas were expelled as early as the first century B.C.E. by a king who stated his motive to be the protection of Buddhism. Buddhists on the island maintained contacts with the Buddhist homeland, particularly via Indian west coast ports. Gradually the entire Buddhist Canon was transmitted and written down. The sect of the Theravādins became dominant and is today the sole surviving Hīnayāna sect of Indian Buddhism anywhere. By the beginning of the first centuries of the Common Era, Buddhist culture was flourishing in Ceylon, so that several centuries later, Chinese pilgrims found it famous in other Asian Buddhist countries.

During the third and fourth centuries C.E., Mahāyāna influences reached the country, but its partisans did not enjoy royal favor for very long. During the reign of the fifth-century king Mahānāma, three Buddhist scholars from south India came to Ceylon; one of these was the famous Buddhaghosa. His *Path of Purity* (Pali; *Visuddhimagga*) is an authoritative survey of Buddhist doctrine and meditative practice. By the end of this important period, the doctrine of the Theravādins was firmly fixed.

By the sixth century, the Theravādins had even expanded from Sinhalese ports along India's western coast, and Abhidharma study flourished. But magical practices (chanting protective *paritta*, spells) also appeared. Mahāyāna continued with the support of one monastery; by the eighth and ninth centuries Perfection of Wisdom teachings and Buddhist Tantra had a place on the island, too. Hindu influences also persisted, so that by the eleventh century King Vijayabāhu had first to liberate his island from Coḷa occupation and then revive the state religion, restoring a valid ordination succession (that is, a proper right to ordain as received from a country with an unbroken line of ordination) and appointing the first Saṅgha-director to oversee the Order.

Subsequent Hindu invasions continued to disrupt the country, endangering the Buddhist Saṅgha there. During this time (until the 1500s) land revenues declined, reducing support for Buddhist institutions; and though the king and nobles continued their patronage, the Saṅgha was weaker financially. The old, great monasteries were disbanded, schisms and lack of discipline disrupted the Saṅgha, and the kings had to purge it of undesirables. Hinduism influenced Buddhist institutions and thought, worship of Hindu gods became a part of popular Buddhism, and Brahmanical gods were worshipped by kings and laity in elaborate festivals. In the north and east of the island, Hindu Tamils were in power.

Later, the Portuguese (1505–1658) seized the lowlands, destroyed monasteries, and forcibly converted people to Catholicism. The

Sinhala kings withdrew to Kandy in the mountains, where they ruled from 1592 until 1815, supporting Buddhism insofar as their circumstances and resources would permit. The Dutch, ardent Calvinists, and finally the English followed the Portuguese in dominating the island. The long period of European rule harmed the Buddhist cause greatly. Under the treaty by which they took over from the Sinhala monarchy, the British were bound to protect Buddhism, but evangelical Christian missionaries proceeded to attack it. Before long, Buddhist spokesmen replied, lay associations were formed, training centers for monks were established, and a revival was under way. Two Westerners who aided the cause of Buddhism are especially revered in Ceylon: Henry Olcott, an American Theosophist who traveled around the country exhorting the people to revive their historic religion; and T. W. Rhys Davids, founder of the Pali Text Society, who by rendering Gautama's teachings admirable in European eyes gave confidence and pride to the peoples who had preserved them.

Since Olcott's and Davids's time, Buddhists in Śrī Laṅkā have contributed a great deal of valuable scholarship to the Buddhist world and, since the achievement of independence in 1948, have taken an active role in the affairs of their own country and Asian Buddhism. In 1950, they founded the World Fellowship of Buddhists, trying to unite Buddhists of all nations.

BURMA

Burma, possessing both ports and overland trade routes, was India's trade gateway to Southeast Asia. Sometime around the third century B.C.E., Indian merchants began taking their cultural traditions (religious ideas, political and legal forms) along with their wares to the people who had settled along Burma's rivers. These reshaped native society, art, and thought, combining with the special character of the people to create a dignified culture that was Burmese and Buddhist.

The Buddhist element came when Aśoka sent monks as missionaries to the commercial center of Thaton, where they founded a monastic settlement. By the second century B.C.E., Sinhalese chronicles report that Burmese monks attended an important religious ceremony on the island. With the great expansion of commerce with India during the first century C.E. and following, many Indians came to Thaton not as colonists and exploiters but as friendly traders. Buddhism was well received and soon was firmly established around Thaton, which became a great Buddhist center. Missions came also from south Indian Buddhist centers and, by the third century, overland from east India.

Local cults (of spirits, or *nats*) were adopted into Theravāda; art, including the making of Buddha images, fell under Indian influence, and stūpas were built. Soon, Burma was a flourishing center of Buddhist life, even spreading its Buddhist culture to other areas and enjoying a prosperity that allowed devout Theravāda practice to flower. Education and discipline were available to monks and laity alike in the monasteries.

Later, diverse influences appeared in the area. By the time of the founding of the Pagān kingdom (849–1287), Mahāyāna was coming via overland trade routes from south China, while Bengal in India was a source of Mahāyāna and Tantrism as well as an aggressive Hinduism.

At the time of the Pagān dynasty's greatest king, Anawrahtā (1040–1077), Buddhism in Burma changed its character by turning to Ceylon for inspiration, particularly in response to growing non-Theravāda movements. Tantrism was asserting its practices, the neighboring Khmers were converting en masse to Hinduism, and Mahāyāna gained strength in areas closer to China. A Theravāda monk, Shin Arahan, considered Hindu influence excessive in the south, so he fled Thaton and went to Pagān, where he converted Anawrahtā to Theravāda. The king became its champion. He defeated the northern Mahāyānist kingdom of Nanchao, converted those tribes that had returned exclusively to spirit cults, and conquered Thaton on the pretext of obtaining Theravāda texts denied to him by its king. Though Anawrahtā patronized Theravāda lavishly, archaeological evidence indicates that Mahāyāna and Tantric monks whom he opposed continued to pursue their doctrines alongside the Theravādins. But it was really Theravāda's day. During this time Burma became the most thriving center of Buddhism in the world, since Buddhism was everywhere else under attack or failing. King Anawrahtā had relics brought from Ceylon, and he transformed his capital of Pagān by magnificent religious building programs. By the time of the Sinhalese king Vijayabāhu, Burma was the most prosperous Theravāda country, sending monks in 1065 to Ceylon itself to restore the ordination line that was in danger of extinction there. Later, the Khmers were brought into the Theravāda fold by Burmese efforts.

Pagān was a fabled kingdom (also a city and a dynasty), known even in the West via Marco Polo. The people were prosperous and had splendid monasteries and temples. In a united Burma the citizens made themselves masters of Buddhist thought, so that Pagān was a center of Buddhist culture. The people had made Buddhism their way of life, monks taught children in the villages, spreading Buddhism far and wide; and for three centuries, the city of Pagān was a splendid city with over 9,000 pagodas (stūpas) and temples.

But Pagān was sacked by the Mongols in 1287 and abandoned. Wars and small kingdoms followed, dividing the country. Mahāyāna dwindled, but Theravāda survived. King Dhammazedi of Pegu (later fifteenth century) reformed the Burmese Saṅgha along Sinhalese lines and made his capital a center of Theravāda culture. A new dynasty emerged, ruling a reunited Burma from 1752 until the British deposition of the king in 1886, when Burma was annexed to India. Under the monarchy the Saṅgha was favored and grew in spite of a petty controversy over whether a monk should wear his upper robe over both shoulders or only over the left. The issue bitterly divided the Saṅgha until 1784, when the king decreed that the both-shoulders faction was right. Pali studies flourished in the nineteenth century, and Sūtras were translated into Burmese. The king appointed a hierarchy headed by his chaplain to regulate the affairs of the Order. After the British took over, they declined to appoint a new director of the Saṅgha when the old one died but eventually arranged for the whole Saṅgha to elect a superior for itself. When outside authority was thus removed, discipline in the monasteries deteriorated. Monks played a prominent part in the early days of the independence movement, later faded into the background, and emerged after independence was won following World War II as an ecclesiastical lobby.

Burmese Buddhism, like Sinhalese, did much to preserve Theravāda orthodoxy. Scholarship was extensive in fields related to doctrine; Burmese authors rewrote versions of the Buddha's previous lives (the *Jātakas*) in Burmese, and these became very popular. The Saṅgha remained accessible to the Burmese people. Monasteries and shrines were built close to where the laity resided, giving access to monastic education and training to all who desired it. Today, Buddhism's place in Burma is secure and paramount.

CAMBODIA, THAILAND, AND LAOS

The boundaries of the contemporary countries of Cambodia, Thailand, and Laos do not necessarily correspond with those of the ancient kingdoms of the area. The people associated with them—Khmers, Thais, and Laos—were not necessarily the first in the area to practice Buddhism, but they often left the first records. Cambodian history traditionally begins in the first century C.E., with the rise of the Kingdom of Funan on the India-China trade route. Brahmins and Buddhist traders settled the area, bringing Indian religions, including a Sanskrit variety of Hīnayāna, as well as political and artistic culture. By the end of the fourth century, the region was thoroughly Indianized, with Indian influence extended to the population at large. Sanskrit in-

A votive figure of a person adoring the Buddha. (Cambodian wood figure, sixteenth century.)

scriptions show that Hinduism and Mahāyāna Buddhism existed together by the fifth century C.E. A century later another strong Indianization took place. Though Funanese rulers were Hindu in these centuries, Buddhism was diffused throughout the kingdom and even enjoyed moderate royal patronage. A Chinese embassy came between 535 and 545 to seek Buddhist texts and teachers.

Khmer power increased in the late seventh century, but the accompanying prosperity favored both Hinduism and Buddhism. By 800 a unified Cambodian state was established with a god-king at the head of the state religion, which was distinctly Hindu of the Śaivite sect. Later rulers built monasteries for both Śaivites and Buddhists, and Hindu cults coexisted with Buddhism through the tenth century. Śaivism remained the main royal cult, but Buddhism received continued patronage too. Some rulers in the eleventh century favored and promoted Buddhism, others blended various sects of Hinduism together, and still Buddhism, primarily Mahāyāna, continued.

It was during the late twelfth century that a monk from Burma introduced Theravāda into Cambodia. Later it was supported by Khmer kings and eventually supplanted Mahāyāna. Theravāda Buddhist monks were at the capital by the end of the thirteenth century, by which time the Cambodian state had dropped Hinduism for Theravāda. This situation remains today.

In the thirteenth century, small Thai states developed on the Indo-Chinese peninsula. Previously, Cambodia and other Indianized states had influenced the area. When two Thai states gained dominance, they accepted influences from Burma and the Khmers. Most importantly, the Thais accepted Theravāda Buddhism from Burma. The king, Ramkham-haeng (late twelfth and early thirteenth centuries), was a patron of Theravāda, and inscriptions tell us that all the people were

Buddhists, too. Bronze images of the Buddha produced in Thailand have been some of the finest in history.

Later, Thai kings in the fifteenth century borrowed Cambodian ideas of the ruler as god-king, used court brahmins and Brahmanical ceremonies, and adopted Hindu law. But Theravāda continued, and despite the court Brahmanism, Thais of all social classes considered themselves Buddhists. Buddhism at the popular level included monks who practiced magic, and the Saṅgha filled a valuable social role in education and religion. Ceylon was the source of renewed Theravāda contacts for the Thais; the situation was reversed, however, in the eighteenth century, when Ceylon turned to Thailand for renewal of Buddhist knowledge and the ordination line. A Thai mission visited Ceylon to perform ordinations for monks and novices. Since that time, Thailand has remained Theravāda.

The Lao people emerged by the fourteenth century when, with the help of Khmer power, the first Laotian state was founded and Khmer missionaries introduced Theravāda. Previously, Mahāyāna was also in the area. Later kings defended and supported Theravāda Buddhism, which became the official religion of Laos in the fourteenth century.

INDONESIA

Indonesia was Hinduized by the fifth century C.E. after a long period of sea contacts with ports to its west. By that time Buddhist missionaries were also coming to the island, but brahmins had already brought the worship of Śiva. It was Śaivism that had royal patronage and prestige, and its devotionalism and forms of worship harmonized with preexisting Indonesian religion. In 671 C.E. the Chinese Buddhist pilgrim I-ching, on his way to Nālandā, stopped at Palembang in the kingdom of Śrīvijaya. He found over one thousand monks, mostly Hīnayāna, and studied there before continuing to India. Inscriptions also indicate that Mahāyāna Tantrism was practiced in Palembang before the close of the seventh century, grafting local Malay magical practices onto the imported Tantric methods of attaining power.

On the island of Java, the rulers of the Śailendra dynasty combined Mahāyāna and Śaivism, with Tantrism linking the two. One of them, in about 800, built the greatest and most glorious of all stūpas, the one at Borobuḍur. This was a giant maṇḍala in stone, its bas-relief representing the pilgrim's search for enlightenment. Its circumambulation path leads past two thousand and more reliefs depicting scenes from Śākyamuni's life, the Jātaka tales, and the Mahāyāna Sūtras. The ascent is a ritual journey through the material world, out of saṃsāra and into nirvāṇa. Only half a century later, another Śailendra king

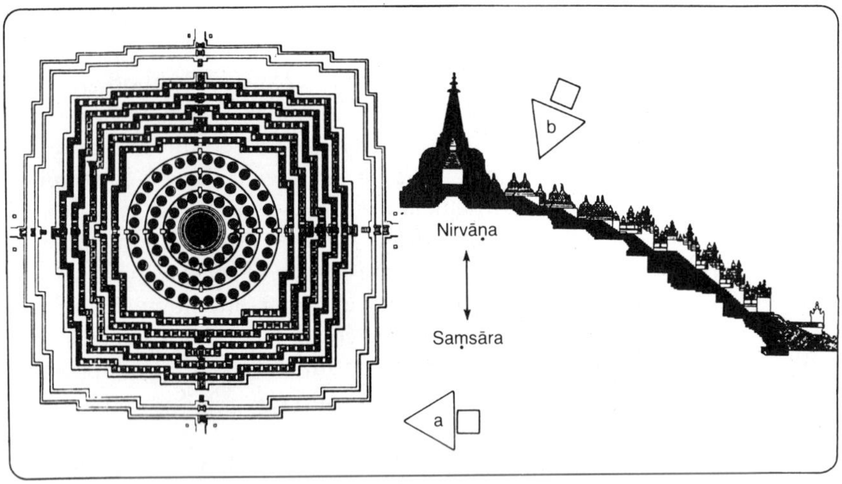

The Borobuḍur stūpa: (a) ground plan, revealing its maṇḍala pattern, and (b) cross-section of the ascent out of saṃsāra to nirvāṇa. (Java, circa 800 C.E.*)*

constructed a great Śiva temple, indicating that both religions had been accepted as showing a way to salvation. The two shrines were also funerary monuments, symbolic of the dead kings' divine ascent to salvation. This form of Buddho-Śaivism continued until, by the end of the fourteenth century, Islam came to the islands and gradually converted all but those on the eastern island of Bali. There a Hindu-Buddhist mysticism survives today.

POPULAR THERAVĀDA BUDDHISM IN RURAL THAILAND

To understand Buddhism as a whole, we need an implicit model to ensure that all dimensions are included or at least acknowledged. Buddhism always existed in several environments, which can be represented as in Figure 2. This model shows monastic Buddhism serving both urban and rural populations and their separate concerns, varying from the royal cult to farmers' rituals. Other religious actors and systems exist in monastic Buddhism's immediate environment, including vestigial Brahmanism, spiritism, indigenous agrarian rituals, and the practices of lay ritual specialists. Thus, monastic Buddhism functions on a continuum with two poles. The urban pole includes the esoteric, soteriological pursuits of the monks and their servicing of the state Buddhist cult (rituals performed for the benefit of the state and the royal family) and of wealthy lay people. The rural pole serves agrarian peasants, bringing monks into the popular sphere of religion.

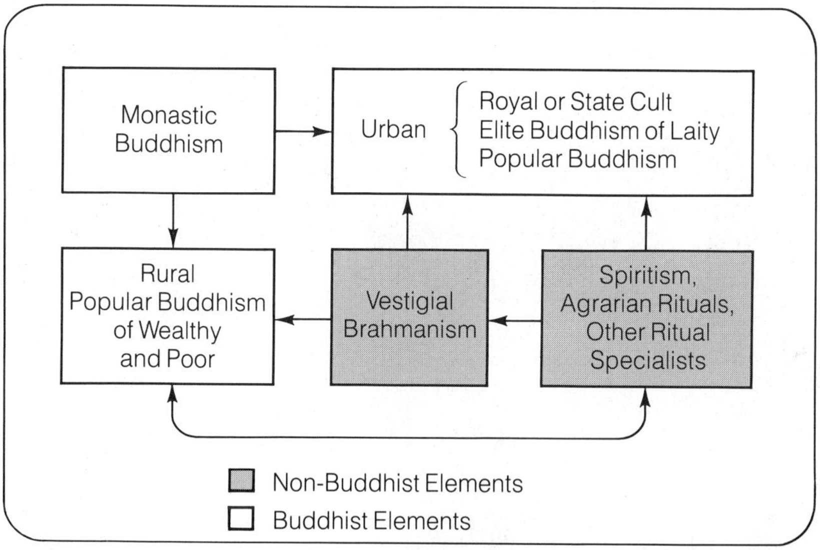

Figure 2. A model of Theravāda Buddhism in its traditional religious environment.

Since we have already seen in historical sources how Buddhism expressed its spiritual goals, the discussion which follows will focus on how monastic Buddhism exists in a contemporary rural setting—in the buildings of the *wad* or temple-monastery, in the activities of the monks, and in the religious life of the monks' supporters, the peasants. This will reveal some of Buddhism's proximate goals and activities in the worldly samsaric sphere (see Terwiel, 1975).

The *Wad*, A Rural Community's Sacred Center

The wad, or temple-monastery complex in rural Thai Buddhism, functions as the sacred center of a number of rice-growing families, usually around a hundred. The family and the wad are the two social institutions that unite the community, linking people together. The laity support the wad for the benefits its sacred activities produce. It is "their wad," since they have donated most of what it is and owns and daily provide the means of its sustenance—rice, robes, and toothpaste included. The monastic rule (Vinaya) forbids monks to engage in worldly life-supporting work so that they can cultivate a special sanctity that, in return, benefits the daily life, security, and prosperity of the supporting families.

Swearer (1976) described a model temple-monastic compound in northern Thailand, the Wad Haripuñjaya. His analysis indicates that the ideal monastic complex has two separate areas. One is reserved for the Saṅgha, including living quarters and buildings for its own esoteric

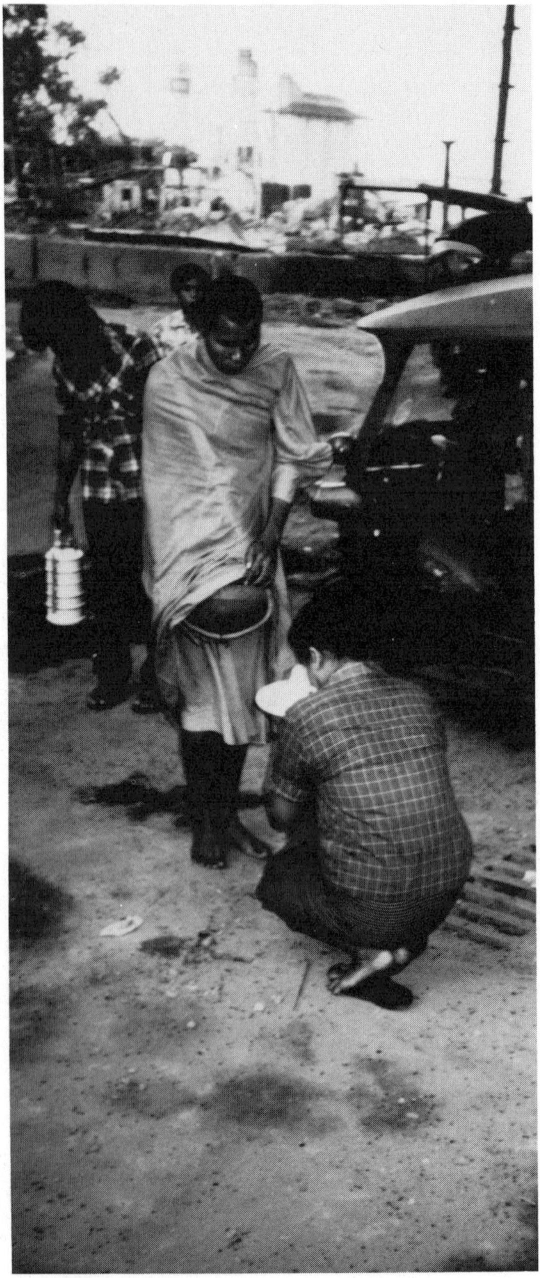

a

b

c

These photographs show scenes from the daily life of popular Buddhism in contemporary Thailand. a) A laywoman in Bangkok kneels to offer a monk food on his early morning rounds; a temple helper behind him carries additional containers for the offerings. b) Donation baskets and goods for sale at a roadside stand in Bangkok. Traditional donations include practical objects such as plates, toothbrushes, soap, toilet paper, and matches as well as customary incense, candles, and flowers. c) Festival throngs offering

e

d

f

candles, flowers, incense, and gold leaf at a ceedii shrine. d) A temple shrine tower (ceedii) commemorating the presence of the Buddha's power to rural Thai Buddhists. e) A recluse sells offerings in a wad complex. f) "Spirit-house" shrine, whose venerable spirit protects the homestead, having been offered flowers, incense, and food; an essential element of popular religion.

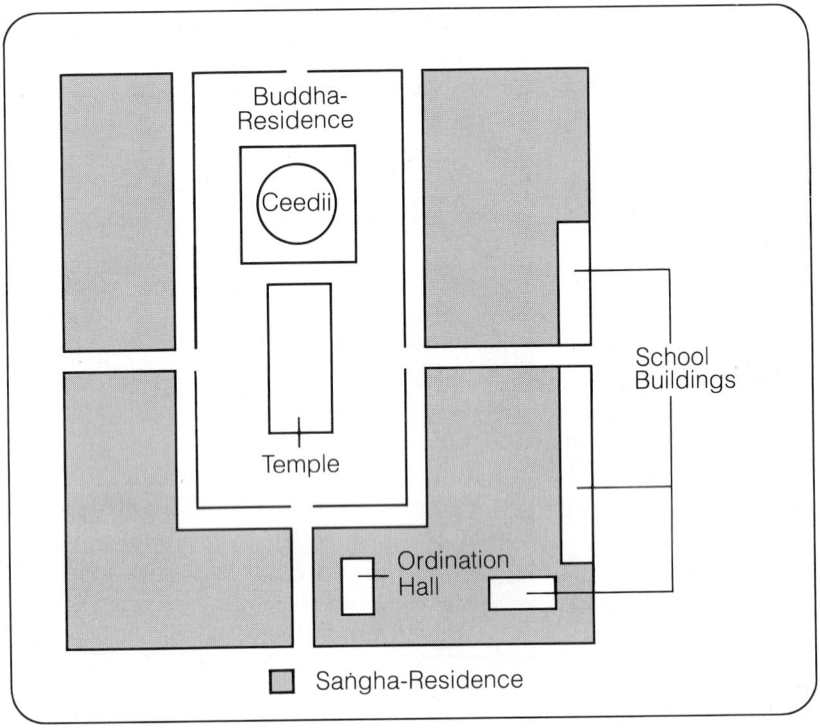

Figure 3. Ground plan of a Thai wad.

ritual and its educational endeavors. The other is devoted to the Buddha, containing the *ceedii* (memorial monument) and several temples where the majority of the wad's exoteric ceremonies and rituals occur, uniting monks and laity. Simplified, the ground plan of these two areas is presented in Figure 3.

The Saṅgha areas of the complex surround and orient themselves toward the Buddha-residence area, which faces east. At the symbolic center of the entire establishment stands the ceedii shrine, which derives from the old Indic stūpa form and should contain a Buddha-relic. The Buddha area's purpose is ritual service to the Buddha, made present in the ceedii's symbolism and honored in the temple's activities. The temple enshrines Buddha images, to which offerings of candles, flowers, and incense may be made before the ceremonies that regularly unite monks and laity. The Saṅgha-residence area houses the monks' dormitories, school buildings, kitchen, bell tower, library, storage areas, a bodhi tree, and, most importantly, an ordination hall, a holy corporate center. These are essential to the Saṅgha's livelihood and mission.

The ordination hall is the foremost building of the Saṅgha's area, as in it new members enter the order. There, too, the monks gather twice monthly, on the last day of the waxing and waning moons, for the recitation of the Pāṭimokkha rule (see p. 49) by an experienced monk or the abbot. The monks alone attend this fortnightly ritual, following the model of ancient Buddhism, which provides a time for reviewing conduct and enhancing spirituality through recitation of the rule. Through ordination, the order brings male individuals into its acculturative sway, allowing them to follow the model example of Siddhārtha's renunciation.

The wad's school buildings are used to instruct monks and novices in the Dharma, its history, customs, and languages, as well as to provide a secular primary education for local boys and girls. Males who join the wad as monks do so, usually at the age of twenty, for one three-month, rainy-season retreat (Thai, *phansăa*; for Pali, *vassa*). They thus learn the basic rituals of the religion, along with chanting and meditation. Moreover, they see how the monastery runs and what it is like to be a monk. Though most leave the monastery to resume work in the fields and begin a family, they have a full experience of Saṅgha life, its rituals and mysteries. The experience functions as an initiation into the sacred community that lives at the center of the secular; they return to life transformed into a full member of the adult community.

The main temple in the Buddha-residence area houses at one end a raised set of shiny bronzed Buddha statues behind a railing decorated during ceremonies by burning candles, flowers, and smoking incense. The temple walls recount in vivid paintings the life of the Buddha or episodes from popular Jātaka tales, thus instructing in values such as detachment, loving friendliness, generosity, calm, and the pursuit of the good. Monks come to this building for ceremonies honoring the Buddha, and it is here that they join with the laity on holy days for public ceremonies. The impression of temple ceremony in rural Thailand is one of relaxed unhurriedness combined with mutual respect and sanctity. The wad's peasants come there for the special access to the sacred it provides, to obtain the benefits of religion that it is the duty of the monks to provide. This contact follows a regular pattern in the year's ritual and festival cycle, augmented by numerous irregular special ceremonies that the monastery's lay supporters request.

Two calendars determine the course of the religious year, the one remembering the events of the Buddha's life, the other protecting and celebrating the agricultural cycle so central to the lives of peasants. Their special dates and times bring the laity to the wad for ceremonies much better attended than the regular fortnightly holy days. In midspring comes the traditional New Year festival, borrowed from ancient India, a time at the end of the dry season when all anticipate the rice planting and rains. A month or so later (as determined by the variable lunar calendar), a festival honors the birth, Enlightenment, and death of the Buddha. Clearly, the first festival, with its ritual lustration of the monks and water drenching of one's friends, seeks to induce and promote the expected rains. The second recalls the major events in the Buddha's life. On this latter "Buddha's Day" many people attend an early morning communal food offering to the monks in the largest temple of the complex, and all the monks attend the Pāṭimokkha recitation in their hall. At evening, the temple bell calls the laity to return to the monastery, filling the temple with quiet activity, many candles, and much incense. Proceeding outside, the monks and laity circumambulate the ceedii-reliquary three times in a candlelight procession, then return to formal preaching and the walk home. During the fruit season there are also festivals. In one, special baskets of fruit are given to monks; in another, bathing robes for the rainy season are donated. In June or July the beginning of the rainy-season retreat comes, initiating for the entire community a period of special, intense religiosity ("Buddhist Lent"), when monks must remain at the monastery for special ceremonies and meditation and lay attendance at the wad increases. After the retreat months, donation ceremonies provide the monks with new robes and other mundane necessities.

Elite Monastic Buddhism in its Rural Setting

Rural monastic Buddhism is an elite religious practice, because it keeps its principal actors, the monks, from defiling contact with the ordinary world so that they can acquire, generate, and pass on to the community special spiritual power. Monks are able to serve the community because their Vinaya rule ensures, first, that the world has no hold on them and, second, that they can live in a ritual purity that enables them to acquire spiritual power. The monastery stands at the center of the agrarian community as a spiritual conductor, able to channel numinous power to the ends sought by peasant and monk alike—namely, safety and well-being in this life and good karma for future rebirths. Though monastic membership thus creates an elite practice within the community's Buddhism, nearly all male members of the community have been or are monks in the wad and can join at any time, since either joining or leaving may be repeated. Most adult males participate directly in the community's monastic center, playing major roles in its support, governance (especially elders), and mission in the world. This is how the wad worked in the traditional peasant society of Southeast Asia. Recent figures indicate that relative percentages of Saṅgha membership declined between 1927 and 1970, showing some change in the traditional situation. In the former year, one out of sixteen males was a monk, while in the latter, only one out of thirty-five was. By the middle of the 1970s, maximum population in the approximately twenty-six thousand Thai monasteries (both urban and rural) at the height of membership (the retreat season) was two hundred thirteen thousand monks, of whom perhaps 25 percent were members for that holy season alone; the total population numbered around forty-two million.

Males enter the life of the monastery at several levels. Young boys may become servants to the monks (*dègwád*, numbering one hundred eighteen thousand in 1975), or older boys, up to the age of twenty (when they would become a monk) may become novices (one hundred twenty-two thousand in 1975) through a special ordination service. These latter are ritually lower in status than the monks. Full membership is available to all males after the age of twenty through Buddhism's oldest ritual, ordination. Joining the order requires considerable ceremony and, particularly for wealthier peasants, costly preparations. But it produces equally great rewards. Sponsoring such a ceremony generates great merit or good karma, as does participating in it as the ordinand or even as a supporting relative. Pledges of the food necessary to support the new inhabitant of the monastery must be secured before he will be allowed to join. Here a mother's encouragement and support often help, gaining her immense merit, too, important as she approaches old age. Generally the most important reason given for entering the monastery involves the learning that the experience provides. The ordinand learns the special rules and roles of monkhood, making him aware of his newly acquired exalted ritual status and the purity he must maintain. He immediately learns the esoteric sacerdotal language of the monks, and the laity must thereafter address him with all due respect.

Once ordained, monks adopt the special way of life of the Saṅgha. They are taught to act mindfully (of both thoughts and deeds), to behave beneficially rather than negatively (remaining polite, sober, friendly, calm) or aggressively, practicing concern and compassion. Monks ideally avoid violent or strenuous activities that excite or stupify (running, jumping, dancing, imbibing, and becoming angry, argumentative, rude, or imperious). These features of Buddhist moral training counteract anger, lust, and delusion, along with pride of self and body, just as Chinese Confucian rules of ritual goodness and English etiquette sought to produce a proper personality through rules that correct behavior. The Vinaya rules, furthermore, allow monks to acquire sanctity by keeping them from ritually polluting activities such as killing (even lower forms of life, which is why they do not farm) and engaging in sexual activity or associating with women. Thus, those who become monks practice an elite form of religion (though it is open to all males), whose special esoteric forms (rituals, chanting, meditation) produce beneficial spiritual power for all living beings, but especially for their own community, for their benefactors and sponsors, for their ancestors and family, and for their own karmic heritage, which they will take into future lives.

The scope of the elite, monastic religious practice reaches from the temple-monastery throughout the entire community. The monks chant and meditate privately in the Saṅgha-residence's ordination hall and publicly in the wad's temple; or they travel to households for similar recitations or to other monasteries. On holy worship days (*wanphrá'*), monks perform the regular ritual honor of the Buddha. During the rainy retreat season (from mid-July to mid-October), religiosity increases greatly, as more ceremonies are performed and many more lay people and young monks join in the ritual life of the wad compound. Monks chant four times daily in the temple and additional times in private (transferring some of the merit of those sessions over to their supporters each time). They give sermons on every holy day during the season, and young monks receive meditation instruction as part of the later afternoon chanting session. Participants gain merit-power on all these occasions, both monk and layperson alike. Clearly the special merit-power being generated during the retreat season serves the agrarian supporters of the wad, since it is then that proper weather conditions and the full maturing of crops is their central concern.

Monks leave the monastery on numerous occasions, on request of the laity, to bring the power of their Pali recitation and ritual-meditative purity directly into the community to serve its interests. A chapter of monks may be asked to bless and empower any of the regular (not specifically monastic) family rituals such as those at birth, tonsure, marriage, or death. They do not perform the ceremony, but in one segment of it bring it their special blessings and the power of the sacred word. Monks also may chant for rain, bless the crop on the threshing floor, or pray for the longevity of the sick and aged. They extend their meritorious power through other means as well. In particular, older monks manufacture amulets and talismans, which when blessed convey their power to laymen. One of the rarer irregular ceremonies at times requested by the laity involves the coming together of a chapter of renowned monks to chant and meditate so as to reempower the charms and amulets gathered for the ceremony, the proceeds going to the support of the monks. Love charms also receive monks' blessings, although monks never participate in the more dangerous, that is, more polluting, forms of power manipulation, which are practiced by lay ritual specialists. Another power exchange occurs when a tattoo-specialist monk etches his auspicious designs on the skin of young men over seventeen. In most of these cases, monks expect to be rewarded financially. Behind all their actions lies the single motive of generating and dispersing beneficial karma power to their patrons and sustainers, parents, and ancestors.

Some monks and novices stay on in the Saṅgha, achieving higher ecclesiastical status through the Thai state's centralized examination system. Studies at the various levels focus on the monk's life, Buddhist ethics, Buddhist wisdom (in the form of proverbs—this is still partially an oral tradition, where proverbs and parables work best), the biography of the Buddha, and the Pāṭimokkha rules. The Saṅgha offers the qualified man a status of great prestige in the community, a reasonable income from donations for specific ceremonies, and the possibility that he may become abbot (chosen by the lay supporters of the monastery) or rise even higher in ecclesiastical office. But most return to the fields and family concerns, for crops need tending, and young men want to court. The initiatory symbolism of joining the Saṅgha comes out in its rituals for leaving. In ancient India, once one had taken the vow of the monkhood, the status change was irreversible. The monk left the secular, profane world and could never regain his ritual status in it. In the Thai case, the monk with his advisors selects an auspicious time for his ritual rebirth. He takes leave of his fellow monks, goes through a ceremony, and then, as a secular man again, has several rituals performed to protect him. On returning home he prostrates himself before his elders to share the good karma he has accumulated. The only other legitimate exit from the Saṅgha is through expulsion for rule violations involving sexual intercourse, stealing, killing, or lying about one's psychic powers.

The picture we gain by thus looking at Thai rural monastic Buddhism shows a religion fully integrated into the concerns and means of survival of a local agrarian community. A striking degree of community-monastery interdependence unites the lay followers with the temporary and permanent members of the monkhood. This more empirical picture of the religion's mundane life and livelihood reveals and makes sense of the elite monastic vocation *in situ*. Next, we will look through the eyes of the farmers themselves to understand their religion.

Popular Rural Thai Buddhism

The popular religion of rural Thai Buddhists is an amalgam of indigenous and borrowed ideas and practices that have been integrated into the elite, textual Buddhism of the wad. Since the monks stand aloof from some of its activities, we can distinguish the literary components from this popular religion, though the monks, coming from peasant backgrounds themselves, may in fact not make the distinction as clearly as analysis does. In effect, the religious environment of the wad is complex and diverse; since this is included in the peasants' total religious perspective, it influences their interpretation of monastic Buddhism. The wad's farmer-peasant supporters interpret textual Buddhism's ritual, chanting, and meditative activities from the perspective of the popular religion, a perspective we need to recover to have a complete view of the totality of their "Buddhism." When Buddhism was adopted as the dominant elite religion of Southeast Asia, it became an overlay into which peasant concerns and ideas were integrated. Thus, interpretations of the textual religion based on elements of indigenous origin were introduced, as well as borrowings from Indic Brahmanical and Chinese sources. Also included were other religious forms pertaining to agriculture, healing, placatory activities, and power acquisition, the domain mostly of local nonmonastic ritual specialists.

The popular religion of any peasant society develops practices that respond to people's needs—fertility of women and fields; adequate rains; freedom from disease for crops, animals, and humans; prosperity; happiness, good fortune; and protection from ill of all other kinds. Such a society is characterized by a pervasive *spiritism* (a term used to avoid words such as *magic, animism*, and the current term, *spiritualism*). This explanation of why things happen assumes that spirits (Thai, *phĭi*; parallel to Burmese, *nat*) of all kinds inhabit the invisible environment that is the matrix of life, exercising powers that determine life's fortunes. Spiritism assumes that the material world is twofold, consisting of a gross physical realm perceivable through the five senses and an invisible spirit realm, whose members impinge on the workings of the physical realm in both positive and negative fashion. Spirits (including ghosts, ancestors, demons, and guardians) exist everywhere. Some guard the earth, temple, village, house, or fields. Outside every hamlet and dwelling, a spirit shrine houses its tutelary spirit. In every house, ancestral spirits watch jealously over the actions of their descendants, while other spirits guard the hearth and family compound. As long as the spirits remain happy, honored, fed, and propitiated, they bring good times. But when they are angered by some human action or oversight or if they are malevolent, they cause crop failure, sickness, misfortune, and every other suffering of humankind.

In adapting to this indigenous spiritism, monastic Buddhism maintained its elite perspective. Monks identify their ritual status as being higher than the spirits, so they never give placatory offerings, this being the task of other ritual specialists. Instead they protect the laity from spirits through blessings and the beneficial effects of Pali chanting. Buddhist monks take part in householder and agrarian rituals by coming to them to chant and bless, but otherwise the layperson or ritualist performs the rest of the ritual. Peasants, too, adopt the monastic structure, giving elements of the religion their own interpretation and adapting its forms to serve their immediate concerns. The standard Buddhist view of life's dilemmas—that existence in transient, conditioned reality is a source of suffering (duḥkha) and that nirvāṇa is the solution—is considerably softened in the popular understanding. Though all undeniably are Buddhists, the peasants do not aspire to the ultimate goal of ending the miserable cycle of rebirths. Salvation, rather, is a proximate, worldly concern, involving the continuance of life and deliverance from its present woes and ills through their own meritorious actions and the agency of the community's monks. Life's torments do not derive from the Wheel of Life's recurrent death but from life's unfortunate circumstances brought on by human faults and the ever-present spirit powers. In the popular interpretation, nirvāṇa is an ultimate bliss attained by the Buddha and the arhants, while peasants expect rebirth in similar or somewhat improved life situations. No one really expects to be reborn in the unfortunate realms as a hungry ghost or animal, and popular instruction reminds everyone of the far worse fates in the hells.

This occasions variant interpretations of specific Buddhist rituals. All farmers frequently take or renew their vow to follow the five precepts often, but their interpretation of this act differs from that of monastic practice. As a peasant-farmer, it is impossible to avoid breaking the precepts, which would require never gossiping, telling less than full truths about everyday matters, drinking, killing of mosquitoes and bugs while working, and providing the family with fresh meat on occasion. The peasant reinterpretation comes in the manner of taking the vow and its expected result. By taking the vow, peasants temporarily achieve an elevation out of the world that pollutes them, so the vow serves to purify and cleanse, rather than to promise them to an impossible ideal. Similar popular interpretations occur for all major activities offered by the elite Saṅgha members. Quite distinct from the textually based meaning, these activities are universally thought to be for the purpose of generating beneficial power that can give the community good fortune and protection as well as produce good effects in future lives. Thus, the major soteriological effects, from the peasant perspective, of the monks' actions come from the beneficent power they generate. Everyone, monks and laity alike, seeks to accumulate this beneficial merit-power by living moral lives to one degree or another, by chanting or listening to sacred mantras, by meditation, and through generosity. For peasants, this has the immediate consequence of making their life more safe and happy and the long-term result of better future lives.

Religion of Women and the Elderly

In a peasant society, women, like chattel, count as a means of production. At least until after menopause, women are ritually excluded as major religious actors. They participate in public ceremonies but from birth are taught to shun monks. Women produce a negative spirituality, due to the ritually polluting menstruation. As in ancient India, sexual release and the menses are understood to have a power antithetical to beneficial karma. Women do not receive power tattoos and can wear only second-rate amulets. They participate in ceremonies and can gain merit by sponsoring them, but generally, during productive years, their place is at home.

This situation changes after the duties of the child-bearing years pass. First, women can join groups of female religious practitioners—closely tied to monasteries—though no women enter the Saṅgha. Second, both laymen and laywomen take special Eight Precept vows, particularly at an advanced age when the importance of bettering one's karma store for the next rebirth assumes greater relative importance. Especially during the retreat season, elderly men and women undertake a special overnight vow to follow the first Eight Precepts for the time of their stay in the wad. This enables women to attend, so they are able to participate more in the wad's spirituality. An elaborate ceremony of donation at that time also makes it possible for much greater merit than usual, and peasants interpret the immediate benefit of the event to be longer life for themselves. Special lay chanting occurs, the monks preach, and devout laity have a chance to talk with the monks late into the night, getting to know them better. The activity also assures participants intense generation of good karma for rebirth.

Becoming devout laywomen in this manner opens religion greatly to older women, who are thought to be no longer an attraction to monks and not a threat each month to their sanctity. Women may finally become more knowledgeable of the ritual and its liturgy and participate in it directly. Even more enthusiastic elderly women can join organizations of recluses, not becoming nuns, strictly, but clearly advancing to within one step of monkhood. Some recluses are solitary, while others live in small groups, wearing white robes. In 1967 they numbered around ten thousand, but they declined slightly by the next count in 1970. These women do follow the Five Precepts strictly; thus, they have to avoid most contact with the secular world, living often close to or in a wad complex. They chant the sacred Pali scriptures, some groups becoming specially known for their virtuosity.

The elderly generally have more interest in religion. It is not thought unusual for younger men to want a family and to have little religious interest except on festival days, which offer opportunity to socialize. Beyond taking the special Eight Precept vows, a man may become a monk again if he can find a family to donate his food. Some withdraw for many years in the same monastery, while others maintain close contacts with the laity, giving them advice on all kinds of matters and disputes. Some older monks give special assistance to the abbot, becoming active in community life, and others specialize in medical arts, using herbs or mantra-empowered water to alleviate aches and pains or grinding up sacred objects to make pills. Still other monks practice esoteric skills such as making sacred diagrams and empowering them for their patrons.

FROM TRADITIONAL TO MODERN THERAVĀDA

Traditional Theravāda's roots lie deep in agrarian society. To the extent that Southeast Asia changes to a more urbanized, technological civilization, traditional meanings and ways will be challenged. The Saṅgha, which presupposes that everything changes, now faces changes in its world that characterize many developing countries today. Some see in this process a weakening of belief, brought about by new notions in the human quest for the real, particularly scientific conceptions that deny spiritism's world picture and offer alternate means of adapting to the environment. One wonders how rural Theravāda Buddhism with its popular religion and its monastic wad will survive. Certainly peasant society will not disappear overnight, nor will the rural Saṅgha.

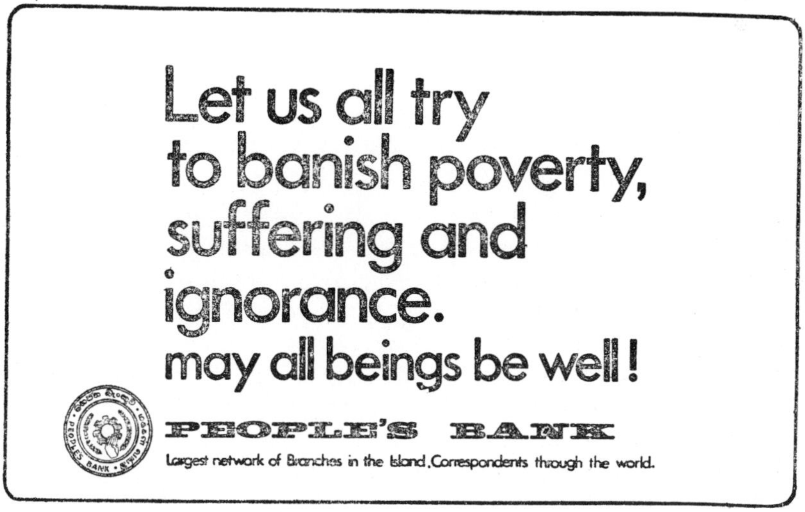

An advertisement for a Śrī Laṅkā bank. (From the publication World Buddhism.*)*

Perhaps, at least in non-Communist countries, rural Buddhism will play a part in the creation of a twenty-first-century society that may combine simple, essential technology and scientific knowledge with traditional ways and wisdom. To the extent that the Saṅgha can provide services that the laity perceive important to their well-being, it will continue to receive their support.

In the rapidly urbanizing centers of Southeast Asia, on the other hand, Buddhism will bear the brunt of secularizing challenges, already far advanced in Communist nations. Some urban Buddhists, at times reluctantly but often enthusiastically, have sensed the changes and the opportunities they bring. The World Fellowship of Buddhists has opened up greater avenues for lay participation in the Saṅgha and fosters a Buddhist ecumenical movement that unites monk and laity, Hīnayāna and Mahāyāna. The sixth Buddhist Council, the most important event in recent Buddhist history, was held in Rangoon, Burma, from 1954 to 1956. Scriptures were reedited, and Buddhists thought about their Dharma together, as they had in the past. Within separate nations, movements such as the Buddhist Sunday School Movement (begun in Thailand in 1958) and lay meditation groups (originating in Burma and Thailand) indicate some renewed interest in bringing traditional Buddhist activities into the modern world. In Thailand, Buddhists have undertaken modernization, and in Śrī Laṅkā and elsewhere monastic education has been improved. Buddhist politicians have become involved in secular affairs, and Buddhists have generally supported neutralism and peaceful coexistence in Southeast Asia.

CHAPTER 9

Buddhism in the Tibetan Culture Area

NEPAL

Nominally, Nepal has the unique position in Buddhism's history of being the birthplace of its founder. It was within the boundaries of contemporary Nepal that the Buddha was born, in the Lumbinī Grove about fifteen miles from his father's capital of Kapilavastu. Legend says that the Buddha returned home after his Enlightenment to declare the new path, converting his own son. In the third century B.C.E., the emperor Aśoka visited the area, and his daughter reportedly married a Nepalese nobleman, bringing Buddhism with her. Thus, it probably has existed in Nepal from a very early time, but we know almost nothing of its history there before the seventh century.

In the early centuries the Buddhism of Nepal most likely developed along the lines of northern India. In the fourth century Vasubandhu visited Nepal. Pātan, a Buddhist center of learning, resembled those of eastern India. Royal favor supported it in the seventh century, and during the two centuries that followed, Nepal developed strong ties with Tibet as many Tibetans came to study in Nepal. Tradition says that King Aṃśuvarman gave his daughter in marriage to the first important Tibetan king, Song-tsen-gam-po (617–650). She introduced the important cult of Tārā ("the Savioress").

After the Muslims invaded Bihar and Bengal in the late twelfth century, many Buddhist monks and scholars took refuge in Nepal, bringing with them Tantrism and large numbers of manuscripts and images. Some of the documents survived until this century, when they

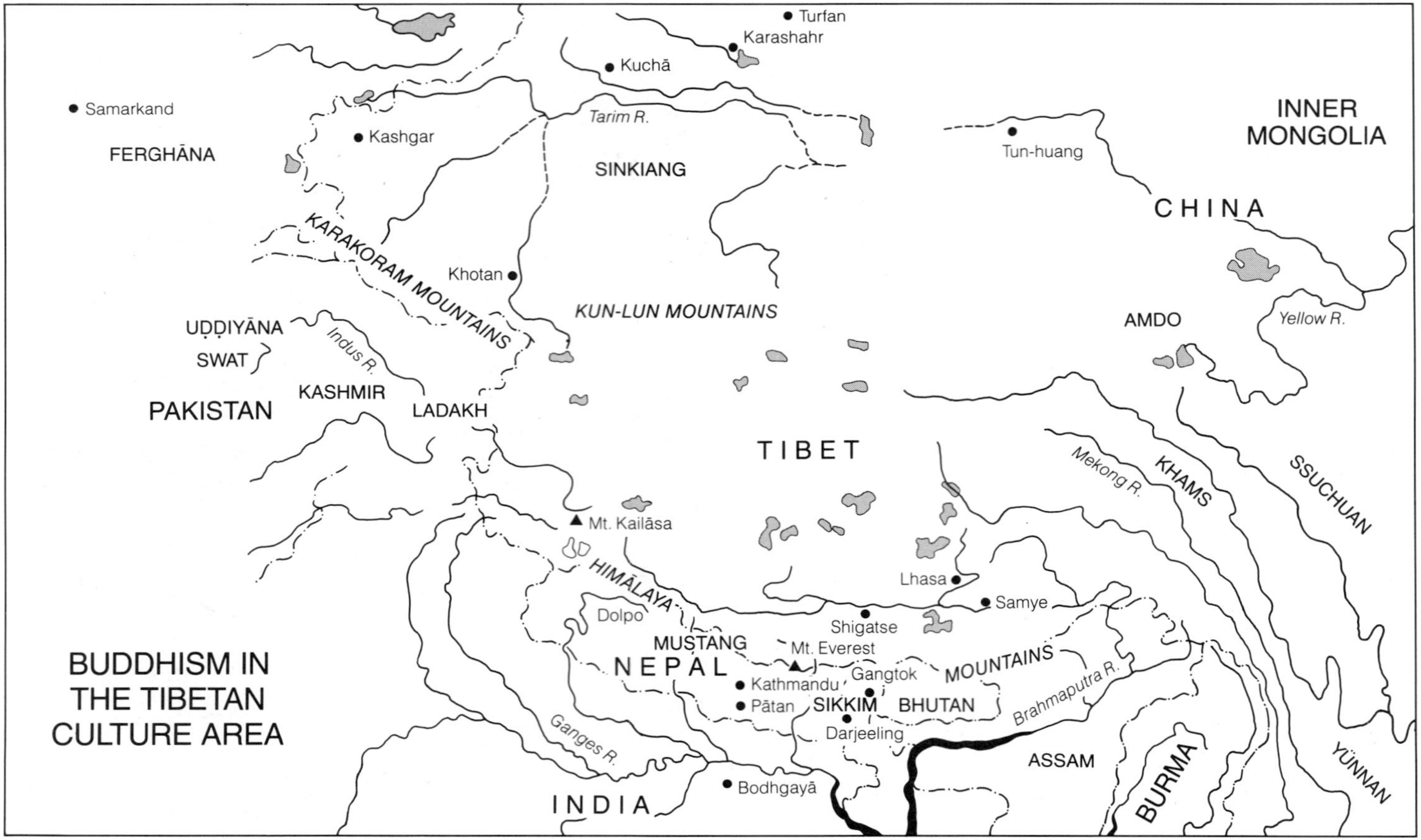
BUDDHISM IN
THE TIBETAN
CULTURE AREA
Samarkand
FERGHĀNA
Kashgar
Kuchā
Karashahr
Turfan
Tarim R.
SINKIANG
Tun-huang
INNER
MONGOLIA
CHINA
KARAKORAM MOUNTAINS
Khotan
KUN-LUN MOUNTAINS
AMDO
Yellow R.
UḌḌIYĀNA
SWAT
Indus R.
KASHMIR
PAKISTAN
LADAKH
TIBET
Mekong R.
KHAMS
SSUCHUAN
Mt. Kailāsa
HIMĀLAYA
Lhasa
Samye
Dolpo
Shigatse
MUSTANG
Mt. Everest
NEPAL
Kathmandu
Gangtok
MOUNTAINS
Pātan
SIKKIM
BHUTAN
Brahmaputra R.
Darjeeling
Ganges R.
ASSAM
BURMA
YÜNNAN
Bodhgayā
INDIA

were retrieved by scholars, adding to our small stock of extant Indian Buddhist manuscripts, most of which were eaten by white ants or otherwise destroyed in their homeland. However, Buddhism in Nepal eventually suffered a fate similar to that of Indian Buddhism, primarily through the weakening of its monastic system. After 1000 C.E., royal patronage sustained the Saṅgha for some time, and the country remained a center of Buddhist culture. Nepal, however, was primarily Hindu, especially the laity, so that once the flow from India stopped, Buddhism declined, merging in part with Hinduism. Around the fourteenth century, Buddhist monks became a high Hindu caste called *banras* (worthy ones), gave up celibacy, and lived in their monasteries as metal workers. Others became *vajrācāryas* (diamond masters), ceremonial specialists who served the ritual needs of the laity, performing rites of birth, death, and other sacraments as hereditary monastery or temple functionaries. Buddhist scholarship declined accordingly during this period, with popular Buddhism syncretizing with Tantric Hinduism. To this day Buddhism survives in two forms in Nepal. One is based on Sanskritic sources, and the other follows Tibetan translations from Sanskrit sūtras and commentaries. The Vajrācāryas of the Kathmandu valley maintain the former. The latter is practiced by the Tibetan people living in the border areas such as Dolpo and Mus-

A "diamond" (vajra, *its hardness symbolizing the absolute) on a lotus (symbolizing the world) in the courtyard of the Buddhist artisans' community temple in Pātan, Kathmandu valley, Nepal. (Photo: Aronson.)*

tang (in northwestern Nepal) and by the Sherpas who migrated from Tibet to live around Everest (in the northeast). Furthermore, Tibetan refugees live in Nepal. Both traditions of Nepali Buddhism still have a handful of first-rate scholars, proficient ritualists, and accomplished meditators. However, with the coming of modernization and the absence of generous donors, the Saṅgha has found it increasingly difficult to attract young Buddhists to serious study and practice and to find financial supporters of these activities.

TIBET: A BUDDHIST CULTURE DISPERSED

In the years after 1959 when the Chinese increased their role and presence in Tibet, one hundred thousand Tibetans became refugees in India, Europe, and America—fully ten thousand of them monks and lamas. In the following two decades one of the least-changed ecclesiastical states in the world, practically untouched by modernizing influences until the middle of this century, was rapidly dismantled in favor of a new society structured along religion-shunning Marxist-Leninist lines. As in many other areas of the world, external forces caused Tibet's traditional order to fall apart. Though the present rulers have maintained a showcase religion (perhaps so as not to appear in an unfavorable light to other Asian Buddhists), the religious culture at home has been obliterated. The mass emigration of Tibetans, especially those high in ecclesiastical hierarchies, has brought the bearers of this religion to western shores and made it available to converts and scholars both here and in Asia. Today, "Lamaism" is the strongest, most unified of the Buddhist groups present and missionizing in Euro-America.

For nearly fifteen hundred years Tibet sat crowning Asia, its plains, fields, and woodlands crossed by a series of formidable mountain ranges. Paradoxically, Tibet existed in splendid isolation but received the influence of many diverse religious cultures. To the south and northeast, the two civilizing giants of Asia, India and China, provided powerful leavening. From the west, Iran and northwestern India contributed their own religious traditions. And across Tibet's north stretched Central Asia, meeting ground (along the fabled silk routes) of peoples and religions, not to mention the much more archaic shamanic horizon of Siberia.

The world's highest country, with an area of a million and a half square miles, was settled originally by Tibeto-Burman speakers, mostly of Mongoloid type. American Theosophists and European occultists discovered Tibet at about the same time that the British became more interested in it politically during the nineteenth century. The

Theosophists transmitted the stock Indian myths about the "land of the snows" (Himālaya) to eager westerners, resulting in the idea that Tibet is the homeland of the lost secrets of past spiritual civilizations. Indian mythology regarded the Himālayas as the realms of the titans (*vidyādhara*, "powerful, esoteric magician or demigod") and gods (residents of the upper-level rebirth realms). Thus, in "forbidden Tibet" (actually it was not, since several non-Tibetan groups, including the Jesuits, established themselves there) resided immortal sages in possession of the lost wisdom. Many of the prophets of Asian religions in the West claimed to have derived their knowledge from these secret Tibetan teachings, and some actually studied there. For their part, the Tibetans thought that the mysterious kingdom (Shambhala) was farther to the north, in little explored mountain ranges.

In the present century, western scholars have begun to investigate Tibetan religion, which is recorded in a vast systematic literature. Further, in the last two decades, Tibetan religious specialists have made this tradition much more available through their writings and teachings, some even in major universities. Far from being the land Theosophists imagined, Tibet turns out to be a Mahāyāna Buddhist country. It is also a mountain agrarian nation (with some nomadic herdsmen), whose culture had little changed from traditional forms when it became more open to western observation. In many ways, it was a feudal society, most resembling medieval Japan or Europe with a stronger communal or tribal consciousness. Tibetan Buddhism before the Chinese invasion provides a good example of how the religion existed before modernizing tendencies changed or destroyed it. In this respect, as does Southeast Asia for Theravāda, Tibet gives us a look at a late Mahāyāna Buddhism in its original context.

TIBET ENTERS HISTORY

In the seventh century C.E., a line of kings became firmly established, enlarging their domain and coming to the notice of China's historians by marching on its borders. A three-century era of political and military greatness accompanied by vigorous territorial expansion brought Tibetans into contact with the major western and eastern civilizations of Asia. Around 634 King Song-tsen-gam-po conquered a Chinese border area and received a Chinese ambassador, followed by a Chinese princess. Later young Tibetan nobles went to China for study. Contacts occurred to the south as well, with Nepal (which sent a princess, too) and with northern India around the middle of the seventh century. Soon thereafter Tibetans took from the Chinese the largely Indianized (and Buddhist) kingdoms of Central Asia (Khotan, Kuchā,

Karashahr, and Kashgar). For the following hundred years, Tibet at times controlled or invaded areas to the southeast (Yünnan) and southwest (Gilgit), even invading the Chinese capital, Ch'ang-an, in 763 and occupying it for fifteen days. In 775–776, the Buddhist Pāla kings of Bengal paid tribute to Tibet, but in the middle of the ninth century Tibetan military power and expansion ended, resulting in a retreat to the homeland.

Throughout this period, Tibetans came into contact with a great diversity of religious traditions, but especially Buddhism, which came from all quarters. China was an important source of civilization, contributing especially Ch'an Buddhism. To the west, Tibet came into contact with Iran, bringing ideas and material culture from as far away as Rome and Greece (medical science) and the Near East (agriculture) as well as Manichaeism, Nestorianism, and Islam. From Central Asia and northern India (present-day Afghanistan and Pakistan), including Gilgit, Kashmir, Gandhāra and Uḍḍiyāna, came Mahāyāna Buddhism (and some Śaivism), along with the new Tantra, which also flourished in Bengal.

INTRODUCTION AND DEVELOPMENT OF BUDDHISM

About 632, according to tradition, King Song-tsen-gam-po sent an emissary to Kashmir to learn writing and devise a script for the Tibetan language. Remarkably, within decades Tibetans had an alphabet and a script adapted to their language in a complicated orthography, the basis for a literate historical culture. Also, as we have seen, Buddhism was becoming known from various directions, though it met with little success because of a lack of royal patronage.

In the mid-eighth century, pro- and anti-Buddhist factions of nobles fought at the court, but forces favorable to Buddhism began to prevail. King Trhisong Detsen (ruled 775–797?), on attaining the throne, became interested in Buddhism, had texts translated from Chinese and Indian sources, and sent a Tibetan to India. Significant missionary activity in Tibet began when he brought the Indian teacher Śāntarakṣita to Tibet from Nepal, though the two had to leave until the principal opponent of Buddhism was murdered. Then both Śāntarakṣita and Padmasambhava, another Indian, reputedly from the Tantric center of Uḍḍiyāna, arrived. The Tibetan tradition reports that Padmasambhava was a fabulous wonder worker, who prepared for the final establishment of Buddhism by defeating and subduing demons and local gods hostile to it, making them into its protectors. The sect of the Nyingma-pa ("Ancient One") claims him as its founder. Soon he left the country, pursued by opposition Bon adherents, but not before

A Tibetan than ka *(painted scroll for visualization) of Beg-tse, Demon Protector of Dharma. (Photo: Antoinette Gordon Collection.)*

cofounding with Śāntarakṣita the Tibetan Saṅgha and the country's first monastic complex at Samye (circa 775?).

At this time, since Sino-Tibetan relations were strong, Ch'an Buddhism, too, became successful. In 781 the king asked two Chinese Buddhist preachers (who probably also acted as spies on Tibetan power) to come to the country. In 791 his edict established Buddhism as Tibet's official religion. Though the common people remained followers of the indigenous shamanism, royal patronage gave the Saṅgha privileges and support, the first step to monastic wealth and independence. The new monasteries and converts became a cult, emerging as a political force outside the state structure. Others emulated the king by making merit-producing donations. The Saṅgha continued the process of opening Tibet outward to wider cultural and religious horizons, expanding even in the area of trade through wandering monks. This growth of the monastic community was opposed by ministers of the state, resulting in persecution.

Before this, however, an event took place that brought together in Tibet representatives of the two great Asian civilizations. By the end of the eighth century, Buddhism in central Tibet had established itself as a result of diverse influences, having come from India (Pāla Bengal, Nepal, and Kashmir) and Indian-influenced areas (present-day Afghanistan and Gilgit and Central Asia) as well as from China. Obviously, ideas foreign to Buddhism were also represented, local cults and beliefs persisted, and indigenous followers of Bon resisted the new power. Furthermore, Indians did not all teach the same ideas. Some favored non-Tantric monasticism, under which monks were vegetarians, abstained from alcohol, and followed the rites of the Sūtras. Others, more Tantric, preferred to follow less stringent rules, using Tantric yoga ritual practices and favoring life in meditation cells. Still others, following Ch'an, supported quietism and spontaneous meditative realizations, as opposed to the Indian emphasis on good works and the long gradual process of achieving Buddhahood.

Faced with problems stemming from the resulting Indian-Chinese doctrinal antagonism, the king adopted the strategy of staging a debate, a familiar Buddhist means for adjudicating such disputes. In 792–794 or thereabouts, Chinese Ch'an and Indian monks met before the king in one of the most remarkable international confrontations of the ancient world. Since Ch'an represented distinctly Chinese religious sensitivities, and Kamalaśīla, the Indian debater, opposed them, a confrontation of two religious traditions took place. The Chinese argued for "sudden enlightenment" and thus the pointlessness of expenditure of great effort and works to achieve the already existing light of the pure mind within. All this made progressive purification a delusive strategy. The Indians countered with their "gradual path," which emphasized the arduous process of attaining spiritual perfection (Buddhahood) through a long succession of rebirths, thus trying to preserve the whole institutional structure of the path to salvation. The event came to be remembered in India, Tibet, and China, but the sources disagree over whom the king chose as the winner. In any case, we know that the influence of Ch'an subsequently declined, while still contributing to later developments and the profusion of interpretations of Tibetan Buddhism. Clearly, though, Tibetan Buddhism was taken predominantly from Indian sources and shared many of the characteristics of Indic religiosity with the mother civilization, as, indeed, did Theravāda in Southeast Asia.

The development of Tibetan Buddhism has been an interaction between scholar-monks leading a conventional celibate life (typified by Śāntarakṣita) and wonder-working yogins wandering freely, often not wearing the monastic robe and not bound to celibacy (typified by Padmasambhava). Spiritual masters of both types are called "lama."

Lama is just the Tibetan translation for *guru* (master, preceptor), and either an eminent monk or an outstanding householder yogin may bear the title.

The work of translating scriptures went forward rapidly in the early ninth century under the patronage of the pious King Ral-pa-can. A commission of Indian and Tibetan scholars standardized the technical terminology and published a Sanskrit-Tibetan glossary. It was decided that, with few exceptions, texts would only be translated from Sanskrit, and works previously translated from vernacular versions were retranslated from Sanskrit. The Tibetan language was stretched, bent, and molded to express a wide range of alien contents and styles. Tibetan translations are often opaque, but they are marvelously consistent and usually match the original point for point.

The king's chief minister, a monk named "Virtue," was first slandered and then executed. Nobles murdered the pro-Buddhist king, whose vicious brother Lang-dar-ma succeeded him (838–842) and by persecution eliminated organized Buddhism from central Tibet. Lang-dar-ma himself was murdered by a monk, but the damage to Buddhism was not repaired for generations. The line of kings terminated, and the religion survived as mundane magic practiced by itinerant yogins. Refugee monks spread Buddhism in other parts of the country, notably in east Tibet (Kham). A descendent of Lang-dar-ma established a strong kingdom in west Tibet in the tenth century, and his successors undertook to promote the Dharma. They chose twenty-one Tibetan boys and sent them to India to learn Sanskrit, study doctrine, and persuade Indian masters to come to Tibet. All but two of the boys died from heat and disease on the Indian plains. Of the two who survived to become scholars, the more famous was Rin-chen Sangpo (958–1055). The illustrious Bengali scholar Atīśa (982–1054), after much persuasion, came to west Tibet in 1042. He was well versed in exoteric and esoteric teachings, and his career crowned the renaissance of doctrine studies in Tibet. He is also famed for the most gracious of all recorded first reactions to Tibetan buttered tea: "This cup contains the elixir of the wish-granting tree."

By this time, central Tibet had recovered from the Buddhist persecution. Monks had come in from Kham and rebuilt the monasteries, and a new line of kings (also descended from Lang-dar-ma) were furnishing patronage. Atīśa's chief disciple, Drom, persuaded him to go to Lhasa, where he spent the rest of his life conferring Tantric initiations and translating. Drom, though a layman, was Atīśa's spiritual heir, and founded the Ka-dam-pa lineage, the first Tibetan sect whose historic beginnings (unlike Nying-ma-pa) are clear.

Drok-mi, a contemporary of Atīśa's, studied in the Tantric university of Vikramaśīla for eight years and then returned to Tibet, where in 1073 he founded the monastery of Sa-kya, whose abbots possessed great learning and temporal power during the twelfth and thirteenth centuries. Clerics from this monastery, Sa-kya-pa abbots, are permitted to marry, and the succession passes either from father to son or from uncle to nephew. The abbot 'Phags-pa (1235–1280), continuing the relations his uncle had established with the Mongols, became prelate to Kublai Khan, from whom he received temporal jurisdiction over all of Tibet.

Another lineage of Tibetan Buddhism, the Kargyüpa, began in the eleventh century with Mar-pa (1012–1097). Mar-pa was a disciple of the great Bengali adept Nāropa, under whom he trained at Nālandā. Returning to Tibet, he took a wife whom he called Nairātmyā, as she also served as his prajñā in the rites of Hevajra (see p. 98). Mar-pa was a man of strong character and strong passions, wrathful and possessive. Only when his own son died did he stop denying the spiritual succession to his long-suffering and gifted disciple, Milarepa ("the Cotton-clad Mila").

Milarepa (1040–1123) is the most popular saint and the greatest poet of Tibet, as well as the Second Patriarch of the Kargyüpa sect founded by Mar-pa. As a youth, he learned magic in order to take revenge on a wicked uncle who had dispossessed and maltreated Mila's widowed mother. Having destroyed his enemy, he was seized with remorse and sought first to expiate his bad karma and then to attain liberation. At thirty-eight he became Mar-pa's disciple. For six years the master put him through cruel ordeals before finally granting him the initiation he sought. Milarepa spent the rest of his life meditating in the caves and wandering on the slopes of the high Himālayas (Kailāsa, Everest). He gradually attracted a following, converted many disciples, and worked wonders for people's benefit. His numerous songs express not only profound Dharma but also the unearthly atmosphere of his mountain home and the cruel rigors and high ecstasies of the ascetic life as well.

The Kargyüpa line was continued by Gam-po-pa (1079–1153), who at thirty-two heard of Milarepa from a beggar and acquired his teachings in thirteen months of study. After Gam-po-pa, the sect split into four branches, one of which converted the people of Bhutan in the seventeenth century and another of which was favored by the Mongol and Ming emperors of China.

The Tibetan scriptures were collected and edited to form a Canon by Butön (1290–1364). This Canon consists of two collections: The *Kanjur*, which comprises the Vinaya, Sūtras, and Tantras, and the *Tenjur*, which contains treatises, commentaries, and works on auxiliary disciplines such as grammar, astrology, and medicine. The first printed *Kanjur* was completed in Peking in 1411, and the first complete printings of the Canon in Tibet were at Narthang—the *Kanjur* (100 volumes) in 1731 and the *Tenjur* (225 volumes) in 1742.

The lama Tsong-kha-pa, in a nineteenth-century Tibetan representation. (Photo: Antoinette Gordon Collection.)

The scene in the early fourteenth century was a welter of sects and subsects. Besides the Ka-dam-pas, the Sa-kya-pas, and the various Kar-gyü-pa branches, there were the Shi-je-pas ("Tranquilizer," or "Peacemaker"), a sect of yogins founded in the late eleventh century by the Indian master Pha-dam-pa Sanggye ("Holy Father Buddha"), and the Nying-ma-pas, revitalized by Guru Chö-wang (1212–1273), who discovered (or claimed to discover) "hidden scriptures" deposited by Padmasambhava and others. Except for the Ka-dam-pas, these sects were lax in discipline, and all were given to politics and magic.

Tsong-kha-pa (1357–1419) was a native of northeast Tibet, where he became a novice in boyhood and received Tantric initiations. Then sent by his teacher to central Tibet, he studied the exoteric Mahāyāna treatises for years and visited all the notable centers of learning there. He was particularly fond of Logic and Vinaya. He took full ordination at twenty-five, began to teach, and through the good offices of a preceptor was able to "meet" Mañjuśrī. In 1393, he had just eight pupils; by 1409, he had a multitude of disciples and controlled the main temple of Lhasa. His new sect, the Gelukpa ("Partisan of Virtue"), professed to continue the strict discipline of the Ka-dam-pas, laid equal stress on the exoteric and the esoteric teachings, and implemented a regular curriculum of systematic doctrinal studies leading to the degree of *Geshe* ("spiritual friend"), equivalent to a doctorate in philosophy or divinity. Three large Gelukpa monasteries were founded near Lhasa in 1409, 1416, and 1419. Tsong-kha-pa was a brilliant scholar, an excellent organizer, and a reformer. His monks had to forgo liquor, sex, evening meals, and long naps. He condemned worldly magic, and his sect practices the Tantras only as a means to enlightenment.

Tsong-kha-pa's third successor was his nephew Gendün truppa, who took office in 1438. He was accepted as an incarnation of Avalokiteśvara, and so started the line of Dalai Lamas. Since they are incarnations in a continuing series, the intermediate stage must pass between the death of the last Dalai Lama and the birth of the next. It is believed to last forty-nine days. Therefore, a search party looks for a child born that long after the death of a Dalai Lama, guided by whatever indications the dying Incarnation has left concerning his next appearance and by the pronouncements of the state oracle. The searchers look for certain physical signs on the infant, prodigies at the time of his birth (for example, a tree that blossoms in winter), and ability to recognize objects belonging to the previous Incarnation. Once the right child is found, he is brought to Lhasa and carefully educated for his future role. Meanwhile, regents rule on his behalf.

The third Dalai Lama (1543–1588) converted the Mongols for the second and last time. He is said to have met the pagan gods of the Mongols, converted them, and made them into Dharma-protectors. The fourth Dalai Lama (1589–1616) turned out, providentially, to be the grandson of the great chief of the Mongols. The fifth Dalai Lama (1617–1682) was a great scholar, surprisingly well versed in Nying-ma-pa literature. He was an energetic and shrewd politician, and with the aid of Mongol armies overthrew the enemies of his sect and became the temporal as well as the spiritual ruler of Tibet. His repressive measures forced many clerics of other sects to take refuge in outlying areas of Tibet, Sikkim and Bhutan. The new Manchu dynasty in China confirmed the Dalai Lama's power and used him and his successors to keep Tibet quiet and safe for China, just as the Dalai Lamas used their status and their wiles to keep the Chinese out of Tibet as much as possible.

The sixth Dalai Lama (1683–1706) was a drinker and girl-chaser and the reputed author of a collection of love songs. He came from a family of Nying-ma-pas, and his apparent debauchery seems to have been part of an attempt to revive the old Tantric ways. Intense opposition to him sprang up. A conclave of lamas decided that Avalokiteśvara had abandoned the body of the incumbent and had entered another lama. Finally a Mongol army burst into Lhasa, killed the regent, and captured the Dalai Lama alive. He died in captivity, perhaps murdered. Subsequent Dalai Lamas were loyal Gelukpas and kept out of trouble with the Chinese. The ninth through the twelfth Incarnations died in boyhood.

The thirteenth Dalai Lama (1874–1933) survived the perils of childhood only to get caught in international politics. He had to flee to Mongolia when the British sent an army to Lhasa in 1904, and in 1910 he fled to India to escape the Chinese, returning in 1912 after the Manchu dynasty fell. The fourteenth Dalai Lama (1935–) was enthroned in 1950, shortly before the Chinese Communists marched in and occupied his country. He fled to India during the anti-Chinese uprisings of 1959. While he lives in exile and serves as *de facto* leader for the tens of thousands of Tibetan refugees, the Chinese grind away the remnants of a medieval culture and religion that, sordid politics notwithstanding, produced a brave, cheerful, and courteous people, many great scholars, and in each generation a few real saints.

TIBETAN BUDDHISM: A MODEL

For the discussion below, the model shown in Figure 1 isolates the basic elements of Tibetan Buddhism and shows how they related to one another. It distinguishes dimensions of the religion and the various participants it served. The monastic establishment, its texts and prac-

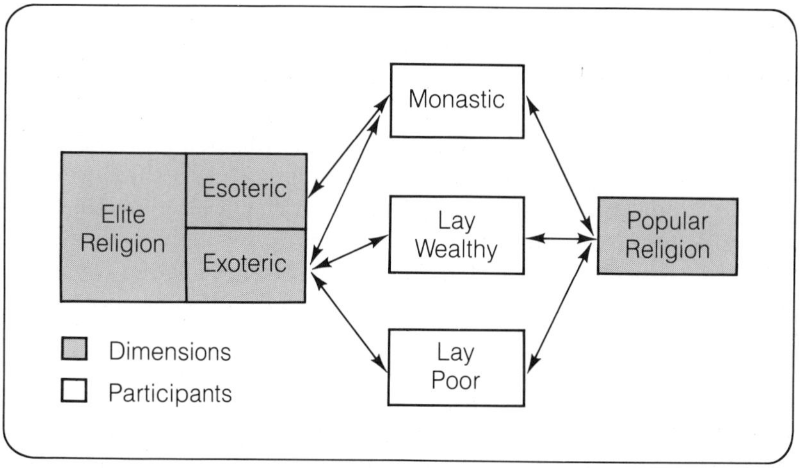

Figure 1. Buddhism in Tibet.

tices, constituted the elite religion and had two parts. The esoteric component, on the one hand, was reserved entirely for initiated monks and lamas, focusing on meditative achievement of ultimate soteriological goals along with the transmission of textual and visual materials and the training of aspirants in these. The exoteric component of the monastic elite religion served, on the other hand, wealthy and poor laity. The second part of Tibetan Buddhism was the popular religion, which primarily served the laity but also interacted with the monks of the exoteric monastic cult as well as influencing the esoteric experience.

The elite religion served monastic and lay participants through its esoteric and exoteric dimensions respectively. Popular Buddhism served primarily the peasants and lay wealthy but also monastic individuals. And these monks, apart from their personal esoteric practice, served the laity with popular religious means and ideas. Also, not included in the diagram are other religious specialists, such as the wandering monks and exorcists, as well as lay functionaries (in the religious practice of the home, for example). These terms will be used in the following discussion, which tries to do justice to Tibetan Buddhism as a unitary phenomenon with distinct subdimensions, practitioners, and concerns.

Means and Goals of Monastic Lamaism

After the demise of the ancient monarchy, Tibet by the eleventh century had become an ecclesiastical state, secular authority being intimately linked to the Buddhist monastic orders that dominated its entire political and cultural history. In 1885 an observer reported that one-fifth the population was monks and nuns, a total of seven hundred sixty thousand in twenty-five hundred monasteries; the census of 1663 conducted by the fifth Dalai Lama counted one hundred thousand monks and nuns in eighteen hundred monasteries. Monasteries, being exempt from taxes and services, existed as independent entities. They owned land and serfs for their support, which also came from the patronage of noble families and lay donations and payments for ritual services. Private property was allowed to the monks, some even engaging in trade, and poor monks served rich ones. Some orders allowed marriage. A person needed wealth to obtain the highest ranks in the religious hierarchy; the impoverished lower clergy usually were unable to reach high position. Many lived as servants, cooks, even athlete-warriors. Those who rose to positions of leadership traveled in quest of books and training, paying for initiations and instruction from teacher after teacher, their lamas. Apart from their political and economic role, monasteries served as universities, teaching religious and secular subjects (such as medicine). They produced art and books in support of the religious vocations. For the lay community, they performed ritual service. And for the elite monks, they were the means of achieving ultimate salvation by providing ascending grades of teaching in book learning, psychic powers, and esoteric ritual.

The primary religious specialists in Lamaism were the masters, or lamas, though others provided special services. Wandering monks and exorcists plied their trade. And hermits, some temporary and others practicing total withdrawal (being completely walled in a cell or cave) also existed, seeking to use the appropriate yogic and Tantric techniques to produce mystic experiences. But primarily, the elite lamas constituted the highest spiritual authority (hence "Lamaism"), both for the performance of ritual and festival activities and for the training of monks who sought to become lamas themselves. The lama transmitted the texts and made them effective through oral instruction and guidance, becoming the spiritual father to the son-disciple. The lama gave both word and power, requiring total submission (owning the disciple's wealth and person). This practice went back to the Indian reliance on the guru as the living god who alone in the world could transmit the teachings and means to salvation. Often, the teacher-disciple relationship included trials for the aspirant and sudden revelations brought about by the charismatic presence of the lama and the disciple's unerring faith and devotion. The lama directed his disciples in the difficult liturgical and meditative disciplines not as something learned about but unforgettably lived and experienced as an initiation into the realms of spiritual reality and activity.

Monastic lamaism practiced an elite and esoteric religion that yet was not entirely divorced from exoteric ceremonials and the popular religion of the laity, peasant and noble alike. Both monks and laity strove to abstain from evil, accumulate merit, and act for the welfare of all living beings, but they used the diverse means open to them. Faith in the religion united lay and monastic, though their experience of it was fundamentally divided. For the lay Buddhist, life provided the opportunity to accumulate merit through pious action in expectation of a better life to come or heavenly rebirth. At the public monastic services and rituals, the laity took no part except as mere spectators. They could not escape the relative reality in which their lives were enmeshed, as the monks aspired to, but could only improve their karmic propensities through making gifts to monasteries, lamas, and the poor or through other pious acts such as lighting lamps for deities, reciting the three refuges, and making pilgrimages. They learned of the karmic mechanism through instruction in the Wheel of Life, popularized by storytellers who supposedly had visited hell (a shamanic theme) and returned. (Such popular moralists were present in ancient India as well.)

Monastic festivals and masked dances enlivened their religious experience but left them outside of the esoteric experience of monastics and monks. The practice of meditation, essential to spiritual transformation and the effectiveness of any ritual, remained reserved exclusively for monks, though the techniques practiced by them were meant to nourish and sustain lay religious life by promoting blessings and transfer of power from monastery to laity.

The esoteric practice of lama and disciple derived from Indian Mahāyāna, both Mādhyamika and Yogācāra, powered by the practice of yogic meditation and Tantric ritualism. Its practice sought to attain the saving transformation of consciousness (its gnostic goal) through doctrine and a rich meditative-ritual praxis that made use of an enormous textual corpus and pantheon with a vast panoply of visualization techniques, rituals, initiations and oral instructions on the most arcane subjects of spirituality. All who practiced vowed to follow the path to Buddhahood, accepting the arduous disciplines required for such a transformation. Following Mahāyāna thought, adepts sought to realize experientially the illusory nature of world experience and the emptiness of every object of cognition. The process assumes a radical disjunction of relative and absolute planes, which can be breached by the innate radiant consciousness (*sems*, for Sanskrit citta) through successive ritual purification and elevation. The archaic Indic problematic assumed that all relative experience is a fall from the desired original absolute state of being, so salvation consists of returning consciousness to the primordial level, transcendent to all relativity. Consciousness has fallen into space and time and must extricate itself through liturgical and meditative exercises until its breakthrough occurs. Such an experience would be ecstatic ("standing outside oneself," the relative "I") and essentially mystical.

By virtue of achieving such mystical transcendance, Tibetan Buddhists claim, the master's consciousness is able to abolish the disjunction of relative (profane) and absolute (sacred), thus not only achieving salvation or release but also the ability to act as hierophant, mediating between the two planes. Meditative visualization produces this goal by temporarily transforming a person into a god. Ecstatically transcendent to one's relative identity, the meditator can replicate experientially the production and dissolution of all phenomena, divesting them of any pretense of substantiality. Through evocations and visualizations, meditators accomplish what Brahmanical priests did when they called the deities to their ritual sacrifice through mantra recitation. But in the Tibetan actualization, consciousness becomes the god and can act as that god, achieving an apotheosis and thus extricating it from the corporality, suffering, and powerlessness of existence. The experience of meditation leads to a realization, uncommunicable in words, of Being itself, a plenitude of emptiness, characterized by bliss and clear light, beyond all dualities. Or the meditator can visualize entire divine reality planes, thus gaining access to the absolute.

One can now see why Lamaism produced an incredible pantheon and a religious art to represent and help make it real. The paintings of maṇḍalas and deities, benevolent and horrific, serve as meditative objects and starting points of meditative visualizations that the texts also minutely describe, a tradition taken from Indian Buddhist Tantric texts. These images reveal to the untrained awareness an esoteric meaning that can be fathomed only by the initiate, who is led to reproduce them as living experience, as reality itself. If understood as the master instructs, these images acquire saving value, even if on the relative plane they seem to represent over and over the horrific, monstrous, fantastic side of divinity. Such techniques go a long way toward making sensible the goal of Tibetan thanatology. The lama adept at transformations into divine beings and onto divine planes can escape the intermediate state (*bar-do*) and rebirth into the Wheel of Life by recalling at the very moment of death such experiences and not falling back into becoming. The widely distributed but little understood Tibetan *Book of the Dead* is a recitation manual used as an aid to help less adept individuals avoid lesser rebirths through a similar mechanism. Thus, for both initiate and noninitiate alike, salvation, always on the Indic model of escape from recurrent death, becomes possible.

Indigenous, Bon, and Popular Tibetan Religion

In addition to the elite and esoteric religion of monastic Buddhism, other subsystems of Tibetan religiosity existed (see the two diagrams and discussions of this model of religion, pp. 119 and 145). Before any literary religious tradition arose, there was an indigenous religious practice, some of which became formulated by the Bonpo or followers of the Bon religion, and some of which were assimilated to later popular (as opposed to elite) Tibetan Buddhism. In much the same way as Buddhism integrated indigenous practices, other missionizing or conquering religions, such as Vedism, Christianity, and Islam, adopted and transformed the local traditions of the areas to which they spread. Tibetan chroniclers refer to the earliest indigenous religion as "the religion of men," opposing it to the systematic organized religions (those "of the gods"—namely, Bon and, later, Buddhism). The first religious specialists mentioned are three, Bonpos, storytellers, and riddle singers. The former were ritualists, while the latter two clearly functioned as transmitters of the oral tradition characteristic of nonliterary transitional religions that come between archaic shamanisms and literary, agrarian historical religions.

Interestingly, from the viewpoint of the history of religions, Bon, like Tibetan Buddhism itself, drew much of its mature content from foreign sources, including Iranian and Śaivite gnostic teachings, archaic shamanism, and even Manichaeism. Buddhism also may have prepared the way for its own introduction by its earlier assimilating of Indo-Iranian elements. Bon existed throughout Tibetan history, having its own texts, cult centers, monasteries, and practices.

It is important for understanding Buddhism not to exclude the popular religion. This often happens, since elite Buddhism can be studied in texts and historical evidence, while popular religion rarely appears in such sources. This in no way means, as some conclude, that popular religion is not Buddhist or is unimportant. Both Bon and Buddhism as religious systematizations incorporated and elaborated indigenous religious practices, and from a numerical point of view, this dimension of Buddhism certainly served many more adherents.

Popular Buddhism continued many indigenous ritual forms, deities, and ideas but throughly assimilated these to the imported Buddhist ideology. It became the religion of the Tibetan people, extending its influence and conceptions from the humblest beggars and peasants to the great nobles and lamas. What we know of the preexisting beliefs comes necessarily from later sources. But it certainly included the usual mythology, dealing with creation and tribal lineages and family genealogies, along with practices to strengthen the security of human livelihood. It featured ancestor worship and gods and goddesses of the striking Tibetan geography (mountains, fields, rocks, and waters). And it had its own forms of worship, including the still familiar burning of fragrant juniper and the festivals of the agrarian cycle (New Year, harvest).

Popular Buddhism involved all classes of Tibetans in the constant struggle of adapting to the vagaries of agrarian living. The highest lamas and the meanest beggars accepted a basic set of notions about reality and how events come about. The common assumption behind both exoteric monastic practices and the popular Buddhism of each community and family was that powers (spirits, local gods, demons) influenced the course of ordinary life, potentially to the favor of humans, but even more potentially to their detriment.

For Tibetans, life seethed with the unpredictable powers and arbitrariness of the invisible component of reality. The invisible deities, spirits, and demons cause every misfortune rained down upon human life, so religion must protect and defend human life, by coercing and defeating the malevolent powers and enlisting the aid of those that are or could be made benevolent. Behind all these efforts of popular religion lay the sure certainty that the law (Dharma) of the Buddha could dominate the potential chaos that ever threatened the human community with suffering and even extinction. What to the esoteric view of the lama were the controlling deities of the cosmos, who held the saving grace of the Buddhist religion, were from the popular religious point of view the powers that through conjuration and piety could be used to ensure the beneficence of life and to gain protection against the destructive forces of nature.

Thus, popular Buddhism incorporated peasant concerns and indigenous as well as Indic religious ideas and practices into the Buddhist scheme. The deities of the indigenous religion, along with its invocations and festivals, joined the Buddhist structure. The Buddhist notion of causality introduced a principle of order, for it was the law that all actions have set consequences. The great deities and personalities of Buddhism, which for the esoteric religion promised ultimate salvation, could just as well be invoked for immediate protection in moments of trial and danger as Avalokiteśvara, Śākyamuni, Tārā, and Padmasambhava were. And the great mantras of salvational Buddhism could equally save one from demons and illness.

In the popular eye, spiritual power is ambiguous and far less controllable than it is for the elite, who are better protected from many uncertainties. This popular religious view of the world assumes that everything is more than physical appearance. Nature teems with conscious entities (such as those seen in the Wheel of Life). Spirits and their powers await the uncautious everywhere, ready to injure, threaten, humiliate, and kill. Popular Buddhism sought to counteract these invisible spirit powers through a comprehensive system of defense and coercion. Proper ritual and recitation generate power, a force to counteract the threats and to foster and enhance life and human goals. The incomparable power of the holy Buddha with his monks and religion assured the Tibetan populace of victory. Rituals and their formulas could produce prosperity and well-being in the material realm and drive out all that threatened them.

Popular religion proposed, and Buddhism agreed, that nothing happens by chance. Nature's powers could and would respond to every human act, some with benevolence and others with anger and vengeance. The powers demanded respect and veneration, nourishment and attention. Offerings and atonements sought to appease and propitiate them. What in scientific civilizations would be explained through physical causation (as in the germ theory of disease) or the chance operation of physical processes was in peasant societies explained as caused by such things as improper human action or pollution.

Popular Buddhism oriented itself specifically to concrete situations. A particular person sponsored a ritual of blessing, purification, or exorcism for the individual, family, clan, or village. Everything at that level was controlled and protected by a profuse system of *lha* (spirits, deities), which resided everywhere. These included personal and tutelary spirits of individuals and the family, the ancestors, the hearth, the home, even the storeroom. In the darkest corner of the kitchen was the interior, or material, spirit, which did not like strangers or exorcists. All could be offended by affront, defilement, or ritual impurity, making the offender liable to ill consequence. Outside the house, the center of security, a host of powers swirled threateningly. Each house (or tent) had a domestic chapel or altar for ceremony, where a lamp was lit and offerings were made by the elders. Every day the layperson took the three refuges and worshipped the guardian deities and the favored figures of the Buddhist pantheon. Paintings, images, and books were also included in household religion, along with various ritual specialists who could be invited for special problems and needs.

These, then, were the realms and powers of the popular religion's "gods of the everyday world," local deities and spirits both benevolent and evil, converted by the coming of Buddhism but concerned not in the least with its goal of ultimate salvation. Popular religion sought to continue life, not transcend it. Everything needed protection. Divination and astrology were used to see how best to act in accordance with the invisible state of affairs, and the techniques of possession and omen and dream interpretation allowed the invisible spirits to speak. Popular ritual sought apotropaic (warding off evil) goals. Rituals offered gifts (or ransom) to hostile powers, seeking expiation and propitiation. Exorcism—through symbolic offerings to the spirits or psychic conflict with the malignant powers—gave human sponsors of the activity the power to intervene, even against the misfortunes that arise from previous karma. Virtuous acts, too, produced merit and numinous power as a defense against misfortune. These included reciting sacred texts, various acts of donation, and aid to local religious figures and institutions. Popular Buddhism considered danger to derive both from past karmic actions and from present infractions (purity/pollution), so a major need or undertaking required offering incense, accompanied by prayers and offerings, which purify and atone. From the strict doctrinal position, all these acts of popular Buddhism belonged to the relative world, the purpose of which was to turn desire away from the phenomenal, but such subtlety offered cold comfort.

Probably one of the reasons why ordinary accounts of Buddhism neglect its popular forms is that these forms tended to espouse notions at variance with elite perception of the doctrine. The inevitability of karmic consequence and the nonexistence of a soul are two such cases in point. Popular Tibetan Buddhism adopted the indigenous (and shamanic) notion of a soul or vital force (*bla*), which can separate from the body, producing unconsciousness or illness or signifying a prelude to death. Specific rituals sought to return this wandering soul to the body and thus to cure or save from death. A malevolent deity or demon could abduct this soul. Divination or dream diagnosis had first to determine the malefactor. Then ritual could ransom the soul, or a ritual specialist could retrieve it in meditative trance, even battling the demon for it. Technically, only karma causes events, but in this case factors strictly not karmic such as local spirits influenced a person's fate. Death, too, supposedly occurs when karmic processes mature sufficiently, yet the goal of the *Book of the Dead* recitation is to intervene in the karmic stream of a person to produce a better result than that merited by the individual's actions. A host of other rituals and pious practices also had the intent of circumventing karmic consequences, including the transfer of merit. Cleansing of karmic consequences or their transformation sought to improve conditions in the next life, in opposition to the spirit and the letter of karmic law, which intended to teach the individual by those very consequences not to make such mistakes again.

Should the question still arise whether this is "really Buddhism," one would have but to ask a Tibetan. The peasants, who would answer affirmatively, do not generally reach the West. The better off would probably answer no, with greater or lesser degrees of condescension, scorn, and embarrassment. History tells us that peasants speak very little in records written by educated individuals who have gone beyond the peasantry. The majority of our evidence indicates that this is Buddhism, as we saw earlier in the case of Thai popular Buddhism. The first rule of the history of religion is to accept the participant's opinion of what is Buddhism; should we then deny the evidence that does come when we do reach the peasant level of society? The conclusion suggests itself that the Buddhism we learn about from texts and archaeology is an elite phenomenon. The full picture appears when one includes in the description the exoteric ritual and popular religion and when one sees how the esoteric, elite religion interacts with the former in a peasant society. One of the deepest changes in extant Buddhism's recent history has been the engulfing of peasant society in a sea of change unlike anything else it has ever encountered.

MONGOLIA

Finally the Mongols, whose original religion was shamanism, were twice brought under the control of Tibetan Buddhism, in the thirteenth century and later in the sixteenth century. After the first conversion, Tibetan Buddhism shared the power of the Mongol Empire and established many monasteries in China, especially in Peking, exerting great power there during the Yüan dynasty (1260–1368). On the whole the people were not won over in this period. Following the second conversion, however, Buddhism adopted for political reasons became very popular, this time gaining the support of the people. Mongolia became a site of great Buddhist monasteries and a center of learning. It is from this period that the term Dalai ("Ocean, All-Encompassing") Lama comes. A Mongol king, Altan Khan, gave it to a Tibetan prelate who claimed primacy in Tibet over his rivals. Buddhist scriptures were translated into Mongol. In time support waned, however, and in the twentieth century a Communist government has taken over.

CHAPTER 10

East Asian Buddhism

THE INDIAN WORLD VIEW IN CHINA

Heavens, hells, karma, transmigration, and bodhisattvas—all became part of the Chinese view of the world, but such a view was not accepted by all Chinese. China never became Buddhist in the way medieval Europe was Christian, and an attitude of rational scepticism persisted. Further, these Indian notions were brought into conformity with the predominant Chinese attitudes. The heavens and hells became replicas of Confucian bureaucracy, karma became strictly the account of merit and demerit and the allotment of lifespan—a pre-Buddhist concern—and transmigration centered chiefly on the status of the dead person and the carrying out of funeral rites to ensure a more propitious rebirth or amelioration of conditions in hells or purgatory. Concern for the souls of the dead was not Buddhist alone, although Buddhism emphasized the welfare of the dead as opposed to native emphasis on the welfare of the living.

The Buddha was another god, more approachable than native gods. Kuan-yin (Avalokiteśvara) became the goddess of mercy, bestowing earthly boons to petitioners. The Dharma in the form of the Chinese translations of Buddhist scriptures was influenced by Chinese concepts and interpretation. In general, the more accurate the translation, the less popular the text. The Saṅgha was the most obviously intrusive element, but despite antipathy from certain quarters it found a niche for itself in Chinese life and society, eventually modelling its relationships after the Chinese family. Rather than being a world and law unto

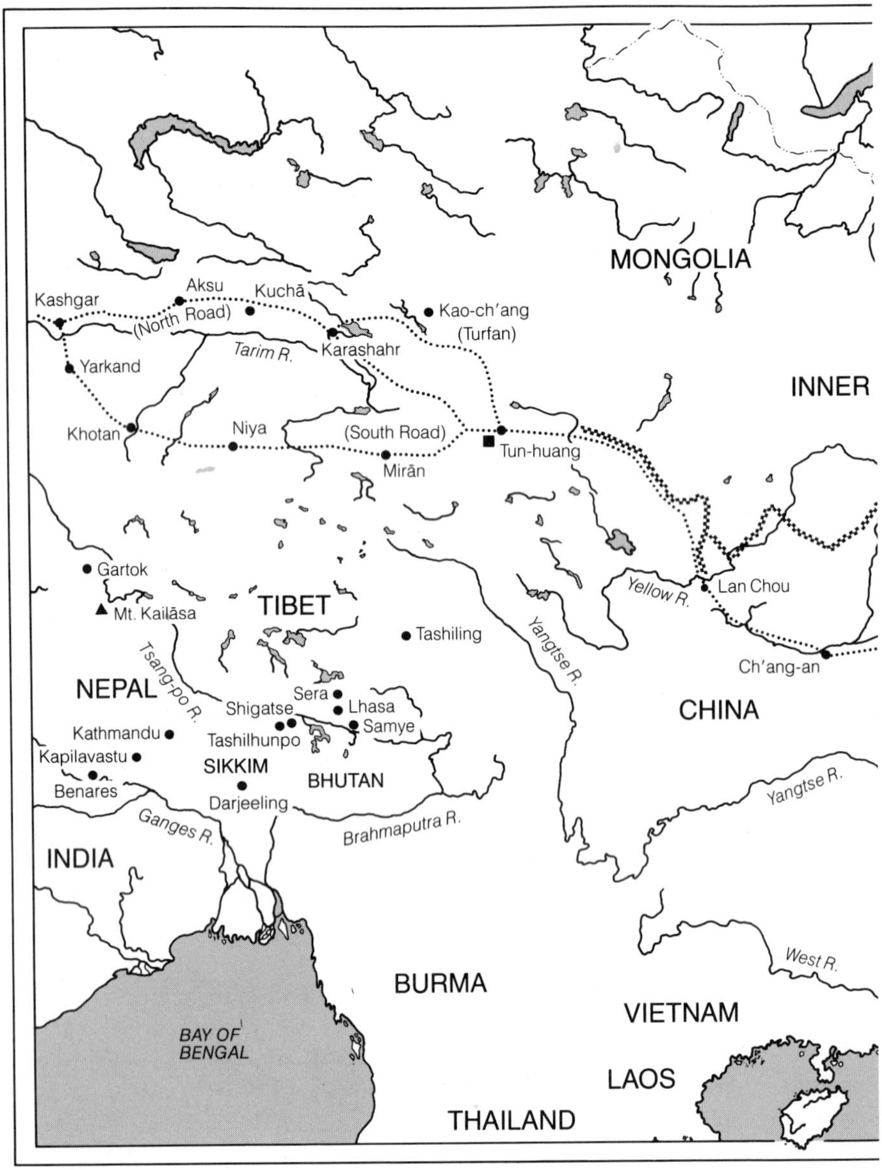

LEGEND

••••••	Ancient Trade Routes between East and West and Eastern Extension into China
▀▀▀▀	Great Wall
▲	Mountains
●	Cities and Towns
■	Rock Sculpture Sites

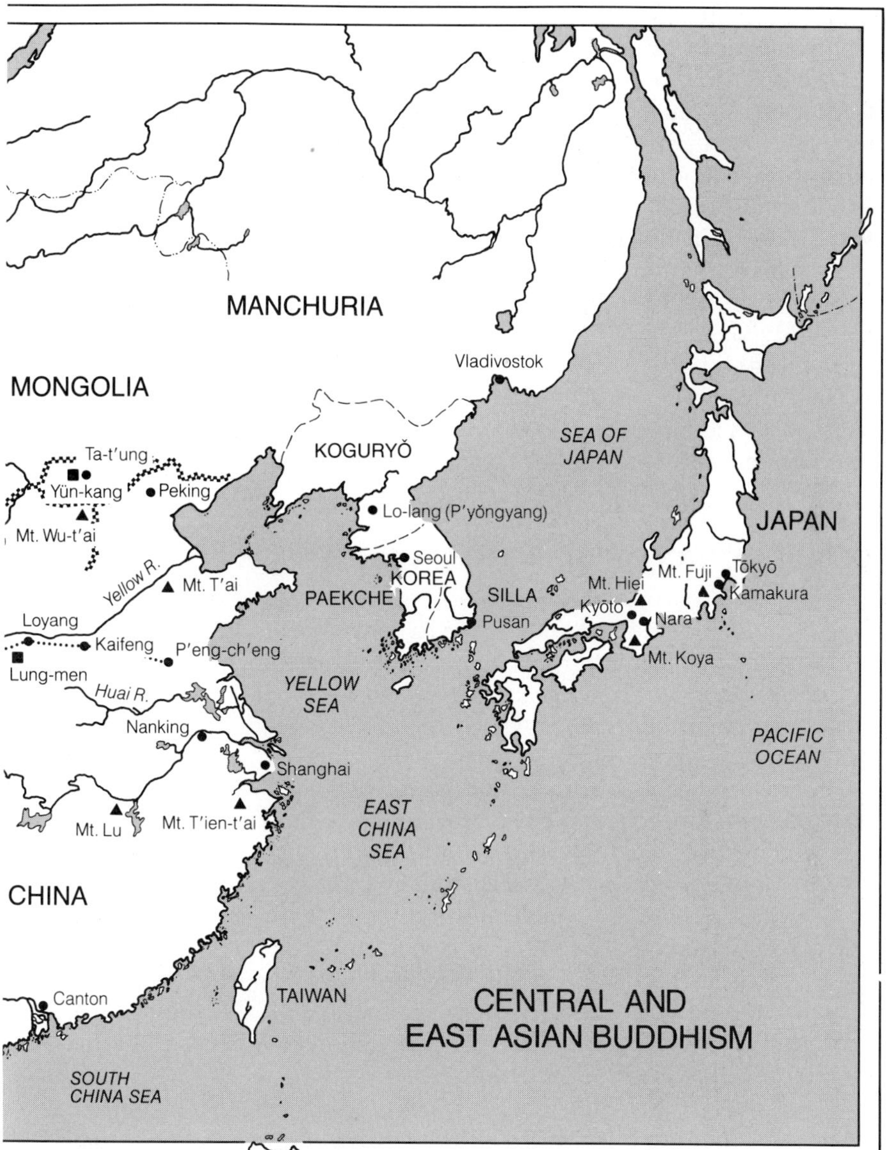
MANCHURIA
MONGOLIA
Vladivostok
KOGURYŎ
SEA OF JAPAN
Ta-t'ung
Yün-kang
Peking
Mt. Wu-t'ai
Lo-lang (P'yŏngyang)
JAPAN
Seoul
KOREA
Yellow R.
Mt. T'ai
PAEKCHE
SILLA
Mt. Hiei
Mt. Fuji
Tōkyō
Kamakura
Kyōto
Nara
Mt. Koya
Pusan
Loyang
Kaifeng
P'eng-ch'eng
Lung-men
YELLOW SEA
Huai R.
Nanking
Shanghai
PACIFIC OCEAN
EAST CHINA SEA
Mt. Lu
Mt. T'ien-t'ai
CHINA
TAIWAN
Canton
CENTRAL AND EAST ASIAN BUDDHISM
SOUTH CHINA SEA

itself—as it ideally was in India—the Saṅgha became part of the Chinese body politic.

Dr. Hu Shih in this century made the most serious accusation against Buddhism in China, saying that the rationalist Neo-Confucianism that received final interpretation at the hands of Chu Hsi (1130–1200) had incorporated Buddhist values, secularized and universalized them, and thereby recast Chinese society in an Indian mode. The question is whether a civilization ever accepts a foreign system inimical or contrary to its native tradition, a question as pertinent for the study of Sung dynasty (960–1279) and subsequent Neo-Confucian orthodoxy as for the study of modern China and its remolding in Marxist-Leninist configurations.

The Indian religion of Buddhism was further modified in Japan, Korea, and Vietnam. It arrived already clothed in Chinese dress and in that form encountered the several native traditions.

INTRODUCTION OF BUDDHISM INTO CHINA

That Buddhism came to dominate the religious life of China by 400 C.E. seems at first sight more remarkable than if the Roman Empire had become Buddhist or the Kuṣāṇa Empire had adopted Christianity. Sea and land communications between India and the Mediterranean were comparatively easy, and trade relations linked the two areas from 2500 B.C.E. onwards. The sea and land routes between India and China were, however, much longer and more arduous, and no direct contact occurred between the two civilizations until about 100 B.C.E., when the Former Han dynasty briefly dominated the Indianized oasis kingdoms of Central Asia.

The concatenation of events that established Buddhism in China is quite traceable and falls within the ordinary scope of historical causality. Nonetheless, the chances against such a sequence are so great that we can well appreciate the conviction of Chinese Buddhist intellectuals that Heaven guided the process.

In the first century C.E., the new and strong Later Han dynasty extended Chinese power into Central Asia, where the various small kingdoms owed their prosperity to the silk trade between China and the West. Serindian (Central Asian) merchant colonies—Khotanese, Sogdians, Parthians, Kucheans, and Kuṣāṇas—settled in an arc of cities from Tun-huang in the northwest to the Huai valley. Their families often stayed in China for generations and became bilingual and bicultural. As some of these people were Buddhists, they welcomed and accommodated the monks who traveled with the caravans. The Chinese, despite their fabled antipathy to learning from foreigners, have always loved exotica; and no doubt the orange-robed monks filled them with the same kind of wonder as parakeets from Cambodia and horses from Ferghāna (Tadžikistan, in Central Asia). China has also cherished throughout the ages an addiction to magic, and the men of Han promptly recognized the kinship between the bhikṣu and the indigenous shaman and wizard-hermit. By mid-century, Chinese patricians were giving donation feasts, and monks were a familiar sight in the capital.

Translating Indian Ideas into Chinese

The first notable translator, An Shih-kao, arrived in 148 C.E. at Loyang, the capital, from Parthia at the eastern reaches of the Silk Road. Buddhism, having become an international religion under the sponsorship of King Aśoka, had spread not only into Southeast Asia from India but also northwestward into Central Asia through the area of present-day Afghanistan.

Buddhism, both Hīnayāna and Mahāyāna, took root in the Central Asian kingdoms, and Buddhist institutions flourished under the influence of, but independent from, the motherland, India. While the role these kingdoms played in the transmission of Buddhism to China is undisputed, the exact details of that role have not been sorted out with certainty. One clear feature, however, is that in the early stages Central Asian monks and missionaries played a much greater part than did those from India.

Another important consideration is the question of Sūtra composition and development. Leaving aside the fanciful tale that Mahāyāna texts were kept hidden in caves and under the sea from the time of the Buddha until it was appropriate that they be revealed, we must recognize that these texts were composed somewhere, and in many instances that somewhere is difficult to locate. If, for example, a text was composed within a Buddhist community in Kuchā, rather than in India proper, is it therefore less than scriptural? Is it to be considered apocryphal? Do texts become more and more apocryphal the further from India their place of composition lies? This question, less trivial than it might seem, relates to Buddhist development within China, the writing of Buddhist scriptures in Chinese, and the attitude of the Chinese to the Buddhist scriptural tradition.

A momentous decision for the history of Buddhism in China was the decision to translate Buddhist texts into Chinese. That this would happen was not necessarily a foregone conclusion. The Vedas are preserved in the now archaic language of early Sanskrit. For centuries the Christian Bible was preserved in Jerome's Latin translation, and after Latin ceased to be a living vernacular, attempts to put the Bible into the language of the people met with fierce resistance. Buddhism, however, has no sacred language. The scriptures themselves suggest that it is all right to translate, that the Buddha's message should be made available to all who are ready to hear. This decision to translate had far-reaching consequences.

It meant first a coloring of the Indian ideas by Chinese thought. Also, it stimulated the Chinese into looking at their own language and resulted in the "discovery" that Chinese is a tonal language. This had great influence on the development of Chinese poetry. Literary forms in the scriptures influenced the development of Chinese colloquial literature. High regard for the written language led the Chinese to preserve as many of the translated texts as possible and gave to posterity the most important literary source for the history of Buddhism. Desire for copies of texts led eventually to printing, and the oldest extant printed book in the world is a copy of the Chinese version of the *Diamond-Cutter Sūtra* dated 868. Wood-block printing was a step away from moveable type, which the Koreans were the first to use in the early fifteenth century. Further, the desire for more or complete texts led Chinese pilgrims to Central Asia and India. Without the Buddhist Canon, there would be no Buddhism, and the Canon is the focal point of Buddhism in China.

For the Chinese, if a Buddhist text was not translated into Chinese from a foreign language, it was not authentic. Therefore, texts now known to have been written originally in Chinese were attributed to a translator, and over the centuries the Parthian An Shih-kao was held responsible for more and more translations. Those texts, however, that can with certainty be attributed to him are very few, and these few reveal no trace of Mahāyāna. He worked for twenty years in the Chinese capital translating short treatises on meditation and Abhidharma. The first known Chinese monk was his disciple, and the beginnings of Buddhist literature in Chinese went hand in hand with the formation of a Chinese Saṅgha.

Lokakṣema, the first known Mahāyāna missionary, also worked in Loyang, between 168 and 188. He translated the *Small Perfection of Wisdom Sūtra* and the *Sukhāvatī-vyūha*. The cult of Amita made little impression at that time, but Chinese familiar with the fourth century B.C.E. Taoist philosopher Chuang-tzu were intrigued by *Perfection of Wisdom* thought and demanded fresh translations of the Sūtras from each successive missionary, though it was not until the early fifth century that they really understood the Buddhist emptiness teachings. Chuang-tzu had prepared the Chinese intelligentsia, giving them a sense of the emptiness of the Absolute as well as the essential meaninglessness of conventional values. Also, his mystical emphasis on becoming one with the boundless *Tao* (see glossary) through contemplative exercises accorded well with Buddhist ideas concerning the ineffable attainment of nirvāṇa.

An Shih-kao and Lokakṣema, the first major translators, built the foundations of one of the most extraordinary religious monuments in the world, the Chinese Buddhist Canon. Not so impervious to the vicissitudes of time as rock sculptures, it lost much over the centuries, especially before the first official printing in the Sung dynasty (960–1279). Much, however, remains of a labor that continued a thousand years from the time of An Shih-kao and Lokakṣema.

The Later Han regime fell apart during the latter half of the second century. As magic is commonly the resort of the desperate, many of the gentry soon followed the path the peasants had taken decades earlier and sought strength and security in the occult. Their interest in Buddhism at this time focused on meditation as a means of obtaining paranormal powers. Only some of these gentlemen became monks; others served as scribes and assistants to the foreign monks or practiced meditation as lay recluses.

The work of translation and evangelization continued through the third century and came to fruition in the period of the Western Chin dynasty (265–316). Dharmarakṣa, "the bodhisattva from Tun-huang," worked in north China from 266 to 308. Born in China of Scythian ancestry, Dharmarakṣa was one of the most important translator-monks during this formative period of Buddhism in China. Being skilled in Chinese as well as Central Asian and Indian languages, he was able to translate a large number of Sūtras. He made the first Chinese version of the *Lotus Sūtra* in 286–290 and also the first translation of the *Large Perfection of Wisdom*. Under him the Chinese Saṅgha reached the takeoff point. His disciples established monasteries, lectured on the Sūtras, ordained monks, and proselytized vigorously. The sacking of the capitals at the end of the western Chin period served to disperse Dharmarakṣa's school to other parts of the country and thus disseminate a new vigorous and intellectual style of Buddhism. The process was repeated often during the centuries of political division. Monasteries and libraries were often burned, but what the Saṅgha lost in security it gained in mobility and communication.

The monks in south China under the Eastern Chin dynasty (317–419) lived peacefully and gradually insinuated themselves into the highest gentry circles by their adroit use of literary wit and personal urbanity. In the north, monks lived dangerously under the rule of "barbarian" chieftains, among a mixed population of Chinese, Tibetans, and Altaic tribesmen. A monk of Central Asiatic origin, the brave and righteous old Kuchean wonder-worker, Fo-t'u-teng, arrived in north China around 310. He became a counselor to Shih Lo, leader of the Hunnish state of Later Chao, and served as court advisor for over twenty years, performing magic, involving monks in politics, mitigating the excesses of the barbarian rulers, and training a cadre of disciplined and enterprising Chinese monks. The Chinese order of nuns was also instituted under his auspices.

Tao-an (312–385) was the most illustrious of Fo-t'u-teng's disciples. Though driven from place to place by the incessant civil wars, he lectured on the *Perfection of Wisdom Sūtras*, collected copies of the scriptures and prepared the first catalog of them, invited foreign monks and supported their translation work, and promoted devotion to Maitreya.

His disciple Hui-yüan (334–416/417) ran a school for gentleman monks and scholars in which he reinterpreted the Confucian and Taoist classics in a Buddhist sense, encouraged the writing of Buddhist devotional poetry in a typical Chinese style, and founded a society for meditation on Amitābha. He settled on Mount Lu and spent the last thirty years of his life there, letting the world come to him (as it did), and the armies pass him by. He staunchly defended the autonomy of the Saṅgha against the state, insisting that the monk is not obliged to kowtow to the ruler.

Thanks to the efforts of Tao-an and Hui-yüan, a sizable intellectual elite in the Saṅgha was ready to receive the great Kuchean translator Kumārajīva (344–413) when he reached the capital, Ch'ang-an, in 401. Already famous as a Buddhist monk well versed in doctrine, Kumārajīva was a major figure whose works were instrumental in transmitting Buddhism, especially Mādhyamika, to China. With the patronage of the king of Ch'in, Kumārajīva and a large team of Chinese collaborators revised (or redid) his predecessors' translations of the most popular Sūtras and translated four Mādhyamika treatises, introducing Nāgārjuna's teachings to the Chinese. His translations were elegant and intelligible, though not always accurate. To this day they are in general use, in preference to the more accurate translations of the later Buddhist pilgrim and translator Hsüan-tsang (circa 596–664).

The three generations of Chinese intellectual monks from Tao-an to Kumārajīva's disciples are called the Buddho-Taoists, because they discussed Buddhism in a Taoist vocabulary and sought in Buddhism solutions to Neo-Taoist problems such as the relation of the Holy Man to the world, whether he really acts, and whether he feels compassion. For example, Seng-chao, in his essay "Prajñā Has No Knowing," tried to communicate the Buddhist idea that the Holy Man acts, but without self-preoccupation or purposive emotion towards the beneficiary, in keeping with Mādhyamika ethics. To convey this idea to his Chinese readers, Seng-chao, employing literary allusion, quoted from Chapter 5 of the familiar Taoist classic of Lao-tzu, the *Tao Te Ching*, writing,

"The Holy Man's good works are as mighty as Heaven and Earth, yet he is not humane." Any Chinese reader would have recognized the allusion in this last phrase, "is not humane," and understood the analogy it draws between the Buddhist Holy Man's compassionate but detached action and that of the Tao ("Heaven and Earth"), which acts without favor or special feeling for one or another of its beneficiaries. The last luminary in this movement was, in fact, Kumārajīva's young disciple, Seng-chao (374–414). His four surviving essays are outstanding expressions of Śūnyavāda in Chinese vocabulary and literary form. Kumārajīva's school was dispersed when the Ch'in kingdom fell. Some of his disciples fled south, and a few went west to the warlord state of Kansu.

The Chinese Saṅgha and the State

Throughout the fifth and early sixth centuries, north and south China pursued separate courses, the south under native dynasties and the north under "barbarian" rulers. Southern Buddhists continued literary activity, producing new translations, debating doctrinal issues, lecturing, and commenting on the principal Sūtras.

Northern Buddhism during the fifth century excelled in works rather than ideas. Intellectual laity and monks had mostly fled south when the northern Wei "barbarians" (386–534) conquered Ch'in and seized Ch'ang-an in 418. The founder of this dynasty favored Buddhism, forbade his troops to pillage the Saṅgha's premises, and ordered the officers in his capital to erect Buddha images and provide dwellings for monks. He appointed a moral and learned monk to the civil service post of Saṅgha-director, thus establishing government jurisdiction over the monasteries in his realm. Unlike Hui-yüan in the south, the monk appointed did not fight for the independence of the Saṅgha from the state but kowtowed to the emperor and justified this seeming contravention of the monastic rule by identifying the emperor with the Tathāgata!

Buddhism flourished and spread in northern Wei until excessive prosperity led to corruption within the Saṅgha and intrigues by jealous Taoists and Confucians. In 446, an edict decreed the destruction of Sūtras, images, and paintings and the execution of monks. Many monks were able to go into hiding, taking Sūtras and images with them; but many temples and scriptures were destroyed, and some monks were put to death.

A new emperor decreed an end to the proscription in 454. From then on, northern Wei rulers patronized Buddhism lavishly and employed monks in responsible civil service posts.

Shortly after 460, the Saṅgha-director persuaded the emperor to undertake one of the world's great religious monuments, the cave temples of Yün-kang. Twenty grottoes were excavated in a limestone cliff several miles from the capital, Ta-t'ung. The earliest caves contain giant stone Buddha images, while the walls of later ones are sculptured profusely with scenes from the Sūtras, the life of the Buddha, bodhisattvas, celestial beings, spirits, and human donors. The project was an act of expiation for the persecution of Buddhism, an indication of imperial favor to the religion, and an attempt to create an expression of the Dharma that would withstand the ravages of time and persecution.

DEVELOPMENT OF SCHOOLS (LINEAGES)

Chinese Buddhism, both northern and southern, sowed the seeds during the sixth century for the great flowering of sects and schools during the seventh. It should be noted that, though Chinese *tsung* is translated "sect" or "school," it denotes a wider range of institutions than either English word. In the classics *tsung* means "clan shrine; clan." Buddhists borrowed the terminology. A tsung consists of people who trace their Dharma-descent to a common *tsu* (ancestor, founder, patriarch).

As translations accumulated, Chinese scholars became puzzled over the discrepancies among the Sūtras. When the commentaries contradicted one another, the Chinese had no trouble accepting that it was simply because at least one author was wrong; but the Sūtras were all supposed to be the word of the Buddha, who could not err and could not genuinely contradict himself. The Sūtras themselves furnished the rudiments of an explanation: the Buddha uses skillful means and preaches different doctrines to suit the conditions of his audience, and each Sūtra was delivered at a particular point in Śākyamuni's career.

This provided the basis for the Chinese method of organizing the apparently contradictory teachings. The method was to divide the teaching of the Sūtras by taking one or a group of similar texts as the most important. Often a monk-scholar would specialize in this way on one set of texts and would begin a lineage by attracting other monks to the same specialization. These lineages, or schools, thus were devoted to the study and exegesis of their particular texts, but members might also learn from other schools that specialized in meditation or monastic discipline. While the lineages harked back to great Indian masters, only two actually attempted to continue schools of Indian Buddhist thought, *San-lun* following the Mādhyamika and *Fa-hsiang* following Yogācāra. Another group of lineages, *Ch'an*, Pure Land, and Third Period focused on specific practices, while a third group, *T'ien-t'ai*, *Hua-yen*, and *Satyasiddhi* placed a heavy emphasis on certain Mahāyāna Sūtras they selected as containing the purest expression of the Buddhist Dharma. Figure 1 diagrams these lineages.

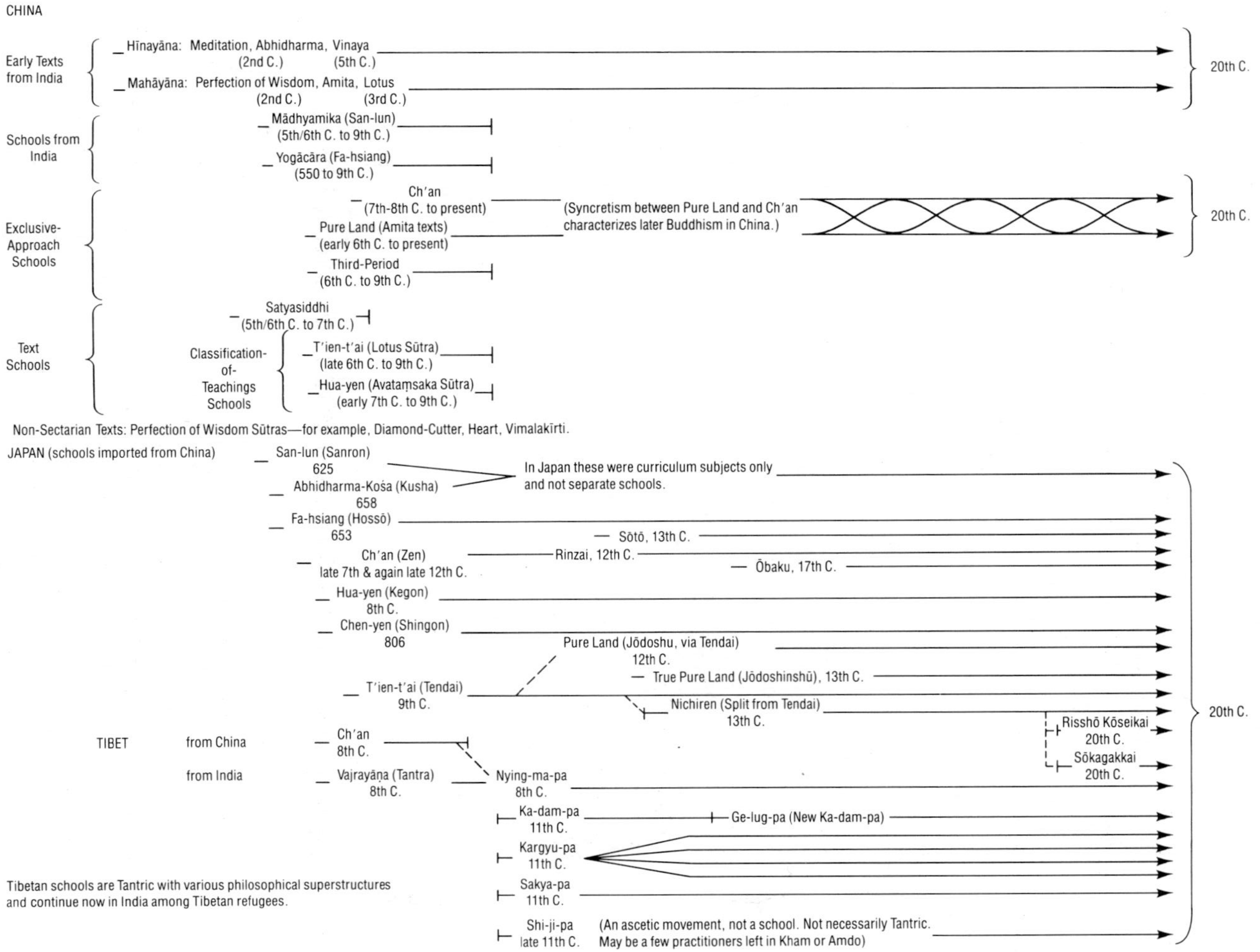

Figure 1. Schools of Chinese, Japanese, and Tibetan Buddhism (all dates are C.E.).

Another notion occupying the thoughts of Buddhists during these turbulent times was that the latter days of Buddhism had arrived. The phrase *Latter-day Dharma* comes from the *Lotus Sūtra*. Indian texts distinguished three Dharma periods: (1) the True Dharma (0–500 After Nirvāṇa); (2) the Counterfeit Dharma (501–1000 or 501–1500 A.N., according to different sources); (3) the Latter-day Dharma (expected to last 10,000 years after the end of the age of Counterfeit Dharma). Sixth-century Chinese put the nirvāṇa of the Buddha at 949 B.C.E., so they thought that the Latter-day Dharma began about 550 C.E. Most of the great sectarian patriarchs offered the advent of the Last Age as a reason why their teaching was necessary and timely. As preachers are always prone to do, they exploited the idea that the current age was sinful and degenerate in order to goad people into religious exertion. The *Lotus*, the *Diamond-Cutter* and other Mahāyāna Sūtras say that people who uphold the True Dharma in the Last Time will earn immeasurable merit. Chinese and Japanese followers of the *Lotus Sūtra* correctly discerned the intent of such passages and often felt that they themselves were called to the leading of holy lives in the last degenerate days of the Buddhist Dharma.

Among the thousands of texts translated into Chinese (or composed in China), there are only a few major ones that set the intellectual and practical life for the schools. Perhaps most important is the *Lotus Sūtra*, but following close behind are the Amita texts, the *Perfection of Wisdom* texts, the *Laṅkāvatāra*, the *Mahāyāna-saṃgraha* (*Compendium of Mahāyāna*), the *Mahāyāna-nirvāṇa* and the *Hua-yen* (*Avataṃsaka*). This last is a collection of texts in itself.

San-lun

The Mādhyamika school from India (see p. 70) was continued in China in San-lun, the Three Treatise sect. The four Mādhyamika treatises translated by Kumārajīva (p. 162) were studied by a few scholars throughout the fifth century. For example, Chih-i, the great T'ien-t'ai master, drew heavily on the fourth, the *Great Perfection of Wisdom Treatise*, for his early lectures on meditation and composed a commentary to it. Nevertheless, for Chih-i, Mādhyamika, the doctrine of emptiness, was just one ingredient among many, and he had little relish for dialectic, the heart of Nāgārjuna's system.

After the demise of Kumārajīva's immediate disciples, interest in the Mādhyamika school waned for a while. But it picked up again in the southern dynasties of Ch'i and Liang, and the greatest master of the San-lun school was Chi-tsang (549–623). In distinction from other masters of Chinese lineages, he rejected "classification of teachings" as a wrongheaded enterprise. His Three Treatise doctrine is quite simply a restatement of Nāgārjuna's teaching in a new vocabulary, with a few additional theses on matters, such as the Two Truths, where Nāgārjuna was too brief and vague.

The Three Treatise lineage died out after Chi-tsang. He was not a meditation master, and the Chinese were not prepared by their type of education to pursue enlightenment through the therapeutic exercise of dialectics. Nevertheless, the theory of the Two Truths was used by other schools, and in India it had even been incorporated in a fundamentally Hīnayāna text, the *Satyasiddhiśāstra*, translated by the San-lun master Kumārajīva.

Satyasiddhi, a Hīnayāna Tradition

Even though the earliest translations into Chinese were Hīnayāna meditation and Abhidharma texts, the edge on the market, so to speak, did not last long. Lokakṣema's translation of the *Perfection of Wisdom* literature (second century C.E.) attracted much attention and set the tone and pace for fervent Chinese adherence to Mahāyāna. In the face of this nearly aggressive attachment to Mahāyāna, Hīnayāna was not so much excluded as absorbed. Hīnayāna texts continued to circulate, and the monastic institution was built on the Hīnayāna Vinaya codes. The Ch'an monastic rule was not to be developed until much later, in the late eighth and early ninth centuries.

Cult practice in the early period of Buddhism in China incorporated Hīnayāna as well as Mahāyāna elements, such as belief in Maitreya and the wish to be reborn into his heaven, and belief in the arhant Piṇḍola, who was ordered by the Buddha to remain on earth as a field of merit for all believers.

In the late fifth and on into the sixth century, when Dharma-masters began to specialize in a particular text, one text that could boast several eminent masters was the *Satyasiddhiśāstra* (*Ch'eng-shih lun*), a Hīnayāna text written by Harivarman in India in the third century C.E. This text was widely studied from the time of its translation by Kumārajīva in the very early fifth century, and many commentaries were written up to the beginning of the T'ang dynasty (618–907), especially in the south. The Ch'i and Liang dynasties (479–557) also saw a revival of interest in the Mādhyamika school of Kumārajīva. The *Ch'eng-shih* was, essentially, a Hīnayāna text. Yet because it expounded a Two-Truth theory, it was believed for some time to be Mahāyāna. It had developed within the group of sects out of which Mahāyāna sprang, so the confusion was easy and understandable. Later the proponents of the San-lun (Mādhyamika) tradition, concerned with purity of teaching, argued forcefully and successfully with the *Ch'eng-shih* specialists. By the beginning of the T'ang dynasty interest in the *Ch'eng-shih* had waned, and it had come to be generally recognized as a Hīnayāna work.

Fa-hsiang

Yogācāra was introduced to China by Paramārtha (arrived in 546), whose most influential translation was that of Asaṅga's *Compendium of Mahāyāna*. A school grew up around this text, and it was perplexity about certain points in it that prompted Hsüan-tsang (596–664) to go to India and study. He spent fifteen months studying Yogācāra at Nālandā, went on a tour through south India, came back to Nālandā and studied some more, was accorded an audience and much honor by the Emperor Harṣa, and returned to China with a large collection of Sanskrit manuscripts. He spent the rest of his life translating the texts he had brought back and teaching Yogācāra to his pupils. His disciple K'uei-chi (632–682) is reckoned as the founder of the Fa-hsiang ("Dharma-mark") school, which soon died out in China. However, it has survived in Japan and was revived in China about 1908 by Yang Wen-hui, the father of the Chinese Buddhist revival.

Though the Fa-hsiang school died out, the great master, traveler, and translator Hsüan-tsang became the focus of legend and miracle tales. His record of his journey to the West in search of the Law is a geography of Central Asia and India in the seventh century. His narrow escapes from death further convinced Chinese Buddhists of the power of Buddhas and bodhisattvas to save one from the evils of the world. Hsüan-tsang left China by stealth and returned a hero, welcomed by the emperor himself. Yet this moment of triumph for Buddhism was also a last hurrah. Hsüan-tsang, rare in his knowledge of Sanskrit, labored over his texts, reproducing accurate translations;

The Chinese pilgrim Hsüan-tsang, with his pack. (From a Chinese painting.)

but despite a monumental output, only his 260-character translation of the *Heart Sūtra* attained general popularity.

Yogācāra theories nevertheless contributed to the development of both the T'ien-t'ai and Ch'an schools.

Hua-yen (Avataṃsaka)

The Hua-yen sect claims Tu-shun, also known as Fa-shun (557–640), as its first master. When a boy he worked as a laborer in a military batallion. At eighteen he went forth and devoted himself to meditation, attaining miracle-working powers. According to tradition, he could charm wild beasts into docility and lure insects away from fields. He studied the *Mahāyānasaṃgraha (Shê-lun) Sūtra* and the *Hua-yen Sūtra*. In the manner of Holy Men his body did not decay after death, and finally his disciples concealed him in a cave-shrine for fear of theft.

Tu-shun's disciple Chih-yen was the teacher of Fa-tsang (643–712), the great architect of the school. In his young days Fa-tsang worked in Hsüan-tsang's translation bureau, and in his old age he assisted Śikṣānanda in the retranslation of the *Avataṃsaka*. He served as preceptor to four emperors and wrote voluminously. One time, to illustrate a difficult Hua-yen teaching to Empress Wu, who usurped the T'ang throne from 684 to 705, Fa-tsang had mirrors set up in a hall in the ten directions (four cardinal, four intermediate, zenith, and nadir), and set a Buddha image and a lamp in the middle of the hall. Another tale tells that the Empress, as dissolute as she was wily, entertained her paramours in just such a room.

Two eminent masters followed Fa-tsang: Ch'eng-kuan (738/737–838/820), and Tsung-mi (780–841), who was also a master in one of the Ch'an lineages. The Hua-yen sect did not survive the general suppression of Buddhism in 845.

The Hua-yen "classification of teachings" assigns top place to the *Avataṃsaka*, and the school's metaphysics centers on the concept of the Dharma-realm expounded in the Sūtra. The Dharma-realm has two aspects: as noumenon (*li*), it is the realm of suchness, of transcendental and immanent Dharma. As phenomenon (*shih*), it is the realm of the dharmas, the conditioned world of rebirth. The Hīnayānist sees the Dharma-realm of phenomena. Mādhyamika and Yogācāra, says Hua-yen, see the Dharma-realm of noumena. T'ien-t'ai and the *Awakening of Faith* (a Chinese Yogācāra text falsely attributed to Aśvaghoṣa) are said to consider a Dharma-realm where phenomena and noumena do not impede each other. The Hua-yen teaching claims to see a Dharma-realm where phenomena do not impede each other but enter into, and are identical with, each other.

The Hua-yen doctrine is not so much a rational philosophy as a galaxy of concepts arrayed for contemplation. This kind of intellectual discipline is a very hard road to samādhi, and in any place or time very few are ready for it.

T'ien-t'ai

The lineage of the T'ien-t'ai sect begins with Hui-ssŭ (515–576). He "went forth" (left his family and social position to join the Buddhist Order) when he was fifteen, and resolved at twenty that it was his vocation to save all mankind. He practiced asceticism and meditation and attained the Dharma-Lotus samādhi, induced by weeks of alternately reciting and meditating on the *Lotus Sūtra*. After much fasting and meditation, he had a dream in which he sat in Maitreya's assembly on a giant lotus flower. He wept, thinking "In the Latter-day Dharma I have received the *Lotus Sūtra*, and now I have met Maitreya." This spurred him to even greater zeal, and many wondrous omens appeared.

To escape the dangers of war, Hui-ssŭ moved south to a mountain, where he spent the rest of his life. Secluded mountain monasteries had been institutionalized by famous monks of Eastern Chin (317–420), especially Hui-yüan. Such an environment favored study and meditation more than the busy metropolitan monasteries that enjoyed imperial favor through their proximity to the court. Most of the great sects, or tsungs, started in the mountain temples and moved into the capital after achieving considerable success in the provinces. And most of the tsungs lost their original purity and spiritual integrity amid the busyness and intrigue that accompanied fame and fortune. Schools that did not maintain a base in mountain monasteries perished when imperial disfavor, persecution, or internal degeneracy overtook them.

While Hui-ssŭ was the first of the T'ien-t'ai lineage, his disciple Chih-i is often recognized as the organizer of this school. Chih-i (538–597), "the great master of T'ien-t'ai," became Hui-ssŭ's disciple, practiced Dharma-Lotus meditation, and attained samādhi when reading a passage in the *Lotus Sūtra* about a bodhisattva who burned his own body in a sandalwood fire as an offering to the Buddha. Later the master appointed Chih-i to lecture on the *Perfection of Wisdom Sūtras* and the *Lotus*; when Hui-ssŭ went south, he turned the leadership of the Community over to Chih-i (who was then twenty-nine).

Chih-i and his followers spent the next eight years in Nanking, the capital of the Ch'en dynasty. Disgusted with the dissolute and turbulent life of the capital, he then withdrew to Mount T'ien-t'ai, in Chekiang, from which the T'ien-t'ai-tsung takes its name.

Chih-i laid equal emphasis on meditation and doctrine study, on self-cultivation and propagating the Teaching. Though he insisted that he was a plain practicer of meditation and not a philosopher, his doctrinal system is an architectonic marvel. It is a vast syncretism designed to comprise and harmonize all Buddhist doctrines. He accepted Hui-ssŭ's thesis that the *Lotus* rather than the *Nirvāṇa Sūtra* contains Śākyamuni's highest teaching and is the authoritative expression harmonizing and explaining all the different doctrines found in the Sūtras. Each of the other Sūtras speaks on several different levels, because it is addressing a mixed audience. T'ien-t'ai distinguishes five periods in Śākyamuni's teaching career; four methods of teaching in Sūtras prior to the *Lotus*: sudden, gradual, secret indeterminate, and explicit indeterminate; and four modes of doctrine: the Tripiṭaka teaching (= Hīnayāna), the pervasive teaching (= Śūnyavāda), the special teaching (= Yogācāra), and the round or perfect teaching (= the *Lotus* doctrine). It also brought into one system the two developing emphases in Chinese Buddhism, the northern penchant for practical action, exemplified in meditation and pious works, and the southern love of philosophical debate, discussion, and elitist intellectualism.

The goal to which this system was directed was enlightenment. The doctrine and practice are "expedient means" designed to direct one along the path, but when the goal is reached, path and goal alike vanish in the transcendent realm. This combines Mādhyamika (Nāgārjuna's metaphysics of emptiness) with soteriology. In the meantime, the great doctrinal synthesis, the classification and explanation of teachings, could well be described as a Chinese Mahāyāna Abhidharma.

The Community on Mount T'ien-t'ai prospered under patronage from the Sui imperial family for two decades after Chih-i's death. But it declined under the T'ang rulers, who did not appreciate the sect's close connections with the preceding dynasty. In the eighth century, T'ien-t'ai revived under the great master Chan-jan (711–781), who inspired some notable lay disciples to encompass Buddhism and Confucianism within one syncretic system. Out of this enterprise arose the Neo-Confucian school, which ironically, became the most enduring and destructive of all Buddhism's enemies.

T'ien-t'ai and Hua-yen succeeded better than San-lun and Fa-hsiang, because they were Chinese adaptations rather than Indian transplants. They did not engage much in formal arguments and proofs, for which the native Chinese tradition had little fondness. In China, gentlemen refrain from argument. Another strength of T'ien-t'ai and Hua-yen was that they gratified the endemic Chinese penchant for harmonizing things, that they assured unity in doctrine while permitting a full panoply of individual options. Since the third century B.C.E. Chinese thought has usually considered unity in ideas as a factor of sociopolitical unity and has abhorred dissension in either realm.

The all-inclusiveness of T'ien-t'ai and Hua-yen diffused the energies of the individual and of the sects. Furthermore, they required a high degree of education and much book study. Starting from similar origins—mountain monks studying one Sūtra and meditating on it—there arose several popular sects during the sixth century, each of which radically simplified its statement of doctrine and advocated the exclusive and intense pursuit of some one practice. Some of these cults professed pessimism about the latter-day world, but they all fostered hope, enhanced faith in the efficacy of devout action, and released a torrent of religious energy. The two chief popular sects were the Ching-t'u-tsung ("Pure Land") and the meditation school Ch'an-tsung (Japanese: Zen).

Pure Land

The roots of the Pure Land school reach back to the Later Han dynasty. The practice of contemplation on the Buddha is described in a text translated in the period 167–186. This practice was a samādhi in which one concentrated on or visualized the Buddhas of the ten directions. Concentration on the Buddha is *nien-fo*, an important term in the later development of Pure Land doctrine.

The Pure Land cult split into the cult of Maitreya, the next Buddha, and the cult of Amita (Amitābha), the Buddha presiding over Sukhāvatī, the Pure Land of the West. Their writings are the Maitreya texts, dealing with the Tuṣita Heaven, and the Amita texts, which come in five categories: (1) Larger Pure Land scripture; (2) Smaller Pure Land scripture; (3) scriptures describing meditation on Amita; (4) commentaries to Amita scriptures; and (5) related texts pertaining to Amita. These early texts and practices of meditation were popular in the north.

Another practice common in the north was the use of magic spells (dhāraṇī). The north had been a hotbed of the practice of magic since the early days of Buddhism there, and dhāraṇī were part of that practice.

Early Taoist texts such as the *T'ai-p'ing ching* (*Classic of Great Peace*) taught that a spirit or spirits of heaven kept a log of everyone's sins, of whatever magnitude, and popular Taoist practice worked toward eliminating sins and attaining long life. Eventually the goal extended from long life to physical immortality. This popular idea of the heavenly spirits' keeping records was incorporated into spurious Buddhist texts, which said that the four guardian kings recorded all the good and bad deeds of all beings, and that the life span of each being was adjusted accordingly.

T'an-luan (476–542), claimed as the first master in the Pure Land lineage, lived in the north, exposed to these popular practices and ideas. He got his religious vocation when, convalescing from a grave illness, he saw a vision of a heavenly gate opening to him. He turned first to Taoism and its recipes for attaining unlimited life, and a treatise he composed describing a Taoist meditation technique is still extant. T'an-luan then met the Indian monk Bodhiruci, who arrived in Loyang in 508. Bodhiruci told him that Buddhism had a superior method for gaining everlasting life and taught him the Amitābha texts. T'an-luan was converted and burned his Taoist books. From this time on the Amita cult eclipsed the Maitreya cult.

Bodhiruci advocated the use of spells for concentration, and T'an-luan's practice under his influence and that of practices already popular in the north gradually developed into recitation of the Buddha's name. The term *nien-fo* in T'an-luan's own writings originally referred to the practice of meditation. There are three possible meanings for the word *nien*: (1) concentration or meditation, samādhi; (2) a length of time equal to one thought; hence, the expression *shih-nien* (ten *nien*) meant the length of time consisting of ten thoughts or moments. This led eventually to a misunderstanding, because *nien* also means (3) vocal recitation, and the phrase *shih-nien* was interpreted as ten recitations of the Buddha's name. The mistake is easy to understand, because in certain Amita texts there is the phrase "holding and maintaining the name [of Buddha]."

T'an-luan advocated teachings or practices already current among the general populace. Pure Land therefore had a popular base from the first. T'an-luan organized societies for recitation of Amitābha's name and propagated the Pure Land cult with great success. He also laid the foundations of sectarian doctrine. He declared that even those who have committed evil deeds and atrocities are eligible for rebirth in the Western Paradise if they sincerely desire it. But he maintained that those who revile the Dharma are excluded—for one thing, because blasphemy is not conducive to aspiration and, for another, because retribution for blasphemy is repeated rebirth in the lowest hell. T'an-luan asserted that even the merit one seems to earn for oneself is facilitated by the overarching power of Amita's vows and that birth in the Pure Land and attainment of Buddhahood there are due to this power. His belief in this power led him to advocate faith and recitation of Amitābha's name rather than meditation.

Times were hard, and intellectual life in the north was not thriving during T'an-luan's career. There was a ready market for easy and efficacious practices. Since it had no tendency to elitism, Pure Land was different from the other Chinese schools. It went to the people, providing easy doctrine and easy practice. In a sense, Pure Land was realistic, recognizing that most people were incapable of meeting the intellectual and financial requirements of the other schools; it also gave a positive reward for practice: rebirth in a blissful utopian paradise. This led to a rather negative view of the world, and there was no claim that this world is the Śākyamuni Buddha's Pure Land, as the *Vimalakīrti*, for example, asserts.

Pure Land practice was found in all classes of society until after the persecution of 842–845 (see p. 188), when it became more and more the practice of ordinary people. Educated gentlemen lost interest in Buddhism.

The next great master was Tao-cho (562–645), and he was succeeded by his disciple Shan-tao (613–681), who gave to Chinese Pure Land its definitive shape. The last two great masters of this formative period were Tz'u-min (680–748) and Fa-chao (late eighth century).

While at first Pure Land was felt to be the "easy" path, suitable for the last degenerate days when only Buddha-invocation (nien-fo) was efficacious, the Buddhist urge to follow a Middle Way began to reassert itself in the work of Shan-tao, who denied that the Pure Land was either an inferior apparition land or a superior place inaccessible to ordinary folk. Nien-fo was still the primary religious act, but other practices were admitted even if only as secondary acts. The exclusive nien-fo practice of the early masters gave way under the direction of later masters to the combined practice of meditation, morality, Buddha-invocation and scholarship, and Pure Land denounced Ch'an for cultivating meditation to the exclusion of morality. This movement of encouraging many practices led eventually to Fa-chao's syncretistic approach, the propensity for which he had received from his earlier training in T'ien-t'ai.

By the ninth century the Amita cult was so fully formed and so widely diffused that it ceased to need great masters. Only Ch'an withstood its influence. Yet by the sixteenth century, Chinese Ch'an was permeated by Pure Land practices, and even now "na-mo a-mi-t'o-fo" (Namo Amita Buddha in Sanskrit, meaning "Homage to Amita Buddha") is chanted regularly in the daily liturgy of Ch'an monasteries.

The two chief Chinese departures from early Indian Amitābhist doctrine were reciting the name rather than meditating on the Buddha and affirming that sinners, too, can go to the Pure Land. It has been noted that reciting sacred names was a popular practice in India, and it was certainly not a part of pre-Buddhist Chinese religion. T'an-luan's motive in explaining away the *Sukhāvatī-vyūha Sūtra*'s statement that grave sinners are excluded from the effect of Amita's vow was the conviction that all living beings possess Buddha-nature. This idea originated in India, but it found such favor in China precisely because no native Chinese philosophy (except Mohism, which became extinct before Buddhism was widely accepted in China) preached universal love and the worth of every person regardless of family or class.

During the eighth century, the Amita cult attracted emperors and slaves, scholars and women, artists and soldiers, monks and laity. The common hope for rebirth in the Pure Land united the otherwise disparate segments of society. From the twelfth century, Neo-Confucian gentlemen disdained to share a cult that was both "vulgar" (since the common people had it) and "foreign"; but their wives continued to recite "na-mo a-mi-t'o-fo," and mandarin boys as they grew up had to expunge the devotion learned from their mothers if they wanted to keep their Confucian orientation pure. No native Chinese god has ever commanded the universal worship that Amita has received.

The Third Period Sect (San-chieh-chiao)

As in Pure Land, latter-day pessimism was basic to the Third Period sect, founded by Hsin-hsing (540–593). He was born after his mother had prayed to the Buddha and dreamed of a spirit who lifted up a child and said, "I'm now giving him to you." When he was four years old he saw on the road an ox trying to pull a cart stuck in the mud. He cried and cried out of pity for it. After seeing many unhappy and evil things he gained insight into the equality of all things, not clinging to affection for some and aversion to others.

Hsin-hsing contended that in the final, degenerate age only his own teachings sufficed. Meditation and monastery life were not enough. So his sect demanded purification through austerities and strict observance of the monastic rules. His followers did not live in monasteries, though. They spent their time with the crowds in the bazaars, placed little value on images and books, and devoted themselves to charitable activities. Hsin-hsing's doctrine emphasized that all things are just manifestations of Buddha-nature, and he concluded that everyone, regardless of species, status, sex, or sect, is worthy of respect. Members of his sect expressed their worship of living beings as future Buddhas by practicing donation lavishly. The sect established an "Inexhaustible Treasury" in Ch'ang-an about 620. The name and the idea of a donation bank come from the *Vimalakīrti Sūtra*. Chinese and Japanese Buddhist lay associations have often operated credit unions and mutual financing societies. The Third Period sect carried this, like other things, to an extreme. Donations poured in faster than the treasurer monks could keep count. Loans were made to people from far and wide. The income was spent on repairing temples, on relief for the sick and the indigent, and on rites of worship.

The Third Period school irked the other sects by insisting that its teaching was the only true one, and it vexed the imperial regime by proclaiming that the glorious age of Sui and T'ang was really a time of decay and depravity. As if this were not enough, the sect went on to say that in the Latter-day Dharma there existed no government that deserved the people's respect and that the imperial power was incapable of saving the country. In 713 the Inexhaustible Treasury was dissolved at the emperor's command. The sect's literature was proscribed. After more than a century of tenuous survival, this movement was extinguished in the general persecution of 845. The marvel is that the government tolerated for so long a teaching that was rankly subversive.

Ch'an

Meditation texts were among the earliest translations, because lay disciples of the second-century C.E. translator An Shih-kao were practicing meditation and needed manuals. Their purpose was to get the superknowledges, especially the mundane ones; and if we are to credit the tales in their biographies, some of them succeeded. The pre-Han Chinese Taoist texts attributed to Lao-tzu and Chuang-tzu mention various meditative techniques, and popular Han Taoism developed and enriched the repertory so that Buddhist meditation found a well-oriented clientele.

Most of the early missionaries and eminent Chinese monks were proficient in meditation. The *Lives of Eminent Monks*, completed about 530, contains biographies of twenty meditators and twenty-one wonder-workers, besides the translators and commentators, who were also noted for meditation. So it is clear that Indian methods of meditation were effective and popular in China. Nevertheless, meditation was just one practice among many in the large monasteries and the famous sects of the late sixth century. The student was involved in lectures and reading, rituals, and sundry pious works to such an extent that he had little time and insufficient encouragement to practice contemplation.

The Ch'an sect arose to meet the demand for a well-grounded and lasting tradition specializing in meditation. It began, like the other Chinese sects, as a lineage of masters devoted to one text, in this case the *Laṅkāvatāra Sūtra*, a Yogācāra text first translated in the fifth century. Ch'an's early history is obscured by legends fabricated in the eighth century and later. It seems a historical fact that Bodhidharma, an Indian meditation master and champion of the *Laṅkāvatāra*, arrived by sea in Canton about 470, stayed briefly in south China, then went north and stayed there until about 520. Legend says that while in the south, Bodhidharma met the pious Emperor Wu of Liang, who asked him: "Have I earned merit by my lifelong temple building, donation, and worship offerings?" Bodhidharma said: "No merit at all." The emperor, disappointed, banished Bodhidharma. The tale is anachronistic, as Bodhidharma was already in the north by 483, and Wu did not become emperor until 502. This encounter, however, points up a central idea of Ch'an, that true merit does not stem from good works and lead to mundane good luck but springs from insight into the Dharma-body, which is one's own true nature. This distinction between finite, or relative, and infinite, or absolute, merit is made repeatedly in the *Perfection of Wisdom Sūtras*.

Bodhidharma settled in a mountain temple near Loyang, where he acquired at least two disciples and taught them the *Laṅkāvatāra*. Legend says that in this monastery he spent nine years gazing at a wall, that he sat continuously until his legs fell off, and that he cut off his eyelids so that his gaze would never falter. The term "wall gazing" occurs in an early pamphlet attributed to Bodhidharma, and the earliest biography says that he taught "wall contemplation." This was probably a kind of "formless meditation" like that recommended in *The Awakening of Faith*, another Yogācāra text, and the Japanese *shikan-taza* ("just sitting") practice.

The Second, Third, and Fourth Patriarchs—Hui-k'o (487–593!), Seng-ts'an (died 606), and Tao-hsin (580–651)—did not contribute significantly to the development of peculiarly Ch'an traditions. Seng-tsan, an especially shadowy figure, is credited with authorship of a long poem, *The Inscription on Faith in Mind*, still extant. The Fifth Patriarch, Hung-jen (601–674), is far better known, at least in legend, because of the supposed contest between his two disciples, Shen-hsiu (606?–706) and Hui-neng (638–713), for the coveted robe of transmission to signify the right to be called the Sixth Patriarch. A suspect tale relates that the Fifth Patriarch, Hung-jen, ordered each of his disciples to write a stanza announcing that Hung-jen would give his robe, Dharma, and succession to the disciple who revealed enlightenment in his verse. Shen-hsiu wrote his secretly on the wall at midnight:

> The body is the Bodhi Tree,
> The mind is like a bright mirror-and-stand.
> At all times wipe it diligently,
> Don't let there be any dust.

He was told to try again. Hui-neng wrote a capping verse:

> Bodhi really has no tree;
> The bright mirror also has no stand.
> Buddha-nature is forever pure; (or: Really no thing exists)
> Where is there room for dust?

We are told that in a private interview in the dead of night, Hung-jen recognized Hui-neng's awakening and gave him the robe of transmission in secret. The details of the struggle for the robe are recorded in the *T'an-ching*, or *Platform Sūtra of the Sixth Patriarch*, a work most likely put together by Shen-hui, Hui-neng's disciple and promoter. Shen-hui secured the title of Sixth Patriarch for his master. We do not know for a fact to whom, if anyone, the robe of transmission was actually given. Be that as it may, the life of Hui-neng became the model for the Ch'an career, and it exemplified many characteristics that became *de rigeur* for Ch'an thought, practice, and legend.

A fragment of Hui-ko's doctrine, preserved in the *Further Lives of Eminent Monks*, expresses succinctly the fundamental Ch'an teaching:

> The deep principle of the True is "utter nondifferent." From of old, one is confused about the Gem and thinks it is a piece of tile. When suddenly "oneself" wakes up, there is the real jewel. Ignorance and wisdom are the same and without difference. Know that the myriad things are all identical with suchness. When you regard the body and do not distinguish it from the Buddha, why go on to seek [nirvāṇa] without remainder?

All these ideas we have seen in the Indian teaching of emptiness and Tantra—the identity of saṃsāra and nirvāṇa, the womb of Tathāgatahood as the gem of intrinsic Buddhahood, this body as the Buddha-body, and the futility of seeking nirvāṇa as if it were another thing among things. The Ch'an masters, like the Tantric poets, did not invent new concepts but extracted the most powerful religious ideas from a diffuse literature and presented them in concentrated, forceful form.

Bodhidharma's austerities, including his cutting off his own eyelids, reveal the extreme intensity of purpose and concentration characteristic of Ch'an. Another example is the legend that Hui-k'o, when Bodhidharma refused him admission as a disciple, stood in the snow until the drifts were up to his knees. When that did not work, he cut off his own arm to give to the master as a token of earnestness. Voluntary bodily mutilation was not a Chinese trait. It was, rather, a form of punishment for certain crimes. Confucians believed that it was the duty of children to preserve from harm the body given them by their parents. Taoists, however, at least as represented in *Chuang-tzu*, often used the mutilated or deformed as examples of virtue and wisdom while at the same time teaching the means to keep one's body intact. Bodily mutilation is still practiced by Chinese Buddhists. It serves several purposes: to encourage intrepid striving, to counteract ordinary timidity, and to arouse energy by fixing the imagination on intense physical pain. It is a manneristic exaggeration of the common Buddhist meditation on suffering.

The private interview, such as that between Hung-jen and Hui-neng, provided the opportunity for the master periodically to evaluate the disciple's spiritual progress. It became a characteristic feature of Ch'an practice. The Chinese character *wu* (*satori* in Japanese) means to awaken, to understand. It translates in Sanskrit as *budh*, the root of *Buddha* and *bodhi*. In Ch'an it signifies an opening of insight, a change to a higher level of understanding similar to the "recognition" that Kauṇḍinya experienced when he heard the First Sermon and to what the audience in a Mahāyāna Sūtra experiences on hearing a Dharma-discourse. Hui-neng had his two awakenings on hearing the *Diamond-Cutter*. This is in accord with the general Indian notion that hearing is the proximate cause of attaining insight. It also shows that early Ch'an acknowledged degrees of awakening and a progression from lower to higher. The school took seriously the Buddha-nature of all beings and sought supreme, perfect enlightenment in this life.

Dialogs that occurred in these private encounters form a substantial part of later Ch'an literature. They are terse, often witty, sometimes bizarre and obscure. The master usually had a lot of students, and only two or three short periods a day were set aside for interviews, so the chance was precious. In addition, the student's hopes and fears were usually keyed up by long waiting and intense striving, so that the meeting had the sudden-death quality of a duel. The master diagnoses the student's problem and treats it. Sometimes he simply explains or advises. Sometimes he provokes, shocks, or otherwise manipulates the student. The Ch'an strategy is to catch a person at the critical moment and do the appropriate thing that triggers awakening. Ch'an masters similarly treat each case as *sui generis*, acting and expecting responses with spontaneity and without preconceptions or premeditation.

The awakening that climaxes the Ch'an interview tale is triggered by the master's words but usually seems much stronger than the mere words would warrant. One factor is the spiritual aura, the charisma, of the master. Ch'an is said to be "a special transmission outside doctrines," a direct transmission from mind to mind. Another factor is that the master's instruction is directed to the specific condition of the inquirer, which the ordinary reader is unlikely to duplicate. Ch'an is for those with keen faculties, and the teaching is given only to those who are ripe for it. A third factor is the interaction between master and disciple. The tense, expectant inquirer feels strongly that he is in the presence of a wise man who can read his character and prescribe for him. He is relieved and thankful to have someone concentrate on him, know him as he really is, and "point directly at his nature." And the student is humiliated, disappointed, and stimulated to greater effort when the master candidly criticizes him.

The early Ch'an contemplative exercise was simply striving constantly to have no notions and to see one's nature and become a Buddha. It meant playing a simple, difficult, and fascinating game of cat-and-mouse with one's "fundamental mind." Interviews with the master were a crucial adjunct. As generations passed, sayings and dialogs of the old masters were collected and came to be used as themes for contemplation. The "old case" or "public document" (*kung-an*, Japanese *kōan*) literature and exercise were fully developed by the early twelfth century. Though kung-an meditation is especially associated with the Lin-chi (Japanese, Rinzai) subsect, it is also practiced by the other branches.

An example of a kung-an is the encounter between Ling-yu and his master, Pai-chang. When Ling-yu was twenty-three he came to Pai-chang, who recognized his talent and took him as an attendant. One day the master said, "Who's there?"

"It's Ling-yu."

"Poke and see if there's still some fire in the stove."

Ling-yu poked around and said, "There's no fire."

Pai-chang got up, went to the stove, poked quite a bit, managed to stir up a small glow, and said to his pupil, "Isn't this fire?" Ling-yu was awakened, knelt down, and bowed in gratitude to the master.

This kung-an is readily intelligible. Fire stands for Buddha-nature. The disciple had not found his "nature" because he had not searched hard enough. Pai-chang commented to Ling-yu that seeing Buddha-nature depends on the right moment, the cause (the student's inherent Buddhahood), and the accessory cause (the master's direct pointing at the mind). The beauty of kung-an language is that it coins its vocabulary freshly and impromptu, avoiding scholastic terminology and using natural symbols. But the kung-an is mastered not when the symbols are identified with technical terms but when, for example, Buddha-nature is experienced as directly as the glowing coals.

The myth of Hui-neng as being an untutored genius, illiterate and unschooled in the scriptures, serves a purpose: the school opposed

Hui-neng, the Sixth Patriarch, tearing up a Buddhist Sūtra—since enlightenment is not in knowing the words but having the experience. (From a Chinese southern Sung painting by Liang K'ai.)

book-scholars' pretensions and called the laity and uneducated people to attain awakening simply by using their native talent. The *Platform Sūtra* shows Hui-neng as illiterate, which may be less than true; but it also shows him quoting the Sūtras, handling a large technical vocabulary, and giving sermons that, though not high prose by T'ang dynasty standards, are far from uncultivated.

The traditional legendary history of the formation of the Ch'an school could not be put into proper historical perspective and subjected to critical historical scholarship until the discovery of the Tun-huang manuscripts, one of the most remarkable archaeological discoveries of the twentieth century. Found among these manuscripts were documents indicating that there is no evidence before the early eighth century either for a Ch'an patriarchal tradition or for the name and biography of the Sixth Patriarch, Hui-neng. One of these patriarchal traditions even gives the title of First Patriarch to Guṇabhadra (394–468) as teacher of Bodhidharma, a false assertion since Guṇabhadra was probably dead before Bodhidharma arrived in China around 470.

Also in these documents the line of Shen-hsiu (see p. 177) is followed, giving no emphasis to Hui-neng. Shen-hui, an unknown southerner seeking to make a name for his own school of Ch'an at the expense of the popular and flourishing northern school of Shen-hsiu, declared the heretofore shadowy figure of Hui-neng to be the Sixth Patriarch. Shen-hui elaborated the biography of Hui-neng with such skill and persistence that his fabrication eventually became the version accepted as standard history of the Ch'an school, a version that was regarded as truth until the twentieth-century discovery of the Tun-huang manuscripts. Shen-hui is probably responsible for sections of the *Platform Sūtra*, a work attributed to Hui-neng but compiled some time after his death.

The legendary history of Ch'an was given its final and enduring form during the early ninth century. Nevertheless, both the school of Shen-hui and the school of Shen-hsiu, along with all but two of the other schools or "houses" of Ch'an, died out during the T'ang persecution of 842–845.

During this eventful ninth century, Ch'an not only created a history, but also gave its community life its classic distinctive form. Noteworthy is the requirement that all monks do manual labor: "One day no work, one day no food." Some other Buddhist monasteries owned much land that was tilled by serfs. The Ch'an monks had taken to manual labor to support themselves as early as the Fourth Patriarch. Huai-hai, also called simply Pai-chang, made labor mandatory. The T'ang Ch'an masters acquired numerous tracts of mountain and wasteland and developed them by means of work parties of monks. They grew rice, cut bamboo, and developed tea plantations. These enterprises made the monks less dependent on donors and their whims and obviated the charge that they were parasites on society. But physical work also served as an integral part of the spiritual discipline. The exercise counteracted the lethargy and depression that can come from sitting in meditation. Also, hoeing the fields and picking tea leaves were performed mindfully as part of day-and-night meditation.

Ch'an has been accused of iconoclasm and antinomianism (avowed rejection of the usual, including obligation to moral law). In the eighth century, a lay follower of T'ien-t'ai charged that "those who travel the Ch'an path go so far as to teach the people that there is neither Buddha nor Dharma and that neither sin nor goodness has any significance." He alleged that ordinary people took this as license to sin and were drawn to destruction like moths to a candle. Then there is the tale of T'ien-jan (died 824), who on a cold night took down the wooden Buddha image in the shrine hall and made a fire with it. When he was accused of sacrilege, he said, "I was only looking for a Buddha-relic." "How can you expect to find a relic in a piece of wood?" "Well then, I am only burning a piece of wood, after all."

It may well be that some people took Ch'an teachings as an excuse to sin, just as some have so taken the Pure Land and Christian teachings that sinners may attain paradise. But the Ch'an masters required strict discipline from their clerical followers and sound morality from lay disciples. T'ien-jan's burning the image was indeed an act of sacrilege, and his companions' reaction is sufficient proof that Ch'an at that time did not condone the destruction of sacred objects. He got away with it and it was reported, because he gave his act a transcendental significance and handled the repartee with wit.

Ch'an has kept the monastic system and has not discarded rituals, images, or the pantheon. Its style and language are distinctively Chinese, but its metaphysics is the core teaching of Indian Mahāyāna . In some ways, too, Ch'an runs counter to major Chinese values. The Chinese as a whole have always loved magic, but the lives of the Ch'an masters contain very few references to the magic powers the meditation expert is supposed to attain. Confucian gentlemen and Taoist adepts both consider themselves above manual labor, but Ch'an trainees and masters toil like coolies. The glory of the Ch'an-tsung is not that it made Buddhism thoroughly Chinese but that it extracted, concentrated, and made efficacious the essence of the Dharma.

Ch'an, like Pure Land, did not develop in isolation. In addition to the influence coming from the Yogācāra tradition and the T'ien-t'ai school, another tradition similar to Ch'an is Tantra. As a separate school, the Chen-yen ("True Word") school, Tantrism lasted only a short time in China during the eighth and ninth centuries. Both Ch'an and Tantra were fed by the Yogācāra and Perfection of Wisdom traditions. The model for the Buddha was one's own teacher, or guru. The emphasis was on practice, and the goal was Buddhahood in this lifetime. One strand of Tantra, the formless tradition of using no external supports of any kind, is similar to the early Ch'an iconoclastic rejection of external supports. Further, there was the deliberate use of unconventionality, of permitting formerly forbidden things.

This unconventionality takes us back into early Chinese history and the unconventional and paradoxical postures expressed in *Chuang-tzu*, a Taoist book dating to approximately the fourth century B.C.E. The halt and the lame ridiculed Chinese paragons of conventionality, as many Ch'an masters ridiculed their more staid Buddhist confreres. Taoists, though not mentioned in the Ch'an histories or writings, also helped to shape the Ch'an tradition and ought not to be ignored in trying to understand the particular flavor of Ch'an.

The Taoist Holy Man, or Sage, shares a number of characteristics with the Ch'an master. The Sage retires to the mountains, eschewing the lure of worldly fame. He does not bow down to the king. The Buddhists eventually lost that particular struggle with the state; nevertheless, the principle remained. The Sage's mind is still, and Shen-hsiu and Hui-neng's image of the mirror and dust occurs a millennium earlier in *Chuang-tzu* and *Lao-tzu*. The Sage in trance is like a piece of dry wood or dead ashes and stays that way for days. Ch'an records also note masters who attained such trance states. The Sage must give the appearance of the fool by the standards of the world. Likewise, the accomplished Ch'an master seems foolish. The Taoist Sage teaches by silence, or nose pulling, or kicking and blows, expecting the disciple to learn intuitively what is required of him. The wordless teaching is an old, old tradition in China, not an invention of the Ch'an masters. The Taoist lives in the world, according with the natural succession of growth and decay, life and death. The Ch'an master, too, unlike other Buddhists who sought escape from the flux and changeability of this world, lived in the world; yet also like the Taoist Sage, by living in an eternal now, he was beyond both time and space, birth and death. In Ch'an there is little talk of nirvāṇa and escape from saṃsāra. The Way itself is immortality.

The Ch'an school's changing of the Vinaya indicated both an acknowledgment of China as its locale and an acknowledgment of this world. Though the principle of "no work, no eat" later was honored more in the breach than the practice, the principle still held. The Ch'an masters' writings reveal a style far more similar to native Taoist and other works than to Buddhist scriptures and moral tales. The kung-an remind one of *Chuang-tzu*, *Lieh-tzu*, and the *Shih-shuo hsin-yü*, a book recording witty conversation popular in the south, especially during the Eastern Chin dynasty. This native tradition and the Ch'an "public cases" both have in abundance an element nearly nonexistent in Buddhist writings: humor. The rare exceptions are found in some of the *Perfection of Wisdom* (emptiness) texts. The ox is not a prominent theme in Buddhist scriptures but becomes very important in the Ch'an tradition. This trend culminates in the famous "ox-herding" (or more properly "ox-taming") pictures originating in eleventh- and twelfth-century China, which are claimed to portray the finding of the ox (the practitioner's original nature, truth, or self-nature).

Ch'an Buddhism fit into the same niche of society as did Taoism and served the same social function as an alternative to the Confucian bureaucratic career. It is not surprising that a fierce rivalry developed between the two.

BUDDHIST CULT PRACTICE IN CHINA

Buddhist cult practice took some unusual directions in China, influenced by indigenous and Taoist ideas and practices. Taoism and Buddhism both contained shamanistic elements in practice, though not necessarily in thought, and thus had a similarity in certain areas that made it easy for Buddhist practice to be adopted.

The search for magic power motivated both Taoists and Buddhists. The Buddhist texts first sought after by the Chinese dealt with meditation, because one of the side effects in meditation is the development of psychic or supernatural powers.

Devotionalism was less pronounced in Taoism than in Buddhism, and Buddhist devotional cults grew rapidly from the time of the fall of Han (220 C.E.) through the Three Kingdoms and Six Dynasties period (220–584). The most popular objects of devotion were Kuan-yin (who had not yet metamorphosed from male to female), Amitābha, and Maitreya. Kuan-yin saved one from dangers and disasters here on earth, and Amitābha and Maitreya welcomed one after death to a paradise and a heaven, respectively.

The Chinese Saṅgha, though recruiting members from the time of An Shih-kao, was hampered in its organization and development for well over a century for lack of complete Vinaya texts. Tao-an in particular was concerned with a sound monastic institution, and for lack of authoritative scripture he developed his own monastic code. It was not until the early fifth century that complete Vinaya texts were made available through the efforts of Kumārajīva (in the north) and Fa-hsien, Guṇavarman, and Saṅghavarman (in the south).

Members of the Chinese Saṅgha, as in Tibet, did not as a rule beg for their food. They were supported by income from monastic landholdings or by gifts from lay donors. Therefore, they had a choice in food, and Taoist practice influenced certain dietary notions found among Chinese Buddhists. The practice of eating only pine needles was borrowed directly from the Taoists. The pine-needle diet was frequently observed by individuals who offered themselves to the Three Treasures of Buddha, Dharma, and Saṅgha in a fire sacrifice. This practice is explicitly described and encouraged in the *Lotus Sūtra*, a Mahāyāna text that became enormously popular in China. Religious suicide by fiery death is, in the *Lotus*, a means of transmutation from earth to a Pure Land. The Taoists also accepted transformation by fire, though it is not certain whether any Taoists actually set fire to themselves, and thus the notion was not utterly foreign to the Chinese. The mastery of fire is a characteristic power of a shaman and is a concept and practice older than either Buddhism or Taoism. So far as is known, this suicide by fire was practiced only in China or areas within the Chinese cultural sphere such as Vietnam.

Another dietary practice was vegetarianism. The Vinaya does not forbid the eating of meat. It does forbid the killing of animals for the purpose of feeding the Saṅgha. If a monk in a Theravāda country finds meat in his begging bowl he must eat it. A Chinese monk, however, must not eat meat. Strict vegetarianism in a Buddhist context is a practice peculiar to Chinese Buddhism, and again, in addition to Buddhist sources such as the *Mahāyāna-parinirvāṇa Sūtra*, Taoist precedents can also be found.

During the third to fifth centuries, Buddhist cult practice was to a great degree eclectic, drawing from different sources and scriptures. Specialization in one particular practice was not apparent. Intellectuals were also devotionalists, and devotionalists were also meditators. The separation of meditation from other activities could well have been merely a side effect of the growth of monasteries in number, size, and, consequently, noise. By the late fifth century, individuals were seeking quiet meditation retreats to escape the clamor of the main monastery or convent.

The Chinese Buddhist Saṅgha for women was not established exactly according to Vinaya regulation until the middle of the fifth century, when a group of Sinhalese nuns arrived in China and made up the quorum of ten fully ordained nuns of ten years' standing that was necessary to impart the orthodox transmission and lineage. This Chinese lineage continues to the present. All other female lineages have ended.

The Saṅgha in China eventually developed a "family" and "clan" system parallel to the secular clans of blood lineages, with an elaborate hierarchy of relationships based upon tonsure, the first act required of one leaving the household life. The newly tonsured individual moved from secular to Buddhist family complete with "father," "uncles," "brothers," and "cousins" (or the female versions of the relationships).

Other practices attested to in early times and continuing to modern days are the Lantern Festival, which has no Indian counterpart; the Buddha's birthday; All Souls' Day; vegetarian feasts; image procession; and releasing living beings.

The Lantern Festival is the fifteenth day of the first lunar month. Buddhist festivals in general occur on days of the changing phases of the moon, while native Chinese festivals more often occur on months and days consisting of double numbers—as, for example, the fifth day of the fifth month. The legend is that, in order to determine whose doctrine was true and whose was false, three altars were set up: one for Buddhist scriptures, one for Taoist scriptures, and one for local gods to whom sacrifices were offered. These were set on fire, and only the Buddhist scriptures did not burn. The reigning emperor then ordered that on the day of the trial by fire, lamps were to be lit symbolizing the great light of Buddhism. This day also marks the conclusion of festivities celebrating the New Year.

The Buddha's birthday is celebrated the eighth day of the fourth month. It is also known as the day for bathing the Buddha in commemoration of the gods' bathing him immediately after his birth. A tiny image of the baby Buddha is placed in a basin of fragrant water, often with flower petals in it. The baby Buddha stands with his right arm raised up as he announces that he is born for the last time and is a Buddha. Worshippers ladle three dippers full of water over the image, reverence him three times, and again ladle three dippers of water. This is a very joyful event, as are most Buddhist festivals, and there is much talk, laughter, and general gaiety.

Vegetarian feasts are meals donated by a layperson for a specific purpose or vow. A certain number of monks or nuns are invited to a vegetarian meal for so many days in a row, often seven. Lay societies also hold communal vegetarian meals, which take on the aspect of a church potluck supper.

Image procession is simply the parading of an image of the Buddha or a bodhisattva either around a temple or monastery grounds or through the streets of a village or town. The occasion can be the Buddha's birthday or any other special day.

All Souls' Day is the fifteenth day of the seventh month, and it originated on the pattern of the *Ullambana Sūtra* (a text composed in China). It commemorates the arhant Maudgalyāyana's (Chinese, Mu-lien) search in hell for his mother. Lanterns are lit, placed on little boats, and set adrift on a river to float where they will. If there are no rivers, then lanterns are made for the one occasion and lit for everyone's enjoyment. The festival, while still a commemoration of the dead, is a happy get-together, and layfolk visit temples and monasteries, which are opened to the public for the occasion. This being the month when the ghosts of the dead return, a common autumnal theme in peasant societies, it is a dangerous time as well, so everyone must make the proper offerings to transfer merit to the revered ancestors. It is one festival in the year when Buddhists can express their cultural need to fulfill filial piety and to aid the dead in their proper journey, keeping them from becoming malevolent and thereby dangerous to the living. The dead are even preached the Dharma, to give them proper direction in their interlife sojourn.

Releasing living beings is an ancient practice, and monastic compounds in China soon had "releasing living beings ponds," in which the laity put fish, turtles, eels, and other aquatic creatures originally destined for the cooking pot. Birds were also released, the pious layman buying them from a vendor and then setting them free. This ritual of saving the lives of living beings did not, however, create in China an attitude of kindness to animals.

An interesting Buddhist cult practice in China is relic worship. The relic may be the famous finger bone of the Buddha presented to an emperor of the T'ang dynasty and scathingly ridiculed by Confucians at the court; or it may be an entire mummified body of an especially holy monk or nun. Many of these mummies still exist, the earliest with a known continuous history dating back to 713 C.E. This is the mummy of Hui-neng, the Sixth Patriarch, whose body did not decay after death. It was eventually covered with a lacquer coating and exists to this day in a special grotto built for it in south China. In the early biographies of monks and nuns, dating from the Later Han dynasty to the Liang dynasty (150–519), we frequently read that a certain monk or nun, known to be especially holy, did not decay after death. Eventually, it became part of a test of a revered monk's holiness. His body would be placed in a large jar and checked after a certain length of time. If it had not decayed, he was truly a saint. This curious practice was first made known to English-speaking people under the quaint name "the potted Chinese."

One notable feature of these public festivals is that, with the exception of a funeral service, all are very joyful, with the feeling of a neighborhood party—which, indeed, many are. The laughter and talking does not indicate lack of respect for the religion but rather its genuine integration into one's life and outlook.

A practice that developed somewhat later, especially during the Ming dynasty (1368–1644) was the keeping of merit books. Detailed lists of good and bad deeds were evaluated in terms of merits and demerits. These books helped the faithful to keep track of their moral and spiritual progress. These books were for layfollowers who more and more took the initiative as the early vigor of monastic institutions drained away after the T'ang.

THE GREAT T'ANG PERSECUTION OF 842–845

The most decisive catastrophe in the history of Chinese Buddhism was the proscription of 845. The external causes were rivalry between the Buddhists and the Taoists and factional strife at the imperial court between the administrators on the one hand and the eunuchs on the other. In addition, the Saṅgha had accumulated a disproportionate share of the nation's wealth; had taken out of use large quantities of bronze and iron to make images; and had acquired tax-exempt status for some 260,000 clerics, 100,000 temple serfs, and a host of lay employees. Taoists' malice and bureaucratic concern for the national economy sufficed to persuade the emperor, who, in 841, ordered that clerics who practiced magic, kept women, or otherwise violated the Discipline should be laicized and that money and real estate owned by monks or nuns should be confiscated by the government. This is no more than a devout Buddhist monarch would do to purify the Saṅgha. But in 845, the emperor, after first ordering a census of the clergy and its property, decreed the destruction of all except a few designated temples, confiscation and melting down of metal objects, return of monks and nuns to lay life, and confiscation of the Saṅgha's lands and serfs. This proscription, unlike the previous ones, was effective throughout all of China. But the emperor died in 846, probably poisoned by the longevity pills his Taoist mentors had been feeding him. The new emperor started by executing the Taoist leaders who had instigated the persecution, and he soon gave permission for the restitution of Buddhism.

Many sects perished entirely during this short, severe persecution. Ch'an suffered like the other sects, but it survived because it was less dependent on libraries, images, and the pomp and circumstance of temple cult. Pure Land was the only other sect to survive, embraced as it was by laymen from all levels of society. Ennin, a Japanese Buddhist monk who lived in China from 838 to 847, has given us a lively, entertaining account of the years of the persecution in his diary. It is a unique, and therefore extraordinarily important, description of T'ang China as seen by a foreigner (see bibliography, p. 248).

Hui-yüan had defended the autonomy of the Saṅgha against the state, but this policy was not generally tolerated. Religions exist in China at the pleasure of a state that does not admit the principle of being "in the world" but not "of it." According to custom and decree, it was the right of the state to regulate and control any aspect of the life of its citizens, including religious organizations. Buddhism never developed a proper organization for defending itself; its structure was congregational rather than papal. The state manipulated Buddhism when expedient, as for example it used Shen-hui, the eighth-century disciple of Hui-neng, the Sixth Patriarch, to drum up money and support for the loyalist effort during the An Lu-shan rebellion. Often in the succeeding centuries certificates of ordination were sold by the state to raise money. When Buddhism competed too strongly and well with the state for money and labor, it did not hesitate to "sift and winnow" the Saṅgha, confiscating its wealth; defrocking the monks and nuns, thereby returning them to useful (income- and tax-producing) labor; and confiscating land that the Saṅgha held tax-free. This pattern of tolerance and persecution persisted up to the present regime in China, and there are indications that it is continuing.

The great T'ang persecution destroyed the economic base of the Saṅgha. Those monasteries whose income base was coveted by the state were cut off with no support. Monks and nuns were sent away, often to a fate of wandering and starvation. The schools of the intellect—as T'ien-t'ai, Hua-yen, and Fa-hsiang might be described—were destroyed. Pure Land, being all-pervasive and not tied to monasteries and libraries, survived. Ch'an persisted because of a greater degree of freedom from monastic paraphernalia but also because of geographical fortune. The surviving houses of Ch'an were located in remoter areas controlled by overlords of considerable autonomy, who were strong enough to ignore the edicts of the emperor (Hupeh, Kiangsu). The urban Ch'an houses died out. Of the eight known Ch'an sectarian lines, only two survived.

After this persecution, Buddhism in China never again regained its former glory and prestige. A revivified Confuciansim, nurtured in part by Buddhist thought, became the dominant intellectual and social force. Taoism too suffered losses in the face of Neo-Confucianism, but Taoism had the advantage of being a native tradition and frequently acted as a complement to Confucianism.

Buddhism was never fully accepted by all parts of Chinese society, and from the first to the last there were critics who used the same arguments over and over: Buddhism was unfilial, it was foreign, it was superstitious, it took wealth away from the state, it was a haven for criminals and ne'er-do-wells, and it was parasitic—taking wealth but creating none. The Buddhists had indeed given the Chinese elements lacking in early Confucianism, especially in the realm of metaphysics. Confucianism appropriated these, and Buddhism lost out. The Confucians controlled the educational system, and the Buddhists did not develop any of their own. A Confucian education underlay the Buddhist learning of a great number of Buddhist monks. Biography after biography relates that such and such a monk was educated in the (Confucian) Classics and the Sūtras.

After the persecution Buddhism ceased to be either an intellectual matrix or an intellectual threat. The Ch'an school developed its own distinctive style and literature, the models for which are to be found in native Chinese literary traditions rather than in Buddhist ones. The Pure Land school had become the religion of the masses, and therefore the elite classes wanted no part of it. Bright, talented men strove to enter the bureaucracy, whose examination system was based on the Confucian classics.

Nevertheless, Buddhism had permanently altered the course of Chinese development. In the arts, Buddhism stimulated sculpture to a high degree of craftsmanship and sophistication. The extraordinary wall paintings in the caves of Tun-huang and other areas of far northwest China date back to the late Six Dynasties (sixth century) and T'ang. Buddhism not only stimulated the art of printing but also contributed to new developments in Chinese literary forms. Buddhist medical missionaries to China brought botanicals and new therapeutic techniques. Buddhists from China carried Chinese civilization to Japan, and over the centuries many Japanese traveled to China in search of the Dharma, just as Chinese had gone to Central Asia and India.

The decline of Buddhism in China cannot be attributed solely to the great persecution. A regenerated Confucianism was already asserting itself more and more. Further, there were no more fresh developments of Buddhism in India and no more missionaries. The land route to India through Central Asia had been closed by the Muslim invasions. Without fresh foreign impetus, the Chinese Saṅgha seemed little able to maintain its former momentum. After the T'ang there were no more major translations made and no more major pilgrimages abroad.

FROM SUNG TO THE PRESENT

The story of Chinese Buddhism from 900 to 1900 is one of a golden later summer (900–1300), an Indian summer in the fifteenth century under the early Ming dynasty, and a fall shading into winter thereafter. No generation was without eminent monks, and yet the place of Buddhism in national life declined under government restrictions on entrance to the monastic orders, curtailment of monasteries' activities, and relentless anti-Buddhist propaganda from the Neo-Confucians, who controlled the education system and the imperial examinations.

The Ch'an school, so vibrantly alive during the T'ang (618–907), began to fossilize during the Sung (960–1279). The spontaneous, witty interviews between master and disciple, the kung-an, became set texts for later generations. Ch'an began to look back to a golden age, its creativity drying up in the process. Pure Land was more and more an affair of the masses. It was Pure Land, not Ch'an, that inspired the Buddhist revival in the Ming dynasty (1368–1644) under the leadership of a monk, Chu-hung (1535–1615). Two new features developed: (1) greatly increased lay participation in religious activities such as printing and distributing texts, and (2) harmonizing of the two schools of Pure Land and Ch'an into one system. Ch'an monks recited Buddha's name, and Pure Land adherents treated such recitation as a kung-an. This syncretism became a permanent feature of later Chinese Buddhism.

The Chinese Buddhist Canon was first printed in the Sung dynasty, a monumental enterprise requiring the cutting of one hundred thirty thousand wood blocks and eleven years for completion. Not only was the Buddhist Canon being reproduced at state expense, it was also thereby closed, another mark of Chinese Buddhist senescence. There were many more state-sponsored printings of the Canon, plus the printing and circulation of individual texts by pious individuals or groups.

The Ming dynasty activities were a forerunner of a modest revival begun in the late nineteenth century, stimulated initially by the need to rebuild monasteries and reprint scriptures destroyed in central China during the T'ai-p'ing rebellion (1850–1864). The rebels, who fervently professed a kind of Christianity, looted and burned most of the great monasteries in the areas they occupied. The shock stimulated both monks and laity. Soon scripture-printing societies and study clubs were active. Some young monks who acquired modern ideas through lay-inititated schools became revolutionaries and participated in the overthrow of the Manchu dynasty in 1911. However, these radicals were not approved of by the majority of the Saṅgha, who believed that a monk should stay out of politics and should study the scriptures rather than modern secular subjects.

The most famous of these radicals was the modernist monk T'ai-hsü (1890–1947). He was never accepted by the abbots of the great Ch'an monasteries of central and south China, who held the real power in the Saṅgha and who were carrying out extensive revitalization of their institutions along traditional lines. But he set up schools; introduced Western-style classroom instruction; taught secular subjects and foreign languages, including Tibetan and Pali; and revived the study of the scholastic treatises, especially of the Fa-hsiang school. T'ai-hsü and his followers opened up relations with coreligionists abroad and promoted the idea of a world fellowship of Buddhists. They announced an ambitious program of education, preaching, welfare, and economic development work, and attempted to implement it insofar as their resources and the troubled state of the country allowed.

The Nationalist regime in Mainland China fluctuated between mild hostility and mild support for Buddhism, but by and large it allowed proponents of the Dharma a freedom they had not had during two and a half centuries of Manchu rule, when all private associations were under suspicion of treason. When the Communists took over the mainland in 1949, they were committed to wiping out all religion as soon as it could be done expediently. First, they declared that the clergy were parasites on society. Then, in 1951, they confiscated the land holdings of the monasteries and so deprived the monks and nuns of the means to carry on religious activities. Young monks and nuns were returned to lay status, and the older clerics were put to work farming, weaving, running vegetarian restaurants, or teaching school. They were subjected to brainwashing to cleanse their minds of non-Marxist ideas. Then, in 1953, a Chinese Buddhist Association was organized so that the government could supervise and manipulate the still sizable Buddhist community and so that China could reap the diplomatic advantages of representation at international Buddhist gatherings. Famous and beautiful old temples were maintained at government expense, Buddhist art works were safeguarded, and sites such as the Yün-kang caves were designated national treasures. Then, when the Great Cultural Revolution got under way, Red Guards proceeded to destroy Buddhist buildings and monuments along with other reminders of China's past. The state of Buddhism in China in the 1980s is still precarious. Some Buddhist landmarks destroyed by the excesses of the Red Guard are being reconstructed. Many are left in ruins. Visitors to China are permitted to photograph "monks" performing services in selected temples. Perhaps once again the state sees a political use for Buddhism with regard to its policies concerning Buddhist countries. The epitaph for Buddhism in China has yet to be written.

In 1930, there were said to be 738,000 monks and nuns and 267,000 Buddhist temples in China. This was by far the largest clergy in China, or in any national church in the world. The majority did not live in strictly run monasteries, but at least 50,000 did. There was much idleness and laxity, but also much diligence and rigor. Buddhism was not a prominent force in national life, but insofar as Republican China was religious, it was more Buddhist than anything else.

Many monks have fled from China to Hong Kong and Taiwan, where Buddhist associations operate freely and show a certain amount of vitality. Both as a popular religion and as a monastic vocation, Buddhism on Taiwan has recently entered a period of genuine renewal. In addition, Buddhism has some following among overseas Chinese communities in Malaysia, Singapore, the Philippines, and North America.

VIETNAM

Buddhism came to the area of Vietnam from both Chinese and Indian spheres of influence, but it was the Chinese Mahāyāna forms that finally prevailed. Chinese civilization was a major force in shaping Vietnamese development, with secondary influences coming from the Indianized states of Funan, Campā, and the Khmers.

Indian colonists helped found Campā on the east coast in the late second century C.E., and under them Buddhism came to the area, along with economic and cultural ties with India. Judging by a bronze Buddha image in a south Indian style, Theravāda Buddhism was probably present by the third century. In the later centuries, Mahāyāna and Tantric monks came. By the ninth century, Buddhism was receiving royal patronage, but the dynasty probably supported Hindu Śaivism as well, creating a syncretistic Buddho-Śaivism similar to that of Cambodia. Mahāyāna continued in Campā up until the fifteenth century, when Annamites, formerly settled in Tonkin, invaded, bringing with them Chinese forms of Buddhism more characteristic of the north. These eventually replaced earlier forms, except for Theravāda survivals on the Cambodian border.

In the north, successive Chinese invasions led to long centuries of Chinese domination after the first century B.C.E. The Chinese brought their state Confucianism and imposed their culture, stressing Taoist and Confucian learning. Nevertheless, Chinese Buddhists did begin coming to the area in the second century C.E. In following centuries other missionaries arrived by sea from India and overland through China from as far away as Central Asia. Hīnayāna and Mahāyāna were both represented. Due to the proximity of China, Ch'an (Vietnamese, *Thiền*) became dominant. It was introduced by the famous Indian meditation master Vinītaruci at the end of the sixth century.

Vinītaruci came to Vietnam in 580 after a brief sojourn in China, where he supposedly received the seal of approval from the Third Patriarch, Seng-Ts'an, and settled in Ha-Dong Province in northern Vietnam. He translated Buddhist texts into Chinese characters, the only script used in Vietnam until the Trần dynasty (1275–1400), when a system called *chu-nom*, similar in principle to Egyptian demotic, was developed for popular literature. Vinītaruci's lineage flourished until the thirteenth century, after which it fades from historical records. The Venerable Vạn-hạnh (died 1018) of the twelfth generation of the lineage was especially revered, and Vạn-hạnh University, founded in Saigon in 1964, was named after this illustrious monk. The seventeenth generation of this lineage counts a nun as one of the twenty-eight recorded patriarchs. Bhikṣuṇī Diệu-nhân (died 1115) is perhaps unique in the annals of Buddhism as the lone female patriarch.

A second school of Thiền (Ch'an) in Vietnam was brought by Vô-Ngôn-thông, a Chinese who received enlightenment under Pai-chang (see p. 181). He later traveled to northern Vietnam, where he eventually attracted disciples, establishing a lineage that flourished for fifteen generations. The fifteenth patriarch (in the seventh generation) was a king, and the fortieth patriarch in the lineage was a layman.

These two sects were established before the great persecution in China (842–845). The third is another Chinese import, first propagated in Vietnam by King Ly-thanh-ton (ruled 1054–1072), a disciple of Ts'ao-t'ang (Thao-Duong). He, in turn, was a disciple of Hsüeh-t'ou, whose lineage goes back to the two surviving Chinese Ch'an houses (see p. 181). The list of eighteen patriarchs includes princes, kings, and laymen. Pure Land practices became a part of the Thiền tradition, and deliberate syncretism was a policy of Thao-Duong, followed by his disciple King Ly-thanh-ton.

Chinese emperors sent Buddha-relics to be enshrined in stūpas, and temples and shrines were constructed in the countryside. Amitism (Pure Land) came to dominate village-level Buddhism, while monastic institutitons remained Thiền. The split continued after the Chinese rule of Vietnam ended in 939, and Buddhism in Vietnam became more and more an expression of national feeling and culture. The Truc-lam sect was founded by a Vietnamese king, Tran-nhan-ton (1258–1308). This sect deliberately brought together Buddhism, Taoism, and Confucianism, attempting to establish a Buddhism that would be effective in the personal, social, and political realms. From this time until the eighteenth century Thiền continued to be a significant part of the developing Vietnamese culture, and there was much less of the attitude of withdrawing from worldly affairs than there was among Chinese Ch'an monks and schools.

Two new sects arose in the eighteenth century, one founded by a Chinese and one by a Vietnamese, and both related to the Lin-ch'i (Japanese, Rinzai) sect. This influx revitalized Vietnamese Buddhism and produced more masters, whose eminence often lay not only in religious excellence but also in literary and artistic ability.

In the centuries after the Ly (1010–1225) and Tran (1225–1400) dynasties, during which Buddhism reached an apogee of influence and power, the Vietnamese Buddhist clergy suffered first under Confucian-trained government administrators and then under the colonialism of the French, preceded by and then moving hand-in-hand with Roman Catholic missionaries. The Vietnamese Catholics have always found themselves caught in the middle. The French colonial government used them in administration, and often Vietnamese royalty and Buddhist clergy made attempts to overcome French rule. They did not succeed. French colonialism brought Western-style education into Vietnam, and this gradually eliminated the use of Confucian classics as the basis for political position.

Buddhism underwent a revival in the 1930s, inspired partly by the Chinese Buddhist revival, and in 1951 an all-Vietnam Buddhist Association was formed. It was this unified Buddhist Church that founded Vạn-hạnh University in 1964, established publishing houses, and tried many endeavors in social services that its leaders were, by previous experience and training, not fully equipped to carry out. A lack of funds also hindered their efforts, and the succession of regimes in South Vietnam after 1954 systematically worked to thwart Buddhist leadership. The Americans did not credit Buddhist leaders, for fear that they would not adhere to "democratic" principles to which the basically Roman Catholic South Vietnamese regimes gave lip service. The Communists used Buddhists when necessary and otherwise sought to destroy Buddhist institutions and the people's allegience to the faith. The mixture of religion and politics in Vietnam has a long history, and Buddhism was a major factor in the shaping of Vietnamese culture. Since 1975, the Buddhist clergy has been severely persecuted, their "crime" being that they advocate peace, nonviolence, harmony, and tolerance. As our generation has seen the death of Buddhism in other countries, we may also see its death in Vietnam.

KOREA

The earliest Korean religion was shamanism, which survives today as a cult of spirits. As early as the first century B.C.E., Chinese colonies were established in the north in the area that became the kingdom of Koguryŏ, one of the Three Kingdoms of early Korean history. The most famous of these outposts of Chinese civilization was at Lo-lang, now the site of the capital of North Korea, P'yong-yang. According to tradition, Buddhism was brought to this northernmost Korean kingdom in 372 C.E. by the Chinese monk Shun-tao (Korean, Sundo). A short time later a Serindian (Central Asian) monk took the teaching to the kingdom of Paekche in the southwest, which tended to maintain relations with southern rather than northern China. The third kingdom, Silla, less influenced by China at first, only gradually received Chinese ideas in rule and administration. By the beginning of the sixth century, however, Buddhism was accepted as the officially favored religion. In the sixth century it was well enough established in the Korean peninsula that emissaries from Paekche took Buddhist statues and texts to Japan, officially introducing the Dharma there.

In the mid-seventh century, after a series of military maneuvers tying in with the Chinese unification of the Sui dynasty (589–618), the kingdom of Silla emerged as the sole ruler of the former Three Kingdoms. Silla consciously modelled itself after the early T'ang (618–907) government and institutions, and this meant the introduction of Confucianism, closely associated as it was with the bureaucratic system.

From the time of these beginnings of Buddhism in Korea, its fate hinged on association with politics and the aristocracy. For the latter, Buddhism provided support for autocratic monarchy, the common people being most attracted to the Pure Land teachings of bliss in the next world, while the lower-level aristocrats followed Confucianism.

Many Korean monks traveled to China to study the Law and to bring back scripture. A few even went on to India. During the eighth and ninth centuries after the Silla unification, Buddhism became a major institution, producing great works of art and fine temples. Ch'an (Korean, *Sŏn*) was introduced from China, becoming the most popular form of monastic Buddhism. The religion held sway in splendid ascendency until its peak in the eleventh century under the Koryŏ dynasty (918–1392). In the early tenth century the Koreans first printed the Buddhist Canon. From the late tenth through the fourteenth centuries Buddhism flourished, with government patronage resulting in new monasteries and works of art. Aristocrats followed both Buddhism and Confucianism, the former for its personal and spiritual aspects, the latter for its political and ethical content. The government built new institutions for both. In the twelfth century Buddhism was suppressed by bureaucratic forces not satisfied with it or its internal corruption, turning instead to Neo-Confucianism. The Buddhist Canon was printed for the second time in the thirteenth century. The wood-blocks for this printing are still preserved, and a new printing is gradually being made from them. These blocks are also the foundation for the Japanese Taishō edition of the Chinese Canon, printed in the late 1920s.

The foundation of the Yi dynasty (1392–1910) coincided with the early Ming dynasty in China (1368–1644), noted for its rigid adherence to orthodox Confucianism as interpreted by the Chinese Confucian scholar Chu Hsi (1130–1200). Under the Yi dynasty, after being subjected to an erratic policy up to the mid-sixteenth century, Buddhism was severely suppressed, reducing the number of sects and monasteries, and state support for Buddhism ended, instead going to Confucian developments. By the nineteenth century, Buddhism, once the state religion of Korea, was at a low point in its history. The Sŏn, or meditation, school dominated what was left of the Saṅgha there, following ancient Korean and Chinese forms of monastic practice.

The policy of severe restriction by the government, however, began to ease near the end of the last century. In 1895, monks were no longer banned from the capital. With the advent of Japanese control, Korean Buddhism began to enjoy a renewal, but Japanese direction often went against Korean practice. The Japanese imported their own forms of Buddhism, eventually causing a split in the Korean Saṅgha between those who followed the more traditional Korean practice of not allowing monks to marry and those who, like the Japanese, accepted married priests. Japanese policy in the decades to follow did not favor the Korean monks who were more nationalistic. By 1935 however, a single sect united Buddhists in Korea.

Following World War II and the end of Japanese control, the Korean Saṅgha was threatened with a serious loss of income because of land reform. In the south, government support restored a viable financial base to the monasteries, but in the north the reform probably ended the presence of Buddhism there.

South Korean Buddhism was still disturbed by dissension over the problem of married monks, though the issue was somewhat resolved in 1962. Some progress has been made by virtue of a national organization and the leadership of two councils. Buddhists have become active recently in education, youth groups, and lay organizations. Today, the Buddhist Canon is being fully translated into modern Korean, and Buddhism is beginning to take a new role in the life of the country.

Two Americans in Japan encounter a group of traveling Korean nuns.

JAPAN

The Buddhism of Korea and Vietnam is Chinese in its origin, sects, doctrines, and institutions. To this day, Korean and Vietnamese monks read the scriptures in Chinese. The religion has taken on a pronounced national coloring in each of these countries and has played an interesting part in their histories, but it has departed from Chinese models no more than Hungarian Presbyterianism and American Lutheranism have deviated from the original churches of Calvin and Luther.

Japanese Buddhism, too, follows its Chinese parent, using the older culture's language for its Canon and drawing from it for its models and inspiration, as well as its sectarian divisions. Nevertheless, its institutions and social character differ as much from those of Chinese Buddhism as Japanese society differs from Chinese.

Between 550 and 600, various Korean kings sent Buddha images and Sūtras to the Japanese imperial court. Some Korean monks were already resident in Japan, and the first Japanese nuns and monks were ordained in this period. The first Korean gifts were accompanied by a memorial extolling Buddhism as productive of merit and wisdom. The Japanese got the idea that worshipping these foreign deities would bring good luck to the nation and at first judged the new religion entirely on short-range consequences; when a plague broke out, the Buddha image was dumped into a moat, and the first temple was razed. When another plague broke out later, images were again thrown into the moat and the nuns were defrocked. When the plague still did not stop, the emperor agreed to permit the Buddhist cult to be practiced freely.

Japan was in the process of consolidating a centralized monarchy out of a federation of tribes when Buddhism arrived, bearing the high culture of China and motivated to convert and civilize. Confucians did not like to go abroad and teach among "barbarians," so in Japan the Buddhists had the field to themselves for centuries. Desire for mundane fortune and cultural prestige made the Japanese hospitable to the Dharma, and from the first it was accepted that religion is primarily an organ of national life and only secondarily a ministration to the individual's needs. Buddhist missionaries were also Chinese, which meant that they brought with them a number of Chinese values; these, along with Buddhism, became part of the fabric of Japanese life.

During the seventh century, under a series of devout emperors, Buddhism was developed as part of the state apparatus. Temples were founded, monks ordained, and public ceremonies sponsored, all for the well-being of the nation. Tradition says that Prince Shōtuku (574–622) wrote the first "constitution" of Japan under Buddhist inspiration and personally lectured on the Sūtras. He is called the founder of Japanese Buddhism. Four Chinese sectarian systems were imported. In 625, a Korean who had studied under Chi-tsang introduced the study of the San-lun (Japanese, Sanron) and the Hīnayāna Ch'eng-shih (Jōjitsu) treatise. In 658, two Japanese monks who had studied under Hsüan-tsang introduced the study of Vasubandhu's *Abhidharmakośa (Kusha)*. A Japanese monk went to China in 653, studied the Fa-hsiang (Hossō) teaching under Hsüan-tsang for over ten years, then returned and introduced it to Japan. Other Koreans as well as Japanese returned from abroad and reinforced the initial transmissions. Kusha, Jōjitsu, and Sanron were never more than curriculum subjects, but Hossō became a wealthy ecclesiastical corporation and has maintained an institutional existence to the present day. In 1948, it had about eighty temples and a thousand clerics. These scholastic treatises must have puzzled early Japanese students, whom we can imagine reading them with the same attitude of knowledge-is-good-for-you-especially-if-it-hurts with which their modern compatriots often tackle Hegel, Heidegger, and Tillich.

In the eighth century, when the capital was fixed at Nara, the Hua-yen (Kegon) sect was introduced by several teachers—Korean, Chinese, and Indian—and rapidly acquired great influence. The Hua-yen world view was adapted to political ideology by equating Vairocana with the emperor and the fourth Dharma-realm, that of phenomena not impeding one another, with Japanese society. The implicit metaphor of the spider and her web fits to perfection the society that the Japanese have created over the intervening centuries, and a study of Kegon renders more intelligible the peculiar Japanese blend of individualism and collectivism. Abstract philosophy was beyond the grasp of Nara intellectuals, but Kegon presented a concrete world vision giving spiritual elevation and political orientation.

In 752, a colossal bronze image of Vairocana was dedicated at the Tōdaiji (Eastern Great Temple) in Nara, where two years later the Chinese Vinaya master Ganjin established an ordination center. The Japanese government permitted ordinations only at approved centers, which were kept few, and so it maintained some control over the Saṅgha. This system, though, gave certain sects a monopoly, enhanced their power, and led to a typically hierarchical, sectarian structure. In such an arrangement the branch temples were ritually dependent on the head temple to provide properly ordained monks, since only it could perform legitimate ordinations. On the other hand, the local temples sent money or goods to the head temple. If the latter had insufficient income of its own, then it depended on the client temples for its living. The Great Buddha is still in Nara, but his network has been small for many centuries. The Kegon sect now counts about 125 temples and 500 clerics.

Buddhism strongly influenced Japanese social customs and material culture during the Nara period (710–784 C.E.). Arts and crafts—architecture, sculpture, painting, carpentry, metal-casting, calligraphy, and papermaking—were stimulated to bigger and better production by the demand for cult articles. Artisans were brought from China and Korea, and Japanese craftsmen were trained. Monks also introduced the Chinese mundane sciences and wizardry: calendar making, astronomy, geomancy, and magic. Buddhist ritual permeated court observances. The public bath and cremation, two of the most notable features of Japanese life, were introduced under Buddhist influence at this time. Monks served as scribes and clerks, providing the literate skills necessary for the Chinese-style administration that the imperial regime was trying to institute. They also acted as engineers in building roads, bridges, dikes, and irrigation systems. Wandering monks explored distant parts of the country and drew the first Japanese maps.

During this period, the imperial authority was virtually the only large entrepreneur in the country that did not yet have either an independent landed aristocracy or a sizable merchant community. As part of the colonization process, the emperor ordered each province to build a seven-storied pagoda, a monastery for twenty monks, and a convent for ten nuns. Copies of the *Golden Radiance Sūtra* were distributed to each province. Before this the monks and court officials who could understand the scriptures in Chinese were a tiny elite. The copying and distribution of Sūtras did much to spread a knowledge of Chinese, even though the immediate aim was to create talismans rather than to acquire knowledge.

The capital was moved to Heian (Kyōto) in 794 in order to rusticate the corrupt and politically meddlesome Nara monks, one of whom, Dōkyō, was accused of plotting to usurp the imperial throne. Six years earlier, in 788, a young monk named Saichō (767–822) had built a little temple on Mount Hiei, northeast of Kyōto. He soon received the patronage of the emperor, who sent him in 804 to study in China. During his year there, he studied primarily T'ien-t'ai but also other schools: Ch'an, Vinaya, and especially the then popular Tantric Buddhism. Upon returning he combined these into a single system, Tendai. Thus, Japanese Tendai is broader in scope than the original Chinese T'ien-t'ai, containing two components, one exoteric and the other Tantric. Saichō kept his monks in seclusion on Mount Hiei while they underwent a twelve-year period of study and meditation. Some of his graduates stayed on the mountain, while others left to serve the state as scribes, engineers, and teachers. Saichō tried hard to get an ordination center established on Mount Hiei; but, due to the opposition of the Nara clerics, the center was only authorized by 827, five years after his death. He received the posthumous title Dengyō Daishi ("Great Master Who Transmitted the Teaching").

Mount Hiei flourished. In its heyday there were three thousand buildings in the temple complex and thirty thousand monks. Initially the court asserted its superiority to the mountain, but eventually the monasteries took to enforcing their demands on the government by mass demonstrations in the streets of the capital and kept armed retainers to lend force to their claims. Even when Mount Hiei became worldly, thought, art, scholarship, and devotion continued to flourish there. The founders of all the new sects of the twelfth and thirteenth centuries were Tendai monks, which testifies to the vitality of Saichō's lotus even after it had begun to rot.

Another Buddhist school that was organized in the early Heian period was *Shingon*. It was founded by a well-educated man, Kūkai. Whereas Saichō was a good monk and a fine teacher, Kūkai (774–835) was a genius. Born a Nara aristocrat, he studied Buddhism, Confucianism, and Taoism during his teens. He sailed for China in 804 and there studied the Chen-yen (Japanese Shingon) sect, a Tantric system introduced to China about 720. Chen-yen ("Truth Word") translates mantra. The sect's practices include not only mantras, but initiations, ritual gestures, maṇḍalas, and contemplations as well. Kūkai returned to Japan in 806 and was granted many honors by the emperor. In 816, he founded a monastery on Mount Kōya, and it eventually became the headquarters of the Shingon sect. Brilliant disciples flocked to take initiation from Kūkai. He wrote prolifically and systematized the doctrines that he had received from his teacher in China. He accorded a high place to the arts and so furthered the aestheticism that distinguishes Japanese Buddhism and general culture. Famous as a calligrapher, he set up a popular school and is said to have invented the cursive syllabary (*hiragana*) of forty-seven signs in which, alone or mixed with Chinese characters, Japanese is written. Kūkai died in 835 on Mount Kōya, where he lies buried. There is a popular belief that he is merely in samādhi and will rise up again when Maitreya returns. His posthumous title is Kōbō Daishi ("Great Master Who Propagated the Dharma").

Shingon became even more popular than Tendai. Mount Kōya is said to have had 990 temples in its heyday. Shingon teaching was received even on Mount Hiei, which rivaled and soon bested Mount Kōya as an esoteric center. By the eleventh century, superstitions and heresies had contaminated Shingon and brought esotericism into disrepute, thus setting the stage for the resolutely exoteric popular sects of the Kamakura period (1192–1338).

By the end of the Heian period, in the twelfth century, Tendai was coming apart at the seams. Saichō had drawn all the Chinese systems

Kūkai, shown on a formal seat with a vajra in his right hand and a rosary for counting mantra recitations in his left.

into a catholic synthesis, and his successors reached out to encompass even Japan's native Shintō by identifying its deities with figures in the Buddhist pantheon. But being so all-sided consumed a lot of energy and slowed the student's progress. So earnest monks desiring realization in this life, or at least assurance of rebirth in Sukhāvatī, took to exclusive pursuit of one or another path. Thus, Japan in the twelfth and thirteenth centuries underwent the same sort of fission into sects that China had in the sixth and seventh.

The chief social cause for the rise of new sects about 1200 was the shift in balance of power between the capital and the provinces, with a new class of provincial small landowners and samurai claiming their share at court and on the battlefield. They were inclined to support their local temples but were reluctant to give lavishly to the head temples in the distant capital area. Moreover, the new samurai class provided an effective link between the old aristocracy and the peasantry. For the first time the higher culture was diffused to the lower classes throughout the country, and some aristocrats, including the founders of most of the new sects, took the task of popularization seriously.

The cult of Amida was encompassed in the Tendai synthesis. Very early, though, a few Tendai monks became evangelists of the Pure Land teaching exclusively. One of these, Kūya (903–972), danced in the streets singing simple Japanese hymns about Amida, organized self-help projects among the common people, and even spread the Amidist gospel among the Ainu. Another Tendai monk, Ryōnin (1072–1132), similarly spread the practice of *Nembutsu* (nien-fo) in song and attracted followers in court and countryside. Yet a third, the learned Genshin (942–1017), wrote an enormously influential treatise, *The Compendium on Rebirth*. He favored the Nembutsu way, not because he considered other paths wrong but because it was open to all, whether saint or sinner, monk or layman, man or woman, emperor or peasant.

Hōnen (1133–1212), founder of the Jōdo-shū (Pure Land sect), might have followed the same course as Genshin within the Tendai fold if hostile reactionaries had not forced him and his followers into secession. An orphan, he went forth at fifteen and during the next decade, spent on Mount Hiei, he excelled in the wide erudition esteemed by Tendai. Yet he was distressed that he and the people of his age were not able to reach enlightenment or become free from their sins. When he was forty-three, he became convinced through studying Shan-tao and Genshin that only complete reliance on Amida would save him. He wrote a treatise setting forth his faith, but when it was published, monks from Mount Hiei seized and burned all available copies and the printing blocks. Hōnen continued to teach his message humbly and without ostentation and converted an emperor, a regent, noblemen and ladies, monks and commoners. Old-line monks intrigued against him until, in 1206, when he was seventy-four, they had him exiled to a remote area from which he was allowed to return only a year before his death. The Jōdu-shū lineage remains strong and active today, but not as much as the school founded by Shinran.

Shinran (1173–1262), founder of Jōdo-shin-shū (the True Pure Land sect), was one of Hōnen's disciples exiled when his master was. His early career resembles Hōnen's. His parents died while he was a child. He went to Mount Hiei as a novice and studied there for twenty years, gradually despairing of finding a passable way through the jungle of scholasticism and syncretisms. At twenty-nine, he left Mount Hiei and the Tendai teachings to follow Hōnen. Kwannon (Avalokiteśvara) appeared to him in a dream and told him to marry. With Hōnen's approval, he married a young noblewoman, demonstrating that monasticism was not necessary to salvation and showing by example that the family should be the center of religious life. Shinran described himself as "neither a monk nor a layman," which aptly categorizes the married clergy of the sect he founded. They continued to live in temples and perform religious services, but they led a family life and expected the eldest son to take over the temple from his father. But Shin-shū (the shortened form of Jōdo-shin-shū) has not proclaimed the household life as an arena in which the great bodhisattva surpasses monks in wisdom and holiness. Shinran considered himself a sinner and thought of his marriage as an admission of weakness, a recognition that he could not save himself through his own power but must depend on Amida's grace.

Shinran was exiled to the northern province of Echigo, where he propagated the Nembutsu among the common people. Although he was soon pardoned, because Hōnen was dead he did not return to Kyōto but traveled through the towns and villages of east Japan (Kantō), spread the teaching, and founded temples. During this period he composed his chief work, *Teaching, Practice, Faith and Attainment*, which was published in 1224. In 1235, he returned to Kyōto and lived quietly there until his death.

Shinran interpreted, elaborated, and in some ways modified Hōnen's teaching. Hōnen had eliminated the element of meditation and merit-gathering from the Nembutsu in order to deepen one's devotion. Shinran stressed that Nembutsu was basically a response to the power of Amida, and thus he held that a single sincere invocation suffices for salvation. Subsequent repetitions are just expressions of gratitude to Amida for assured salvation. The power to exercise faith, says Shinran, is a gift from Amida and not an intrinsic possession of man.

The last point is the general Mahāyāna idea that religious initiative is possible only because the germ of Buddhahood is innate to living beings and is irradiated by the grace of the Buddhas. The radical feature of Shinran's teachings is his utter rejection of the cult of merit and his apprehension lest the deliberate pursuit of virtue or wisdom either prevent faith or impair one's gratitude to Amida.

Shinran was not a saint in the usual Buddhist sense. He did not keep an austere regimen, was not celibate, did not practice meditation, did not exercise superknowledges, and used his great erudition only to reinforce the simple Nembutsu faith that he propagated. Nevertheless, he is revered by his followers with as much fervor and more sentiment than Tantra accords its great preceptors or Zen its famous masters. He was a good and humble man, compassionate and sentimental, sincere in his words and candid about his feelings. Though an aristocrat by birth, he made common cause with the lower classes, shared their way of life, and forewent the display of upper-class learning.

At Shinran's death there was no Jōdo-shin sect because he had never tried to organize one. He left behind many loose associations of followers, whom his blood descendants organized into a sect. Rennyo (1415–1499) defined the religious position of the school more clearly and shaped its adherents into a feudal domain with armies and territorial control. They fortified their temples and in the sixteenth century they withstood Nobunaga's siege of their temple in Ōsaka for ten years before surrendering, only to be slaughtered by the perfidious Shōgun.

Another Buddhist sect was founded by Nichiren (1222–1282), who also studied at Mount Hiei but became dissatisfied with traditional Buddhist methods. Nichiren was the son of a fisherman. While still a boy he entered a local monastery, and at twenty he was studying on Mount Hiei. Like Hōnen and Shinran, he was appalled at the corruption around him and frustrated with a teaching that offered all paths to all men yet rendered none of them effective. His solution, though, was to return to the root of Chih-i's and Saichō's teaching, to the *Lotus Sūtra*. He left Mount Hiei after ten years and went back to his native district. In 1253, he launched his campaign to conquer Japan with the pure *Lotus* gospel. He began chanting "Namu myō-hō-ren-ge-kyō" ("Salutation to the *Lotus Sūtra*"), which formula he held to be a sufficient means of salvation. Anyone who pronounced it would attain Buddhahood, acquire moral virtue, and become on this earth an embodiment of paradise. Nichiren identified himself as an incarnation of the Bodhisattva Superb Conduct, a leader of the bodhisattva hosts whom Śākyamuni summoned out of the earth and commanded to worship the *Lotus Sūtra*. He was convinced that it was his mission to save the Japanese nation from social and political disorders that he viewed as the consequences of wrong religion. He condemned Shingon because it worshipped Vairocana and neglected Śākyamuni. Amidism he castigated for worshipping Amida rather than Śākyamuni. His criticism of Zen was that it revered only the historical Śākyamuni and not the eternal Buddha of the *Lotus Sūtra*. When he went to Kamakura (the seat of the Shōgun's government) and broadcast his virulent denunciations of all other sects, the government was shocked and the religious world outraged. He was twice exiled and once narrowly escaped execution. Each suffering was in his eyes a glorious martyrdom: "Indeed every place where Nichiren encounters perils is a Buddha-land." He achieved recognition as a prophet when the Mongol invasion that he had predicted in 1260 and 1268 was attempted in 1274. Many followers were attracted by his courage, his single-minded zeal, and his vision of Japan as an earthly Buddha-land from which the revived and purified Dharma was to spread throughout the world.

Ch'an (Japanese: Zen) was introduced to Japan as early as the seventh century and taught by a few masters in the eighth and ninth; but it did not catch on until the early Kamakura period, when concentration on a single path came into fashion. Eisai (1141–1215), a Tendai monk and scholar of Mount Hiei, who went to China and trained in the Lin-chi (Rinzai) house, established this sect in Japan on his return in 1191. He won the favor of the Shōguns and forged the alliance with the military class that has ever since been the social foundation of Japanese Zen. By compromising expediently with Tendai and Shingon, he managed to win acceptance for Zen without exacerbating sectarian strife. He appealed to nationalist interests to get Zen accepted, writing a tract, *Propagate Zen, Protect the Country*. He is also venerated as the father of Japanese tea culture. Chinese Ch'an monks engaged in tea planting and also drank tea, as a stimulant to aid meditation and as a social alternative to wine. Kūkai is said to have brought tea from China, but it was Eisai who brought the seeds, planted them in the temple grounds, and fostered the use of the beverage. Fifteenth-century Zen people developed the tea ceremony as a social art and a spiritual discipline. Like flower arrangement, archery, jūdō, and kendō, it is a secularization of Buddhist ritual and contemplation. The goal in these arts is to realize a perfect fusion of aesthetic perception and noumenal awareness, of stillness and motion, utility and grace, conformity and spontaneity.

Dōgen (1200–1253), who established the Ts'ao-tung (Sōtō) house of Zen in Japan, is revered to this day by Buddhists of all sects and by many non-Buddhists as a great thinker, an admirable man and a gifted contemplative. His early life is much like that of the other sect-founders of his time. He was born to a noble family, lost his father when he was two and his mother when he was seven, and was awakened religiously by this encounter with suffering and impermanence, reinforced by his mother's deathbed plea that he become a monk. At twelve he left home, and a year later be became a novice on Mount Hiei, where he studied hard until he became engrossed in an enigma: if all living beings have Buddha-nature, then why do the Buddhas and bodhisattvas all aspire to bodhi and engage in practices? He went around seeking an answer and so came in 1214 to enter a Zen temple in Kyōto under Eisai's successor. He and his teacher set out for China in 1223, where he trained under two eminent masters. Dōgen returned to Japan in 1227 and soon settled in a small rural temple where he would be free from the intrigues and contention of temples in Kyōto. He taught *zazen* ("sitting meditation"), wrote, and attracted so many followers that he had to move several times to more spacious temples. Rather than do battle with the hostile and envious monks of Mount Hiei, he moved to east Japan, was for a while the Shōgun's guest in Kamakura, and settled in the nearby mountain temple, Eihei-ji, which was built especially for him. He was ill for several years with a lung disease and died at the comparatively young age of fifty-three.

During the Ashikaga period (1333–1568), when the country was divided among powerful feudal lords and, after 1400, rent by civil wars, the two Zen sects were the only major religious bodies that did not resort to arms to defend themselves and to further their cause. Zen monasteries were peaceful havens for thinkers, teachers, and artists. But the monks were also business entrepreneurs. They engaged in trade with China, maintained their own ships, and sold their imports. Zen monks devised new methods of accounting. Other Zen monks managed academies that taught not only Buddhism but Neo-Confucianism and classical Chinese literature as well. At the same time, Zen masters wrote tracts in colloquial Japanese, using the forty-seven-sign syllabary so that they could be easily read and easily understood when read aloud. Provincial temples disseminated these tracts and their teachings to the people at large.

The Shōgun Nobunaga put an end to Buddhist militancy by destroying all fortified monasteries. He razed the temples on Mount Hiei in 1571, burning the libraries and chapels and beheading or taking captive all the inhabitants. The Tokugawa Shōgunate (1603–1868) gave Japan peace, but at the price of civil and religious liberty. Christianity, which had made headway in the late sixteenth century, was stamped out brutally in the early seventeenth century. As part of the anti-Christian proceedings, every family was required to register as adherents of a Buddhist temple. This *danka*, or "parishioner" system divided the territory and the population into parishes and incorporated the Buddhist clergy into the state apparatus as census takers, registrars of vital statistics, and government informers. Sects were forbidden to proselytize; conversion from one sect to another was obstructed by bureaucratic means. The government did not contribute financially to the temples, however, but laid the burden on the parishioners. The Buddhist sects became "established" churches, protected from both growth and collapse, spiritually discredited in the eyes of the populace.

Nonetheless, there was a great deal of scholarship, and the sects kept their traditions alive. The temples ran primary schools for children and deserve much of the credit for the comparatively high rate of literacy with which Japan ended the Tokugawa era. A new Zen sect, the Ōbaku, was introduced from China in the seventeenth century. This stimulated a reform movement within Sōtō Zen in the late seven-

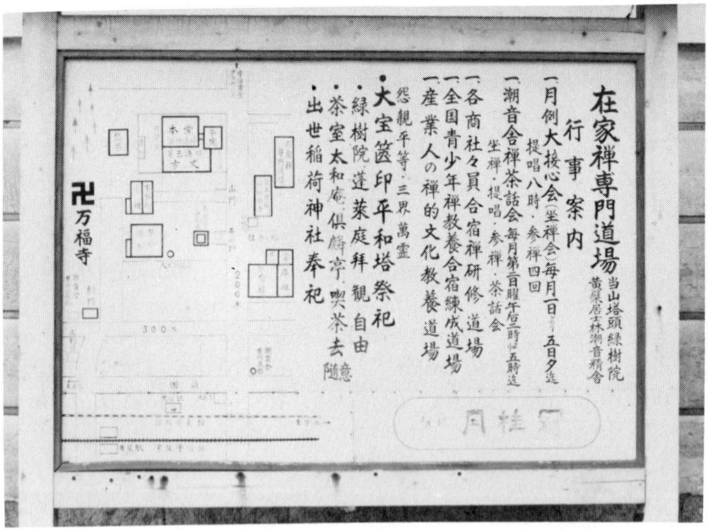

Bulletin board outside the main temple of the Ōbaku sect of Zen in Kyōto, Japan. On the left is a diagram of the temple ground plan, while an advertisement for saké adorns the right bottom. A free translation of the writing (by Shinzen Young) is on p. 209.

teenth and early eighteenth centuries. Japan's greatest poet, Matsuo Bashō (1644–1694) was a lay disciple of Zen. Late in his life (1694), Bashō composed this reflection on the Buddhist experience of no-self:

> On this road
> With no traveler
> Autumn night falls.

In such lapidary haiku, he secularized several salient Buddhist insights and stamped them indelibly into Japanese culture—transiency, loneliness and silence, compassion for living things, and awareness of the transcendental in the mundane and natural. Hakuin (1685–1768) revitalized Rinzai Zen, teaching peasants and children and founding a line of eminent meditation masters.

The Meiji Restoration of 1868 was inspired by a Shintō nationalism hostile to Buddhism. After a brief spell of persecution and the expropriation of temple lands, the Buddhists were roused to assert themselves, recovered much of their prestige, and took steps to modernize, such as founding schools and universities and giving the clergy modern educations. The Meiji government decree that the clergy of all sects be allowed to marry has been observed so well that nowadays there are very few celibate monks in Japan except for young men in training. The various sects have taken on a panoply of modern lay

Zen Practice for the Laity
(At the Householder's Center, Mt. Ōbaku, Kyōto)

Intensive Zen Meditation Retreats

First to fifth of each month. Lectures daily at 8 P.M.

Private interviews four times a day.

Talks on the Zen Tea Ceremony

From 3 to 5 P.M. on the second of each month.

Group Zen Meditation for Company Employees

Youth Hostel

For character development of the nation's youth in the spirit of Zen.

Center for Fostering Zen Culture among Industrialists

Peace Memorial Stūpa

Dedicated to the dead spirits of enemies as well as allies throughout the Three Realms.

Tea garden open to public.

Sip tea and leave.

Shintō Shrine of the God Inari, who confers worldly success.

Drink Gekkeikan Saké

Matsuo Bashō ("Banana Tree"), foremost of Japan's Buddhist poets.

organizations, Sunday Schools, Boy Scout troops, meditation clubs, and young people's societies. There are many popular Buddhist magazines; popular books on Buddhism and translations of the Sūtras are found in every neighborhood bookstore; and a plethora of scholarly books and journals continues to be published. Busloads of tourists visit the old temples of Nara. Kōya-san and Hiei-zan, the ancient centers of the Shingon and Tendai schools, are accessible by cable car; women are no longer excluded from their premises. The old sects possess an impressive number of temples, clerics, and lay followers. They are apprehensive about the new lay movements such as Sōkagakkai and Risshō-kōseikai, both outgrowths of Nichiren-shū, which appeal to some Buddhist texts and insights but bypass the old ecclesiastical apparatus and often use aggressive methods that are offensive to traditional Buddhists. These new sects have attracted millions of members and have placed Buddhism in the central arena of national life for the first time since the sixteenth century. But they are not likely to jeopardize the future existence of the historic sects. Since the Nara period, no sect that acquired independent institutional status has ever become extinct.

EAST ASIAN BUDDHISM IN THE TWENTIETH CENTURY

In countries that have become Communist, official party policy discourages any observance of the Buddhist religion. What this will mean for the future of Buddhism in North Korea, Vietnam, Laos, Cambodia, China, and Tibet is not apparent at the present time. Some scholars foresee the end of Buddhism in China and Tibet. The Chinese New Constitution of 1965 included strictures against Buddhism designed to hasten its disappearance from Chinese life. The Buddhist community

The Japanese Buddhist ritual for feeding and thus appeasing the hungry ghosts. During the ritual a few grains of rice are offered at mealtimes. The very unusual wooden hands are used in this ritual at Mampuku Temple on Mt. Ōbaku, headquarters of the Ōbaku Zen sect near Kyōto.

was the target of severe repression during the Red Guard movement (1966–1969) in China and Tibet. Committing genocide against the Tibetan people, the Chinese have effectively ended Buddhism there. Tibetan Buddhism survives today in the West and in India, where the government gave fleeing refugees a place to settle in a country that, in 1956, had just celebrated the 2500th anniversary of the Buddha. The official policy of Communist governments is that religion perpetuates social injustice and that religious thought and culture do not serve the people's proper (material) needs. Given this climate the survival of Buddhism is in considerable doubt.

The situation in contemporary Japan is paradoxical. Though no official policy condemns the Buddhist religion, Western-style modernization has turned many of its people away from their temples, leading especially to neglect of such important practices as serious meditation.

Zen meditation halls lack full contingents of participants, even though they are open to the laity; and priests leave their hereditary positions in the temples for secular pursuits. On the other hand, the laity is gaining a greater role in Japanese Buddhism. Secular meditation groups and new sects like Sōkagakkai give laypeople new opportunities to act within a Buddhist context. Japan, like Śrī Laṅkā and Thailand, has shown interest in sending missions abroad. It is perhaps significant that Japanese Buddhist scholarship is voluminous and substantially furthers the cause of Buddhist studies the world around. Recently, major philosophers in Japan, such as Nishida Kitarō, have been Buddhists.

The Buddhist experience in the Vietnamese war is too recent to assess. All the world remembers the newspaper and television images of Buddhist monks burning themselves to death. In all, over thirty self-immolations took place. Actually, the Buddhist Saṅgha did not become involved in politics there until partisan Roman Catholic anti-Buddhist leaders abused it. Militant Buddhists responded by supporting the coup against their oppressor, Ngo Dinh Diem, in 1963, though during the war Buddhists were split between moderate and militant factions. Buddhist calls for peace were thought treasonous by the Saigon government's tough anti-Communist leaders, a stand that precluded real Buddhist participation in peace-making efforts, which remained in the hands of the military.

Buddhism in Vietnam, Laos, and Cambodia suffers from the policy or whim of the present government of Vietnam. The strange fratricidal and genocidal war in Cambodia, fomented and furthered by the Vietnamese army, has brought to the once relatively peaceful and prosperous country the all-too-real threat of extinction—of a culture and an entire people. The traditional Vietnamese imperial dream of dominating all of Southeast Asia may yet be realized, and under Communist leadership, there is no place for Buddhism in that dream. Perhaps, eventually, Buddhism will be used in Southeast Asia as it is now used in China—for political propaganda among foreigners. If it should come about that there are no longer any Buddhist nations to woo, then Buddhism would perhaps be flung out to the dust heap of time past, a fate not out of keeping with Buddhist prophecy.

Certain of these prophecies foretell the demise of Buddhism in Asia and its preservation in "the land of the red-faced people," a place identified by some as North America. Only change is constant, and it is a Buddhist virtue to maintain equanimity in the face of ceaseless change. Ironically, Buddhism in Asia probably faces a bleaker future than in the West, since it is only beginning to face the challenges hurled at Western religions by scientific rationalism for the past two centuries. Perhaps Asian Buddhism will further weaken, as the attack has only just begun in most areas that are not today Communist; and in countries now Communist, the attack is already institutionalized as party doctrine. In Japan the process is more advanced, which may be one reason why Japanese teachers are leaving their temples for Western countries. A prosperous economic base is requisite for most cultural or spiritual achievement, but this is lacking today in nearly all Asian Buddhist countries. Only one thing now is sure: that the forces determining Buddhism's future fate are no longer confined to Asia, because Buddhism has successfully come West.

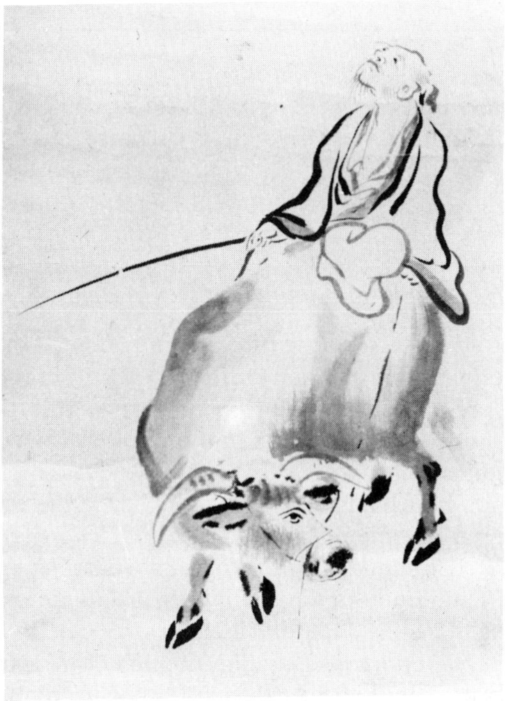

The meditator tames (disciplines) the unruly ox (the karmic individuality) to turn attention to the quiet.

CHAPTER 11

Buddhism Comes West

EUROPE'S EARLY KNOWLEDGE OF BUDDHISM

Little can be said of Europe's earliest acquaintance with Buddhism. There were certainly no extensive direct or accurate reports of Buddhism in the pre-Christian or early Christian periods. Through the Middle Ages, Europeans remained ignorant of Buddhism. There may have been Indian influence on early Greek thought, expressed in Gnosticism and Manichaeism. Some wonder whether Plato's doctrine of the transmigration of souls and his notion of knowledge as remembrance originated in India. The Buddha's first night watch vision, crucial to his Enlightenment, has both these elements in it, but there is no certainty that it inspired Plato. It is also quite possible that there was Buddhist influence on early Christian theology in Alexandria. Later, Islamic civilization, the first to stretch all the way from Europe to the Indus since Alexander's empire, brought Indian tales to Christendom, but the influence was not important religiously. The Catholic saints Barlaam and Josaphat (a corruption of the word *bodhisattva*) derive, curiously, from the Buddha legend, which became increasingly garbled as it traveled west from India.

The First Exchanges

The first of the spiritually inclined visitors to the East were figures such as the later Pythagorean Apollonius of Tyana, who possessed yogic powers and reputedly studied with the Brahmins in India. During the Hellenistic age, wandering philosophers like Apollonius infused the religious traditions of Gnosticism with elements borrowed perhaps from India. But it was not until the age of western exploration that anyone could retrace such archetypal journeys.

The East first lured European explorers, traders, missionaries, and government and church officials before attracting those in search of Buddhism. Beginning in the thirteenth century and as a result of the Crusades, Europeans gradually began to travel to Asian Buddhist lands. But these were only occasional ministers to the Khan or an adventurous merchant such as Marco Polo. Vasco de Gama's oceangoing explorations made such tortuous land journeys as Marco's appear old fashioned, and the Jesuits reached India, Japan, and China in the sixteenth century and Tibet (Father Ippolito Desideri) in the seventeenth century. Latin versions of some Buddhist texts reached Europe along with the all-important dictionaries and grammars of Asian languages. By the 1800s, scholars had brought back substantial materials from the various European colonies, and the academic study of Buddhism commenced in France, the United Kingdom, and Germany as well as in the United States, Russia, and Hungary. Manuscripts were taken to Europe, with some accurate translations already appearing in the late part of the century and increasingly so during the early decades of the twentieth. Both these texts and easier access to Buddhists, both at home and abroad, gave Euro-Americans the possibility of finding Buddhism attractive as a religion, even though knowledge of it was often incomplete and faulty.

Although Buddhist ideas, however imperfectly transmitted, have had some influence on Western intellectuals, they probably have had very little on the public. European philosophers adopted a few ideas from the somewhat inadequate sources available to them in the nineteenth century. Schopenhauer thought he saw a pure pessimism in Buddhism and, in turn, influenced Wagner and Nietzsche. Though he referred occasionally to Buddhism, Nietzsche knew little of it, even though some of his later works have a Zen ring to them. Spengler was also influenced, and in the United States, Emerson and Thoreau were interested in Indian ideas, some of which had a Buddhist flavor. But in actuality, Thoreau had few books in Harvard College library or Emerson's collection that gave substantial ideas on Buddhism, and his sources were much richer from the Hindu side, as his references to Hindu texts indicate. Similarly, Walt Whitman's 1871 epic call for a "Passage to India" spoke of the desire for Eastern wisdom, but its author had little concrete knowledge of it. Whitman expressed a longing typical of some Westerners of that time.

Theosophy

Theosophy ("knowledge of the divine"), born of a Russian mother, Helena P. Blavatsky (1831–1891), and an American father, Colonel H. S. Olcott (1832–1907), marks American religion's most serious turn East in the century, going far deeper than Thoreau or Whitman. Inspired by spiritualist experiences, Blavatsky claimed to have wandered out of Russia and spent time at the feet of spiritual masters in Egypt, Mexico, Canada, Inner Asia, and even Tibet before arriving in New York City. She announced that she had come to America for the birth of Spiritualism and sent the image of a mysterious Buddhist country, Tibet, flowing through American veins.

Buddhism entered the stream of American religion because Theosophy had borrowed much from Buddhist systems and set up the myth of sacred India and enigmatic Tibet, circulating their ideas widely. Theosophy developed a particular interpretation of Indian religion, involving masters and occult brotherhoods of adepts (and their powers), so its descriptions mixed Buddhism with materials from many other sources. Within five years of their first meeting, the Theosophical leaders, Blavatsky and Olcott, made the first Western spiritual pilgrimage to the East, in search of the sacred land and contact with its true religion. In this they followed other pilgrims, like the Chinese and Tibetans, who before had visited the birthplace of the Buddha to study with Indian masters.

Theosophy lasted for some time in the United States, notably in San Diego's Point Loma experimental spiritual community in the first part of the twentieth century. More importantly, it set to work forces in American and European religion that would lead eventually to the introduction of Buddhism as a religion. Its founders fixed into the Euro-American mythic consciousness the image of the sacred East (as in Hesse's novels) to which pilgrimage could be made, bringing transformation and contact with a source of gnōsis, or saving wisdom.

WESTERN BUDDHISM IN THE TWENTIETH CENTURY

A turning point in Americans' perception of Buddhism came just before the twentieth century began. At the Chicago World's Fair in 1893, the World Parliament of Religions gathered representatives from around the world, including two Buddhists, one a Rinzai Zen master and the other a Sinhalese monk influenced by Olcott. The latter sponsored an important society for disseminating knowledge of Buddhism to the West, and the former returned to the United States, invited by supporters to San Francisco in 1905.

The visit resulted in three of his closest disciples coming to America. One founded Zen groups from the 1920s to the 1950s on the West coast. The second founded a Zen group in New York City by 1930 (the Buddhist Society of America, which became the First Zen Institute of America). The third, D. T. Suzuki (1870–1966), became by his writings and the influence of his personality a major source of knowledge and conversion to Buddhism, particularly Zen.

Though Suzuki wrote and lectured more than he set up groups to promote the tradition, he had an enormous impact on American and British Buddhists and those becoming Buddhist. In England alone this included such important figures as Christmas Humphries, Alan Watts, and Edward Conze, all of whom wrote autobiographies in which we learn of Buddhism in their times. Another Suzuki student—a Sussex woman, Peggy Teresa Nancy Kennett, born in 1924 to Buddhist parents—became in November 1970 the founder of the Zen Mission Society near the foot of Mount Shasta in northern California.

Humphries, Watts, and Conze, along with their Japanese mentor, Suzuki, brought Buddhism to the West as no Theosophist had ever imagined possible. Conze and his colleagues, a distinguished international group of scholars including Russians, Italians, British, French, and Americans, brought equally important academic changes to the Euro-American world. During the twentieth century Buddhology became an accepted, international discipline at the university level. Eventually, by the 1950s, academic scholarship had considerably opened Buddhism to Western students. Scholars came to know it in all its dimensions, much more accurately describing its situation in history and society, translating its texts scientifically, and carrying out the scholarship required for valid, accurate knowledge.

The actual number of Euro-American Buddhists during most of the twentieth century has been small, but one could see, by mid-century, a new form of religion emerging. In the early decades groups formed, and individuals made contact with Asians; but much growth was precluded by the limitations on travel, communication, and access to valid knowledge. By the later decades many conditions had changed, allowing greater contact with Buddhists by Westerners. World War II sent millions of Westerners to exotic lands far from Iowa cornfields, and it also promoted the growth of transportation and communications. After the war, cultural prosperity freed many to found institutes (such as San Francisco's American Academy of Asian Studies) or pursue research on Buddhism. By the 1960s, universities began programs in Oriental and even in Buddhist studies (as at the University of Wisconsin in 1965), training many new scholars. Some of these were themselves Buddhists, using the tools of the University to study their adopted religion.

In the mid-1950s very few Americans had heard of Buddhism or knew that American Buddhists existed. In the fifteen years to 1970, so many conditions changed that one could hardly have expected the results. Americans went to war in two Buddhist countries of the East once again (Korea and Vietnam). Even before that, Buddhism began to attract attention through the media. Part of the generation of Americans born during World War II grew up reading books on Edgar Cayce and reincarnation or Jack Kerouac's *The Dharma Bums* and *On the Road*. Their younger brothers and sisters encountered Buddhism when Southeast Asia became prominent during the war in Vietnam. It is too early to epitomize what happened in the 1960s in American religion, but for Buddhism the roots extend back to Theosophy and Western universities' discovery of the non-Western world. By the 1970s, students of American religion could no longer ignore the presence of small but growing Buddhist communities in many North American population centers.

THE CONTEMPORARY SITUATION OF NORTH AMERICAN BUDDHISM

When determining Buddhism's place in American religion in terms of membership, the number of Buddhists is found to be very small, even counting the immigrant communities of the Japanese and Southeast Asians. Prebish (1979) estimated the number of American Buddhists to be around several hundred thousand, perhaps a generous figure and certainly impossible to substantiate. By subtracting the number of American Buddhists in immigrant communities, the much smaller number of recent converts to Buddhism and members of longer standing groups reveals that as a religious community, Buddhism is not very large.

Two kinds of Buddhist groups exist today in the United States and Canada. The first, located mostly on the West Coast, are the churches of the descendants of Japanese immigrants. Organized as the Buddhist Churches of America, they continue to follow the Japanese Jōdo Shinshū tradition (see Kashima, 1977). More than seventy-five years after their founding, these churches count between forty thousand and one hundred thousand members, mostly from the Japanese-American community. As their designation *churches* suggests, they have adopted the standard Protestant American style of worship, meeting on Sundays for services conducted by a minister in black robes. The organization links sixty independent churches, located mostly on the West Coast but with some in the East, and sponsors educational programs

The San Jose, California, Buddhist Church (1975).

and publications. Thus, these American Buddhists have made up a small sector of the richly diverse pluralism of American religion for many decades.

The other kind of Buddhists prevalent in the United States today are Caucasians influenced by the rapid influx of information about Buddhism following World War II. Although groups had formed in the early decades of the century, two waves of missionizing brought Buddhists in their various robes to permanent homes on American soil. The first resulted in the founding of groups roughly deriving from the Sino-Japanese tradition, mostly Zen, in the large cities of California, with sporadic beginnings from other traditions, including Theravāda in Washington, D. C., and Tibetan in New Jersey. The explosion of the 1960s resulted in the second wave: it was part of the "hippie" revolution, which created a genuine, organized (non-Beat) counterculture in America. In this wave came the exotics, like Tibetan Tantrism, and the less established groups. Some were offshoots from popular Japanese religion, and others came from different Buddhist home countries, including Korea (Sŏn), Vietnam (Thiền and Pure Land, brought especially after 1975 by immigrant refugee populations), Burma, Thailand, and Śrī Laṅkā (especially meditation groups). California probably ranks first in total Buddhists (never formally counted), and "Tibet in the Rockies" (Boulder, Colorado) seems to be a major Tibetan Buddhist center, appropriately backed up against the onset of the eastern Rocky Mountain uplift.

The Reverend Sunya Pratt, who served the Japanese Buddhist community in Tacoma, Washington, for more than 30 years. (Photo: Boris Erwitt.)

In effect, in these groups, Buddhism has accomplished the same step that established it centuries ago in Central Asia, China, and Śrī Laṅkā. Valid lineage lines of ordination mark some of the more orthodox of these groups. And all have the one essential individual, a teacher from one of the Asian original traditions—Zen or Tibetan or Theravādin—whose main functions involve not only leading and instructing the group but also the teaching of Dharma-successors to carry on after the master's death.

These groups include transmissions from all the major divisions of Buddhism existing today. From the Japanese sources, Jōdo-shū (Pure Land), Jōdo-shin-shū (True Pure Land), Rinzai and Sōtō (and combinations), Nichiren Shōshū, and Shingon all have members and an institutional presence. All four Tibetan lineages find homes here, as well as Ch'an and Ching-t'u (Pure Land) from China, Chogye Chen or Sŏn (a Zen form) from Korea, and Theravāda from Śrī Laṅkā and Southeast Asian sources, especially Thailand. This constitutes an impressive representation for such a young phenomenon as American Buddhism, the result of its incredible growth from 1965 to 1980. Many of these groups exist primarily because they teach meditation, a major avenue of entrance for Americans to Buddhism as well as Hinduism. But once established, they tend to acquire land and buildings and embark on translation and publication projects, as well as other occupations. Some have built or acquired impressive establishments, taking over entire sets of buildings from defunct communities (or even an old hot springs) or acquiring a block of buildings on a city street.

Many Buddhist communities provide meditation training for residents close by, offer standard forms of Buddhist worship, and organize conferences and special sessions for meditation, generally in settings that obviously derive from Asia but are to greater or lesser degrees Americanized. Most groups stress how indigenous they have become in living habits (often communal) and ways of life, remaining thoroughly American while being Buddhist all the while, too. Members work mostly in the surrounding community.

Most remarkably, as we have seen, these groups, especially the longer existing Zen groups, have produced American Dharma-successors to their Asian mentors. American students have been ordained and trained to transmit Buddhism with the full legitimacy of the lineage succession. In the 1960s, perhaps a dozen of these masters existed, while today they number perhaps fifty, mostly males. But females have also achieved the status of teaching master.

As in ancient India, Buddhism appeals to urban individuals who have lost a sense of the spiritual. The more advanced centers have evolved complete institutions, like their Asian models, integrated into the community in service and training capacities. In a Los Angeles Zen group (Zen Center of Los Angeles) one finds ten main buildings. There are meditation halls; two residences for teachers and their families; a kitchen-dining hall and social center; four residences for staff and trainees; and one building devoted to office and business space, including a medical clinic, bookstore, art gallery, and sewing room. Funds derive from resident trainee fees, nonmembership contributions, retreat and workshop donations, the center's business ventures and services, along with general donations and interest on savings. The community has a travel agency and legal office and offers diverse services of a spiritual nature. These include three to four and one-half hours of meditation daily, private interviews with teachers, thrice daily Sūtra chanting, public Dharma lectures once a week, renewal of vows twice monthly, public Dharma dialogue with a teacher once or twice a month, Zen life intensives every few months, intensive meditation retreats twice a month, regular meditation instruction, and three meals a day. The center publishes a monthly newsletter and calendar, a twice-yearly newspaper, translations and books of the teacher's lectures, Zen texts, and other material on the Buddhist life.

Observing these groups, one finds their membership to be mainly in their 30s and 40s, people who joined in the late 1960s and after, with some members in the 15-to-25 bracket and some 55 and older. The groups apparently realize that the period of rapid growth is now slowing down and are putting down deeper roots and trying to solve the problems of financial survival.

BUDDHISM AS AN EMERGENT, "EXCURSUS" RELIGION

How should we interpret the presence of Buddhism in American religion? In reviewing the photographs in the gallery section (see pp. 224–225) one senses that had we visited these Buddhists in 1966–1967 with the photographer, the Reverend Boris Erwitt, we could have identified them as emerging from the pattern of the established pluralism that made up American religion. This trend led Ellwood (1979), an astute observer of alternative religions in America, to call Buddhism an emergent, "excursus" religion. Many have tried to describe just what American Buddhism is; it could be part of America's turning East (also a political and economic reality), or a feature of a counterculture born in the 1960s, or some kind of escape from secularism and the despair resulting from its rejection of spirituality.

In Ellwood's view, a feature of the religious fabric of a society becomes emergent when it "appears suddenly and unexpectedly" to stand "out from the sea of established religion." Furthermore, those who become involved in an emergent religious group seek an "excursus" away from the experience and norms of their cultural religion. This accomplishes a shift in the structure of transformation (following Streng's definition of religion as means of ultimate transformation), allowing an experience that is novel and that promises renewal, special gnōsis, or self-discovery. Part of the excursus involves experiencing a state of "liminality" in a new community whose meanings and symbols reverse those of one's ordinary culturally consensual view of reality. Many religious aspects of culture foster such experiences, including countercultures, pilgrimages, church services, as well as personal mystical experiences and membership in monastic and communal settlements. The excursus that Buddhism makes possible for Americans leads them, as it did Blavatsky and Olcott, to the mystic East, now brought home and adapted to live in its latest environment. As to the future of excursus religion, Ellwood speculated: "But in the religious folk culture of a technological society, among the spiritual peasantry of a postindustrial nation, excursus religion could have a strange and important role" (1979, p. 172).

Buddhism is only one component of American excursus religiosity, finding itself among other minority forms from the West (Hasidism, Christian monasticism), Near East (Sufism, Black Muslims) or southern and eastern Asia (Hinduism, Buddhism, Taoism in the form of Zen), along with native spiritualism, UFO cults, meditation, psychic-development and human-potential groups, and, in fact, the entire assemblage of groups that Roszak (1975) called the "Aquarian Frontier." Ahlstrom considers many of these part of American "Harmonial Religion," which seeks to achieve a harmony with nature and the cosmos rather than to dominate it. In the striking creativity of contemporary American religion of all forms, excursus, emergent Buddhist groups now play a part.

a

c

b

d

Gallery on emergent American Buddhism. In 1966–1967, the Reverend Boris Erwitt, an American Pure Land priest and a professional photographer, took these photographs as part of his Survey of Buddhism in the U.S.A., sponsored by Professor Kenneth Morgan of Colgate University. a) Buddhist nuns at the New York Chinese Temple. b) Sister Kumi of New Orleans. c) Meditation at the

f

e

g

First Zen Institute in New York. d) An American Buddhist before his home shrine. e) Abbot McDonough of the Zen monastery in Stockton, California. f) The "Red Lama" and his daughter at their home in New York. g) Meeting of the Buddhist Fellowship of New York. In mid-first row are the Sinhalese ambassador and a Chinese monk.

APPENDIX

Buddhist Meditation by Shinzen (Steven) Young

Shinzen (Steven) Young was ordained a Shingon monk at Kōyasan, Japan, in 1970. At present he is senior meditation teacher at the International Buddhist Meditation Center in Los Angeles. The following has been excerpted and adapted, by permission, from his book *Stray Thoughts on Meditation*.

> "There are many paths for entering the reality of nirvāṇa, but in essence they are all contained within two practices: stopping and seeing. Why?
>
> Stopping is the primary gate for overcoming the bonds of compulsiveness.
> Seeing is the essential requisite for ending confusion.
> Stopping is the wholesome resource that nurtures the mind.
> Seeing is the marvelous art which fosters intuitive understanding.
> Stopping is the effective cause of attaining concentrative repose.
> Seeing is the very basis of enlightened wisdom.
>
> A person who attains both concentration and wisdom has all the requisites for self-help and for helping others. . . . It should be known, then, that these two techniques are like the two wheels of a chariot, the two wings of a bird. If their practice is lopsided, you will fall from the path. Therefore, the Sūtra says: To cultivate onesidedly the merits of concentrative repose without practicing understanding is called dullness. To cultivate onesidedly knowledge without practicing repose is called being crazed. Dullness and crazedness, although they are somewhat different, are the same in that they both perpetuate an unwholesome perspective.
>
> *Hsiao Chih-Kuan*
> by Master T'ien-T'ai
> China, Sixth Century C.E.

Despite three distinctive meditative traditions—from southern and southeastern Asia, Tibet, and eastern Asia—the overall Buddhist orientation toward meditation can be divided into two interrelated components. The first, called *śamatha* in Sanskrit, is the step-by-step development of mental and physical calmness. The second, *vipaśyanā*, is the step-by-step heightening of awareness, sensitivity, and clarity of things. The corresponding Pali terms are *samatha* and *vipassanā*; in Tibetan, *zhi gnas* ("peaceful abiding") and *lhag mthong* ("penetrating vision"); and in Chinese, simply *chih* (stopping) and *kuan* (seeing). These two components complement each other and should be practiced simultaneously. Some techniques primarily develop calming, others, clarity, and still others, both equally. It is of the utmost importance, however, that one component not be enhanced at the *expense* of the other. To do so is no longer meditation. Tranquillity at the expense of awareness is dozing; awareness at the expense of calm is "tripping."

Śamatha, if taken to an extreme, leads to special trance states; these may be of value, but they are not the ultimate goal of Buddhism. The practice of clear observation, on the other hand, if developed with sufficient intensity and consistency, leads to a moment of insight into the nature of the identification process. At that moment, awareness penetrates into the normally unconscious chain of mental events that gives us rock-solid convictions such as "I *am* so-and-so" or "such-and-such *really* matters." This insight brings with it a radical and permanent change in perspective, a refreshing sense of freedom that is not dependent on circumstances. The attainment of this perspective and the full manifestation of its implications in daily life are the goals of Buddhist meditation.

Śamatha is the practice of stilling the mind through letting go. In Buddhist usage, it is virtually synonymous with the term *samādhi*. This latter term is usually translated as "one-pointedness," or concentration. Unfortunately, the word *concentration* often carries the connotation of repressing the mind, forcing it not to wander from a certain object. Such a tug of war between the desire of the mind to hold an object and its desire to wander is exhausting and produces unconscious tensions. This is the very antithesis of the śamatha state.

The nature of concentration is detachment. Realizing this marks an important step along the path to the attainment of mental power. In real concentration, one simply rests the mind on the object at hand and then proceeds to let go of everything else in the universe. The mind then remains on that object until it is appropriate to shift attention. Thus, the ability to focus, to concentrate totally on one thing, is essentially equivalent to the ability to let go of everything. But, in order to do this, it is necessary to relax the body in a special way.

First, one learns to keep the body upright and utterly motionless entirely through balance and relaxation, without using muscular effort. The traditional Buddhist posture for this is the cross-legged "lotus," although satisfactory results can be achieved with a variety of postures, even sitting in a chair. The important thing is to align the vertebrae, find a position of equilibrium, and simply let the body hang from the spine by its own weight. This feeling of letting go then extends to the breath and finally to the mind itself.

Since śamatha has the dual nature of letting go and one-pointedness, two approaches to the mind are possible. One is simply to allow the emotional and conceptual content of the mind to settle of its own weight. A way this can be achieved is through the elegant technique of "analogy" (*anumāna*). One feels a part of the body, such as the arm, relaxing, then discovers the mental analog of that feeling—that is, what it feels like to relax thought.

The second approach is to rest the attention on a specific object and gently return it there each time it wanders off. Eventually this wandering habit weakens, then disappears. The object may be physical or visualized, outside the body or within.

It is common in all Buddhist traditions to give beginners some form of meditation that brings the mind to rest on the breathing. In Zen this usually involves counting the breaths or following the breath in and out. In the Theravāda approach, one typically cultivates awareness of the touch or feeling of the breath at the nose tip or lip. Here no attempt whatsoever is made to control the breath. In Tantra, elaborate channels for the breath are visualized in the body, and cycles of inhalation, retention, and exhalation in fixed ratios are practiced as in Haṭha yoga.

Chanting is also common to all Buddhist traditions. When done with proper posture and intention, it can be very tranquilizing. In east Asia, chanting Amitābha's name (Chinese, *nien-fo*; Japanese, *Nembutsu*) is especially popular. Many Tibetans incessantly chant mantras aloud or silently. Even in Theravāda countries, the chanting of special Suttas called "pirit" represents a major event in the monastic year, often going on unbroken for many days and nights. The mind-stabilizing nature of chant and mantra recitation was also recognized in Christianity as witnessed by the "prayer of the heart" so popular in Eastern Orthodox spirituality. Chanting has a strong śamatha effect, but, as usually practiced, there is little of the vipaśyanā component; thus, its power to bring liberating insight is weak.

As body, breath, and mind settle, a distinctive slowing down of the overall metabolism begins to take effect. One may need to sleep less, eat less, breathe less. The spontaneous slowing of breath is probably the most easily observed physical barometer of depth of samādhi. Normal adults at sea level breathe about fifteen times a minute. During seated meditation, at a middle level of śamatha, the breathing rate may drop to only two or three breaths a minute. Because śamatha practice produces such conspicuous changes in the body's function, there has recently been a good deal of physiological research on meditators.

Śamatha is thus a continuum of states of progressive settling of the mind associated with growth in detachment, concentration power, and a distinctive set of physiological changes. At the deep end of this continuum, these phenomena become extreme, and states called in Pali "jhānas" (Sanskrit, dhyāna) are entered. In deep jhāna the drives to which everyone is normally subject are suspended, though not necessarily extinguished. This may last for a few hours or several days. One does not feel driven to move, eat, sleep, or think. Indeed, the metabolism so slows that the breath *seems* nonexistent. The mind, which in its uncultivated state is like a torrential cataract, becomes a rippleless, limpid lake. The deepest jhāna is a kind of trance, but by no means is every trance a jhāna state. The characteristics of the jhānas are distinct and well-defined in the Abhidharma literature. In all, nine levels are distinguished.

Śamatha is best developed by a daily sitting meditation practice. What are the typical experiences of a person who takes up such a practice? How is it likely to affect his or her day-to-day life?

At first, the body strains to remain upright during sitting, the breath is rough and pistonlike, and the mind wanders. One may even feel more agitated than usual. Actually, one is just becoming aware for the first time of the appalling extent and intensity of the chaos within. This awareness is the first stage of progress. In the Tibetan tradition, it is called "realizing the mind as a waterfall."

As with any other art, however, time and regular practice bring skill at śamatha. Body learns to settle into the posture, breath becomes smooth and slow, and irrelevant thoughts no longer scream for attention but whisper and are more easily ignored. By the end of each half-hour or hour meditation period, one experiences a noticeable calm, lightness, and openness. Then the task is to remember this calm state and to keep it somehow throughout the activities of the day!

At first, it may be possible to recapture this settling effect only during the simplest mechanical tasks such as walking, sweeping, or gardening. The emphasis on manual labor in all forms of monasticism, East and West, is meant to provide situations wherein it is relatively easy to preserve inner silence while moving the body. After sufficient experience, the awareness of calm can be preserved throughout the day, though its depth may vary depending on circumstances. One can drive a car or make love, even have arguments and write books, without leaving the śamatha state. One even dreams in it.

Even a person with no meditation experience can appreciate the advantage of a calm and concentrated mind in carrying out physical or mental tasks. With the deepening of śamatha, most activities of daily life are enhanced as one brings this ever more powerful, ever more stable mind to bear on them. In addition, the associated settling of the body produces energy. And śamatha is a state of openness and acceptance, key factors in successful interpersonal relationships. The detachment associated with śamatha makes it much easier to stick to one's principles and approach one's moral ideal.

For many śamatha practitioners the events of the day are seen as a sequence of opportunities to deepen and apply skill at one-pointedness. Peculiar inversions in values may take place. Normally unpleasant situations turn into gold. Overwork and physical discomfort tell a person something. Uncomfortable? Go deeper! Chaotic and fearful situations are accepted as challenges to one's meditative prowess. Wasting time is no longer conceivable. Being unexpectedly kept waiting for an hour somewhere means an hour of "secret use, hidden enjoyment." The Sung dynasty Ch'an master Wu-Men summed it up when he said, "Most people are used twenty-four hours a day; the meditator uses twenty-four hours a day."

The states along this "śamatha continuum" from superficial calming to total trance are known outside Buddhism. Indeed, they are central to the systematic cultivation of mystical experience in all religious traditions. For example, in the Roman Catholic church, terms for such states are *oratio quies* ("prayer of quiet") and *recollection*. Sometimes these states are referred to as "nondiscursive prayer," as opposed to usual prayer, which uses words and thoughts. There is a copious literature on the subject in both the eastern and western churches. Different authors use different terminologies to distinguish benchmarks along the continuum. The deepest trance level of prayer of quiet was sometimes called *infused contemplation* or simply *contemplation*. After the sixteenth century, the practice of nondiscursive prayer declined in the western church.

Nor is the experience of śamatha found only within the context of religious mysticism; it sometimes crops up in the arts, sports, and other "secular" activities that require intense concentration and relaxation.

It is interesting to see how beliefs and attitudes influence people's perceptions of the śamatha process. The musician who sometimes experiences a light transient samādhi while performing will probably associate this state only with the art and, being unaware of its broader potentials, will not strive to deepen and maintain it. In this case, the artist's daily life will never be engulfed and transformed by the experience.

For Buddhists, the attainment of samādhi at its various depths is more a skill than a preternatural grace. Like piano playing or golf, it is something that can be learned reasonably well by most people with sufficient motivation and regular practice. Of course, it is a special skill because of its great generality and power. Other skills can be enhanced by this one skill. More important, it is special because of the changes it brings to one's life. Śamatha, no matter how deep, is not the ultimate goal of the Buddhist. The intensity and enrichment that habitual one-pointedness brings to daily life are but pleasant by-products of the meditative process. Even the jhānas, though purifying and refreshing, are conditioned, impermanent and ultimately unsatisfying. They may even become a hindrance to realizing the true Buddhist goal, nirvāṇa, the undriven life. Śamatha is merely a tool that facilitates the attainment of nirvāṇa.

The word *nirvāṇa* literally means extinction, not the extinction of self but the extinction of the *kleśas*, the "afflictions" that prevent spiritual happiness. The kleśas may be broadly grouped under three headings: *rāga, dveṣa*, and *moha*. Rāga ("desire") is the drive to repeat pleasant experiences. Dveṣa ("aversion," or "antipathy") is the rejection of unpleasant experience. Moha is confusion and lack of clarity. Moha is responsible for our sense of limited identity and prevents us from noticing the subtle malaise and discomfort that underlie all experience.

Concerning rāga and dveṣa, an important point is sometimes missed. Rāga means hankering for mental and physical pleasure, not the pleasure itself. The serious Buddhist seeks to eliminate this hankering, because it is a source of suffering. Pleasure of itself is most definitely not evil and need not be abjured. Likewise, dveṣa is the reaction of rejecting psychologically and physically painful situations. Fighting with pain causes suffering. Pain, if not frantically rejected, causes no suffering. One who has come to grips with rāga and dveṣa, then, enjoys the pleasant without feeling frustrated when the pleasant cannot be had. Likewise, he or she naturally avoids hurt yet does not feel imposed upon when hurt is unavoidable.

So nirvāṇa is what life feels like to a person for whom:

> No matter how assailed, anger need not arise.
> No matter what the pleasure, compulsive longing need not arise.
> No matter what the circumstances, a feeling of limitation need not arise.

Such a person is in a position to live exuberantly, to experience life fully, and also to experience death fully. The former is called "nirvāṇa with a remnant," the latter "nirvāṇa without a remnant."

There are two ways in which śamatha serves as the tool for attaining nirvāṇa. Firstly, it confers a sense of letting go, which aids in the gradual renunciation of desire and aversion. Secondly, it gives the mental stability and one-pointedness necessary for effective vipaśyanā practice. Vipaśyanā destroys moha.

Moha means basically not knowing what is going on within oneself. According to Buddhism, it is the fundamental kleśa, lying at the root of all one's problems. The cure is extending clarity and awareness into the normally unconscious processes. This sounds like much of western psychology. The difference lies in the fact that, in meditation, awareness is cultivated within the śamatha state, that distinctive, profound settling of mind and body described above. This allows for an exposing of the unconscious that may be keener than that usually attained in psychotherapy. Not surprisingly, the results are somewhat different. Therapy, when successful, solves specific problems. Meditation, when successful, provides a general solution applicable to any problem, even important ones such as guilt, failure, intractable disease, old age, and death. Psychology tells us something about how a person's problems arise. Meditation reveals something about how the idea of "person" arises and, in doing so, frees one from the necessity of always identifying with being a particular person. Within the context of such radical objectivity, personal problems can then be dealt with very efficiently.

Sustained vipaśyanā leads to a moment of liberating insight when a huge mass of moha falls away like a chunk of concrete, revealing a vista of freedom. In Abhidharma, this is called "entering the stream of nobles." The Rinzai Zen school speaks of kenshō ("seeing one's nature") or satori ("catching on"). Sometimes in English it is referred to as initial enlightenment or breakthrough. At that moment, the wisdom eye opens, but wider for some than for others. In any case, it never closes again. This is no "peak experience" that later fades. It is a permanent change in perspective, a turning around of the basis of the mind.

A breakthrough of insight into mystical oneness sometimes occurs spontaneously to people who have never practiced meditation and may not even be particularly "spiritually" inclined. However, without some background in cultivating calm and clarity, it is difficult to hold on to and integrate such an insight, and the experience usually fades into a pleasant memory after a few moments, hours, or days. Occasionally, such an unsought experience does work a permanent transformation, but even then without systematic practice it is difficult to realize its full implications in daily life.

According to Buddhist concepts, at this first breakthrough one realizes "no-self." But this expression (anātman), which Buddhists are so fond of, can be very misleading. At first blush, the idea seems uninviting if not absurd. It sounds like a negation of individuality, a frightening loss of controlling center, or a kind of deluded regression. But what is meant by no-self is becoming free from the concept of self (*satkāyadṛṣṭi*). And this is not quite the same thing as losing self, nor does it necessarily even imply the absence of a concept of self.

What is meant by "becoming free from a concept"? One is free from a particular thought or concept if that thought always arises without the slightest unconscious tension, repression, or break in awareness of the thought as thought. Then one experiences the thought so fully that there is no time for the mind to tense and solidify the thought, so the thought ceases to be in one's way. In other words, a thought, concept, mental image, or memory has no hold over us if we always experience it totally (vipaśyanā) and yet remain relaxed (śamatha). This is no easy matter in any case. Initial enlightenment comes when we discover that it is possible to allow our deepest moment-to-moment image of "me and mine" to arise in this full, empty way. From then on, the distinction between self and other (or between enlightenment and nonenlightenment) loses its hold.

Most people, even after such a breakthrough, still find themselves becoming confused, doing wrong things, feeling bad, giving in to unwholesome habits, and the like, though they are no longer constrained to identify with these negativities. So they continue to practice, even more assiduously than before, working to eliminate rāga and dveṣa, rooting out subtle remaining moha, eradicating the stubborn sway of old habits.

Along the way, as one moves closer and closer to complete nirvāṇa, there may come a point at which priorities shift from "wisdom" to "compassion"—that is, from meditation to action.

If you really feel oneness with everything, it is only natural to take responsibility for all your parts. Helpful words and actions begin to flow forth spontaneously.

Although in Mahāyāna, compassion (more accurately, love) is conceived of on a par with wisdom, in practice priority is usually initially given to gaining liberation. It's just more efficient that way. Clearing away some moha first makes it less likely that one's efforts to help others will be misguided. Eliminating rāga and dveṣa makes it less likely that one's zeal will lead to aggressiveness and the sacrificing of principles for an end. Further, after one is free from the concept of helper, helped, and helping, there need be no feeling of chagrin or loss of enthusiasm when one's efforts to help fail.

The specific direction that such activities take depends on the culture, circumstances, abilities, and personality of the individual. They have ranged from wizardry to political activism.

To summarize, śamatha and vipaśyanā are tools for attaining "enlightenment," a non-self-centered perspective. That perspective is a tool that facilitates the achievement of nirvāṇa. According to some Mahāyāna conceptualizations, nirvāṇa itself is a kind of tool, a tool that allows a person to exert effortlessly and efficaciously a beneficial influence on others. If one is free and one's influence is such that it benefits a great many people at the very deepest level, as did Śākyamuni, one is a Buddha.

Following are a few specific techniques for developing the liberating awareness described above, according to various Buddhist teachings.

A common approach used in the Theravāda tradition is to flood the consciousness with more and more complete and precise information about matter-of-fact mental and physical events. Typically, one first learns to experience this intense "vipaśyanā mode" of observation for a single simple event. Once learned, this can be generalized and applied to any aspect of experience. With practice, a suppleness is developed that allows one to perceive each event in the stream of daily life in this totally aware way.

Take, for example, the act of walking. Most people do it unconsciously. There's nothing wrong with that, but suppose one would like to enhance awareness of this event "walking." One could start by mentally noting which foot is swinging at any particular time. This gives one a tiny bit more information about the reality of walking than doing it unconsciously. Next, with regard to each foot, try to note the very instant when the foot begins to rise and the instant when it again touches the ground. Left up, left swing, left down, right up, right swing, and so on. For still more detailed observation, it is useful at the beginning to walk much more slowly than normal and perhaps to pause between each component of the walking. Now, note the instant the left heel rises, note the sweep of tactile sensation as the sole lifts away from the ground. Note the moment the toes leave the ground, the beginning of the forward swing, the swing itself, the end point of the swing, the beginning of lowering the foot, the lowering, the instant the foot touches ground, again the sweep of tactile sensation and the instant when the foot has completely returned to the ground. Now pause. Note when the will to move the right foot arises. Now begin to move the right foot, observing each component as before.

Such an exercise builds much samādhi, but this is a by-product. The important thing is increased clarity about the process. After more practice, it is possible to apply an even finer analysis. Within each component of the motion (lifting, swinging, lowering, and so forth) can be distinguished numerous subcomponents: tiny jerks, each with distinct beginning and end points and each preceded by a separate will to move.

If this keen observation is sustained, alterations in perception begin to occur. The event seems to slow down, a subjective sensation independent of any actual physical slowness. Each component of the event seems to contain vast expanses of time and space within which to perceive information in an unhurried way.

But wait. As one's information about the foot gets fuller and fuller, the foot seems to be less and less there! It expands, becomes light and hollow, merges with things, disappears, and reappears. Without being seduced or frightened, just keep on noting the simple reality of the foot's moment-to-moment motion.

This vipaśyanā mode of awareness can be applied to every type of experience. One can gently move the eye over an object, drinking in information about it so rapidly and fully that the consciousness has no time to solidify the object. Likewise with the other senses—touch, taste, smell, and hearing. This is the fundamental paradox of meditation: see something fully, and it is transparent; hear fully, and there is silence. The feeling of solidity and separateness of objects, which most people take for granted, turns out to be merely an unnecessary and toxic by-product of the process of perception. It clogs the flowing stream of life. One can function quite well without it.

Applying this total mode of awareness to emotions, concepts, and mental images is the most difficult but most productive exercise of all. The stream of a person's thoughts and feelings is unpredictable and gripping, not at all like raising and lowering a foot! Yet with the detachment and one-pointedness of śamatha, one can catch a thought at its very onset and note each minute permutation until the very end in that same slowed-down, complete, unsolidified mode of awareness. A person who can unrelentingly apply this mode to his or her deepest images of self will enter a refreshing new world.

The meditator attempts to establish direct contact with deep processes. One approach is to pose a question that can be readily answered by the deep spontaneous mind but is utterly intractable for the discursive surface. This approach was developed within certain schools of the east Asian Ch'an-Zen tradition. Nowadays, it is particularly associated with Rinzai, one of the two major schools of Japanese Zen. Such a conundrum is called a kōan in Japanese; "What is the sound of one hand?" and "Mu" are two famous ones. The kōan question is mercilessly pressed to deeper and deeper levels, and in the process great samādhi power is developed. When an answer wells up, it carries with it a valuable insight. In this way, by answering many such kōans, the wisdom faculty is gradually exercised. However, if the question is pressed deeply enough, the insight accompanying its solution will be sufficient to crack moha and bring kenshō (initial enlightenment). It is important to remember, however, that there are many kōans for specific purposes and that individual teachers use kōans in different ways.

Meditation is sometimes described as a journey from the surface mind to the unobstructed Mind, a journey made by progressively extending calmness and awareness to subtler and subtler levels, eliminating layer after layer of unconsciousness in great sheets. But along this journey one may experience various phenomena that have significance even though they are not in themselves the goal. The meditator may experience warm, blissful energy flowing in parts of the body, see dazzling light, hear symphonies of internal sound, seem to float out of the body, and the like. Or one may encounter what appear to be archetypal entities: gods, goddesses, sages, and demons. In most traditions of Buddhism, such experiences are denigrated as stray paths and impediments along the "main line" to liberation. Zen teachers usually dismiss them as *makyō* (obstructive hallucination) and recommend simply ignoring them.

The Tantric tradition takes a different tack. The Tantrics systematically explored and cultivated these visualization phenomena. But—and this is really the point—they interpreted these experiences in Buddhist terms and skillfully harnessed them towards the realization of the twin ideals of Mahāyāna, wisdom and compassion. Herein lies the distinctive and powerful contribution of Buddhist Tantra. It successfully incorporates experiences from the subtle "realms of power" in a way that is both philosophically and practically consonant with the goals of Buddhism. This is part of what is meant by "skillful means," of which the Tibetans so often speak.

Tibetan tradition has thus preserved and developed a rich repertoire of contemplative techniques, one of which is "visualization," which perhaps could be more accurately described as mental creation.

We have pointed out how Buddhist meditation seeks to counteract the process of identification with a particular self. One way to go about this is, step by step, to build another self from scratch! One visualizes body parts and imputes mental states, speech, and personality until one can see this artificial being as vividly as anything in the natural world. This is no easy task, but it is made possible through practice and the great mental stability that śamatha confers. The practitioner then learns to identify fully with the created being for a specific period of time. This involves a learning process that, when done properly, is perfectly controlled, lucid, and contrived to bring insight into the arbitrary nature of self-identification. But it confers even more, because the alternate self that is created and identified with is an archetype, an ideal image: a Buddha, bodhisattva, or guardian deity. Not only is power of concentration and liberating insight developed by this practice, but one begins to take on the virtues and positive attributes of that ideal, quickly eliminating the subtle remaining kleśa blocks to nirvāṇa. In this way, visualization is a skillful means for rapid progress toward complete liberation. It is, however, also relevant to the compassion aspect of Buddhism, because habitually perceiving oneself as a spiritual archetype has a subtle and pervasive influence on other people, drawing them in and fostering their own spiritual growth.

Liberating insight achieves the Dharma-body (*dharmakāya*), which, being merely the absence of any sense of obstruction, is formless. Within, there is constant identification with an ideal image. This is the enjoyment-body (*sambhogakāya*). Outwardly the visualizer appears to others as a normal human being, the apparition-body (*nirmāṇakāya*)—normal but somehow special, magic in a way that people cannot quite put their finger on.

So far we have spoken of meditation in terms of growth, development, rewards, and attainments. In Japan there is a school that approaches meditation in an utterly different way, refusing to speak of any "attainment" such as samādhi, enlightenment, or nirvāṇa. According to Sōtō Zen, meditation is most emphatically not a tool, a means to an end. Rather it is an expression of the fact that the means and the end are not separate. Sōtō Zen advocates something called "just sitting." If meditation is a journey, it is a journey to where one is. The distance separating starting point and goal is zero. The mystic's freedom is none other than noticing that the bonds do not exist to begin with. In ultimate terms, to create in people's minds a solidified concept of enlightenment as a future goal is already to mislead them in some way. Sōtō Zen refuses to speak in any but ultimate terms. This is the perspective of the so-called "original enlightenment" school of thought that Dōgen, the founder of Japanese Sōtō Zen, had studied as a youth under Tendai masters.

Then if everything is already perfect, what should one do? Sōtō Zen says, every day, for a period of time, place the body in meditation posture and just sit. Let go of everything but the reality of sitting. Do not daydream, do not seek Buddhahood. In a sense, Sōtō Zen is the ultimately simple form of vipaśyanā practice in which one is simply totally aware from moment to moment of the fact of the body sitting. But it is much more, because this is done within the context of the Mahāyāna philosophy of original enlightenment and, moreover, with the deepest faith that such sitting is the perfect expression of that inherent perfection. This last element, faith, characterized the ethos of the Kamakura period (1192–1338), during which Dōgen lived and during which pietistic sects such as Pure Land and Nichiren-shū flourished.

Finally, a few words about misconceptions and misapplications of meditation. To begin with, it is common for people to fool themselves into thinking that they meditate. One often hears statements such as "I meditate with kung-fu" or "life is my meditation." This is possible but rare. By Buddhist criteria, only a practice that palpably and relentlessly destroys the grip of desire, aversion, and confusion is worthy of the name meditation.

Another mistake is to identify meditation with a particular way of life. Obviously, if one's daily life is seamy and chaotic, it will be difficult to attain peace of mind, but it is ludicrous to think that a person must be a vegetarian or enter a monastery to make headway in meditation. Such externals can help. They can also distract. The path to freedom is systematic and open to all. One does not need to be a Buddhist to profit from Buddhist meditation.

Excessively glorifying the master, or guru, is another possible aberration. True, one needs guidance and encouragement, but people who are searching for *the* guru often fail to make solid progress. The Buddha Śākyamuni urged self-reliance and downplayed the role of authority in the spiritual life.

Some people meditate for one-upmanship and special powers. They think that meditation will give them an edge on the other person. Actually, the purpose of meditation is to learn to embrace failure as enthusiastically as success. As for special powers, Buddhism (particularly Tantric Buddhism) holds that it is legitimate to explore those realms in order to help others. However, in general, it is best to do this after liberation has been glimpsed. Only then do special powers cease to be seductive, frightening, or at all impressive.

Everyone who develops habitual śamatha will sometimes misuse it. If one does something wrong, it will be done wrong very one-pointedly! There is even a technical term for this, *micchā samādhi*. Also, it is easy to use the withdrawal of śamatha to avoid facing unpleasant realities. In particular, one can silence the internal voice of conscience with it. This is why cultivating śīla ("wholesome character, morality") is a prerequisite to cultivating samādhi. It is also another reason why vipaśyanā awareness should accompany śamatha detachment.

"If some is good, more is better" is not necessarily true of sitting meditation. Some people who sit all day and night for years have amazingly little to show for their effort.

One of the most insidious traps on the meditative path is getting stuck in a good place. By this is meant achieving some good results and becoming complacent, not moving on to the better results that lie ahead. In Zen, a person who gets a taste of enlightenment and does not move forward is referred to as "a worm in the mud."

Deep contemplative attainment does not make a person perfect; it confers mind-power, a sense of happiness that is not dependent on circumstances, and a basically loving orientation toward one's environment. It does not, however, guarantee immunity from stupidity, poor judgment, or cultural myopia.

Furthermore, each meditative system has its characteristic weaknesses. Theravāda "vipassanā" meditation could make one humorless and depersonalized if not balanced with "friendliness meditation." Tantric practice can easily degenerate into manipulativeness, sterile ritual, and obscurantism. Belief in original enlightenment and "just sitting" could get in the way of rapid growth. In Japan, Zen training, particularly Rinzai, can be brutal and imbue a tendency towards authoritarianism. In fact, Zen suffered a temporary eclipse in Japan following World War II precisely because it had been widely used as an underpinning for militarism. The practice of meditation in order to get tough and the cultivation of detached repose so that one can kill and be killed without fear or compunction represents a tragic perversion.

That these aberrations and misdirections exist should not in the least surprise, dismay, or discourage us. Every tool can be misapplied. The fact is that each of the above approaches to meditation, if skillfully and persistently cultivated, produces a well-balanced, fulfilled individual whose very presence benefits his or her fellows. As such, they represent a significant and powerful contribution to human culture.

Glossary

Foreign-language or specialized technical terms that appear in the text are defined below. As for the Sanskrit terms, this is an interlocking glossary; all of the key doctrinal terms that occur in the text in their original Sanskrit form are defined in it, often using other terms that are also explained in the glossary. If not already known, these other terms, which are italicized, must be consulted as well. Learning about another vision of life, such as that of Buddhists, requires learning some of the language in which the religious experience is conceptualized. Often our English equivalents carry connotations unwarranted for a different world view. Understanding the terms in this glossary and how they relate to one another can substantially aid in your understanding of the Buddhist religion and the textbook you are using. Students should try to learn or be able to recognize all these terms. Teachers can help, especially with proper pronunciation, by reading them aloud and rehearsing them with the class. When the Pali form of the term is sufficiently different from the Sanskrit as to cause possible confusion, the Pali form follows in parenthesis. A term immediately following in quotation marks is the literal English meaning of the word, but not necessarily a good translation equivalent. Generally, the first word that follows is the translation equivalent chosen for this text; when such a word occurs in the text in English, it stands for the Sanskrit term with which it is here joined.

References immediately after the definition are first to this text, then to the following three works: Stephan V. Beyer, *The Buddhist Experience: Sources and Interpretations*, in this same series; Henry Clarke Warren, *Buddhism in Translations* (New York: Atheneum, 1963); and Edward Conze, *Buddhist Thought in India* (Ann Arbor: The University of Michigan Press, 1967). In the matter of defining crucial features of religions, students may also want to consult Keith Krim (general editor), Roger A. Bullard, and Larry D. Shinn, *Abingdon Dictionary of Living Religions* (Nashville, Tennessee: Abingdon Press, 1981).

Abhidharma. Scholastic ordering and elaboration of the meaning of ideas, involving especially psychology-metaphysics, from the *Sūtras*. See p. 40.

Abhidharma Piṭaka. Collection of seven

scholastic works of the *Theravāda* school, one of the three traditional portions of the Pali Canon.

Anātman (Anattā). Devoid of self (*ātman*), a term applied to all phenomena including the sense of "I" or personhood, indicating the Buddhist view that everything is transient and insubstantial, being without underlying reality or independent, substantial, continuing substrate. As applied to personhood, the anātman doctrine states that there is no ātman in the five *skandhas*. See also *śūnyatā*. Warren ("no-ego") pp. 129–159; Conze pp. 36–39, 122–134.

Anitya (Annica). Impermanence, flux, change; characteristic of everything that arises and continues to exist due to causes and conditions and is thus subject to eventual disappearance. See also *anātman*. Conze, pp. 34, 134 ff.

Arhant (Arahant). "One who is deserving (of reverence and offerings), worthy"; perfected saint, a person who has attained *nirvāṇa*, destroyed the *āsravas*, achieved the goal of *bodhi*, and who will be released at death from rebirth in *saṃsāra*. This term is used by *Hīnayāna* traditions; see *bodhisattva* for a corresponding *Mahāyāna* ideal.

Āsrava (Āsava). Outflow, binding influence, the destruction of which is equivalent to attaining release (arhant-ship), the final goal of Buddhist practice. Listed as four: the outflows of sensual desire, desire to exist, wrong (or speculative) views, and ignorance.

Ātman (Attā). Self; substantial, independent entity existing apart from the phenomenal personhood (the *skandhas*, in the Buddhist view), giving continuity and essential identity to individual beings. Against this ātman view espoused by Hinduism (in the Upaniṣads and the Bhagavad Gītā, for example), Buddhism propounded its anātman doctrine.

Avidyā (Avijjā). Ignorance, particularly of the Four Holy Truths, the root cause of *duḥkha* and the first link in the causal chain of *pratītya-samutpāda* leading to recurrent rebirth in saṃsāra; its opposite is bodhi or prajñā. See Warren, pp. 170–179.

Bar-do (Tibetan). "Intermediate state"; in Tibetan Buddhist thanatology, the passage from one life to the next.

Bhikṣu (Bhikkhu). Buddhist monk.

Bhikṣuṇī (Bhikkhunī). Buddhist nun.

Bhikṣu-saṅgha. Order of Buddhist monks; Bhikṣuṇī-saṅgha, order of Buddhist nuns.

Bodhi. "Awakening"; enlightenment, the special knowledge of a *Buddha*, the ultimate goal of Buddhist practice.

Bodhicitta. Thought or mind of (that is, intentness upon) *bodhi*; the mental attitude the candidate "puts forth" or "arouses" when aspiring to the *bodhisattva* path. See p. 76; Beyer, pp. 101–103.

Bodhisattva. Being who is to become fully enlightened (possess *bodhi*); especially as applied to Gautama, the future *Buddha*. More generally, in Mahāyāna Buddhism the term applies to those who have experienced enlightenment (bodhi) but who have taken a special vow to continue being reborn into *saṃsāra* (rather than entering *nirvāṇa*) so as to deliver others from their suffering by aiding in their attainment of enlightenment. This contrasts with the older ideal of the *arhant*, who was the product of a monastic community of individuals striving primarily for their own salvation. The *Mahāyāna* ideal of the bodhisattva stressed the return of the enlightened being to the world, where the suffering of others demanded compassionate action on their behalf. See "The Bodhisattva Path," pp. 74–78; Beyer, pp. 38–45, 99–115, 217–225, 229–235.

Bon (Tibetan). The semi-indigenous religion of Tibet, with which Buddhism interacted; had its own monks, cult practice and places, texts, and liturgy.

Brāhmaṇa. Ritual priest of the old Indic religious tradition; continued into classical times as the upper, sacerdotal class of the Hindu social system. Anglicized form: brahmin; related religion: Brahmanism.

Buddha. "Awakened"; an enlightened one; Gautama's title after his Enlightenment visions. Beyer, pp. 1–6, 238–240.

Ch'an (Chinese). The first syllable of the Chinese Ch'an-na, which transliterates Sanskrit *dhyāna*, and refers to the Chinese meditation school of Buddhism; in Japanese, pronounced "Zen." See pp. 176–184.

Dependent co-arising. See pratītya-samutpāda.

Dhāraṇī. "Holding"; a spell or incantation

used to fix the meditator's mind or to invoke a god or goddess (= *mantra*); verse or syllable charm to generate beneficial karma or power.

Dharma (Dhamma). Has many meanings in Buddhist texts, the proper one being determined by context and use. Meanings occurring in this textbook are: (1) Dharma, the teaching of the *Buddha*, the Truth; (2) the Real; (3) dharmas, the immediate constituents of all phenomena (things, mental and physical events) in the conditioned realm. Also, dharma can mean moral law, the right, duty, or religion.

Dhyāna (Jhāna). Meditative trance ("trance" here is not used to designate an unconscious or dazed state, but a special meditative attainment of calm, firm mental control, and clarity, achieved through rigorous meditative training); sometimes more loosely used to mean meditation in general rather than the specific meditative trances. See pp. 11–12 ("four stages of dhyāna"); Appendix, p. 228; Beyer, pp. 85–86, 107–108, 206–211 (adds further formless dhyānas); Warren, pp. 109–110, 288, 291, 347–348, 374, 384–385.

Duḥkha. "Dis-ease"; usually translated as suffering or ill; the transmigratory misery that, as the first Holy Truth states, characterizes all conditioned reality; all the dis-ease humans experience because of attachment to *saṃsāra* through the five *skandhas*. *Duḥkha* is equivalent to saṃsāra; its opposite, sukha, true happiness, is a synonym of *nirvāṇa*. Warren ("misery") pp. 170, 204, 369, 438–440; Conze pp. 34–36.

Elite religion. As used in this text, the normative textual religion of literate religious specialists (monks, literati) and the higher classes; has an esoteric (private) side requiring special training or initiation and an exoteric (public) side; contrasts with *popular religion*. See models, pp. 119, 145.

Guru. Spiritual preceptor, master, teacher.

Hīnayāna. The Small Vehicle or Course; the whole set of sects that arose between the first and fourth centuries after the death of the *Buddha*. Hīnayāna sects and monks were numerically the majority in Indian Buddhism; one of these, the *Theravāda*, survives today in Śrī Laṅkā and Southeast Asia. See p. 65 with note; Conze, pp. 119–191.

Karma (Kamma). Act, action, deed performed by body, speech, or mind, which, according to the intention it embodies, will have a set consequence (vipāka, result or phala, fruit), experienced in this or a future rebirth. Warren, pp. 179–182, 194–202, 209–279.

Kuan-yin (Chinese). The Chinese translation of Avalokiteśvara, the *bodhisattva* of compassion. In China during the Sung dynasty (960–1279) the bodhisattva changed from male to female. Kuan-yin is petitioned for earthly boons such as money, good luck, and children.

Lama (Tibetan). Master, spiritual preceptor in Tibetan Buddhism (Sanskrit, *guru*).

Lamaism. A term derived from *Lama*, sometimes used to refer to Tibetan Buddhism.

Lha (Tibetan). God, deity, spirit in popular Tibetan Buddhism.

Mahāyāna. The Great Vehicle or Course; the general term for the sects that arose in India after the Sthavira-Mahāsāṅghika schism of the second century following the death of the *Buddha*. Today Mahāyāna, or northern Buddhism, is associated with Tibet, Mongolia, China, Korea, Japan, and Vietnam. See pp. 65–99; Conze, pp. 195–274.

Maṇḍala. Magic or sacred circle; cosmoplan used in *Tantric* meditation and ritual. See pp. 92, 95–98 *passim*.

Mantra. "Instrument of mind"; short verse or collection of syllables used to evoke (visualize, actualize) a deity, gain protection against evil or adverse forces, or as a meditative object, especially in Buddhist *Tantra*. See pp. 93–94.

Māra. Killing, death, "Destroyer," "Tempter," the personification of evil or attachment to transient conditioned reality (the Wheel of Life); this world as an obstacle to the attaining of enlightenment; the god of desire and death. Sometimes in Buddhist iconography Brahmā, Viṣṇu, Śiva, and Indra are four forms of Māra, indicating the Buddhist antipathy for the Hindu gods of worldly continuance.

Māyā. Illusion, trick, wile; a term favored by *Mahāyāna* writers to describe the apparent "reality" of *saṃsāra*, which being only relatively real, or dependent on causes and conditions, is like an illusion (not nonexistent but deceptive), a magic show, a trick, a bubble, or a mirage, since it lacks any substantial independent reality, and soon disappears. See *śūnyatā*. Beyer, pp. 215–217, Conze, pp. 220–225.

Mudrā. Sign, seal, token; especially a position of the fingers and hands characterizing images of the Buddha or other Buddhist figures and practiced in ritual performance (especially in Tantra). See p. 245.

Neo-Confucianism (Chinese). A renewal and development of Confucianism in the Sung dynasty (960–1279) inspired partly by reaction to Buddhism and also by incorporation of Buddhist metaphysics. This "new" Confucianism received definitive interpretation in the hands of Chu Hsi (1130–1200) and remained the official state orthodoxy until the Republic (1912).

Nien-fo (Chinese). "Reciting Buddha's name," "concentrating on the Buddha"; eventually the practice of reciting the Buddha's name as a means of attaining grace and salvation.

Nikāya. Collection of *Sūtras* found in the *Sūtra Piṭaka*, also called *Āgama*, text, scripture. See p. 39.

Nirvāṇa (Nibbāna). "Blowing out, quenching (as of a fire)"; the goal of Buddhism, the extinguishing of passionate attachment or desire (rāga), fearful hostility or hatred and anger (dveṣa), and confusion or delusion (moha), the primary causes of *karma* and hence bondage to *saṃsāra*. Attained when the *āsravas* are stopped, it is the unconditioned state, emancipation, or release from rebirth and *saṃsāra's* limiting conditions (*duḥkha, anitya, anātman*, recurrent death); structurally equivalent to the Hindu goal of mokṣa (release), given the hybrid designation brahmanirvāṇa, or nirvāṇa in the absolute, in the Bhagavad Gītā. See p. 229; Beyer, pp. 199–206, 212–215; Warren, pp. 59, 281 ff., 331–353, 377–383, 389–391; Conze, pp. 69–79, 159–166.

Pāramitā. "Supremacy"; perfection, practice of a virtue to the point of supremacy, especially by a *bodhisattva*. See pp. 77–78; Conze, pp. 211–217.

Parinirvāṇa. "Full nirvāṇa"; loosely, the complete and final release attained at the death of a *Buddha* (see pp. 33–35), or more accurately, complete release from ignorance, desire, and attachment through the five *skandhas* to material phenomena.

Perfection of Wisdom. In this text the translation equivalent used for the Sanskrit term *prajñā-pāramitā*.

Popular religion. In the context of any historical, peasant civilization, the religion incorporating indigenous *spiritism* that is integrated into the normative literary overlay (like Buddhism in Theravāda countries or Tibet), generally seeking proximate rather than ultimate salvational goals (protection, fertility of women and fields, health, happiness, prosperity); contrasts with elite religion. See models, pp. 119, 145.

Prajñā (Paññā). Wisdom, insight, understanding of the true nature of conditioned reality and the Four Holy Truths, and clearing the mind of the *āsravas*, the goal of the Buddhist path. Made possible by the disciplined practice of *śīla* and *samādhi*, and leading to release from bondage to rebirth in *saṃsāra*, the final step in the three trainings leading to *nirvāṇa*. A synonym is insight (vipaśyanā). See p. 37; Beyer, pp. 197–198 and Part III; Warren, p. 330.

Prajñā-pāramitā. The perfection of *prajñā*, the *Mahāyāna* designation of the supreme degree of *prajñā*, which sees that all *dharmas* are *śūnya*, devoid of *svabhāva*; also the designation of the earliest Mahāyāna Sūtras.

Pratītya-samutpāda (Paṭicca-samuppāda). Dependent co-arising, also translated in other works as "conditioned co-production," "conditioned genesis," and variations on these; the specific formula analyzing the causal links (preconditions, nidāna) in the chain connecting *avidyā*, the root cause, with the consequents, birth, aging, and dying (and the whole mass of samsaric *duḥkha*). See also *saṃsāra*. See p. 16; Beyer, pp. 194–197; Warren ("Dependent Origination") pp. 84, 165–208; Conze, pp. 156–158.

Private Buddha (Pratyekabuddha). A Buddha "for himself alone" who has achieved enlightenment but remains solitary, not teaching the truth to others; distinct from both arhant and bodhisattva.

Pudgala. "Person," a self neither identical with the five *skandhas* nor different from them who nonetheless knows, transmigrates, and enters *nirvāṇa*; the doctrine asserted by the Pudgalavādins (Personalists).

Samādhi. Concentration; the state that is

the goal of Buddhist meditation, characterized by "one-pointedness of thought (on the meditative object)," calm, stability, and absence of distraction or mental disturbance; the senses are controlled, mindfulness (smṛti) is attained, false notions of "I" and "mine" (associated with a notion of a substantial independent selfhood) are stopped, and *prajñā* is possible. A synonym is calm (śamatha); more loosely used, meditation in general. See p. 37; Beyer, Part II; Warren, pp. 291 ff.

Saṃsāra. "That which turns around forever," "the great run-around"; the round of existence, transmigration, the realm into which *karma*-laden beings are reborn and die recurrently; made up of six rebirth realms as illustrated in the Wheel of Life (see p. 14; saṃsāra is characterized by *duḥkha, anitya, anātman* (the three marks, lakṣaṇa, of all conditioned things) and *śūnyatā*; it is often synonymous with *pratītya-samutpāda*, while its opposite is *nirvāṇa*; a term used by both Buddhists and Hindus.

Saṅgha. "Assemblage"; the Order or Community of Buddhist monks, nuns, and laity. In *Theravāda* it often refers only to the monastic order. See p. 30; Beyer, pp. 65–73; Warren, pp. 392–486.

Satori (Japanese). The Japanese reading of the Chinese word *wu*.

Sems (Tibetan). Mind, spirit; the innately pure mind, which by essence is undefiled; the principle allowing transcendence in Tibetan *soteriology* (for Sanskrit, citta).

Śīla. Morality, virtue, conduct conducive to progress on the path to *nirvāṇa*; rules (especially the ten precepts, p. 53) to correct and purify a person's karmic endowment, preparatory to the double practice of *samādhi* and *prajñā*. See p. 136; Beyer, Part I; Warren, pp. 285–287.

Skandha (Khandha). "Heap, mass"; appropriating group or personality aggregate, a term used to indicate that all aspects of personhood that exhibit permanence or unity, either separately or as a group, giving a sense of "ego" or "self," are in reality only impermanent, causally produced aggregations or groups. The five skandhas are (1) form (rūpa, the body or physical skandha), (2) feeling (vedanā), (3) conception (saṃjñā), (4) karmic dispositions (saṃskāras, plural), and (5) consciousness (vijñāna). The five skandhas constitute the phenomenal world-and-person; are the five bases for clinging to (appropriating) existence which results in continued rebirth; are characterized as well by *duḥkha, anitya*, and *anātman*. See pp. 24, 28; Conze, pp. 107 ff.

Soteriology. The study or doctrine of salvation; studies of or theories about savior figures such as the Mahāyāna *bodhisattvas*.

Spiritism. The form of religion characteristic of primal and historical peasant cultures; conceives the immediate invisible environment to be thronged with spirits (including those of the ancestors), whose actions account for events in the visible physical environment, including misfortune and disease as well as prosperity and well being; a precursor of spiritualism.

Śramaṇa. "Striver"; a member of the renunciant sects of early India (after 800 B.C.E.) whose rule (as the Buddhist *Vinaya*) usually required abandoning concerns in the mundane world (including social and ritual status), and practicing mendicancy, sexual abstinence, and austerities; one śramaṇa, the *Buddha*, gathered a large following, founded an order (the *Saṅgha*) and a missionizing world religion.

Srotāpanna. Stream-winner, one who has entered the stream leading to *nirvāṇa*, and will not relapse; one who has been "converted" to Buddhism; the lowest of the four stages or grades of saint; these four stages or paths of sanctification are, in ascending order, (1) srotāpanna, (2) sakṛd-āgāmin, once-returner, one who will have to be reborn in this world as a human being only once more to become an *arhant*, (3) anāgāmin, nonreturner, one who will never have to be reborn in this world as a human being but will be spontaneously reborn in the highest heavens until attaining *nirvāṇa*, and (4) *arhant*, one who will never be reborn again in any rebirth realm. See pp. 25–26; Warren, p. 287.

Sthavira. "Elder," for Pali Thera; see Theravāda, Theravādin.

Stūpa. Memorial shrine or reliquary, especially to the deceased *Buddha*.

Sukhāvatī. "Happiness-having"; Pure Land or land of happiness of Buddha Amitābha (Amita). See pp. 86–88; Beyer, pp. 123–124.

Śūnya. "Swollen, hollow"; empty, devoid, that is, of any *ātman* or substantial independent underlying reality (cf. *svabhāva*), the favorite Mahāyāna explication of the older *anātman* doctrine; the claim is that on the surface things appear substantial, but, when seen with penetrating insight (*prajñā*), they are found to be empty inside, without independent reality or enduring substantiality.

Śūnyatā. Emptiness (see *śūnya*); characteristic of all *dharmas*. See pp. 67–71; Conze, pp. 59–61, 242–249.

Śūnyavāda. The teaching that all *dharmas* are *śūnya*.

Śūnyavādin. "Empty-ist," follower of the Śūnyavāda.

Superknowledge. (Sanskrit, abhijñā). Knowledge attained through meditation. The six superknowledges of the enlightened person are (1) magic powers; (2) ability to hear anything anywhere; (3) knowledge of others' minds; (4) memory of one's own former lives; (5) ability to see anything anywhere; and (6) extinction of outflows or knowledge of the cessation of one's own rebirths.

Sūtra (Sutta). A Buddhist text, especially the dialogs or discourses (in Pali) of the *Buddha*, collected in the *Sūtra Piṭaka*, the Basket of Discourses, and the principal texts of the early *Mahāyāna* (in Sanskrit), also attributed to the *Buddha*. See pp. 38, 65–67, 270.

Svabhāva. Own-being (as opposed to a state of being dependent on causes and conditions); the notion held by some Indian thinkers (Svabhāvavādins, followers of the svabhāva theory as opposed to the Śūnyavādins) and perceived through ordinary common sense that things somehow have independent, continuing, substantial reality—that is, svabhāva; countered by the Buddhist assertion that everything arises in dependence on causes and conditions and therefore has no independent, or substantial, unchanging existence or reality. See pp. 69–71; Conze, pp. 220–225.

Tantra. Ritual manual, for which the school of Buddhist Tantra is named. See pp. 91 ff.; Beyer, pp. 124–161, 258–261.

Tao (Chinese). The way; the order of the universe; the way one ought to travel to be in harmony with the cosmos.

Taoism (Chinese). A complex of several systems of practice all claiming as authoritative the early works attributed to Lao-tzu and Chuang-tzu, including philosophical Taoism, alchemical Taoism, and magical or popular Taoism, the latter two being very much interested in physical immortality.

Tārā. "Savioress"; female manifestation of the protective divine in Buddhism, especially Tibetan; perhaps her name, taken to mean "star," relates her to the Babylonian Ištar, "saving or lucky star."

Tathāgata. "He who has come or gone thus (that is, on the path of all the *Buddhas*)," or "He who has reached what is really so, the True"; the term used by the Buddha to speak of himself after Enlightenment. See p. 23.

Theravāda (Pali for Staviravāda). The teaching of the Elders; originally an early sect which established in Śrī Laṅkā, at the Great Monastery of Anurādhapura, about 240 B.C.E. Today the term is used to designate the older, more conservative school of southern or Pali Buddhism found in Śrī Laṅkā, Burma, Thailand, Laos, and Cambodia. Contrasts with *Mahāyāna*. See pp. 65, 101 *ff*.

Theravādin. One who holds to the teaching of the Elders.

Tṛṣṇā (Taṇhā). "Thirst"; desire, craving, the cause of *duḥkha*; includes desire for sensual pleasure, for continued becoming, and for no becoming. To gain *nirvāṇa*, tṛṣṇā must be eliminated, since it binds a person to its objects, thus causing continued rebirth in *saṃsāra*.

Tsu (Chinese). Ancestor, founder, patriarch.

Tsung (Chinese). "Clan shrine, clan"; in the Buddhist *Saṅgha* refers to those who trace their Dharma-descent to a common *tsu*.

Upaniṣad. Sanskrit speculative texts, the earliest of which were roughly contemporaneous with early Buddhism; later identified with Hinduism, the alternate spiritual tradition.

Vinaya. Monastic discipline and the collection of texts, originally included in the Pali Canon, containing rules for monastic discipline; more generally, the rules of Buddhist morality and canon law. See pp. 38, 49–53; Beyer, pp. 69–73.

Wad. In Thai Buddhism, the temple-monastery complex usually surrounded by a wall.

Wu (Chinese). "Awakening"; the term used for enlightenment, especially within the *Ch'an* tradition.

Yogācāra. The "yoga practice (that is, the following of the yoga or discipline of the

Bodhisattva's path)" school of Buddhism, which thought nothing exists outside the mind (hence: "Mind-Only School"). See pp. 71–73. Yogācārin, follower of the Yogācāra School.

Yogin. Practitioner of yoga and meditative self-discipline.

Zen. The Japanese pronunciation of Chinese Ch'an; the meditative school of Buddhism whose popularity in the west began with the writings of D. T. Suzuki. See pp. 176–184, 206–210.

Selected Readings

This book is a short introduction to the Buddhist religion. Because of its brevity, many important subjects have received only passing reference. Even major doctrines have been but briefly explained; it is hoped that many students will want to read more. The Glossary already includes some references to further readings. For those desiring a deeper knowledge, the following bibliographies select materials that substantially add to the picture of Buddhism presented here. Note: books listed with a French or German title require a reading knowledge of the language, since English translations are lacking.

GENERAL SOURCES

Since this book was closely tied by its authors to textual sources, students can easily supplement it by reading selected Buddhist texts, using it as a guide to understanding. Stephan V. Beyer's companion volume to this book, *The Buddhist Experience: Sources and Interpretations*, in this same Wadsworth series, is the best single source of such texts. Beyer's collection includes texts translated from all major Buddhist canonical languages. Carefully organized and clearly introduced, they make up an invaluable companion to this introduction to the Buddhist religion.

A second source for a student who wants to learn more is *Buddhism: A Modern Perspective*, edited by Charles S. Prebish (University Park and London: Pennsylvania State University Press, 1975, both paperback and hardcover; henceforth it is referred to as Prebish, *Buddhism*). This book, written by former students of Richard Robinson, has summaries of almost all major topics in Buddhist history and thought. Included is an extensive glossary with many proper names, titles of texts, and brief historical sketches, as well as a long bibliography. This is a fine one-book guide to more advanced studies of Buddhism. In it a student can immediately find more information on almost all the subjects introduced in this textbook, so it is the reference to turn to first.

The following works, almost all available in paperback editions, should provide beginning students with sufficient materials to supplement what has been presented in this book.

Bapat, P. V., ed., *2500 Years of Buddhism.* New Delhi: Government of India, Publications Division, 1956. Issued to commemorate the 2500th anniversary of the Buddha's Final Nirvāṇa, this book is a good source of information on the whole of Buddhism.

Basham, A. L., *The Wonder That Was India* (hereafter referred to as *Wonder*). New York: Grove Press, 1959. A survey of the culture of the Indian subcontinent before the coming of the Muslims; a many-splendored classic. Contains much historical information on the background and context of Buddhism in India, comparisons with Hinduism, and material on Buddhism itself. Includes examples of art and literature.

Coomaraswamy, Ananda K., *Buddha and the Gospel of Buddhism.* New York: Harper Torchbooks, 1964. Though written many decades ago, this reissue is an excellent survey of Indian Buddhism, including many subjects omitted by others; thoughtful, engaging presentation, beautifully illustrated. A book about Buddhism, with heart.

Conze, Edward, *Buddhism: Its Essence and Development.* New York: Harper Torchbooks, 1965. Succinct introduction to major Buddhist ideas written by a world-famous Buddhist scholar obviously committed to the Buddhist vision; mixes insight with controversy.

———, *Buddhist Meditation.* New York: Harper Torchbooks, 1969. A useful introduction to Buddhist meditation through texts.

———, ed., *Buddhist Texts through the Ages* (hereafter referred to as *Texts*). New York: Harper Torchbooks, 1964. Collection of texts, including translation of Pali excerpts by I. B. Horner, of Mahāyāna texts by Edward Conze, of Buddhist Tantra by David Snellgrove, and of Chinese and Japanese texts by Arthur Waley. Excellent translations, but somewhat difficult to use due to lack of continuity and introductory materials.

———, *Buddhist Thought in India.* Ann Arbor: University of Michigan Press, 1967. The best survey of Indian Buddhist thought, comprehensive, well-documented. A detailed, more advanced source than others; should be of interest to those who like philosophy and doctrine.

de Berval, René, ed., *Présence du bouddhisme.* Saigon: France-Asie, 1959. Articles of varying quality in French and English on Buddhism in most countries. Now somewhat dated. Many photographs, maps and charts.

Horner, I. B., *The Living Thoughts of Gotama the Buddha.* London: Cassell, 1948. Excellent anthology from Pali sources, with a brilliant introduction by Ananda K. Coomaraswamy. Miss Horner has also written an excellent, succinct summary of Theravāda Buddhism, "Buddhism: the Theravāda," in R. C. Zaehner, ed., *The Concise Encyclopedia of Living Faiths*, pp. 267–295 (Boston, Beacon Press, 1967). In the same source, Edward Conze summarizes Mahāyāna, pp. 296–320; and Richard H. Robinson describes Buddhism in China and Japan, pp. 321–347.

Johansson, Rune E. A., *The Psychology of Nirvana.* New York: Doubleday, 1970. Careful study of early Pali Buddhist thought on nirvāṇa and its attainment; systematically covers major points of doctrine, closely tied to representative Pali texts.

Morgan, Kenneth W., ed., *The Path of the Buddha.* New York: Ronald Press, 1974. Good survey of Buddhism throughout Asia written by prominent Asian Buddhist scholars. Similar to, but less complete than, P. V. Bapat, *2500 Years of Buddhism*, cited above.

Rahula, Walpola, *What the Buddha Taught.* New York: Grove Press, 1974. A very popular work, read widely both in the West and Southeast Asia.

Warder, A. K., *Indian Buddhism*, 2nd ed. rev. Delhi: Motilal Banarsidass, 1980. A recently published survey of Indian Buddhism. Usefully supplements this textbook; good bibliography and index.

Warren, Henry C., *Buddhism in Translations*. New York: Atheneum, 1963. Judicious, comprehensive selections from Pali texts in graceful but dated translations.

Watts, Alan, *The Way of Zen*. New York: Vintage, 1957. This is only one of Watts's many books available, not always on Buddhism, but one of the best by this late, popular writer. Some caution is required when reading Watts to distinguish what he says that derives from his own thought and what he writes that attempts more strictly to describe Buddhism itself. This latter is often very little.

OTHER SOURCES FOR THE STUDY OF THE BUDDHIST RELIGION

The books listed above are good, scholarly accounts of the Buddhist religion. But there are other ways of learning about it, too. Some different kinds of sources are listed below to help those beginning their study of the subject.

On Buddhist Art

Art has always been a major part of religious practice and a major expression of religious experience. Buddhist art is particularly rich, since it is multicultural and has a tradition that spans more than two thousand years. Buddhists have produced an enormous amount of art; the books listed below are only a sample.

*Various seating postures (*āsana*) and hand gestures (*mudrā*) of Buddhist sculpture, including (a) the Buddha in full lotus seating posture, his hands in the teaching gesture ("turning the wheel of the law" mudrā); (b) the "half-lotus" leg position for seated meditation. Additional hand gestures: (c) meditation; (d) assurance against fear; (e) reasoning and explaining; (f) veneration and reverence; (g) touching the earth; (h) boon-bestowing.*

The most complete single source on Buddhist art is P. M. Lad, *The Way of the Buddha* (New Delhi: Government of India, Publications Division, 1956). Issued on the occasion of the 2500th anniversary of the Buddha's Final Nirvāṇa, this book selects art from all sources to describe the background of Buddhism, the Bodhisattva's life and message, the growth of Buddhism, the pantheon, and the spread of Buddhism beyond India. Complete notes accompany the many illustrations. A book that duly honors not only the Parinirvāṇa but all Buddhist artists too.

A very useful work for the study of Buddhist (and Indian) art and iconography is Gösta Liebert's *Iconographical Dictionary of the Indian Religions: Hinduism, Buddhism, Jainism* (Leiden, Netherlands: Brill, 1976). This book defines carefully the terms, iconographic forms, and deities met in Buddhist art and literature.

Other worthwhile studies of Buddhist art are:

Buddhadasa, Bhikkhu, *Teaching Dhamma by Pictures*. Bangkok: Social Science Association Press of Thailand, 1968. This book presents a traditional Thai manuscript that illustrates the Buddhist Path, with commentary on its rich symbolism by the author.

Bussagli, Mario, *Painting of Central Asia*. Geneva: Editions d'Art Albert Skira, 1963. Magnificent Buddhist paintings from the rich finds of Central Asia.

Coomaraswamy, Ananda K., *Elements of Buddhist Iconography*. Cambridge, Mass.: Harvard University Press, 1935. An early interpretation of symbolism in Buddhist art.

———, *History of Indian and Indonesian Art*. New York: Dover, 1965. Excellent survey, including Buddhist art.

Dagyab, Loden Sherap, *Tibetan Religious Art*. Wiesbaden, Germany: Otto Harrassowitz, 1977. Excellent two-volume work, the first introducing the art, the second showing it in color plates.

Davidson, J. Leroy, *The Lotus Sutra in Chinese Art*. New Haven, Conn.: Yale University Press, 1954.

Fickle, Dorothy H., *The Life of the Buddha: Murals in the Baddhaisawan Chapel National Museum, Bangkok, Thailand*. Bangkok: Fine Arts Department, 1972. Includes color illustrations.

Fontein, Jan, *The Pilgrimage of Sudhana: A Study of Gaṇḍavyūha Illustrations in China, Japan and Java*. The Hague: Mouton, 1968. The *Pilgrim's Progress* of Buddhism in art and literature, spanning several civilizations.

———, and Money L. Hickman, *Zen, Painting and Calligraphy*. Boston: Museum of Fine Arts, 1970. Attractive selection of and commentary on Zen art.

Ghosh, A., ed., *Ajanta Murals*. New Delhi: Archaeological Survey of India, 1967. Beautiful illustrations, sensitively interpreted.

Gray, Basil, *Buddhist Cave Paintings at Tun-huang*. Chicago: University of Chicago Press, 1959.

Griswold, Alexander, et al., *The Art of Burma, Korea, Tibet*. New York: Crown, 1964. A good survey of little known areas.

Hisamatsu, Shin'ichi, *Zen and the Fine Arts*. Tokyo: Kodansha International, 1971. Large selection of Zen-related arts.

Krom, N. J., *The Life of Buddha on the Stūpa of Barabudur According to the Lalitavistara Text*. The Hague: Martinus Nijhoff, 1926. An excellent retelling of the biography with photographs of the episodes from the great Javanese stūpa.

Lyons, Islay, *Gandhāran Art in Pakistan*. New York: Pantheon, 1957. Records an important phase of Buddhist art, the product of Indo-Greek culture.

Marshall, Sir John, *The Monuments of Sāñchi*. London: Probsthain, 1940. One of the most important remaining Buddhist stūpas is the subject of this book.

Mitra, Debala, *Buddhist Monuments*. Calcutta: Sahitya Samsad, 1971. Excellent description of sacred Buddhist sites in India.

Rawson, Philip, *The Art of Southeast Asia*. New York: Praeger, 1967.
Roland, Benjamin, *The Art of Central Asia*. New York: Crown, 1974. Good analysis of the art record, revealing its many interesting Buddhist features.
———, *The Evolution of the Buddha Image*. New York: Abrams, 1963.
Saunders, E. Dale, *Mudrā, a Study of Symbolic Gestures in Japanese Buddhist Sculpture*. New York: Bollingen Foundation, 1960.
Singh, Madanjeet, *Himalayan Art*. New York: Macmillan, 1971.
Sivaramamurti, Calambur, *The Art of India*. New York: Abrams, 1977. Includes many Buddhist pieces and puts them in the context of Indian civilization.
Snellgrove, David L., *The Image of the Buddha*. Tokyo: Kodansha International, 1978.
Weiner, Sheila, *Ajaṇṭā: Its Place in Buddhist Art*. Berkeley: University of California Press, 1977. Short but comprehensive analysis of the painting, sculpture, and architecture of one of the most famous of Indian Buddhist sites.
Wray, Elizabeth, *The Ten Lives of the Buddha*. New York: John Weatherhill, 1972. Features Jātaka-tale temple paintings so important to Thai religious instruction.

The interested student should also consult works on the arts of each Buddhist country. This short bibliography only begins to list sources for the study of the Buddhist religion through its artistic heritage.

Audio-Visual Resources on Buddhism

Many good films on Buddhism exist, catalogued and reviewed by experts in Robert A. McDermott, ed., *Focus on Buddhism* (1981), available in cloth or paper from Anima Publications, 1053 Wilson Avenue, Chambersburg, Pennsylvania 17201. This book spans the entire Buddhist experience by cultural area, listing other aids such as slide sets and recordings as well.

Apart from the rich, strictly textual Buddhist tradition, Buddhism can also be studied through other types of literature composed by Buddhists. From Beyer's selection of passages in *The Buddhist Experience*, a student can gain some idea of the great diversity of literary genres Buddhists have used. Discussed below are a few samples.

Traditional Biographies of Buddhists

One can learn much from the biographies of famous Buddhists. Two remarkable works have come to us from the biographies of eminent Tibetans: Herbert V. Guenther, (trans.), *The Life and Teaching of Nāropa* (London: Oxford University Press, 1963) and W. Y. Evans-Wentz, *Tibet's Great Yogi Milarepa* (London: Oxford University Press, 1969). A new translation of this latter is Lobsang P. Lhalungpa's *The Life of Milarepa* (New York: Dutton, 1977).

The great Buddhist biographical tradition of China remains, for the most part, untranslated, and what little has been translated often appears in sources difficult to find.

Chavannes, Edouard, *Mémoires sur les Religieux Eminents*, Paris, 1894.
Gernet, Jacques, "Biographie de Maître Chen-houei du Ho-tso," *Journal Asiatique*, vol. 239 (1951), pp. 29–68. This is the biography of Shen-hui who established his master Hui-neng as the Sixth Patriarch of Ch'an.
Liebenthal, Walter, "A Biography of Tao-sheng," *Monumenta Nipponica*, vol. 11 (1955), pp. 64–96.
Link, Arthur, "Biography of Shih Tao-an," *T'oung Pao*, vol. 46 (1958), pp. 1–48.
———, "Shih Seng-yu and His Writings," *Journal of the American Oriental Society*, vol. 80 (1960), pp. 17–43.

Soymié, Michel, "Biographie de Chan Tao-k'ai," *Mélanges publiés par L'Institut des Hautes Études Chinoises*, Tome Premier, Paris, 1957, pp. 415–422.
Tsu, Y. Y., "Diary of a Chinese Buddhist Nun: Tz'e-kuang," *The Journal of Religion*, vol. 7 (1927), pp. 612–618. Reprinted in *The Chinese Way in Religion*. Belmont, Calif.: Wadsworth, 1973, pp. 120–124.
Weinstein, Stanley, "A Biographical Study of Tz'e-en," *Monumenta Nipponica*, vol. 15 (1959), pp. 119–149. This is a study of K'uei-chi, the last great master of the San-lun sect.
Wright, Arthur, "Biography of the Nun An Ling-shou," *Harvard Journal of Asiatic Studies*, vol. 15 (1952), pp. 193–196.
———, "Fo-t'u-teng, A Biography," *Harvard Journal of Asiatic Studies*, vol. 11 (1948), pp. 321–371.

Biographies of three Chinese nuns are translated by Arthur Waley in *Buddhist Texts Through the Ages*, pp. 291–295. The entire *Kao-seng chuan (Lives of Eminent [Chinese] Monks)* has been translated by Arthur Link, but this translation remains in manuscript form only. The biography of Hui-yüan appears in Erik Zürcher, *Buddhist Conquest*, vol. 1, pp. 240–253. Biographies of Korean monks are in Peter Lee, *Lives of Eminent Korean Monks*, Harvard University Press, 1969. Three Chinese Tantric masters have been studied by Chou I-liang in "Tantrism in China," (see reference in bibliography). Fascinating glimpses of the Chinese Tantric monk I-hsing, mathematician, astronomer, and cartographer of the late seventh and early eighth centuries, can be found in Joseph Needham, *Science and Civilisation in China*, vol. 3, Cambridge, 1959, *passim.*

The biographies and records of the Chinese Buddhist pilgrims and travelers have been given much more attention.

Beal, Samuel, *Buddhist Records of the Western World*, London, 1885; Paragon, New York, 1968. This book includes the *Hsi-yu-chi* of Hsüan-tsang, *Fo-kuo-chi* of Fa-hsien, and travels of Sung Yün from *Lo-yang ch'ieh-lan chi*.
———, *Life of Hsüan-tsang*, London, 1911. His materials are taken from Hsüan-tsang's biography.
Chavannes, Edouard, "Voyage de Song-yun dans l'Udyana et le Gandhara," *Bulletin de l'École Française d'Extrême-Orient*, vol. 3 (1903), pp. 1–63.
Giles, H. A., *The Travels of Fa-hsien*, Cambridge, 1877, 1923.
Grousset, René, *In the Footsteps of the Buddha*. London: Routledge and Kegan Paul, 1932; Hertford: Stephen Austin and Sons, 1971. This is a narrative account of Central Asian and Indian history and religion woven together from the record of Chinese Buddhist travelers to these lands.
Legge, James, *The Travels of Fa-hsien*. Oxford, 1886.
Lévi, Sylvain, "Les missions de Wang Hiuen Ts'e dans l'Inde," *Journal Asiatique*, 9th series, vol. 15 (1900), pp. 297–468.
Reischauer, Edwin, *Ennin's Diary*. New York: Ronald Press, 1955.
———, *Ennin's Travels in T'ang China*. New York: Ronald Press, 1955, especially pp. 164–271. The *Diary* is a translation of Ennin's diary and *Travels* puts Ennin and his diary into context. Both books are recommended highly.
Takakusu, J., *A Record of the Buddhistic Religion*. Oxford, 1896; Delhi, 1966; Taipei, 1970. This is the account of I-tsing, a Chinese Buddhist pilgrim who traveled to India and back by way of Southeast Asia.
Watters, T., *On Yüan Chwang's Travels*, (2 vols.). London, 1904. His materials are taken from Hsüan-tsang's own account of his travels.

Buddhist Autobiographies, Asian and Western

There are not (yet) many Buddhist autobiographies, but their number is growing and has come to include those by Western Buddhists.

Traditional Autobiographies

One extended autobiographical account of at least part of a Buddhist's life was written in the seventeenth century by Japan's most famous *haiku* poet, Matsuo Bashō. A lay Buddhist who practiced Zen meditation, Bashō at the relatively late and frail age of forty became a wanderer, going against all personal inclinations to settle down in his older years. He left five sketches of his resulting travels, which filled the remaining ten years of his life. They are a magnificent literary self-portrait of a Buddhist, as great as the one left by Henry David Thoreau in *Walden*. Bashō made his wanderings to see faraway parts of Japan into an extended journey of (Buddhist) self-discovery, much as Thoreau did, though ostensibly he described only his stay at Walden Pond. Bashō's sketches are translated by Nobuyuki Yuasa in *Bashō: The Narrow Road to the Deep North and Other Travel Sketches* (Baltimore: Penguin, 1966). Hidden below the surface of his compressed writing are some of the best glimpses into a Buddhist's experience of the Path ever recorded.

Another Japanese Buddhist poet (1763–1827) also left a lyric diary; it, too, has been translated by Yuasa: Issa's *The Year of My Life* (Berkeley: University of California Press, 1960).

Another valuable set of traditional Buddhist autobiographies has been recovered and translated by David Snellgrove under the title *Four Lamas of Dolpo*. Volume I is *Introduction and Translations* (Cambridge, Mass.: Harvard University Press, 1967). This is a complete book, with suitable introduction, ample photographic illustrations, texts, and critical commentary and annotation. The autobiographies reveal how it was, in the sixteenth and seventeenth centuries, as remembered by four lamas of the Dolpo region, which today is in western Nepal but which has always been a cultural borderland of Tibet.

Diaspora Tibetan Autobiographies

The mass exodus from Tibet of monks and lamas after 1959 has resulted in quite a few autobiographies of refugees. These accounts help us grasp the meaning of the diaspora as well as to glimpse the traditional lives of important individuals. The Dalai Lama wrote *My Land and My People* (New York: McGraw-Hill, 1962). And his brother, Jigme Norbu Thubten, now a professor at Indiana University, recorded his experiences in *Tibet Is My Country* (New York: Dutton, 1961). Chögyam Trungpa, leader of most Buddhists in Boulder, Colorado, contributed *Born in Tibet* (New York: Harcourt, Brace & World, 1968). Rato Khyongla Nawang Losang wrote his fascinating *My Life and Lives: The Story of a Tibetan Incarnation* (New York: Dutton, 1977), with interesting chapters on Lhasa, monastery study, debating sessions (Chapter 7), the New Year, Tantric studies, and his flight to India after being forced to teach in a Communist school. B. Alan Wallace translated another monk's memoirs in *The Life and Teaching of Geshe Rabten* (London: George Allen & Unwin, 1980), subtitled *A Tibetan Lama's Search for Truth*. It traces his life from a farm in Kham into the monastic life and training and finally to his flight to India.

Autobiographies by Western Converts to Buddhism

A growing category of Buddhist autobiographies is those composed by Western Buddhists. John Blofeld's *The Wheel of Life: The Autobiography of a Western Buddhist* (Berkeley, Calif.: Shambhala, 1972) records the author's wanderings around China, life in a Zen monastery, and a Tibetan initiation. Although the work is not a full autobiography, D. P. E. Lingwood, or Maha Sthavira Sangharakshita, wrote *The Thousand-Petalled Lotus: An English Buddhist in India* (London: Heinemann, 1976).

Of great importance to our knowledge of the early development of Buddhism in Euro-American culture are three autobiographies published in the 1970s. Christmas Humphries wrote *Both Sides of the Circle* (London: George Allen & Unwin, 1978), describing his transition from Theosophist to Zen Buddhist. He became known as the "Leader of Western Buddhism" and "the man who has done more than anyone to bring Buddhism to the West" (Edward Conze's report, which also describes him as "a prominent representative of Western Sectarian Buddhism" and "well known Buddhalogue"). Alan Watts describes how he became the prophet of Zen, along with Suzuki (who directly influenced all three of these autobiographers), calling his work *In My Own Way* (New York: Vintage, 1973). He makes it clear that his brand of Zen did not even require being a Buddhist, a designation that made him uncomfortable, as did disciplined meditation and moral sentimentalists of all stripes. Conze's autobiography is *The Memoirs of a Modern Gnostic:* Part 1, *Life and Letters*; Part 2, *Politics, People and Places* (Sherborne, England; Samizdat Publishing Company, 1979). Part 3, *Forbidden Thoughts and Banished Topics*, had to be delayed in publication to await the demise of all the principals, thus releasing the publisher from libel suits. The work is a lively description of a twentieth-century life, which Watts matches in his own right, though from a different class and point of view. Conze considered Watts's haven, California, to be the realm of the destructress incarnate (as in Kalifornia).

Poetry and Fiction

There have been many Buddhist poets. Han-shan's poems have captured the reality of the experience of Buddhist transformation. The poems, as arranged by his translator, Burton Watson, in *Cold Mountain, 100 poems by the T'ang* [Chinese] *Poet Han-shan* (New York: Columbia University Press, 1970), describe his transformation from a carefree youth and subsequent life as a family man through difficult, bitter years which led eventually to the "Cold Mountain"—both a place where he took refuge and his own state of mind. Like Bashō, Han Shan never became a monk but remained a lay Ch'an Buddhist. His poems similarly go to the heart of the search for nirvāṇa.

Another Chinese Buddhist poet, one who deserves to be read more by Westerners, is Li Ho: J. D. Frodsham, translator, *The Poems of Li Ho* (791–817) (Oxford: Clarendon Press, 1970).

Recently, William LaFleur has given us a selection of poems from Saigyō (1118–1190) in his *Mirror for the Moon* (New York: New Directions, 1977). And from Burton Watson comes *Ryōkan: Zen Monk-Poet of Japan* (New York: Columbia University Press, 1977). Ryōkan (1758–1831) avoided institutional Zen, too, preferring to be a mountain recluse. He begged to devote full time to meditation and poetry.

New translations are making the sixteenth-century Chinese folk novel *Monkey* more available to Westerners. Arthur Waley translated selections of Wu Ch'eng-en's novel (New York: Grove Press, 1958), and now Anthony C. Yu (*The Journey to the West*, Chicago: University of Chicago Press, 1977 and following) is bringing out a complete translation. Berkeley's Asian Humanities Press is publishing the sequel by Tung Yueh under the title *The Tower of Myriad Mirrors* (1978).

Monkey is the best of popular Chinese Buddhist literature, a work of consummate fantasy. Supposedly the account of Hsüan-tsang's journey to India to fetch Buddhist scriptures for the Chinese emperor, the novel tells of a fabulous stone monkey who, in typical Indian fashion, (the book uses a Sino-Buddhist world view) pursued and gained power (*siddhi*) from a venerable patriarch. Running amok on a spree through Heaven, he made too many powerful enemies and was only released from imprisonment in a mountain when he was forced by the goddess of compassion, Kuan-yin, to accompany the priest Tripitaka (Hsüan-tsang) to India, thus putting his formidable power to practical purpose. The "real" story of Hsüan-tsang is equally fascinating, and is told by Waley in *The Real Tripitaka* (New York: Macmillan, 1952). It is well worth reading as the semilegendary history of a famous Asian Buddhist's life.

Modern Buddhists have written novels, too. One, by Michio Takeyama, *The Harp of Burma* (Rutland, Vt.: Charles Tuttle, 1968), describes in poignant terms a Japanese soldier who becomes a Burmese monk rather than return to Japan at the end of World War II. It was also made into a fine Japanese film, *The Burmese Harp*. Both call forth deep feelings.

Popular Books on Buddhism

A bibliography for student readers of a textbook such as this should comment somewhere on the mass of popular books on Buddhism that are available in libraries and bookstores. Best be advised to use some caution in reading these, since their factual reliability often leaves much to desire. Some are outright forgeries—at least that is the opinion of scholars who argue, for instance, that T. Lobsang Rampa's series of books beginning with *The Third Eye* was written by a Londoner who did not grow up in Tibet, as his writings claim. (He naturally countered that his body had been inhabited, with his permission, by a transmigrating Tibetan whose experience in that remote land his writings describe.)

On the other hand, many popular books on Buddhism are worth reading. No one can be exclusively "right on Buddhism," since there must be as many ways of being "right about it" as there are adequate interpretations or real-life experiences of it.

Adventurers have left us exciting records of their experiences in Buddhist countries. An example is Sven Hedin's, *Trans-Himalaja* (Leipzig, 1909, English edition, New York: Macmillan, 1909). Hedin roamed over Central Asia in the early twentieth century. Another example is Heinrich Harrer's *Seven Years in Tibet* (New York: Dutton, 1954). He escaped from an Allied prison camp in India where he was interned at the outbreak of the Second World War. Rather than staying in India, he made his way to Tibet and personally witnessed that closed society until the end of the war, eventually reaching fabled Lhasa itself. Fosco Maraini wrote *Secret Tibet* (London: Hutchinson, 1952; New York: Grove Press, 1960), an exciting, perceptive book on his experiences in Buddhist monasteries. Lama Anagarika Govinda, a European convert to Buddhism who lives in Asia, recounted his wanderings in Tibet in *Way of the White Clouds* (Boulder, Colo.: Shambhala, 1978). Another European Buddhist, John Blofeld, reminisces about his own experiences in pre–Second World War Buddhist China to illustrate his impressionistic, faithful accounting of the *Bodhisattva of Compassion: The Mystical Tradition of Kuan Yin* (Boulder, Colo.: Shambhala, 1978); Kuan Yin's cult is widespread in popular Chinese Buddhism, so Blofeld's descriptions hold some interest.

Traveling scholars have also written accounts of their journeys, such as Snellgrove's *Buddhist Himālaya: Travels and Studies in Quest of the Origins and Nature of Tibetan Religion* (Oxford: Bruno Cassirer, 1957) and his reissued *Himalayan Pilgrimage: A Study of Tibetan Religion* (Boulder, Colo.: Prajna Press, 1981). Similarly, Marco Pallis wrote *Peaks and Lamas* (London: Woburn Press, 1957), describing his travels in Buddhist areas of India, Sikkim, and Ladakh in the 1930s. A new group of travelers, those who journey to Asia (particularly to Japanese Zen Buddhist temples) to meditate, have produced a considerable number of books on their experiences, accounts which are often found in bookstores today. An example of one of these is Peter Matthiessen, an American naturalist and adventurer, who accompanied the field biologist George Schaller one fall on a trek to Shey, in Dolpo. There, around the Crystal Mountain Monastery (also described by Snellgrove), the rare bharal (Himālayan blue sheep) had not been hunted into extinction. *The Snow Leopard*, Matthiessen's remembrance of the journey into Dolpo, was published by New York's Viking Press in 1978. This book expands the genre of Buddhist travel literature, since its author is ecologically aware. Matthiessen missed the elusive snow leopard he sought, on his "true pilgrimage, a journey of the heart" (the San Diego zoo has a pair), and describes his somewhat frustrated pursuit of meditation. The reader sees in this book how one American's Buddhism goes.

Many authors have written on Buddhism, from adventurers to churchmen-turned-lecturers (like Watts). The discerning reader should examine each book and read it for what it is, relying on scholars for the most accurate knowledge. Such authoritative sources follow.

SELECTED SOURCES FOR MATERIAL IN SPECIFIC CHAPTERS

The following is a selected bibliography on the main topics presented in this book, following its outline.* This is not an exhaustive listing of sources. More extensive bibliography on specific subjects can be found in Prebish, *Buddhism*; Frank E. Reynolds, *Guide to the Buddhist Religion* (Boston: G. K. Hall, 1981); *Bibliographie bouddhique* (Paris: 1928 and following); S. Hanayama, *Bibliograpy on Buddhism* (Tokyo, 1961); and Yushin Yoo, *Books on Buddhism: An Annotated Subject Guide* (Metuchen, N. J.: Scarecrow Press, 1976). Other sources are issues of *Buddhist Text Information* and *Buddhist Research Information*, available from the Institute for Advanced Studies of World Religions (5001 Melville Memorial Library, SUNY at Stony Brook, Stony Brook, New York 11794). Another bibliographic series comes from the *Institute Belge des Hautes Études Bouddhiques*, which issues the *Série bibliographies* (Brussels, starting in 1969), including *Bibliographie du bouddhisme zen* (1969), *Bibliographie du bouddhisme* (1971), and *Bibliographie de la littérature prajñāpāramitā* (1971), all by Pierre Beautrix. For German-language publications, consult Hans Ludwig Held's *Deutsche Bibliographie des Buddhismus* (Hildesheim/New York: G. Olms, 1973).

A useful bibliography of journal articles is Yushin Yoo's *Buddhism: A Subject Index to Periodical Articles in English, 1728–1971* (Metuchen, N.J.: Scarecrow Press, 1973). Journals that often contain articles about Buddhism and are likely to be easily available are *History of Religions, Journal of the American Oriental Society, Harvard Journal of Asiatic Studies, Journal of Asian Studies, T'oung Pao, Philosophy East and West, Journal Asiatique, Bulletin of the London School of Oriental and African Studies, Bulletin de l'École Française d'Extrême Orient, Journal of the American Academy of Religion, Journal of the International Association of Buddhist Studies*, and *Indo-Iranian Journal*.

* On occasion, this bibliography identifies a book by an incomplete reference (lacking place, publisher, or date) or lists a book that may have been reprinted at a later date. Readers can ascertain the book's availability with the author and title citation.

Chapter 1. Gautama's Enlightenment

Antecedents of Buddhism

For background on the setting of Gautama's Enlightenment, students can consult the following works.

Basham, A. L., *History and Doctrines of the Ājīvikas*. London: Luzac, 1951. Excellent, detailed survey of the Buddha's competitors.

Fairservis, Walter A., *The Roots of Ancient India*. Chicago: University of Chicago Press, 1975. Detailed archaeological study of early Indic civilization.

Hopkins, Thomas J., *The Hindu Religious Tradition*, 2nd ed. Belmont, Calif.: Wadsworth, 1982. See especially the first chapters and their bibliography.

Jaini, Padmanabh S., *The Jaina Path of Purification*. Berkeley: University of California Press, 1979. Treats another stream of Indic religion from the Buddha's time.

Jayatilleke, K. N., *Early Buddhist Theory of Knowledge*. London: George Allen & Unwin, 1963. A masterpiece. Sometimes hard reading, always rewarding. Excellent survey of śramaṇa movement, pp. 69–168.

Johnson, Willard, *Poetry and Speculation of the Ṛg Veda*. Berkeley: University of California Press, 1980. Describes the early development of the Sanskrit world view, discussing many Buddhist themes.

Keith, A. B., *The Religion and Philosophy of the Vedas and Upanishads*. Cambridge, Mass.: Harvard University Press, 1925. Authoritative survey.

Gautama the Buddha: Birth to Enlightenment

Bareau, André, *Recherches sur la biographie du bouddha*. Paris: Adrien-Maisonneuve, 1963. Exhaustive comparative study of the Pali sources.

Conze, Edward, *Buddhist Scriptures*. Baltimore: Penguin, 1959. Gives a condensed translation of Aśvaghoṣa's *Buddhacarita (Acts of the Buddha)*, pp. 34–66.

Cowell, E. B., trans., "The Buddha-Carita of Aśvaghoṣa," in *Buddhist Mahāyāna Texts*. Delhi: Motilal Banarsidass, 1965. (Reprint of vol. 49 of *Sacred Books of the East* [SBE]).

Foucher, A., *The Life of the Buddha*. Middletown, Conn.: Wesleyan University Press, 1963. A poor English translation of *La vie du bouddha* (Paris: Payot, 1949). The author, a great historian of Buddhist art, expresses many questionable opinions on doctrine and religion.

Johnston, E. H., *The Buddhacarita, or Acts of the Buddha*. Part 2, Translation. Calcutta: Baptist Mission Press, 1936. Chapters 1–14, in scholarly and readable translation; the best. (Reprinted, New Delhi: Oriental Books Reprint Corporation, 1972). The rest of the text is translated by Johnston in *Acta Orientalia*, vol. 15 (1937).

Nakamura, Hajime, *Gotama Buddha*. Los Angeles: Buddhist Books International, 1977. A short, scholarly retelling of the life.

Ñāṇamoli, Bhikkhu, *The Life of the Buddha*. Kandy, Śrī Laṅkā: Buddhist Publication Society, 1972. Life and teachings of the Buddha selected from Pali sources.

Nārada, Thera, *The Buddha and His Teachings*. Colombo, Śrī Laṅkā: Vajirārāma, 1964. Good translations of basic Pali texts, with authoritative commentary by a Theravāda scholar-monk. On the Buddha's life, see pp. 1–64, 318–331.

Thomas, E. J., *The Life of the Buddha as Legend and History*. London: Routledge & Kegan Paul, 1927. Readable, scholarly, standard.

Warren, *Buddhism in Translations*, pp. 38–83, 331–349.

The Twelve Preconditions of Dependent Co-arising

Jayatilleke, *Theory of Knowledge*, pp. 445–457. Sets Keith straight.
Johansson, Rune E. A., *The Dynamic Psychology of Early Buddhism*. London: Curzon, 1979. Pali sources on dependent co-arising.
Kalupahana, David J., *Causality: The Central Philosophy of Buddhism*. Honolulu: University Press of Hawaii, 1975.
Keith, Arthur Berriedale, *Buddhist Philosophy in India and Ceylon*, 1st ed., 1923. (Reprinted, Banaras, India: Chowkhamba, 1963.) Masterly but quirky. Causation, pp. 96–114.
Nārada, *Teachings*, pp. 418–431.
Thomas, E. J., *The History of Buddhist Thought*. London: Routledge & Kegan Paul, 1933. Very good as an account of early Buddhist thought according to the Pali Canon. On dependent co-arising, see pp. 58–70.

The Wheel of Life and the Hierarchy of Beings

Haldar, J. R., *Early Buddhist Mythology*. New Delhi: Manohar, 1977. A study of little-known subjects relating to early Buddhism.
Law, B. C., *The Buddhist Conception of Spirits*. Varanasi, India: Bharatiya Publishing House, 1974. (Reprint from 1923).
Matsunaga, Daigan and Alicia, *The Buddhist Concept of Hell*. New York: Philosophical Library, 1972. From the Vedas through Mahāyāna.
Nārada, *Teachings*, pp. 432–452.
Renou, Louis, et Jean Filliozat, *L'Inde classique*. Tome 1 (Nos. 1–1357). Paris: Payot, 1947. Tome 2 (Nos. 1358–2494). Paris: Imprimeri es Nationale, 1953. The standard topical encyclopedia of Indology. Tome 2, pp. 315–608, presents everything the fledgling scholar should learn about Buddhism and much that is new to veterans. On pantheon, see Nos. 1029, 1077–1079, 1086–1087, 2266–2272.
Waddell, L. A., "The Buddhist Pictorial Wheel of Life," *Journal of the Asiatic Society of Bengal*, vol. 61 (1893), pp. 133–155. Describes in detail the Tibetan Wheel of Life.
Warren, *Buddhism in Translations*, pp. 289–291, 308–330.

Chapter 2. The Buddha as Teacher

Commentary on the First Sermon

Dutt, Nalinaksha, *Aspects of Mahāyāna Buddhism and Its Relations to Hīnayāna*. London: Luzac, 1930. A great book. Doctrine of nirvāṇa, pp. 129–202.
Jayatilleke, *Theory of Knowledge*, pp. 382–401. On faith.
Nārada, *Teachings*, pp. 74–102.
Poussin, Louis de La Vallée, *Nirvāṇa*. Paris, 1925. His mature view, well developed.
———, *The Way to Nirvāṇa*. Cambridge, 1917. Popular lectures by one of the greatest modern Buddhologists.
Robinson, Richard H., "The Classical Indian Axiomatic," in *Philosophy East and West*, vol. 17 (1967), pp. 139–154. On being, nonbeing, and the Middle Way.
Stcherbatsky, Theodore, *The Conception of Buddhist Nirvāṇa*. Leningrad: Office of the Academy of Sciences of the U.S.S.R., 1927. An attack on La Vallée Poussin by another great master.

Warren, *Buddhism in Translations*, pp. 117–128, 380–391.
Welbon, Guy Richard, *The Buddhist Nirvāṇa and Its Western Interpreters*. Chicago: University of Chicago Press, 1968. A readable and discerning history of the West's intellectual encounter with Buddhism as instanced in the problem of nirvāṇa.

On Early Buddhist Meditation

Ñāṇamoli, Thera, trans., *The Path of Purification* (Buddhaghosa's *Visuddhimagga*). Colombo, Śrī Laṅkā: R. Semage, 1956.
Nyanaponika, Thera, *The Heart of Buddhist Meditation*. New York: Samuel Weiser, 1973. Deals with Satipaṭṭhāna (mindfulness) meditation.
Swearer, Donald K., *Secrets of the Lotus*. New York: Macmillan, 1971.
Vajirañāṇa, Mahāthera, *Buddhist Meditation in Theory and Practice*. Colombo, Śrī Laṅkā: Gunasena, 1962.

On Buddhist Abhidharma

(See also below, "Early Schisms and Sects.")
Guenther, Herbert V., *Philosophy and Psychology in the Abhidharma*. Berkeley, Calif.: Shambhala, 1976.
Jacobson, Nolan Pliny, *Buddhism, the Religion of Analysis*. London: Feffer & Simons, 1974.
Ñāṇatiloka, Mahāthera, *Guide through the Abhidhammapiṭaka*. Colombo, Śrī Laṅkā: Bauddha Sāhitya Sabhā, 1957.
Nyanaponika, Thera, *Abhidamma Studies*. Kandy, Śrī Laṅkā: Buddhist Publication Society, 1965.
Rhys Davids, Mrs. C.A.F., *The Birth of Indian Psychology and Its Development in Buddhism*. London: Luzac, 1936.

Founding the Saṅgha

Nārada, *Teachings*, pp. 103–225.
Thomas, *Life*, pp. 89–142.

The Parinirvāṇa

Nārada, *Teachings*, pp. 233–269.
Thomas, *Life*, pp. 143–164.
Warren, *Buddhism in Translations*, pp. 95–110.

Chapter 3. Development of Indian Buddhism

General Sources

Horner, I. B., *Women Under Primitive Buddhism*. Delhi: Motilal Banarsidass, 1975 (reprint). Useful early study.
Kloppenborg, Ria, *The Paccekabuddha: A Buddhist Ascetic*. Leiden, Netherlands: Brill, 1974.

Law, Bimala Churn, *Buddhaghosa*. Bombay: Bombay Branch Royal Asiatic Society, 1946.

Ling, Trevor, *The Buddha: Buddhist Civilization in India and Ceylon*. Baltimore: Penguin, 1976.

Narain, A. K., *The Indo-Greeks*. Oxford: Clarendon Press, 1957.

Pande, G. C., *Studies in the Origins of Buddhism*. Allahabad, India: University of Allahabad, 1957.

Pardue, Peter, *Buddhism: A Brief Account*. New York: Macmillan, 1971. Social history of Buddhism.

Perez-Ramon, Joacquin, *Self and Non-Self in Early Buddhism*. The Hague: Mouton, 1980.

Tarn, W. W., *The Greeks in Bactria and India*. Cambridge, England: Cambridge University Press, 1951.

Varma, Vishvanath Prasad, *Early Buddhism and Its Origins*. Delhi: Munshiram Monoharlal, 1973.

Wagle, Narendra, *Society at the Time of Buddha*. New York: Humanities Press, 1967. The social structure of India in the Buddha's time, based on the Pali Canon.

Yu, Chai Shin, *Early Buddhism and Christianity: A Comparative Study*. Delhi: Motilal, 1980.

Formation of the Canon

Conze, Edward, *Thirty Years of Buddhist Studies*. Oxford: Cassirer, 1967. A collection of articles. The first, "Recent Progress in Buddhist Studies," first published in 1959–1960, summarizes the state of scholarship on the Buddhist scriptures.

Inde Classique, Nos. 1940–2169. The best scholarly précis on Buddhist literature.

Law, Bimala Churn, *A History of Pāli Literature* (2 vols.). London: Kegan Paul, Trench, Trubner & Co., 1933.

Macdonell, A. A., "Literature (Buddhist)," in Hastings's *Encyclopaedia of Religion and Ethics* (ERE), vol. 8, pp. 85a–89b.

Nārada, *Teachings*, pp. 270–278.

Thomas, *Thought*, pp. 261–287. A survey of the Pali Canon and other Buddhist scriptures.

Winternitz, Moriz, *A History of Indian Literature*. Calcutta: University of Calcutta, 1933. Vol. 2, pp. 1–21, 34–165.

Early Schisms and Sects

Aung, Shwe Zan, trans., and C.A.F. Rhys Davids, ed., *Compendium of Philosophy*. London: Luzac, 1910 and 1956. Translation of the *Abhidhammattha-saṅgaha*, a medieval Theravāda textbook on Abhidhamma. Excellent introduction and notes.

Banerjee, Anukul Chandra, *Sarvāstivāda Literature*. Calcutta: World Press, 1979.

Bareau, André, *Les sectes bouddhiques du Petit Véhicule*. Saigon: École Française d'Extrême-Orient, 1955. A definitive scholarly work.

Conze, Edward, *Buddhist Thought in India*. Ann Arbor: University of Michigan Press, 1967. Hīnayāna sects, pp. 119–191.

Dutt, Nalinaksha, *Buddhist Sects in India*. Calcutta: Firma KLM, 1977.

Frauwallner, E., *The Earliest Vinaya and the Beginnings of Buddhist Literature*. Rome: Istituto Italiano per il Medio ed Estremo Oriente, 1956.

Funahashi, Issai, et al., "Abhidharmakośa-śāstra," in *Encyclopaedia of Buddhism (EB)*, vol. 1, pp. 58a–63.

Karunaratne, W. S., H. G. A. van Zeyst, and Kōgen Mizuno, "Abhidhamma," fascicule 1, pp. 37b–49a, in *EB*, ed. G. P. Malalasekera, published by the Government of Śrī Laṅkā. Fascicule 1 appeared in 1961. Subsequent fascicules (parts) come out from time

to time. This encyclopaedia is an outstanding piece of Asian international cooperation. The best articles in it are really excellent.
Kao Kuan-ju, "Abhidharma-mahāvibhāṣā," *EB*, vol. 1, pp. 64b–80a.
Mizuno, Kōgen, "Abhidharma Literature," *EB*, vol. 1, pp. 64b–80a.
Poussin, Louis de La Vallée, *L'Abhidharmakośa de Vasubandhu*. Paris: Geuthner, 1923–1931. Annotated translation of the crowning masterpiece of the Abhidharma movement.
Stcherbatsky, Theodore, *The Central Conception of Buddhism and the Meaning of the Word "Dharma."* London: Royal Asiatic Society, 1923. Reprint by Susil Gupta, Calcutta, 1956. A brief interpretive exposition of the *Abhidharmakośa's* doctrine.

Aśoka

Bhandarkar, D. R., *Aśoka*, 3rd ed. Calcutta: University of Calcutta, 1955.
Nikam, N. A., and Richard McKeon, *The Edicts of Aśoka*. Chicago: University of Chicago Press, 1959. Translates the edicts.
Przyluski, Jean, *The Legend of Emperor Aśoka in Indian and Chinese Texts*. Calcutta: Mukhopadhyay, 1967.

Religious Life in the Early Centuries

Anesaki, M., "Ethics and Morality (Buddhist)," *ERE*, vol. 5, pp. 447b–455b.
Auboyer, Jeannine, *Daily Life in Ancient India* (from approximately 200 B.C.E. to 700 C.E.). New York: Macmillan, 1965. Contains information on early Indian (including Buddhist) worship and life.
Davids, T. W. Rhys, *Buddhist India*. Delhi: Motilal Banaradass, 1980. Religious life in the early centuries.
Dutt, Nalinaksha, *Early Monastic Buddhism*. Calcutta: Calcutta Oriental Book Agency, 1960.
Dutt, Sukumar, *Buddhist Monks and Monasteries of India*. London: George Allen & Unwin, 1962.
———, *Early Buddhist Monachism*. Bombay: Asia Publishing House, 1960.
Geden, A. S., "Monasticism (Buddhist)," *ERE*, vol. 8, pp. 797a–802b.
Horner, *Living Thoughts*, pp. 74–75, 88–138.
Prebish, Charles S., *Buddhist Monastic Discipline*. University Park and London: Pennsylvania State University Press, 1975. Translates two discipline texts, with an introduction on the rise of Buddhist monasticism.
Warren, *Buddhism in Translations*, pp. 91–94, 392–421, 441–481.

Chapter 4. The Beginnings of Mahāyāna Buddhism in India

Bareau, *Les sectes bouddhiques*, pp. 296–305.
Conze, *Buddhist Thought in India*, pp. 195–204.
Dutt, Nalinaksha, *Aspects of Mahāyāna Buddhism*. London: Luzac, 1930.
Lamotte, Étienne, "Sur la formation du Mahāyāna," in *Asiatica (Festchrift F. Weller)*. Leipzig, 1954, pp. 381–386.

The Teaching of Emptiness

Conze, Edward, *Buddhist Wisdom Books*. London: George Allen & Unwin, 1958 (also New

York: Harper & Row, 1972). Contains *Diamond-Cutter Sūtra* and *Heart Sūtra*; translation with commentary.

———, *The Prajñāpāramitā Literature*. The Hague: Mouton, 1960.

———, *Selected Sayings from the Perfection of Wisdom*. London: Buddhist Society, 1955.

———, *Buddhist Thought in India*, pp. 238–249.

Inada, Kenneth K., *Nāgārjuna, A Translation of His Mūlamadhyamaka-kārikā with an Introductory Essay*. Tokyo: Hokuseido Press, 1970.

Kiyota, Minoru, ed., *Mahāyāna Buddhist Meditation: Theory and Practice*. Honolulu: University Press of Hawaii, 1978. A volume of studies dedicated to Richard H. Robinson.

Lamotte, Étienne, *L'Enseignement de Vimalakīrti* (Vimalakīrtinirdeśa). Louvain, Belgium: Publications Universitaires, 1962. Excellent French translation, with copious notes and introduction, of one of the most important and well-written Mahāyāna Sūtras.

Mookerjee, Satkari, *Buddhist Philosophy of Universal Flux*. Delhi: Motilal Banarsidass, 1980. On the school of Dignāga.

Murti, T. R. V., *The Central Philosophy of Buddhism*. London: Unwin, 1980. A great book on Mādhyamika, somewhat obscured by the author's thinking in Sanskrit and writing in the vocabulary of 1910-ish British idealism.

Ramanan, K. V., *Nāgārjuna's Philosophy as Presented in Mahā-Prajñāpāramitā-Śāstra*. Tokyo, 1966; Delhi: Motilal Banarsidass, 1978.

Robinson, Richard H., *Early Mādhyamika in India and China*. Madison: University of Wisconsin Press, 1967. Read pp. 21–70.

Sprung, Mervyn, trans., *Lucid Exposition of the Middle Way*. Boulder, Colo.: Great Eastern, 1980. Translates the essential chapters of Candrakīrti's *Prasannapadā*.

Sprung, Mervyn, ed., *The Problem of Two Truths in Buddhism and Vedānta*. Boston: Reidel, 1973.

Streng, Frederick J., *Emptiness: A Study in Religious Meaning*. Nashville, Tenn.: Abingdon Press, 1967. A study of Nāgārjuna and his vision with respect to the relation between religious awareness and symbolic expression. Contains complete translations of Nāgārjuna's two chief works.

The Doctrine of Mind Only

Chatterjee, Ashok Kumar, *The Yogācāra Idealism*. Banaras, India: Hindu University Press, 1962. A weak book, but the only one in English.

Conze, *Buddhist Thought in India*, pp. 250–260.

Fukaura, Seibun, "Ālaya-vijñāna," *EB*, vol. 3, pp. 382b–388b.

Lamotte, Étienne, *La somme du Grand Vêhicule d'Asaṇga* (Mahāyānasaṃgraha). Tome 2. Traduction et commentaire. Louvain, Belgium: Muséon, 1938. A basic manual of Vijñānavāda.

Poussin, Louis de La Vallée, *La Siddhi de Hiuen-tsang*. Paris: Geuthner, 1928–1948. Translation of Hsüan-tsang's *Ch'eng-wei-shih-lun*, a synthesizing commentary on the *Thirty Verses* of Vasubandhu.

Rahula, Walpola, "Asaṅga," *EB*, vol. 2, pp. 113b–146b.

Suzuki, D. T., trans., *Laṅkāvatāra Sūtra*. London: Kegan Paul, 1932 and 1956.

———, *Studies in the Laṅkāvatāra Sūtra*. London: Routledge, 1930. A fine treatment of the Sūtra's version of Yogācāra.

Willis, Janice Dean, *On Knowing Reality*. New York: Columbia University Press, 1979. A specialized study translating part of Asaṅga's *Bodhisattvabhūmi*.

Chapter 5. Soteriology and Pantheon of the Mahāyāna

The Bodhisattva Path

Batchelore, Stephen, trans., *Shantideva: Guide to the Bodhisattva's Way of Life*. Delhi: Motilal Banarsidass, 1979.
Dayal, Har, *The Bodhisattva Doctrine in Buddhist Sanskrit Literature*. London: Kegan Paul, 1932. (Reprinted, Delhi: Motilal Banarsidass, 1975.)
Guenther, Herbert V., trans., *The Jewel Ornament of Liberation*, by Sgam-po-pa. London: Rider, 1959. An excellent Tibetan manual of the Bodhisattva Course. Hard to read because the translator uses nonstandard equivalents for technical terms.
Matics, Marion, trans. *Śāntideva: Entering the Path of Enlightenment*. New York: Macmillan, 1970.

The Celestial Bodhisattvas

Inde Classique, Nos. 2336–2339.
Lamotte, Étienne, *Histoire du bouddhisme indien*. Louvain, Belgium: Publications Universitaires, 1958. Great scholar, great book. Maitreya, pp. 775–788.
———, "Mañjuśrī," *T'oung Pao*, vol. 48 (1960), pp. 1–96.
Warren, *Buddhism in Translations*, pp. 480–486.

The Celestial Buddhas

"Akṣobhya," *EB*, vol. 3, pp. 363–368a.
"Amita," *EB*, vol. 3, pp. 434a–463b.
Hurvitz, Leon, *Scripture of the Lotus Blossom of the Fine Dharma* (the *Lotus Sūtra*). New York: Columbia University Press, 1976.
Kern, H., trans., "The Saddharma-puṇḍarīka or the Lotus of the True Law," *SBE*, vol. 21. Oxford: Clarendon, 1909. An obsolete masterpiece.
Müller, F. Max, trans. (1) "The Larger Sukhāvatī-vyūha," *SBE*, vol. 49, pp. 1–72. (2) "The Smaller Sukhāvatī-vyūha," *SBE*, vol. 49, pp. 89–103.
The Shinshu Seiten ("The Holy Scripture of Shinshu"), compiled and published by the Honpa Hongwanji Mission of Hawaii, Honolulu, 1955. The three chief Pure Land Sūtras translated from the standard Chinese versions, plus other texts from Chinese and Japanese.
Takakusu, J., trans., "The Amitāyur-dhyāna-sūtra," *SBE*, vol. 49, pp. 161–201.

Chapter 6. Buddhist Tantra

Bharati, Agehananda, *The Tantric Tradition*. New York: Weiser, 1975. Treats both Buddhist and Hindu Tantra; dense.
Dasgupta, Shashibhusan, *An Introduction to Tantric Buddhism*. Berkeley, Calif: Shambhala, 1974.

———, *Obscure Religious Cults*. Calcutta: Firma K. L. M., 1962.

Guenther, Herbert V., *The Tantric View of Life*. Boulder, Colo: Shambhala, 1976. Almost as dense as Bharati on same.

———, *The Royal Song of Saraha*. Berkeley, Calif.: Shambhala, 1973.

Kvaerne, Per, *An Anthology of Buddhist Tantric Songs*. Oslo: Universitetsforlaget, 1977. Translation with introduction to late Buddhist Tantric songs (*Caryāgīti*).

Lessing, Ferdinand, and Alex Wayman, trans., *Fundamentals of the Buddhist Tantras*, by Mkhas-grub-rje. The Hague: Mouton, 1968. Useful translation of a schoolman's marginalia on Tsongkhapa's Tantric writings.

Pott, P. H., *Yoga and Yantra*. The Hague: Martinus Nijhoff, 1966. Helpful work for the study of Buddhist Tantra.

Robinson, James B., *Buddha's Lions: The Lives of the Eighty-Four Siddhas*. Berkeley, Calif.: Dharma, 1980.

Snellgrove, David L., *The Hevajra Tantra*. Part I, *Introduction and Translation*. London: Oxford University Press, 1959. The only complete Tantra available in English. Readable and well-informed introduction.

Tucci, Guiseppe, *The Theory and Practice of the Mandala*. New York: Samuel Weiser, 1973.

———, *Tibetan Painted Scrolls*. Vol. 1, *The Religious Ideas: Vajrayāna*. Rome: Libraria dello Stato, 1949.

Chapter 7. Facets of Later Indian Buddhism

Aiyappan, A., and P. R. Srinivasan, *Story of Buddhism with Special Reference to South India*. Madras, India: Government of Madras, 1960.

Banerji, Aparna, *Traces of Buddhism in South India*. Calcutta: Scientific Book Agency, 1970.

Basu, N. N., *Modern Buddhism and Its Followers in Orissa*. Calcutta, 1911.

Joshi, Lalmani, *Studies in the Buddhistic Culture of India*, 2nd rev. ed. Delhi: Motilal Banarsidass, 1977.

Mishra, V. B., *Religious Beliefs and Practices of North India during the Early Mediaeval Period*. Leiden, Netherlands: Brill, 1973. On Buddhism, pp. 138–145.

Naudou, Jean, *Buddhists of Kashmir*. Delhi: Motilal Banarsidass, 1980.

Central Asia

Emmerick, R. E., *A Guide to the Literature of Khotan*. Tokyo: Reiyukai, 1979.

Nagel's Encyclopedia—Guide to China, 4th ed. Geneva: Nagel, 1979. Good description of present-day Central Asia, with detailed history and description of the caves of Tun-huang.

Soper, Alexander C., trans., *Arts of China, Buddhist Cave Temples, New Researches*. Tokyo: Kodansha, 1969.

Stein, Sir Aurel, *Serindia* (5 vols.). Oxford: 1921; *Ancient Khotan*, Oxford: 1907; *Innermost Asia*, Oxford: 1928; *On Ancient Central Asian Tracks*, London: 1933.

Waley, Arthur, *Ballads and Stories from Tun-huang*. London: George Allen & Unwin, 1960.

General Works for Part Two

Conze, Edward, *A Short History of Buddhism*. Bombay: Chetana, 1960. A fine synoptic history of Buddhism in India and its spread throughout Asia.

Dutt, Sukumar, *Buddhism in East Asia*. Bombay: Bhatkal Books, 1966. Good introduction to Buddhism beyond India.

Zürcher, Erik, *Buddhism, Its Origin and Spread in Words, Maps, and Pictures*. Leiden, Netherlands: Brill, 1959; New York: St. Martin's Press, 1962. Very useful for tracing the spread of Buddhism from its beginnings in India throughout the rest of Asia.

Chapter 8. The Buddhism of Southeast Asia

Aronson, Harvey B., *Love and Sympathy in Theravāda Buddhism*. Delhi: Motilal Banarsidass, 1980.

Bechert, Heinz, *Buddhismus, Staat und Gesellschaft in den Ländern des Theravāda-Buddhismus*. Weisbaden: Otto Harrassowitz, 1966, 1967, 1973.

———, "Saṅgha, State, Society, 'Nation': Persistence of Tradition in 'Post-Traditional' Buddhist Societies," *Daedalus*, Winter 1973, pp. 85–95.

———, "Theravāda Buddhist Saṅgha: Some General Observations on Historical and Political Factors in Its Development," *Journal of Asian Studies*, vol. 29 (1969–1970), pp. 761–778.

Bunnag, Jane, *Buddhist Monk, Buddhist Layman*. London: Cambridge University Press, 1973.

Byles, Marie M., *Journey into Burmese Silence*. London: George Allen & Unwin, 1962. A plucky Australian lady in Burmese meditation centers. Informative about Burma and its religion, as well as about what happens when one meditates.

Cabaton, Antoine, "Cambodia," *ERE*, vol. 3, pp. 155a–167a. An overall picture of Cambodian religious life.

Coedès, George, *The Indianized States of Southeast Asia*. Honolulu: East-West Center Press, 1968.

———, *The Making of Southeast Asia*. Berkeley: University of California Press, 1966.

Damais, Louis-Charles, "Le bouddhisme en Indonésie." In *Présence du bouddhisme*, by René de Berval, pp. 813–824. Saigon: France-Asia, 1959.

Evers, Hans-Dieter, *Monks, Priests and Peasants: A Study of Buddhism and Social Structure in Central Ceylon*. Leiden, Netherlands: Brill, 1972.

Gombrich, Richard F., *Precept and Practice: Traditional Buddhism in the Rural Highlands of Ceylon*. London: Oxford University Press, 1971.

Gomez, Luis, ed., *Barabuḍur: History and Significance of a Buddhist Monument*. Berkeley, Calif.: Asian Humanities Press, 1980.

Jayatilleke, K. N., *The Message of the Buddha*. New York: Free Press, 1974. Discussions of Buddhist topics from a sophisticated Theravāda point of view.

Jones, John Garret, *Tales and Teachings of the Buddha*. London: George Allen & Unwin, 1979. Study of Jātaka tales important for study of Theravāda.

King, Winston L., *A Thousand Lives Away: Buddhism in Contemporary Burma*. Cambridge, Mass.: Harvard University Press, 1964. A perceptive outsider assesses the state of Theravāda thought and values in contemporary Burma.

———, *Theravāda Meditation*. University Park: Pennsylvania State University Press, 1980.

Kornfield, Jack, *Living Buddhist Masters*. Santa Cruz, Calif.: Unity Press, 1977. Theravāda masters described.

Lerner, Eric, *Journey of Insight Meditation: A Personal Experience of the Buddha's Way*. New York: Schocken Books, 1977. An experience of vipaśyanā meditation.

Lester, Robert C., *Theravāda Buddhism in Southeast Asia*. Ann Arbor: University of Michigan Press, 1973.

Ling, Trevor, *Buddhism and the Mythology of Evil: A Study in Theravāda Buddhism*. London: George Allen & Unwin, 1962.

Ludowyk, E. F. C., *The Footprint of the Buddha*. London: George Allen & Unwin, 1958. Description of the monuments of "old Ceylon."

Malalgoda, Kitsiri, *Buddhism in Sinhalese Society, 1750–1900: A Study of Religious Revival and Change*. Berkeley: University of California Press, 1976.

Rahula, Walpola, *History of Buddhism in Ceylon*. Colombo, Śrī Laṅkā: M. D. Gunasena, 1956. Treats period from third century B.C.E. to tenth century C.E.

———, *The Heritage of the Bhikkhu*. New York: Grove Press, 1974. Description of the monk's life in Ceylon, with illustrations.

Ray, Niharranjan, *Theravāda Buddhism in Burma*. Calcutta: University of Calcutta Press, 1946.

Reynolds, Mani and Frank, *The Three Worlds According to King Ruang*. Berkeley, Calif.: Asian Humanities Press, 1980.

Sarkisyanz, E., *Buddhist Backgrounds of the Burmese Revolution*. The Hague: Martinus Nijhoff, 1965.

Schecter, Jerrold, *The New Face of Buddhism*. New York: Coward, McCann, & Geohegan, 1967. Buddhism's involvement in social and political change.

Seneviratne, H. L., *Rituals of the Kandyan State*. Cambridge, England: Cambridge University Press, 1978. Describes the ritual at the Palace of the Sacred Tooth Relic in Śrī Laṅkā.

Smith, Bardwell L., ed., *The Two Wheels of Dhamma*. Chambersburg, Pa.: American Academy of Religion, 1972. Important work on Śrī Laṅkan Buddhism.

———, *Religion and Legitimation of Power in Śri Laṅka; Religion and Legitimation of Power in Thailand, Laos, and Burma*. Both Chambersburg, Pa.: Anima Books, 1978.

Soni, R. L., *The Only Way to Deliverance*. Boulder, Colo.: Prajna Press, 1980. Uses Theravāda materials to discuss Buddhist meditation.

Spiro, Melford E., *Buddhism and Society*. New York: Harper & Row, 1970. Excellent survey of Buddhism in Burmese society.

———, *Burmese Supernaturalism*. Englewood Cliffs, N. J.: Prentice-Hall, 1967. An anthropologist looks at the total religious system of the Burmese. See especially "Supernaturalism and Buddhism," pp. 246–280. Good, up-to-date bibliography.

Swearer, Donald K., *Buddhism and Society in Southeast Asia*. Chambersburg, Pa.: Anima Books, 1981. Best overall summary to date.

———, *Buddhism in Transition*. Philadelphia: Westminster, 1970.

———, *Wat Haripuñjaya, A Study of the Royal Temple of the Buddha's Relic, Lamphun, Thailand*. Missoula, Mont.: Scholars Press, 1976. Excellent study of a northern Thai temple complex and its varied activities. Good interpretive work.

Tambiah, S. J., *Buddhism and the Spirit Cults in Northeast Thailand*. Cambridge, England: Cambridge University Press, 1970.

———, *World Conqueror and World Renouncer*. Cambridge, England: Cambridge University Press, 1976. Important study of the Thai Saṅgha and Buddhist polity.

Terwiel, B. J., *Monks and Magic, An Analysis of Religious Ceremonies in Central Thailand*. London: Curzon Press, 1975. Gives the rural Thai rice farmer's view of the "Crystal Sky Monastery" by a participant-observer anthropologist who joined the Saṅgha to describe the power exchange between monk and peasant.

Wells, Kenneth E., *Thai Buddhism, Its Rites and Activities*. Bangkok: Christian Bookstore, 1960. A straight description of ceremonies, liturgies, and festivals.

Yoe, Shway (pseudonym of James George Scott), *The Burman, His Life and Notions*. London: Macmillan, 1896. Now in paperback. A sympathetic and informative classic.

Chapter 9. Buddhism in the Tibetan Culture Area

Bernbaum, Edwin, *The Way to Shambhala*. New York: Anchor, 1980. Subtitled *A Search for the Mythical Kingdom beyond the Himalayas*; good, detailed study.

Beyer, Stephan V., *The Cult of Tārā*. Berkeley: University of California Press, 1973. The first treatment of Tibetan Tantric ritual-meditations as they are actually practiced. The author based his account on field work among Tibetan refugees in India. An excellent work.

———, *Tibetan Mystic Song* (Lyricord Disc LLST 7290) and *Songs of Gods and Demons: Ritual and Theatrical Music of Tibet* (Lyricord Disc LLST 7291). Recorded in Tibetan communities in India, these long-playing records present some lesser-known Tibetan music from the traditions of mystic song and the Tibetan opera and epic. Each record has complete translations of texts, as well as photographs and commentary.

Blofeld, John, *The Tantric Mysticism of Tibet*. New York: Dutton, 1970.

Bu ston, *History of Buddhism* (2 vols.), trans., E. Obermiller. Heidelberg: 1931–1932.

Chakravarti, B., *Cultural History of Bhutan*. Vol. 1, *From Pre-History to Padmasaṃbhava*. Chittaranjan: Hilltop Publishers, 1979.

Chang, Garma C. C., trans., *The Hundred Thousand Songs of Milarepa* (2 vols). Boulder, Colo.: Shambhala, 1979.

Dargyay, Eva M., *The Rise of Esoteric Buddhism in Tibet*. Delhi: Motilal Banarsidass, 1977.

Demiéville, Paul, *Le Concile de Lhasa*. Paris: Imprimeries Nationale de France, 1952. Describes the debate held in Lhasa between representatives of Indian Mahāyāna and Chinese Ch'an.

Douglas, Nik, *Tibetan Tantric Charms and Amulets*. New York: Dover, 1978.

Douglas, Nik, and Meryl White, *Karmapa: The Black Hat Lama of Tibet*. London: Luzac, 1976. Describes the incarnation line of the Karmapa Black Hats, teachers of the Kargyüpa sect, with its current center in Sikkim.

Ekvall, Robert B., *Religious Observances in Tibet: Patterns and Function*. Chicago: University of Chicago Press, 1964.

Evans-Wentz, W. Y., *The Tibetan Book of the Dead*, 3rd ed. Oxford: Oxford University Iress, 1960.

———, *Tibetan Yoga and Secret Doctrines*, 2nd ed. Oxford: Oxford University Press, 1960.

———, *Tibet's Great Yogi Milarepa*, 2nd ed. Oxford: Oxford University Press, 1951. Evans-Wentz was a Theosophist who worked with bilingual Tibetans to produce translations that are readable and notes that are often inane.

Fremantle, Francesca, and Chogyam Trungpa, trans., *The Tibetan Book of the Dead: The Great Liberation Through Hearing in the Bardo*. Boulder, Colo.: Shambhala, 1978.

Govinda, Li Gotami, *Tibet in Pictures*. Berkeley, Calif.: Dharma, 1979.

Guenther, Herbert V., *Tibetan Buddhism without Mystification*. Leiden, Netherlands: Brill, 1966. Translations of four eighteenth-century Gelukpa tracts, with introduction and notes.

Heissig, Walter, *The Religions of Mongolia*. Los Angeles: University of California Press, 1979. Interesting account, especially of Buddhist missionary activities.

Hoffman, Helmut, *Quellen zur Geschichte der tibetischen Bon-Religion*. Wiesbaden: Franz Steiner Verlag, 1950. Best work on Bon.

———, *The Religions of Tibet*. London: George Allen & Unwin, 1961. A standard work, weak on doctrine.

Houston, Gary W., *Sources for a History of the bSam yas Debate*. Sankt Augustin, VGH Wissenschaftsverlag, 1980. Important work on the Lhasa debate.

———, *Wings of the White Crane: Poems of Tshangs dbyangs rgya mtsho*. Delhi: Motilal Banarsidass, 1981. Only good book in English on the life and poetry of the sixth Dalai Lama.

James, E., *Tibetan Treasury of Aphoristic Jewels*. Bloomington: Indiana University Press, 1968.

Karmay, Heather, *Early Sino-Tibetan Art*. Warminster, England, 1975.

Kongtrul, Jamgon, *The Torch of Certainty*. Boulder, Colo.: Shambhala, 1976. Describes meditation practices of Tibetan Buddhism. Some interviews with contemporary teachers.

Lauf, Detlef Ingo, *Secret Doctrines of the Tibetan Book of the Dead*. Boulder, Colo.: Shambhala, 1977. Good on Tibetan thanatology.

Lhalungpa, Lobsang P., *The Life of Milarepa*. New York: Dutton, 1977. A new translation that updates Evans-Wentz.

Ortner, Sherry B., *Sherpas through Their Rituals*. Cambridge, England: Cambridge University Press, 1978. Interesting study of Tibetan Buddhists in Nepal who came to settle near Mount Everest 450 years ago.

Poppe, Nicholas, *The Twelve Deeds of Buddha*. Seattle: University of Washington Press, 1967. Translation of a Mongolian version of the Lalitavistara.

Ram, Rajendra, *A History of Buddhism in Nepal A.D. 704–1396*. Delhi: Motilal Banarsidass, 1978.

Sierksma, Fokke, *Tibet's Terrifying Deities*. The Hague: Mouton, 1966. An interpretation of aspects of Tibetan art and culture, perhaps too Freudian.

Snellgrove, David L., *The Cultural Heritage of Ladakh*. Vol. 1, *Central Ladakh*. Boulder, Colo.: Prajna Press, 1977.

———, *The Nine Ways of Bon*. London: Oxford University Press, 1967. Short introduction, mostly translated texts.

———, and Hugh Richardson, *A Cultural History of Tibet*. New York: Praeger, 1968. Readable. Gives a prominent place to religion.

Sopa, Geshe Lhundup, and Jeffrey Hopkins, *Practice and Theory of Tibetan Buddhism*. New York: Grove Press, 1976. Translations on meditation systems and doctrine.

Stein, R. A., *Tibetan Civilization*. Stanford, Calif: Stanford University Press, 1972. Excellent one-volume treatment; includes much on religion.

Tucci, Giuseppe, *The Ancient Civilization of Transhimalaya*. Geneva, 1973.

———, *The Religions of Tibet*. Berkeley: University of California Press, 1980. The best detailed treatment to date.

Chapter 10. East Asian Buddhism

General Reading on Chinese Buddhism

Birnbaum, Raoul, *The Healing Buddha*. Boulder, Colo.: Shambhala, 1979. Discusses the celestial Buddha "Master of Healing," associated with lapis lazuli.

Ch'en, Kenneth, *Buddhism in China, A Historical Survey*. Princeton, N. J.: Princeton University Press, 1964. Has at least something on everything. Excellent on historical facts, weak on doctrine and interpretation; extensive bibliography.

———, *The Chinese Transformation of Buddhism*. Princeton, N. J.: Princeton University Press, 1973.

de Bary, Wm. Theodore, ed., *Sources of Chinese Tradition*. New York: Columbia University Press, 1960. Pages 306–408 contain Chinese Buddhist texts, well-chosen and well-translated by Leon Hurvitz.

Hsü Sung-peng, *A Buddhist Leader in Ming China: Life and Thought of Han-Shan Te-Ch'ing, 1546–1623*. University Park: Pennsylvania State University Press, 1979.

Overmyer, Daniel L., *Folk Buddhist Religion, Dissenting Sects in Late Traditional China*. Cambridge, Mass: Harvard University Press, 1976.

Paul, Diana, *Women in Buddhism*. Berkeley, Calif.: Asian Humanities Press, 1980.

Robinson, Richard H., *Chinese Buddhist Verse* (hereafter referred to as *Verse*). London: John Murray, 1955. Didactic and liturgical hymns from the Chinese Canon.

Takakusu, Junjiro, *The Essentials of Buddhist Philosophy*, 3rd ed. Honolulu: Office Appliance Co., 1956. Data-rich but opaque textbook material on the Sino-Japanese sects.

Thompson, Laurence G., *Chinese Religion: An Introduction*, 3rd ed. Belmont, Calif.: Wadsworth, 1980. Places Buddhism within the panorama of Chinese religiosity.

Waley, Arthur, "Texts from China and Japan," in Conze, *Buddhist Texts*, pp. 269–306. Choice morsels that Waley happened to like.

Wright, Arthur F., *Buddhism in Chinese History*. Stanford, Calif: Stanford University Press, 1959. Readable, strong on history, weak on doctrine. See review by Richard H. Robinson, *Journal of the American Oriental Society*, vol. 79 (1959), pp. 311–318.

Yang, C. K., *Religion in Chinese Society*. Berkeley: University of California Press, 1961. Sociological approach to the study of Chinese religion.

Yü Chün-fang, *The Renewal of Buddhism in China: Chu-hung and the Late Ming Synthesis*. New York: Columbia University Press, 1980.

First to Sixth Centuries

Robinson, *Early Mādyamika*. Concerns the years around 400 C.E., the Buddho-Taoists, and the first serious Chinese attempt to master an Indian treatise system.

Zürcher, Erik, *The Buddhist Conquest of China*. Leiden, Netherlands: Brill, 1959. Social and doctrinal history till 400 C.E. A great book, perspicacious on all facets of the subject.

T'ien-t'ai

de Bary, *Chinese Tradition*, pp. 349–368.

Hurvitz, Leon, *Chih-i (538–597): An Introduction to the Life and Ideas of a Chinese Buddhist Monk. Mélanges Chinois et Bouddhiques*, XII, Bruges, Belgium, 1963. The only good book in English on T'ien-t'ai.

Takakusu, *Essentials*, pp. 126–141.

San-lun

de Bary, *Chinese Tradition*, pp. 333–343.

Liebenthal, Walter, *Chao Lun, The Treatises of Seng-chao*, 2nd rev. ed. Hong Kong: Hong Kong University Press, 1968.

Takakusu, *Essentials*, pp. 96–107.

Fa-hsiang

de Bary, *Chinese Tradition*, pp. 343–349.

Takakusu, *Amitāyur-dhyāna-sūtra*, pp. 80–95.

Hua-yen

Chang, Garma Chen-chi, *The Buddhist Teaching of Totality: The Philosophy of Hwa-yen Buddhism*. University Park: Pennsylvania State University Press, 1971.

Cook, Francis H., *Hua-yen Buddhism, The Jewel Net of Indra*. University Park: Pennsylvania State University Press, 1977.

Kao Kuan-ju, "Avataṃsaka Sūtra," *EB II*, vol. 3, pp. 435a–446a.

Suzuki, D. T., *Essays in Zen Buddhism*, Third Series. London: Rider, 1953. Zen and the Gaṇḍavyūha, pp. 21–214.
Takakusu, *Essentials*, pp. 108–125.

Pure Land

de Bary, *Chinese Tradition*, pp. 374–386.
Robinson, *Verse*, pp. 41–45, 64–74. The Pure Land liturgical hymns.

Ch'an (Zen)

Briggs, William A., ed., *Anthology of Zen*. New York: Grove Press, 1961. A handy collection of Zen writings by contemporary Asians and Westerners. Contains translations from Japanese and other materials difficult to find elsewhere. The section on Buddhism in the West is interesting but dated.
Chang, Chung-yuan, *Original Teachings of Ch'an Buddhism*. New York: Vintage, 1971. Useful translations from the *Transmission of the Lamp*.
Chang, Garma Chen-chi, *The Practice of Zen*. New York: Harper & Row, 1959. Presents Zen from the viewpoint of a modern Chinese practitioner who has also worked with Tibetan Tantra. Contains some good practical tips on meditation, in addition to history and teachings.
Dumoulin, Heinrich, *A History of Zen Buddhism*. Boston: Beacon Press, 1969. Readable and scholarly, though the author's interpretations sometimes depend on Catholic apologetic concepts.
———, *Zen Enlightenment: Origins and Meaning*. Weatherhill, 1979.
Graham, Dom Aelred, *Zen Catholicism*. New York: Harcourt, Brace & World, 1963.
Hoffmann, Yoel, *The Sound of the One Hand: 281 Zen Koans With Answers*. New York: Basic Books, 1975. Answers?
Hoover, Thomas, *Zen Culture*. New York: Vintage, 1977. A useful survey of the manifestations of Zen in Japanese culture.
Johnston, William, *Christian Zen*. New York: Harper & Row, 1971.
———, *Silent Music—The Silence of Meditation*. New York: Harper & Row, 1974. Father Johnston has practiced Zen in Japan for over twenty years and has done much to introduce the use of some Buddhist techniques into Catholic contemplation. He is a major participant in the Christian-Zen dialog.
Kapleau, Philip, *The Three Pillars of Zen*. Boston: Beacon Press, 1967. How Zen is practiced in modern Japan. Lectures by Zen masters, interviews, letters, testimonials. Especially good for its numerous accounts of meditation experiences of both Japanese and Westerners. A lotus among the thistles of writings by western Zen enthusiasts.
Lancaster, Lewis, and Whalen Lai, eds., *Early Ch'an in China and Tibet*. Berkeley, Calif: Asian Humanities Press, 1980. Collection of eighteen essays on the development of Ch'an; influences of Indian Buddhism, Taoism, and Confucianism considered.
Luk, Charles, *Ch'an and Zen Teaching*. Series 1, 2, 3. London: Rider, 1960–1962. Sloppy translations of many important texts otherwise not accessible. See review by Richard H. Robinson, *Journal of Asian Studies*, vol. 21 (1962), p. 368.
Satō, Giei, *Unsui: A Diary of Zen Monastic Life*. Honolulu: University Press of Hawaii, 1973. Ilustrates all aspects of Rinzai training in Japan, based on the artist's experiences; a humorous, insider's view of Zen.
Schloegl, Irmgard, *The Zen Teaching of Rinzai*. Boulder, Colo.: Shambhala, 1979.
Shibayama, Zenkei, *A Flower Does Not Talk*. Rutland, Vt.: Charles E. Tuttle, 1970.

Contains an interesting set of six ox-herding pictures that contrasts with the more common set of ten.

Suzuki, D. T., *Essays in Zen Buddhism*. Series 1, 2, 3. London: Rider, 1949, 1953. A treasure of information and insights by the man who made *Zen* an English word.

Suzuki, Shunryū, *Zen Mind, Beginner's Mind*. New York: Walker/Weatherhill, 1970. The author's approach is that of Sōtō Zen—"just sitting" without seeking to become a Buddha. The book serves as a balance to the writings of D. T. Suzuki, who, following the Rinzai tradition, emphasized grasping satori (enlightenment) through intense struggle.

Thich Nhat Ḥanh, *Zen Keys: A Zen Monk Examines the Vietnamese Tradition*. New York: Anchor Books, 1974. Another view of Zen from the Vietnamese tradition.

Welch, Holmes, *The Practice of Chinese Buddhism*. Cambridge, Mass.: Harvard University Press, 1967. Based on interviews with refugee Ch'an monks. Readable, scholarly, reliable. The best book on any regional variant of modern Buddhist monastic life.

Yampolsky, Philip, *The Platform Sutra of the Sixth Patriarch*. New York: Columbia University Press, 1967. Translation, introduction, notes. The best scholarly treatment in English of this major scripture.

———, *The Zen Master Hakuin: Selected Writings*. New York: Columbia University Press, 1971.

Modern China

Chan, Wing-tsit, *Religious Trends in Modern China*. New York: Columbia University Press, 1953.

Welch, Holmes, *Buddhism under Mao*. Cambridge, Mass.: Harvard University Press, 1972. Excellent information on Buddhism in China since 1949.

———, *The Buddhist Revival in China*. Cambridge, Mass.: Harvard University Press, 1968. Readable and authoritative.

Vietnam

Thich Nhat Ḥanh, *Vietnam: Lotus in a Sea of Fire*. New York: Hill & Wang, 1967. Modern Buddhist response, Vietnamese style, to political and military aggression of many varieties.

Thich Thien-An, *Buddhism and Zen in Vietnam, in Relation to the Development of Buddhism in Asia*. Rutland, Vt.: Charles E. Tuttle, 1975. Survey of Buddhism in Vietnam. Illustrated.

Korea

Busnell, Robert E. *The Collected Works of Chi-nul*. Berkeley, Calif.: Asian Humanities Press, 1980. Works of a traditional Korean Sŏn (Ch'an) master who lived from 1158–1220.

Lancaster, Lewis R., *The Korean Buddhist Canon: A Descriptive Catalogue*. Berkeley: University of California Press, 1980.

Lee, Peter H., *Lives of Eminent Korean Monks*. Cambridge, Mass.: Harvard University Press, 1969. Collection of traditional biographies.

Mitchell, Stephen, *Dropping Ashes on the Buddha*. New York: Grove Press, 1976. Contemporary stories and teachings of the Korean Sŏn master Seung Sahn, who has taught in the United States since 1962.

San, Ku, *Nine Mountains*. Song Kwang Sa Monastery, 1978. Dharma letters of a contemporary Korean meditation master.

Japan

Anesaki, Masaharu, *Nichiren, the Buddhist Prophet*. Cambridge, Mass.: Harvard University Press, 1916. A fine book on a fascinating personality.

Cleary, Thomas, *Record of Things Heard*. Boulder, Colo.: Prajna Press, 1980. Translations from Dōgen.

Cook, Francis, *How to Raise An Ox*. Los Angeles: Center Publications, 1979. More translations from Dōgen.

de Bary, Wm. Theodore, ed., *Sources of the Japanese Tradition*, New York: Columbia University Press, 1958. Essayettes and translations of Buddhist texts, pp. 93–110, 116–175, 190–266. Basic and excellent.

Dumoulin, *History of Zen*, pp. 137–268. The best part of the book.

Earhart, H. Byron, *Japanese Religion*. 3rd ed. Belmont, Calif.: Wadsworth, 1982.Treats Buddhism as a major strand in the overall complex of Japanese religion. The best thing to read next on Japanese Buddhism.

Eliot, Charles, *Japanese Buddhism*. London, 1935 and 1959. A great book in its day. Obsolete but not superseded.

Hakeda, Yoshito S., *Kūkai, Major Works*. New York: Columbia University Press, 1972.

Kamstra, J. H., *Encounter or Syncretism: The Initial Growth of Japanese Buddhism*. Leiden, Netherlands: Brill, 1967.

Kitagawa, Joseph M., *Religion in Japanese History*. New York: Columbia University Press, 1966. Up-to-date, well-informed and informative.

Kiyota, Minoru, *Shingon Buddhism: Theory and Practice*. Los Angeles: Buddhist Books International, 1978.

Kodera, Takashi James, *Dogen's Formative Years in China*. Boulder, Colo.: Prajna Press, 1980.

Matsunaga, Daigan and Alicia, *The Foundation of Japanese Buddhism* (2 vols.). Los Angeles: Buddhist Books International, 1974, 1976.

Pilgrim, Richard B., *Buddhism and the Arts of Japan*. Chambersburg, Pa.: Anima Publications, 1981.

Renondeau, G., *Le bouddhisme japonais—Textes fondamentaux de quatre grands moines de Kamakura*. Paris: Albin Michel, 1965.

Suzuki, D. T., *Zen and Japanese Culture*. New York: Pantheon, 1959.

Contemporary Asian Buddhism

Dumoulin, Heinrich, and John C. Maraldo, *Buddhism in the Modern World*. New York: Macmillan, 1976.

Lester, Robert C., *Theravada Buddhism in Southeast Asia*. Ann Arbor: University of Michigan Press, 1973.

Ling, Trevor, *Buddha, Marx, and God. Some Aspects of Religion in the Modern World*. New York: St. Martin's Press, 1966.

Schecter, Jerrold, *The New Face of Buddha*. New York: Coward-McCann, 1967. First-hand reporting by a journalist who has seen much but understood little.

Chapter 11. Buddhism Comes West

Albanese, Catherine L., *America: Religions and Religion*. Belmont, Calif.: Wadsworth, 1981. Sets the coming of Buddhism in context.

Campbell, Bruce F., *Ancient Wisdom Revived, A History of the Theosophical Movement*.

Berkeley: University of California Press, 1980. Describes the movement in whose wake many Eastern ideas came into Euro-American culture.
Conze, Edward, *Buddhist Studies, 1934–1972*. London: Bruno Cassirer, 1967.
Cox, Harvey, *Turning East: The Promise and Peril of the New Orientalism*. New York: Simon & Schuster, 1977. A somewhat superficial look at Eastern spirituality in America.
de Silva, Lynn, *The Problem of the Self in Buddhism and Christianity*. New York: Harper & Row, 1979.
Dickstein, Morris, *Gates of Eden: American Culture in the Sixties*. New York: Basic Books, 1977.
Ellwood, Robert S., *Alternative Altars: Unconventional and Eastern Spirituality in America*. Chicago: University of Chicago Press, 1979. Though only one chapter treats the Zen of the "Beat Generation," this is an important work on "excursus religion" in America.
———, *Religious and Spiritual Groups in Modern America*. Englewood Cliffs, N.J.: Prentice-Hall, 1973. Classic account of cults, with appropriate setting of context in first two chapters; valuable comments on Asian imports and the religio-environmental niche they occupy.
Gudmunsen, Chris, *Wittgenstein and Buddhism*. London: Macmillan, 1977.
Humphries, Christmas, *Sixty Years of Buddhism in England (1907–1967)*. London: Buddhist Society, 1968.
———,*Zen Comes West: Zen Buddhism in Western Society*. London: Curzon Press, 1977.
Hunter, Louise, *Buddhism in Hawaii: Its Impact on a Yankee Community*. Honolulu: University of Hawaii Press, 1971.
Johnson, Willard, *Riding the Ox Home*. London: Rider, 1982. Places meditation in the context of its worldwide history as well as in the frame of the Sino-Japanese ox-taming pictures and contemporary civilization.
Kashima, Tetsuden, *Buddhism in America: The Social Organization of an Ethnic Religious Institution*. Westport, Conn.: Greenwood Press, 1977. Describes in detail the Jōdo Shinshū Buddhist Churches of America (BCA).
Lang, David Marshall, *The Balavariani (Barlaam and Josaphat)*. Berkeley: University of California Press, 1966.
———, *The Wisdom of Balahvar: A Christian Legend of the Buddha*. New York: Macmillan, 1957.
Layman, Emma McCloy, *Buddhism in America*. Chicago: Nelson-Hall, 1976. Impressionistic description; not as useful as Prebish on same.
Merton, Thomas, *The Asian Journals of Thomas Merton*. New York: New Directions, 1975. Records his final visit to Asia.
———, *Zen and the Birds of Appetite*. New York: New Directions, 1968. Collection of essays on Buddhism and Christianity.
Oliver, Ian P., *Buddhism in Britain*. London: Rider, 1979.
Prebish, Charles S., *American Buddhism*. Belmont, Calif.: Wadsworth, 1979. The best book to date; complete, detailed, and well-informed. Discusses a good variety of groups and assesses Buddhism's place and future.
Riepe, Dale, *The Philosophy of India and Its Impact on American Thought*. Springfield, Ill.: Charles Thomas, 1970.
Roszak, Theodore, *Unfinished Animal: The Aquarian Frontier and the Evolution of Consciousness*. New York: Harper & Row, 1975. A perceptive interpretation of the spiritual meaning of the awakening of "transcendent energies" in America.
Sedlar, Jean W., *India and the Greek World: A Study in the Transmission of Culture*. Totowa, N. J.: Rowman & Littlefield, 1980. Detailed analysis, often with little concrete result.
West, Martin L., *Early Greek Philosophy and the Orient*. Oxford: Clarendon Press, 1971. Read with Sedlar.
Willson, A. Leslie, *A Mythical Image: The Ideal of India in German Romanticism*. Durham, N.C.: Duke University Press, 1964.

An Overview of the Buddhist Scriptures

A. The Pali Canon: The *Tipiṭaka* ("Three Baskets")
  See Thomas, *Thought*, pp. 265–276, and *Inde Classique*, Nos. 1947–1979.
  I. *Vinaya-piṭaka* ("Basket of Discipline")
    1. *Sutta-vibhanga* ("Division of Rules")—the rules of the Pātimokkha code with explanations and commentary.
      a. *Mahāvibhaṅga* ("Great Division")—the 227 rules for monks.
      b. *Bhikkhunī-vibhaṅga* ("Division Concerning Nuns")
    2. *Khandhaka* ("Sections")
      a. *Mahāvagga* ("Great Group")—rules for ordination, Observance Day, rainy-season retreat, clothing, food, medicine, and procedures of the Saṅgha.
      b. *Cullavagga* ("Small Group")—judicial rules, miscellaneous rules, ordination and instruction of nuns, history of the First and Second Councils.
    3. *Parivāra* ("The Accessory")—summaries and classifications of the rules. This is a late supplement.
  II. *Sutta-piṭaka*, ("Basket of Discourses")
    1. *Dīgha-nikāya* ("Collection of Long Discourses")—34 suttas.
    2. *Majjhima-nikāya* ("Collection of Medium Discourses")—152 suttas.
    3. *Saṃyutta-nikāya* ("Collection of Connected Discourses")—56 groups of suttas.
    4. *Aṅguttara-nikāya* ("Collection of Item-more Discourses")—over 2300 suttas.
    5. *Khuddaka-nikāya* ("Collection of Little Texts")
      Khuddaka-pāṭha ("Little Readings")—a breviary.
      b. *Dhammapada* ("Verses on Dharma")—423 verses in 26 chapters.
      c. *Udāna* ("Utterances")—80 exalted pronouncements of the Buddha, with circumstantial tales.
      d. *Itivuttaka* ("Thus-saids")—112 short suttas.
      e. *Sutta-nipāta* ("Collection of Suttas")—short suttas, mostly in verse of high poetic quality.
      f. *Vimāna-vatthu* ("Tales of Heavenly Mansions")—gods tell the deeds that earned them celestial rebirths.

g. *Peta-vatthu* ("Tales of Ghosts")—how various persons attained that unfortunate rebirth.
h. *Thera-gāthā* ("Verses of the Elders")—stanzas attributed to 264 male personal disciples of the Buddha.
i. *Therī-gāthā* ("Verses of the Eldresses")—stanzas attributed to about 100 female personal disciples of the Buddha.
j. *Jātaka* ("Lives")—tales ostensibly reporting the former lives of Śākyamuni. The verses in each tale are supposed to have been uttered by the Buddha, and so are considered canonical; but the 547 tales themselves are extracanonical.
k. *Niddesa* ("Exposition")—verbal notes to part of the *Sutta-nipāta*. The *Niddesa* is second or third century C.E.
l. *Paṭisambhidā-magga* ("The Way of Analysis")—Abhidharma-style treatment of some doctrinal topics.
m. *Apadāna* ("Stories")—lives and former lives of the saints.
n. *Buddhavaṃsa* ("Lineage of the Buddhas")—lives of 24 previous Buddhas, of Śākyamuni, and of Maitreya, presented as being told by Śākyamuni.
o. *Cariyā-piṭaka* ("Basket of Conduct")—verse retellings of Jātakas illustrating the Bodhisattva's practice of the perfections.

III. *Abhidhamma-piṭaka* ("Basket of Scholasticism")
1. *Dhamma-saṅgani* ("Enumeration of Dharmas")
2. *Vibhaṅga* ("Divisions")—more on sets of dharmas.
3. *Dhātu-kathā* ("Discussion of Elements")
4. *Puggala-paññatti* ("Designation of Persons")—classifies people according to their spiritual traits and stages.
5. *Kathā-vatthu* ("Subjects of Discussion")—arguments about theses in dispute among the Hīnayāna schools.
6. *Yamaka* ("The Pairs")—arranged in pairs of questions; deals with the basic sets of categories.
7. *Paṭṭhāna* ("Activations")—24 kinds of causal relation.

B. The Chinese Canon: The *Ta-ts'ang-ching* ("Great Scripture-Store")

See Ch'en, *Buddhism in China*, pp. 365–378, and *Inde Classique*, Nos. 2107–2162. The first printed edition was produced in Szechuan, in 972–983 C.E. It consisted of 1076 texts in 480 cases. The standard modern edition is the *Taishō Shinshū Daizōkyō* (*Ta-ts'ang-ching* newly edited in the Taishō reign-period). It was published in Tokyo, 1924–1929, and consists of 55 Western-style volumes containing 2184 texts. A supplement consists of 45 volumes. The following analysis is of the Taishō edition.

I. *Āgama* Section, vol. 1–2, 151 texts. Contains the Long, Medium, Mixed (= Connected) and Item-more Āgamas (Nikāyas), plus some individual texts corresponding to parts of the Pali Khuddaka.
II. Story Section, vol. 3–4, 68 texts. *Jātakas*, lives of various Buddhas, fables, and parables.
III. *Prajñā-pāramitā* Section, vol. 5–8, 42 texts.
IV. *Saddharma-puṇḍarīka* Section, vol. 9, 16 texts. Three complete versions of the *Lotus Sūtra*, plus some doctrinally cognate Sūtras.
V. *Avataṃsaka* Section, vol. 9–10, 31 texts.
VI. *Ratnakūṭa* Section, vol. 11–12, 64 texts. A set of 49 Mahāyāna Sūtras, some in more than one translation.
VII. *Mahāparinirvāṇa* Section, vol. 12, 23 texts. The Mahāyāna version of Śākyamuni's last days and words.
VIII. Great Assembly Section, vol. 13, 28 texts. A collection beginning with the Great Assembly Sūtra, which is itself a suite of Mahāyāna Sūtras.
IX. Sūtra-collection Section, vol. 14–17, 423 texts. A miscellany of Sūtras, mostly Mahāyāna.

X. Tantra Section, vol. 18–21, 572 texts. Vajrayāṇa Sūtras, Tantras, ritual manuals, and spells.
XI. Vinaya Section, vol. 22–24, 86 texts. Vinayas of the Mahīśāsakas, Mahāsāṅghikas, Dharmaguptakas, Sarvāstivādins, and Mūla-sarvāstivādins. Also some texts on the Bodhisattva discipline.
XII. Commentaries on Sūtras, vol. 24–26, 31 texts—on Āgamas and on Mahāyāna Sūtras, by Indian authors.
XIII. Abhidharma Section, vol. 26–29, 28 texts. Scholastic treatises of the Sarvāstivādins, Dharmaguptakas, and Sautrāntikas.
XIV. Mādhyamika Section, vol. 30, 15 texts.
XV. Yogācāra Section, vol. 30–31,49 texts.
XVI. Collection of Treatises, vol. 32, 65 texts. Works on logic, anthologies from the Sūtras, and sundry treatises.
XVII. Commentaries on the Sūtras, vol. 33–39, by Chinese authors.
XVIII. Commentaries on the Vinaya, vol. 40, by Chinese authors.
XIX. Commentaries on the Śāstras, vol. 40–44, by Chinese authors.
XX. Chinese Sectarian Writings, vol. 44–48.
XXI. History and Biography, vol. 49–52, 95 texts.
XXII. Encyclopedias and Dictionaries, vol. 53–54, 16 texts.
XXIII. Non-Buddhist Doctrines, vol. 54, 8 texts. Sāṃkhya, Vaiśeṣika, Manichean, and Nestorian Christian writings.
XXIV. Catalogs, vol. 55, 40 texts. Successive catalogs of the Canon beginning with that of Seng-yu published in 515 C.E.

C. The Tibetan Canon

See *Inde Classique*, Nos. 2033–2044, and Kenneth Ch'en, "The Tibetan Tripiṭaka," *Harvard Journal of Asian Studies*, vol. 9 (1945–1947), pp. 53–62.

I. *Bka'-'gyur (Kanjur)* ("Translation of Buddha-word"). The number of volumes and order of sections differ slightly from edition to edition. The following is according to the Snar-thang (Narthang) version.
1. *Vinaya*, 13 vols.
2. *Prajñā-pāramitā*, 21 vols.
3. *Avataṃsaka*, 6 vols.
4. *Ratnakūṭa*, 6 vols. A set of 49 Mahāyāna Sūtras.
5. *Sūtra*, 30 vols., 270 texts, three-quarters Mahāyāna Sūtras and one-quarter Hīnayāna ones.
6. *Tantra*, 22 vols., over 300 texts.

II. *Bstan-'gyur (Tenjur)* ("Translation of Teachings"). In the Peking edition, this consists of 224 volumes and 3626 texts, divided into:
1. *Stotras* (hymns of praise), 1 vol., 64 texts.
2. *Commentaries on Tantras*, 86 vols., 3055 texts.
3. *Commentaries on Sūtras*, 137 vols., 567 texts.
   a. *Prajñā-pāramitā* commentaries, 16 vols.
   b. *Mādhyamika* treatises, 17 vols.
   c. *Yogācāra* treatises, 29 vols.
   d. *Abhidharma*, 8 vols.
   e. Miscellaneous, 4 vols.
   f. *Vinaya* Commentaries, 16 vols.
   g. Tales and dramas, 4 vols.
   h. Technical treatises: logic (21 vols.), grammar (1 vol.), lexicography and poetics (1 vol.), medicine (5 vols.), chemistry and sundry (1 vol.), supplement (old and recent translations, indices; 14 vols.).

Concept Index

References to illustrations are printed in boldface type.

27, 36–37; in Tibetan Buddhism, 148–149
Epic hero: bodhisattva as, 78; Buddha as, 6, 36
Euro-America, Buddhism of, 214–223

Faith: of laity stream-winners 58; in Buddha as beginning of path to salvation, 25–26; and rebirth in Sukhāvatī, 88; required for refuge taking, 30
Final Nirvāṇa (parinirvāṇa) of Buddha, 33–35
Four Holy Truths, 24, 26 (Table 1) 27–29; in dependent co-arising, 17; understood in Buddha's enlightenment vision, 12
Full moon as symbolic motif in Buddha's enlightenment experience, 14

Gnōsis (saving knowledge): in Ch'an, 180; Four Holy Truths as, 28; as transformation of consciousness in esoteric Tibetan Buddhism, 148
God denied as cause of world experience, 18
Golden Mean compared to Middle Way, 27
Guru: essential in Tantrism, 93, 99, 147, 183; excessive glorification of, 234

Habit: in Buddha's enlightenment, 11; counteracted by discipline of Middle Way, 27; and meditation, 231
Happiness: in Buddha's search for enlightenment, 10; as goal of power manipulation in popular Thai Buddhism, 129; of liberated arhant, 30; transience of, 8; in worldly life, 28
Hatred: as source of rebirth in Wheel of Life, 19; as "aversion" counteracted in meditation, 229–231
Heavens: and attaining nirvāṇa as nonreturner, 26; not nirvāṇa or deathless realm in Indic world view, 16; as rebirth realm on Wheel of Life, 19–20
Hells as rebirth realm on Wheel of Life, 15, 19
Holy Eightfold Path: Buddha's explanation of, 26 (Table 1), 27, 29; as Buddhist Middle Way, 24; completion of, and arhant-ship, 12
Holy person as object of faith in Buddhism, 25
Householder (household life): Buddha's rejection of, 8–9; or lay bodhisattva in Mahāyāna, 74–75; leaving, through ordination, 53; life of, as blessed, 28; as not propitious for highest attainment in early Buddhism, 41; return to, in Thai Buddhism, 127; Vimalakīrti as householder-bodhisattva, 75
Hungry ghosts: as objects of Japanese feeding ritual, **211**; in popular Thai Buddhism, 129; as rebirth realm in Wheel of Life, 19

Identity: personal, and karmic continuity, 15–16; in meditative experience, 230–232
Ignorance as cause of rebirth and world experience, 17. *See also* Avidyā
Impermanence: Buddha's first experience of, 8; as characteristic of Wheel of Life, 19; of skandhas, 24; of world results in choice for ultimate transformation, 36
Indonesia, Buddhism in, 117–118
Indulgence: as meaning of Buddha's early life, 36; sensual, rejected by Buddha, 10–11, and condemned by his Middle Way, 23
Initiation, temporary membership in Theravāda Saṅgha as, 123
Insight (vipaśanā): in dhyāna, 12; liberating, in meditation, 230–232; required for release from samsāra, 16
Intention in Buddhist view of ethical consequence, 15

Japan, Buddhism of, 198–213
Jina. *See* Victor

Karma: and bondage to continuation of personal identity, 15–16; in Buddha's self-transformation, 36–37; in causation and bondage, 17; in Chinese Buddhism, 155; only improved through donations and pious acts by laity in Tibetan Buddhism, 147; and rebirth realms, 18–20; reinterpreted in popular Tibetan Buddhism, 152–153; understood in Buddha's enlightenment visions, 12
Kleśa (affliction) interpreted in terms of meditation, 229–231
Knowledge: as counteractive to bondage to rebirth, 16–17; of Four Holy Truths as saving, 24; reverses karmic outflows, 27; and salvation and spiritual maturity in Buddha's life, 36–37. *See also* Gnōsis
Kōan (meditative conundrum): in Ch'an, 180–181, 183–184; in meditation, 232
Korea, Buddhism of, 195–97

Laity: in Ch'an, 181; in later Chinese Buddhism, 191; not usually instructed in meditation and wisdom in early Buddhism, 60; religious life of, in early Buddhism, 57–61; support of temple-monastery in Theravāda, 119; in Zen, **208–209**. *See also* Laity-monk relations
Laity-monk relations: in Chinese cult practice, 184–188 passim; in early India,

Subject and Name Index

Pāṭimokkha rules, 127
Patriarchs, 177
Paul, 15
Peace Memorial Stūpa, 209
Pegu, 115
Peking, 142, 154
Perfection of Wisdom (emptiness) texts, 184
Perfection of Wisdom ideas, 91
Perfection of Wisdom literature, 167
Perfection of Wisdom Sūtras, 78, 98, 162, 170, 177
Perfection of Wisdom Texts, 166
Perfection of Wisdom Traditions, 182
Persia, 69
Personalists, 44
Pha-dam-pa Sanggye (Pha-gdams-pa saṅs-rgyas), 143
'Phags-pa, 142
Philippines, 192
Piṇḍola, 167
Pipal (Bodhi Tree), 61
Piṭakas, 38
Platform Sūtra, 181
Platform Sūtra of the Sixth Patriarch, 177
Plato, 214
Point Loma, Caliornia, 216
Portuguese, 112
Prajāpatī, 8, 33, 57
Prajñā-pāramitā Sūtras, 69, 94
Pratt, Sunya, 220
Prayāga, 98
Prebish, C., 218
Pre-Han dynasty, 176
Pre-muslim Persia, 102
"Propagate Zen, Protect the Country," 206
"Public Document" (kung-an), 180
Pudgalavādins, 42
Purāṇas, 67
Pure Land, 73, 164, 174–175, 182, 185, 188–189, 191, 196, 219, 224, 234
Pure Land cult, 173
Pure Land lineage, 172
Pure Land practices, 194
Pure Land school, 190
Pure Land sects, Chinese and Japanese, 88
Pure Land teachings, 203
P'yong-yang, 195
Pythagorean, Apollonius, 214

Quaker, 31, 65
Quan-ân, 82
Queen Kṣemā, 33
Queen Māyā, 61

Rāhula, 8, 32
Rājagṛha, Capital of Magadha, 32–33, 38
Rāma, 79
Rangoon, 132
Ral-pa-can, King, 141
Ramkham-haeng, King, 116
Red Guard Movement, 211
Red Guards, 192
"Red Lama," 225
Rennyo, 205
Republican China, 192
Ṛg Veda, 93
Rhys-Davids, T. W., 113
Rin-chen Sangpo (Rin-chen Bzaṅ-po), 141
Rinzai Zen, 194, 206, 208, 220, 230, 232, 235
Risshō-kōseikai, 210
Rock edicts, 47
Roman Catholic Church, 229
Roman Empire, 158
Rome, 103, 138
Roszak, 223
Rules of Discipline (Pali, Pāṭimokkha), 49
Russia, 215–216
Ryōnin, 203

Saichō, 90, 200–201, 205
Saigon, 193, 212
Śailendra dynasty, 117
Saint Teresa of Avila, 96
Śaivism, 91, 100, 116–117, 138
Śakas, 45
Śakra, 34, 85
Śākyamuni (Sage of the Śākyas) 7, 88
Sa-kya-pa (Sa-skya-pa), 142–143
Śākyas, 7
Śāla trees, 34
Samantabhadra, 82–83
Samarkand, 102
Saṃvara, 89
Samye, debate at, 105
Samye (Bsam-yas), 139
Samyutta Nikāya, 39
San-chieh-chiao, 175
Sāñcī, 32, 47, 54
Sandhinirmocana, 71
San Diego, California 216
San Francisco, California, 216–217
Saṅgha, 3, 6
Saṅgha director, 112
Saṅghamitta, 48
Saṅghavarman, 184
San Jose, California, 219
San-lun (Japanese: Sanron), 164, 166–167, 171, 199
San-lun (Mādhyamika), 167
Sanron, 199
Sanskrit, 3, 38–39, 102, 141, 159, 168, 174
Sanskrit manuscripts, 168
Sanskrit-Tibetan glossary (Mahāvyutpatti), 141
Sanskrit variety of Hīnayāna, 115
Santarakṣita, 138–140
Saraha, Tantric poet, 78, 97
Śāriputra of Nālandā, 25,32